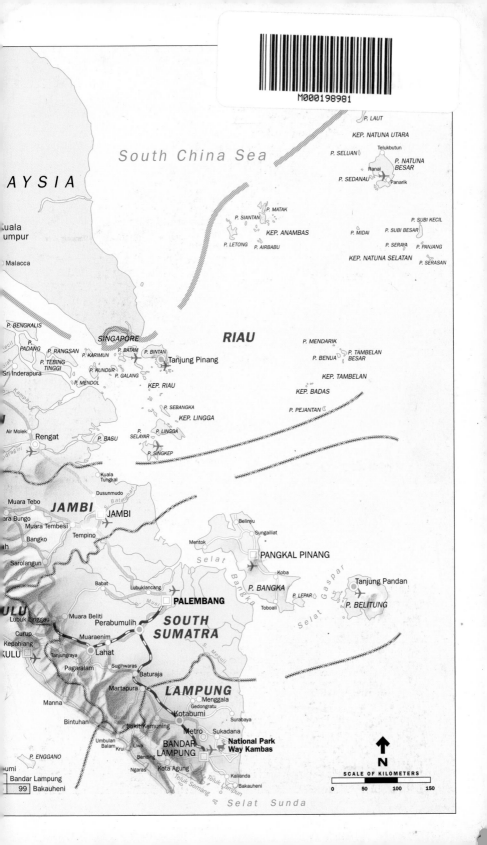

SUMATRA

Edited by

ERIC M. OEY

PERIPLUS
EDITIONS

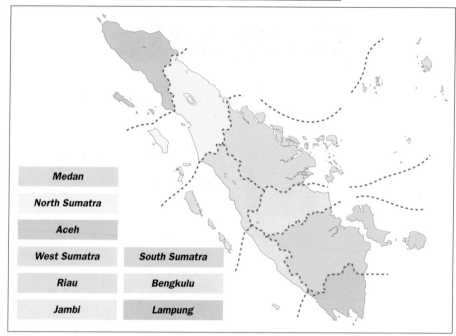

Medan

North Sumatra

Aceh

West Sumatra   South Sumatra

Riau   Bengkulu

Jambi   Lampung

© 1996 by Periplus Editions (HK) Ltd.
2nd edition
ALL RIGHTS RESERVED
Printed in the Republic of Singapore
ISBN 962-593-017-5

Publisher: Eric Oey
Second edition edited by Julie Heath
Cartography: Violet Wong and Kathy Wee
Production: Mary Chia and Teresa Tan

International Distributors:
Benelux Countries: Nilsson & Lamm bv, Postbus 195, 1380 AD Weesp, The Netherlands
Germany: Brettschneider Fernreisebedarf GMBH, Hauptstrasse 5, D-85586 Poing
Indonesia: C.V. Java Books, P.O. Box 55 JKCP, Jakarta 10510
Japan: Charles E. Tuttle Inc., 21-13, Seki 1-Chome, Tama-ku, Kawasaki, Kanagawa 214
Scandinavia: Platypus Förlag, Inspektörsgatan 4, 252 27 Helsingborg, Sweden
Singapore and Malaysia: Berkeley Books Pte. Ltd., 5 Little Rd, #08-01, Cemtex Industrial Building, Singapore 536983
U.K.: GeoCenter U.K. Ltd., The Viables Centre, Harrow Way, Basingstoke, Hampshire RG22 4BJ
U.S.A.: *NTC Publishing Group* (Passport Guides), 4255 W. Touhy Avenue, Lincolnwood [Chicago], Illinois 60646

Cover: A beautiful young lady from Jambi dressed for festivities. Photo by Jill Gocher.
Pages 4-5: Rafting the Alas River in Western Aceh province. Photo by Kal Muller.
Pages 6-7: An elephant safari in Way Kambas Reserve, Lampung Province. Photo by Alain Compost.
Pages 8-9: Woman praying at the back of Banda Aceh's Grand Mosque. Photo by Kal Muller.
Frontispiece: A Minang woman in traditional *adat* costume. Photo by Alain Compost.

The Periplus Adventure Guides Series

BALI
JAVA
SUMATRA
KALIMANTAN *Indonesian Borneo*
SULAWESI *The Celebes*
EAST OF BALI *From Lombok to Timor*
MALUKU *Indonesia's Spice Islands*
IRIAN JAYA *Indonesian New Guinea*
UNDERWATER INDONESIA
A Guide to the World's Greatest Diving
SURFING INDONESIA *(1996)*
BIRDING INDONESIA *(1996)*
TREKKING INDONESIA *(1996)*
WEST MALAYSIA *and Singapore*
SABAH & SARAWAK *with Brunei Darussalam*

DEDICATION

The editor dedicates this book to his parents, Tom and Berenice, whose support and love have been a constant source of encouragement, and also to Oom Tjie Soe and Tante Siew Eng in Pekalongan.

Contents

CONTENTS

PART I

Island of Adventure

Sumatra, fabled "Land of Gold" of the ancients, is unlike any other tropical island on earth. It is neither the largest landmass in the Indonesian archipelago (Irian Jaya and Kalimantan are larger), nor the most populous (Java has three times as many people), but by most accounts it is the most varied and interesting island to visit. Sumatra indeed has something for everyone—lush rainforests, exotic flora and fauna, cascading rivers, sparkling crater lakes, shimmering white sand beaches and an incredibly diverse array of traditional ethnic groups who inhabit some of the most spectacular volcanic landscapes in the world.

Straddling vital waterways at the western end of an immense island chain, Sumatra is a kind of anchor for the rest of the archipelago. It is truly continental in scope: vast lowland rainforests and coastal wetlands are cut by a network of broad, silt-laden rivers that snake across the island for up to 800 km before emptying into the South China Sea. Unlike all the other islands of a similar scale, however, Sumatra is also volcanic—its lofty range of western peaks forming a longitudinal "spine" dotted with lakes and fertile upland valleys.

The island is extremely rich in natural resources. Its coal, tin, bauxite, oil, gold, natural gas, timber, rubber, tea, palm oil, cacao and coffee together account for over half of Indonesia's export income, while its long coastline is dotted with harbors giving access to seas teeming with tropical marine life.

As a result, Sumatra has played a major role in Indonesian history. The first large kingdom in these islands—the Buddhist state of Srivijaya—had its capital on the Musi River near what is now Palembang, and from here controlled a massive volume of trade passing through the Malacca and Sunda straits for over 300 years—conquering all other ports around the coasts and maintaining direct links with harbors in faraway India and China.

Indian civilization, which was to have such a far-reaching cultural impact in the region, entered Indonesia through Sumatran ports in the first millennium AD. In the second millennium the same story was repeated—as Islam arrived from the west along the trans-oceanic trade routes, established a foothold in the ports of northeastern Sumatra, and spread from here to the neighboring islands.

Sumatra was of course inhabited long before the arrival of these foreign priests and traders. Well over a dozen major ethnic groups live on the island, speaking more than 25 different languages and hundreds of dialects. Sumatra today supports 40 million people—over 20 percent of Indonesia's huge population—with a size and density similar to that of California, though far less urbanized.

Found here are some of Indonesia's most dynamic peoples. The Acehnese of the north, for example, are fervent Muslims renowned for their fierce resistance to Dutch rule. The Minangkabau of West Sumatra have migrated throughout Indonesia and today form the economic and intellectual elite in many areas. Sumatra's largest group, the Malays, were the great seafaring traders of Asia in pre-modern times, and their tongue forms the basis for the national languages of Indonesia and Malaysia. Last but not least, the Bataks of the northern highlands around Lake Toba are the nation's most resourceful and flamboyant group.

As a travel destination, Sumatra thus has few peers. Its natural habitats possess an unparalleled variety of wildlife—from elephants and rhinos to the world's largest flower (the foul-smelling rafflesia) and the most expensive aquarium fish (the golden *arowana* or "dragon fish")—while the island's traditional peoples are as fascinating as they are warm and hospitable. In short, Sumatra combines most of the incomparable attractions of the Indonesian islands all rolled into one!

— *Eric Oey*

Opposite: *View of Mt. Singgalang from Panorama Park in Bukittinggi. Photo by Coen Pepplinkhuizen.*

GEOGRAPHY

A Vast Island of Dramatic Contrasts

Sumatra is the fourth largest island in the world after Greenland, New Guinea and Borneo, with a land area of some 473,481 sq km —roughly the size of California or Spain. It is an island of enormous regional diversity, that for administrative purposes has been divided into eight large provinces. To some extent, these divisions have been made along ethnic, and not geographic lines. The provinces of Aceh and Lampung at Sumatra's northern and southern tips, for example, are home to the Acehnese and Lampung peoples, while North and West Sumatra are the Batak and Minangkabau homelands, respectively. Other provincial boundaries, however, have been determined more by the island's lofty central mountain range and the large river systems flowing eastward from it. Sumatra's largest province is South Sumatra, which encompasses a major slice of territory on the east coast and the large islands of Bangka and Belitung.

Migrating continents

Contrary to earlier beliefs, recent geological research has demonstrated that Sumatra once formed part of the great southern continent called Gondwanaland, and not part of Asia. About 160 million years ago it broke away and began to migrate northwards— eventually lodging, with Malaya, Thailand and Burma, against what is now Indochina.

About 40 million years later, India started its own northward journey, crashing slowly but powerfully into Tibet some 80 million years later. The dense oceanic plate on top of which India rested then nudged eastward against the relatively light and rigid Sunda Plate. This caused massive buckling, faulting and shearing—resulting in the formation of a series of small islands to the west of Sumatra, as well as of Sumatra's central Barisan Range and the valleys in between.

Today, part of the Indian Ocean plate continues to slide below the west of Sumatra, causing frequent but minor earthquakes, eruptions and landslides. The stress and shearing has been relieved by a long rift valley stretching from Semangko Bay at the island's southern tip, north through Lake Kerinci, Bukittinggi and the Alas Valley to Banda Aceh. The most famous section of this rift is Bukittinggi's Ngarai Sianok Canyon.

All along its length, the rift has been filled

in by some 65 volcanic peaks, several of which are still active. The fault continues southward into the straits between Sumatra and Java, where it has created the most infamous of Indonesia's many volcanoes—the mighty Krakatau.

Parallel slices

The physical geography of Sumatra is best considered as a series of parallel longitudinal slices running northwest to southeast along the main axis of the island. In the extreme

west is a sparsely inhabited chain of islands —from Simeulue in the north to Enggano in the south—that is separated from Sumatra by a submarine trench which plunges to depths of 2,000 meters.

The western fringe of Sumatra itself is a narrow but complex coastal strip, alternating between fertile alluvial soils where rice is grown, and inhospitable swamps that are gradually being drained for agriculture. Rugged foothills rise steeply from this coastal fringe to the mighty Barisan Mountains— several of which tower above 3,000 meters. The highest non-volcanic peaks (about 3,400 meters) lie within the Gunung Leuser National Park in the northern part of the island. Sumatra's highest volcano is Mt. Kerinci—at 3,800 meters, the highest Indonesian mountain outside of Irian Jaya.

Also found along this central axis is dramatic Lake Tujuh—a spectacular crater lake, 5 sq km in area, perched at an altitude of 2,000 meters atop Mt. Tujuh. It is best seen from the southern slopes of adjacent Mt. Kerinci, but can also be reached directly from the town of Sungaipenuh. Impressive mountains are also found in the limestone areas around Bukittinggi and Payakumbuh in West Sumatra, and in the Lhoknga area of Aceh. These are not particularly high, but the unusual karst formations with steep sides, often studded with caves, are very interesting.

East of the Barisan Range lie irregular

foothills and broad, dry lowlands which have seen rapid development in this century as plantations and as urban and agricultural centers. These lowlands are now also the focus of industrial development based on food processing and fossil fuels.

As you approach the coast, particularly in the central and southern regions, the dry land turns to various types of swamps—the largest extent of swamplands in Indonesia outside of Irian Jaya. These swamps are crisscrossed by large, meandering rivers. Where the peat is not too thick, the land has been cleared for rice cultivation; where it is thicker, pineapples and coconuts grow. Where the peat is really thick—and it can reach an incredible 22 meters in parts of Riau—agricultural crops cannot be grown. Logging continues, however, and land drainage in other areas threatens to eliminate many of these magnificent raised swamps.

Further east, off the central and southern coasts, are the low-lying eastern islands at the southern end of the Malacca Strait. Here, extensive areas are mined for bauxite and tin, but Batam Island is also being developed now as a leisure, business and industrial alternative to Singapore—with everything from industrial estates to luxury beach resorts.

Far out in the South China Sea about 500 km from the mainland are the Natuna Islands. These have little agricultural potential but are important strategically, as well as possessing important fishing grounds and rich reserves of oil and natural gas.

Riches of the earth

Sumatra is extremely rich in fossil fuels—oil, gas and coal. Oil is found mainly in the east, from Riau to South Sumatra, both on land and offshore. New technologies had to be

Opposite: *The jungle-clad slopes of Mt. Merapi (2,891 m), in the heart of the Minang Highlands.*
Above: *Rimba Panti Reserve near Bukittinggi.*

developed to tap this wealth, especially to facilitate drilling in the thick peat deposits of coastal Riau. Roads there are built on top of floating plastic carpets, and derricks perch atop tall piles reaching down to the bedrock below. Almost all of the oil from this central basin is pumped to the port of Dumai on the east coast. In southeast Aceh is the enormous Arun gas field, which ranks as one of the world's most productive. In South Sumatra, at Muaraenim, is a very large open-cast coal mine. The coal is taken from here by rail south to Teluk Betung and thence to Java.

Small amounts of gold are mined, though the important metals are aluminum (bauxite) and tin. Bauxite is mined on Bintan, one of the Riau Islands, then shipped to Japan for processing into alumina, then back to Sumatra again, where it is smelted into aluminum at the Inalum plant on the coast of North Sumatra.

Sumatra's 'big bang'

Huge Lake Toba in North Sumatra is Southeast Asia's largest lake, covering 1,146 sq km, and so far defying efforts to measure its depth—though it is known to be deeper than 450 m. It occupies the caldera of a massive volcano which exploded some 100,000 years ago in the most powerful volcanic eruption ever known. Early man was probably living in Sumatra at the time, and the scale of devastation caused by the explosion is hard for us to imagine— equivalent to hundreds of hydrogen bombs detonating simultaneously.

Shortly before the eruption, a giant boil of a mountain grew above the increasing quantities of molten material below. When the solid ground finally gave way, a searingly hot plume of ash was thrown into the sky—its remains can be traced today over an area of 20-30,000 sq km. Around the volcano the ash settled in a layer more than 600 m thick. This eruption set the world record for the quantity of material ejected—some 1,500-2,000 cubic

km, compared with just 0.6 cubic km for the much-publicised eruption of Mt. St. Helens in Washington State, USA. Because of the massive quantity of ejecta, the empty cone soon collapsed in on itself to form the world's largest caldera. This became an ancient lake, which was itself destroyed about 30,000 years ago when a second, much smaller eruption occurred. The island of Samosir in the center of the lake, and the lake's eastern shore—the main tourist centers today—are all that remain of the shattered cone.

The first Europeans to see Lake Toba were a pair of British missionaries, Messrs Burton and Ward, who traveled here in 1824. They were told that the lake level rose and fell like the sea. Although much of the area was already deforested and under rice cultivation, one area on the eastern shore was still covered with jungle. At the time, the lake's outlet was unknown, but eventually it became clear that the Asahan River flowed out through a "spirit-filled" forest at what is now Porsea on the southeastern shore.

One reason for the forest's mystique may have been the impressive 100-meter Siguragura waterfall, which races through a narrow gorge—now rendered somewhat less dramatic by the presence of a hydroelectric dam. A short distance downstream is the 150-meter Sampuran Harimau waterfall which cascades into a large natural amphitheater near Tangga. Tumbling into this spectacular gorge is Sumatra's highest waterfall, at a point where the small Ponot River drops 280 meters from the mountains above and joins up with the Asahan River below. Although the falls are now used for hydroelectric power to supply the massive Inalum plant, the natural beauty of the area has not been lost. On a clear day these falls can be seen from the windows of

Above, left: *A tea plantation near Lake Kerinci.*
Above, right: *Oil palms are a common sight throughout Sumatra.*

jets plying the Medan-Jakarta route.

The climate of Sumatra has changed dramatically over the past million years. During the ice ages, glaciers covered the higher peaks in the north, in what is now Gunung Leuser National Park. The largest glacier on Mt. Leuser covered some 100 sq km.

Sea levels have also been as much as 50 meters higher and 180 meters lower than they are at present. As a result, the low lying eastern swamps and plains have been inundated and exposed several times. At times of low sea levels, land bridges connected Sumatra with Peninsular Malaysia, Borneo and Java, and the estuaries of large rivers such as the Musi, the Kampar and the Indragiri were situated some 700 km farther east from the present-day coastline, near what are now the Natuna Islands.

Fierce tropical storms

The western parts of Sumatra are by far the wettest; few areas here receive less than 4,000 mm of rain per annum, quite evenly distributed throughout the year. The wettest spots are the hills behind Padang, which receive 5,000 mm, and the northern Bengkulu mountains, which are drenched with more than 6,000 mm (about 10 times the rainfall of London!). The driest places are on the east coast and in the central rift valley, but even most of these receive more than 2,000 mm.

Although the difference between seasons is not very distinct, dry periods often occur in the early part of the year and in June and July. During these periods, wild fires occur, often started by farmers clearing patches of land. The problem is growing worse because the changing world climate is prolonging the dry seasons. Logging has also opened up the moist forests, allowing forested areas to dry out—as have drainage schemes on the east coast, which dry out the peat deposits, causing them to burn out of control. It is not unusual for air traffic approaching Singapore to be re-routed because of the smoke from fires in southern Sumatra.

While there is considerable local variability, winds in Sumatra generally blow from the north between December and March, and from the south between May and September. Many of the seasonal winds are particularly fierce, and have been given names by the local residents. A stormy wind that occurs in the region of Lake Tawar, in Aceh, is given the name Angin Depik—after the *depik* fish that is easily caught in the lake around this time. There are also two warm, dry winds —the Angin Bohorok which blows eastwards from the mountains behind Bohorok (in North Sumatra) and the Angin Padang Lawas which blows east of Padang Sidempuan (in West Sumatra)—which often damage crops and make agriculture in some regions almost impossible because the soils become so dry.

— *Anthony Whitten*

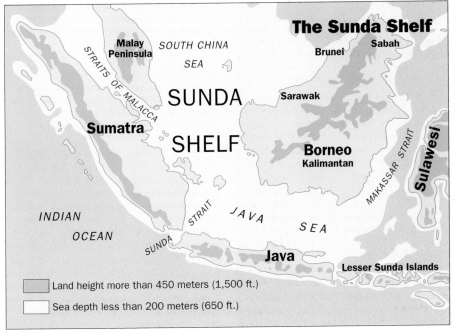

Land height more than 450 meters (1,500 ft.)

Sea depth less than 200 meters (650 ft.)

WILDLIFE

Beasts of the Tropical Jungle

Sumatra's wildlife is the stuff of adventure books. Huge elephants, large skulking cats and elusive rhinos inhabit dense tropical forests amidst a tangle of enormous trees, twisting lianas, and weird and wonderful flowers. Massive human-like apes and beautiful shimmering birds—glimpsed but for a moment—make Sumatra a truly exciting place for naturalists and nature-lovers.

One should not expect the drive-up-and-snap ecotourism of East Africa, however. Good sightings of animals are the result of patience and a considerable investment of time. The ideal way to go about it is to wander slowly through the forest, or find a suitable spot and sit quietly and wait—or rise before dawn and go into the forest with a flashlight.

Sumatra's remarkable biological wealth is partly due to the island's great size and diversity of habitats, and partly to its periodic con-

nections with the Southeast Asian mainland during the past few hundred thousand years. The island has no fewer than 196 different species of mammals—nearly three times the number in Great Britain—20 of which are found nowhere else. These include several species of bats, five primates, the Sumatran rabbit, various squirrels and the elegant Sumatran weasel.

The wide rivers of the east coast are home to dozens of large fish, including a giant catfish that grows to 2 meters in length, and the world's most expensive aquarium fish—the golden *arowana* or dragon fish. Many types of fishes may be seen in the marketplaces in the early morning. Some air-breathing, "walking" species are kept damp and sold alive.

Smaller rivers yield many more species of aquarium fish—heavily striped tiger barbs, the pink-and-brown Kuhl's loach, the orange-and-black clown loach, silver "sharks," half-beaks, gouramis and a variety of rasbora. The guppy was introduced to the region in 1929 by an aquarist in Bandung, West Java, when he accidentally let some escape. Today the guppy is found in ditches and rice fields in most rural areas.

Regional variation

Excavations on Java, where conditions for fossil preservation are better than on Sumatra, have revealed that about 70,000 years ago the Indonesian archipelago was home to many large mammals that are now extinct. Eight species of elephant, a giant pangolin, several pigs, wild dogs, saber-toothed cats, hyenas and a hippopotamus have all left their remains in the fossil record.

Several other species have disappeared more recently—the last confirmed shooting of a Javan rhinoceros on Sumatra was in 1928. The disappearance of the leopard, which still survives in Peninsular Malaysia and Java, is more of a mystery, as it is well-adapted for mountains, forests or plains—with their abundance of monkey and deer.

Sumatra's wildlife is not uniformly distributed throughout its regions. The islands of Simeulue and Enggano—respectively at the top and bottom of the island chain west of Sumatra—have very impoverished wildlife. It is possible that neither has ever been connected to the mainland. Neither island has

ALAIN COMPOST

Left: *The Sumatran tiger.* **Right:** *Sumatran elephants, found in abundance in the southern provinces, have been herded into reserves. Some are being trained to be economically productive.*

any species of squirrel (the main island has 24), but Simeulue has distinctive forms of the long-tailed macaque and forest pig, 3 endemic snakes and 20 endemic subspecies of birds.

The massive explosion of Lake Toba in North Sumatra (see "Geography") may have had an important influence on the distribution of animals in Sumatra, because it spread a broad barrier of dry volcanic material across thousands of square kilometers, forming a kind of barrier. There are clear differences between the mammals found to the north and south of this area. To the north live white-handed gibbons, Thomas' leaf-monkeys, orangutans, the Sumatran wren babbler, Schneider's pitta and the bronze-tailed peacock pheasant. To the south live the agile gibbon, banded leaf-monkey, tarsier, tapir and blue-masked leafbird.

A forgotten eden

More than half a million years have passed since the Mentawai Islands, which lie 100 km off the coast of West Sumatra, were connected with the main island of Sumatra. This long isolation has allowed the evolution of endemic species and the survival of primitive (or relict) species in this region.

Eighty percent of the Mentawai's mammals are endemic. These special Mentawai animals include three species of monkey and a gibbon. Two of the monkeys—the *joja* and the *simakobu*—are unique among monkeys in the Old World in that they live (as the gibbons do) in small family units comprising the mother, father and offsprings.

The people of these islands have a story which tells how humans came into being. At a conference of the *bilou* gibbons, it was agreed that their trees were becoming too crowded. So half the gibbons left the trees to live on the ground, and in time became people. This kind of story represents the closeness felt by the traditional people for their land and its animal inhabitants.

'Men-of-the-forest'

There is an awesomeness and splendor about the primary forest that is difficult to describe in words. The Sumatran forests are disappearing fast, and a walk in one of them should be on every traveler's itinerary.

The easiest forest to reach for the casual visitor is the one at Bukit Lawang on the edge of the Gunung Leuser National Park in North Sumatra, a two-hour ride from Medan. Here captured orangutans (literally meaning "men-of-the-forest") are trained to return to the wild, and it is possible to see these splendid, tousled, russet-colored beasts being educated to adopt a forest lifestyle, though occasionally the forest area near the rehabilitation station is closed to visitors during the time that feeding is stopped to encourage the young animals to find their own food.

Other forest areas are quite easy to reach

ALAIN COMPOST

from Bengkulu, Banda Aceh, Blangkejeran, Kabanjahe, Sidikalang, Pematang Siantar, Bukittinggi, Tebingtinggi and Padang. The basic principle in any of these places is simply to head for the hills.

Mountains and parks

As one climbs a Sumatran mountain, the environment becomes cooler and more exposed. The trees and their leaves become smaller, the boughs and branches become covered in moss. Colorful rhododendrons and other familiar temperate zone plants grace the upper slopes. These plants are found only at the higher elevations, and some bird and other animal species are found only here too.

More adventurous and independent travelers could explore the mountains of Gunung Leuser National Park. Allow at least four days to climb Mt. Kemiri, one of the more accessible peaks, and plan your ascent well. Surprisingly, you will need a number of helpers, and do not forget that temperatures at the peak are only a degree or two above freezing at night.

The mountains are the place where you are most likely to see signs of rhinos and tigers. A word of warning—in this tiger country do not squat down at night to perform your ablutions; women are particularly vulnerable to attacks at night.

The clearance of large areas of lowland forest in recent years has led to conflicts between people and large forest animals such as pigs, long-tailed macaques, bears and elephants. Elephants, which cause the most local damage, have been confined to smaller and smaller areas of the forest as agricultural development and new roads have advanced. These roads often cross traditional elephant migration routes to and from areas with mineral-rich soils. Some populations of elephants are now living at higher densities in Sumatra than anywhere else in the world.

Elephants may be seen in spectacular con-

centrations in the Way Kambas National Park in Lampung province, and in the Air Sugihan Reserve. The reason for this is that elephant drives have been conducted—using helicopters blaring loud rock music, guns firing blank ammunition, and hordes of willing villagers—to persuade the elephants to move from agricultural areas into the reserves. These reserves consist largely of secondary forest, scrub and grasslands which elephants prefer, because their foodplants are more abundant there.

The plight of the elephants symbolizes the plight facing much of Sumatra's wildlife—how to survive when even the forest areas set aside for conservation are facing constant attrition? An attempted solution to the elephant's plight is to take young elephants into "training schools" and to teach them to be economically productive. The oldest of the schools is in the Way Kambas National Park.

Stinking giants

Among the records Sumatra can boast of is the possession of the largest and the tallest flowers in the world. The largest is the peculiar rafflesia, and its size is by no means its only unique feature. It is in fact a parasitic plant that has no leaves, no stem and no roots. It grows on the stem and roots of a particular climbing vine, and apart from the flower it consists only of a few strands of tissue inside the vine. Flower buds, looking like small red cabbages, emerge on the stem but develop slowly—a bud 10 cm in diameter will take about 5 months to open.

When the flower does eventually open there is a powerful smell of rotting meat. Singularly unpleasant to humans, the smell

Above, left: *The tapir, a distant cousin of the rhino.* **Above, right:** *A flying lizard swishes through the air.* **Right:** *A baby orangutan and its mother at the Bukit Lawang rehabilitation station.*

attracts flies and beetles that pollinate the flowers. Since the male and the female flowers may grow some distance apart and remain open for only a week, the odds are clearly stacked against successful pollination. After flowering they decompose and the very small, ripe fruit has to accidentally get caught in the feet of small forest animals so that some of the seeds may happen to be dropped on a vine stem where they can grow. Again, the odds are not exactly in its favor!

The small reserve of Batang Palupuh just outside Bukittinggi in West Sumatra is one of the best places to see this plant. While it is a seasonal plant, it is probably worth visiting at anytime of year—you may never get a chance to see even a Rafflesia bud again!

Another enormous flower with an impressive name is *Amorphophallus titanum*, a type of giant arum lily, of which generally only the leaves are seen. These leaves feed an underground tuber that, when large enough, produces a flower stalk as tall as a man. As with all other lilies, the blossoms are small and packed together on a central spathe.

Like the Rafflesia, the flowers smell of rotting meat and are pollinated by beetles and flies. You have to be lucky to see this plant in full flower, but chances are best in the forests around Mt. Kerinci. The local name is *bunga bangkai*, "corpse flower"—a name that is applied to the *Rafflesia arnoldi* as well on account of the overpowering stench.

And what of tomorrow?

In the forests of Sumatra, the echoing sounds of timber being chopped down at an amazing speed are now as common as the *"ku-ow"* calls of the Argus Pheasant or the drumming of the coucal. The shouts of timbermen are immediately followed by the rustling of a thousand leaves tearing through the forest canopy, and then the ground shudders as the trunk of a centuries-old tree slams to the ground, while the animals shriek with fear. Minor forest products such as rattan, tree gums, etc., are taken away with scant regard to replanting or to future harvests. Tigers, Sumatran rhinos and other game are still shot to provide pleasure for a few hunters, and to appease local villagers. The remaining patches of forest are dwindling fast.

So get out there and explore—climb the mountains, tramp the hills, and enjoy what remains. Take care not to add to the damage, and encourage others to do the same. Sumatra's wildlife is grand and very special, even though time, a certain determination, and a little bit of luck are required to see it. If you are patient and persistent, the rewards are great. But even if all that you can see is the blurred shapes of monkeys crashing through the canopy above you, you will have witnessed at least something of Sumatra's fast-disappearing wildlife.

— *Anthony Whitten*

ALAIN COMPOST

BIRDS

Rare, Colorful Denizens of the Forest

With some 600 species, Sumatra is second only to Irian Jaya in the sheer variety of its birdlife. Fully three quarters of these birds are resident, though only 17 are unique. Sadly, many species are endangered by clearing of land for settlement, logging and hunting, and some are now sighted only rarely.

Calls of the wild

Majestic hornbills attract your attention with their noisy wingbeats and loud calls. Particularly spectacular is the Rhinoceros Hornbill *Buceros rhinoceros*. The male is 1.2 m long, with a huge reddish, up-turned casque and loud honking call. The call of the Long-tailed Helmeted Hornbill *Rhinoplax vigil* consists of a long series of "*hoop*" notes gradually quickening in tempo, then rapidly building to a crescendo, climaxing in a cackling laugh.

Another common call of the forest is the loud "*ku-ow*" of the great Argus Pheasant *Argusianus argus*. When its decorative wing and tail plumes are fully developed, the male pheasant reaches a length of nearly 2 m. Like so many secretive forest birds, you must be very fortunate to see it in the wild.

The colorful kingfishers are mostly inconspicuous forest-dwellers, but the White-throated Kingfisher *Halcyon smyrnensis* lives in open country. This bird was first spotted in 1921 near Medan, but has subsequently spread throughout the island. Along swamps and rivers, watch out for the huge Stork-billed Kingfisher *Pelargopsis capensis*—with its loud, wailing cries.

Mixed dinner parties

If you are lucky enough to chance upon a fruiting fig tree, you will probably see a host of pigeons, hornbills and barbets—all so intent on gorging themselves that they ignore the observer standing below in a shower of discarded fruit debris. Occasionally shattering the cathedral stillness of the noon-time forest, a flock of birds will sweep down upon you, excitedly searching for food. This "feeding party" ranges from woodpeckers, jays and trogons to drongos, bulbuls and babblers. Such parties are believed to be a spontaneous response to food shortages in the dry season. The birds' frenzied activity drives insects from every nook and cranny, to be gobbled up greedily. After just a few minutes, the flock moves on, leaving the equally frenzied birdwatcher frantically trying to remember each species as the last bird departs.

Montane birds

Hill forests are the best birdwatching regions for the casual visitor. Many are accessible, the climate is comfortable, and the birds are less secretive. Here you will hear the rapid, monotonous, three-note call of the Black-browed Barbet *Megalaima oorti* and the curious buzzing note of the Fire-tufted Barbet *Psilopogon pyrolophus*. The lucky birdwatcher will also find the distinctive Yellow-naped Woodpeckers *Picus flavinuchus* and *Picus chlorolophus*, or a party of colorful but secretive Green Magpies *Cissa chinensis*.

Prominent calls are those of the large Cuckoo-dove *Macropygia unchall*, the Mountain Imperial Pigeon *Ducula badia*, and the White-crested Laughing Thrush *Garrulax leucolophus*, with its distinctive hopping gait and beautiful call, which builds to a maniacal climax. The Bronze-tailed Peacock Pheasant *Polyplectron chalcurum* and the Salvadori's

ALAIN COMPOST

Pheasant *Lophura inornata* are endemic to the mountains of Sumatra. The latter was not seen for several decades, but has been sighted recently on Mt. Kerinci in West Sumatra.

Lowland forests

The most popular lowland area for birdwatching in Sumatra is Way Kambas Reserve in Lampung, easily accessible on a weekend trip from Jakarta. A majority of lowland forest species have been recorded here, including the hornbills. Further up the east coast are extensive expanses of swamp forest, but the remaining dryland forests here are greatly in demand for agriculture, and it is increasingly difficult to find good birdwatching localities within easy access of the main roads. It is essential to reach the forest soon after dawn in order to catch the peak activity.

In Way Kambas, the birdwatcher may happen upon a party of Crested Fireback Pheasants *Lophura ignita*, or see the huge White-bellied Woodpecker *Dryocopus javensis*. The Black-and-yellow Broadbill *Eurylaimus orchromalus* is a common songster, with its trilled notes on one pitch that steadily gather speed to a cicada-like buzz.

The best songster of the lowland forest is undoubtedly the long-tailed, scarlet, black and white Shama *Copsychus malabaricus*, a secretive robin of the deep forest. The Eared Nightjar *Eurostopodus temminckii* is also a favorite, with its "*tok-tedau*" calls uttered in flight just above the canopy of trees precisely at dusk and dawn.

The lowland forests have the greatest variety, but even the brightly colored birds are not found easily. A dedicated birdwatcher requires not only skill and patience but also a considerable degree of luck to sight some of the birds mentioned.

Left: A Red-crowned Barbet. *Above:* Storm's Storks looking for fish in a swampy river along the coast. *Right:* A Buffy Fish Owl (ketupa ketupa).

Wetlands

The remote and muddy east coast is a major wintering and transit zone for over 100,000 palaearctic waders from some 25 species. The 4,000 Asian Dowitchers *Limnodromus semipalmatus* sighted here are most exciting, as they represent about half of the world's population of this rare bird.

The Asian Wetlands Bureau is anxiously trying to locate the breeding colonies of Sumatra's 3,000 Milky Storks *Ibis cinereus*, in order to protect this endangered species. The wetlands are also home to large numbers of egrets and herons, Lesser Adjutant Storks *Leptoptilos javanicus*, Black-headed Ibis *Threskiornis melanocephalus*, and a tiny relict population of Spot-billed Pelicans *Pelecanus philippensis*.

Two wetland birds are high on the endangered list. Sumatra and Kalimantan are home to most of the world population of Storm's Stork *Ciconia stormi*—a forest bird of the swamps and rivers. Sumatra is also one of the main strongholds of the forest-dwelling White-winged Wood Duck, whose range formerly extended from Northeast India south to West Java. It is now confined to scattered relict populations. One such population lives in southeast Sumatra, but the wetlands here now possess only a fraction of their former wealth due to human population pressures.

— Derek Holmes

PREHISTORY

From Flaked Glass to Iron and Bronze

We know little of Sumatra's role in the evolution of modern humans. Its forested equatorial landscape has not preserved the same kinds of lake and river-laid deposits which have yielded so many early human fossils in the drier climatic zone of central and eastern Java. Early humans probably avoided the humid rainforests and instead occupied the fertile mountain valleys which run along Sumatra's mountainous spine. Perhaps one day their remains will be found, but so far the record is circumstantial.

The earliest inhabitants

Sumatra, like Java, was joined by dry land to the Malay Peninsula for most of the past million years. Sea levels were generally lower, owing to the great volumes of water trapped in the Pleistocene glaciers. The western part of the Indonesian archipelago has only existed in its present form for the past 6,000 years and for brief intervals during the warmest interglacial periods; the previous interglacial occurred some 120,000 years ago.

Humans probably first entered Sumatra one million years ago across the land bridges of the Pleistocene era (1.6 million to 10 thousand years ago). Archaeological evidence of human activity in Sumatra dates back only 10,000 years. Flake tools of a black volcanic glass called obsidian have been excavated from layers of this age in the cave of Tianko Panjang near Lake Kerinci.

But the most famous remains of the early, pre-agricultural period are gigantic middens of discarded marine shells, animal bones and stone tools once found (most are now destroyed) along the east coast plain between Lhokseumawe and Medan. Little is known of the people who made these mounds, but their skulls suggest that they were of Australomelanesian (similar to the native inhabitants of Australia and inland New Guinea) instead of Mongoloid (East Asian) appearance. They hunted deer, pig, elephant, honey bear and rhinoceros and made their stone tools by flaking one side of a large oval river pebble. Their cultural re-mains are called "Hoabinhian." Similar materials dating back 4,000-13,000 years, but without such large shell middens, also occur in the Malay Peninsula, Thailand and Vietnam.

Austronesian agriculturalists

All the peoples of Sumatra speak Austronesian languages. They are closely related biologically—all belonging to the "Southern Mongoloid" population which now occupies most of Southeast Asia. The Austronesian language family includes almost all indigenous languages of island Southeast Asia and the Pacific islands beyond the Solomons. Starting about 4,000 BC, Austronesian-speaking people began to spread southwards from Taiwan, reaching Sumatra around 2,500 BC.

Most Sumatrans speak dialects of the Malay language, or very closely related languages such as Minangkabau. Languages outside this Malayic group include Gayo and Batak, and the languages spoken in the islands off Sumatra's west coast—Simeulue, Nias, Mentawai and Enggano.

Little archaeological research has been carried out in Sumatra—far too little to allow any useful statements to be made about the prehistoric relationships among these peoples. However, two important observations can be made. First, there is evidence from lakes and swamps in the highlands around Mt. Kerinci and Lake Toba that forest clearance, probably for agriculture, was underway at least 4,000 years ago—perhaps by as much as 7,000 years ago. The evidence comes from palynology: the study of pollens preserved in cores drilled from the ground. It is possible that this forest clearance reflects the arrival of Austronesian-speaking peoples in Sumatra, unless there were other (Austroasiatic-speaking?) agricultural peoples living there before them. This is still one of the big unknowns of the Sumatran past.

The second observation is that languages outside the Malayic group—Gayo and Batak, Simeulue, Nias, Mentawai and Enggano—probably represent localized descent from the initial Austronesian languages established in their respective areas. Acehnese—which is related to the Chamic languages of southern Vietnam—may be an exception.

Right: *A kora-kora outrigger, perhaps similar to the crafts used by ancient Austronesian mariners to settle the islands of Indonesia and the Pacific.*

But the Malayic languages, which also occur in Peninsular Malaysia and coastal Borneo, seem to reflect a later period of cultural and linguistic expansion, perhaps due to the rise of Srivijaya in the late 7th century. This Buddhist kingdom was focused around the area which is now Palembang in South Sumatra. The Malayic languages, therefore, may have replaced older Austronesian languages.

Malay is spoken along the entire eastern lowlands of the island south of Medan—even by the nomadic Kubu peoples. The Kubu foragers, who are of Southern Mongoloid origin, speak a language so closely related to their agricultural neighbors that it is possible that sometime in the recent past their ancestors turned from agriculture to foraging—a reverse of the most commonly-assumed direction of cultural development.

The age of bronze and iron

Like Java, Sumatra has no detailed pre-Bronze Age archaeological record. Our picture for the island really only comes into focus from about 2,000 years ago, when knowledge of bronze casting and iron smelting arrived with the massive bronze drums of Vietnamese ("Dongson") origin.

These drums, with their elaborate surface decorations of boats, raised-floor houses, animals, birds and human warriors have been found at several places in Sumatra—some of these artifacts have been found near Lake Kerinci, in Lampung, in South Sumatra, and near Bengkulu.

The famous Batugajah stone in the Pasemah Highlands of South Sumatra shows a Dongson drum being carried on the back of a man who is apparently subduing an elephant. The Batugajah stone was originally located near Pagaralam in West Sumatra, but is now kept in the museum in Palembang. This carved boulder is one of the fascinating complex of carved megalithic monuments found in the fields around Pagaralam. The bas-relief carvings on these stone monuments show men riding elephants or buffaloes, helmeted human heads, humans wrestling with snakes. There are also many stone mortars, which may have had ritual uses.

Massive underground tombs constructed of large slabs of rock have produced Metal Age artifacts such as glass beads and items made of bronze, iron, and even sometimes gold. Some were painted inside in red, black and white with schematic motifs of horned buffaloes, felines, monkey-like figures and humans. In one case two humans (or possibly a human and a giant cat) are shown holding a Dongson drum. Examples of these grave paintings can be seen in the National Museum in Jakarta. These megalithic carvings and slab stone graves were probably both made during the earlier part of the first millennium AD.

—Peter Bellwood

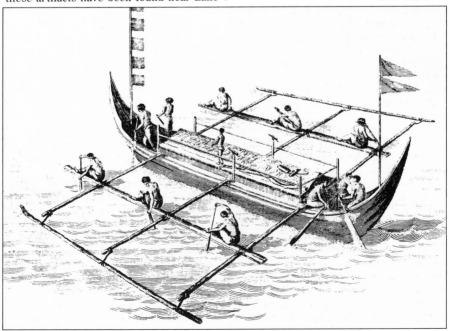

EARLY HISTORY

Svarnadvipa: The Ancient Island of Gold

Sumatra crept slowly and tentatively onto the historical stage. The Indian *Ramayana* epic (3rd century BC) mentions a Svarnadvipa or "Gold Island" which is probably Sumatra, for the island has rich gold deposits that have been mined since antiquity. A Greek scholar of the first century AD named Claudius Ptolemy wrote that cannibals lived on the five Barousai Islands east of India. This is probably a reference to northwest Sumatra—the port of Barus on this coast was famous in later centuries as a source of camphor.

Until about AD 600, foreign writers thought of Sumatra as a forbidding wilderness, inhabited by fierce cannibalistic tribes and wild beasts, but enticingly rich in mineral and botanical wealth. One trading port, located somewhere in the southeast coast, stood out as an isolated outpost of civilization in a savage land. This port, known to the Chinese as Gantoli, maintained diplomatic relations with China between AD 441 and 563.

By the end of the 7th century, several Sumatran kingdoms had established contact with China. These Sumatran courts sent diplomatic missions to China, and Chinese Buddhist monks undertook the hazardous 40-day sea voyage to Sumatra en route to India, bringing back with them glowing descriptions of these kingdoms as flourishing centers of trade and scholarship.

The empire of Srivijaya

The greatest name in ancient Sumatran history is Srivijaya ("Glorious Victory"). In the late 7th century, this kingdom rapidly expanded from its capital near present-day Palembang in southeastern Sumatra, and gained control over the neighboring ports. For the next 400 years Sumatra's history is essentially the story of Srivijaya's golden age.

The name Srivijaya first appeared in AD 671, when a famous Chinese monk, I Ching (also known as Yijing) sojourned in Palembang for six months on his way to India. Palembang was then an active center of Buddhist learning and trade. Yijing states that there were more than 1,000 Buddhist monks in the city, and advised other Chinese monks to go to Srivijaya to study Sanskrit before proceeding to India. Yijing sailed from China to India and back on Srivijayan ships, which were the chief means of transport and communication over this vast distance.

Almost all our accounts of Srivijaya come from records left by foreign visitors. Srivijaya must have had written records, but these would have been written on strips of *lontar* palm leaves, and none has survived. Faint echoes of Srivijayan voices are recorded on a few stone inscriptions found around Palembang and other sites in South Sumatra. Most were written during a critical period between AD 682 and 686 when the kingdom was expanding fast and consolidating its power.

The Srivijayan inscriptions are all similar in content—containing oaths of loyalty to the king coupled with threats of divine retribution against rebels and troublemakers. One inscription from the island of Bangka mentions a military expedition about to depart for Java. Another from Talang Tuo, west of Palembang, commemorates the founding of a park by the ruler—a Buddhist act of virtue

Left: *Srivijayan statue of a boddhisatva, an enlightened being whose every act was designed to contribute to the welfare of all living creatures.*

commited to earn merit for all creatures.

These inscriptions indicate that Srivijaya had a government divided into at least two levels—a central ruler and subordinate governors in outlying districts. They also reveal a complex hierarchy of officials, including generals, tax collectors and scribes attached to the central court.

Srivijayan inscriptions have been found as far north as southern Thailand, and in its heyday the empire seems to have extended all around the coasts of Sumatra, the Malay Peninsula and perhaps western Borneo. Yet these far-flung trading outposts were probably held together by nothing more elaborate than a set of loose ties of loyalty and tribute between the maharaja at Palembang and local rulers who controlled the various ports.

Buddhism and trade

The Palembang inscriptions show that Srivijaya's elite practiced an esoteric form of Buddhism imbued with magical practices. The rulers probably modelled themselves on the Buddhist concept of the *bodhisattva*, an enlightened being whose every act was designed to contribute to the welfare of living creatures. Sumatran, Chinese and later Arab sources paint Srivijaya as a wealthy and powerful kingdom, aggressively pursuing a monopoly over the trade in oriental luxuries passing along the coasts of the island. The hinterlands were never a target for direct control, since their products had to pass through Srivijayan-controlled territory along the coast anyway.

This trade was not a trifling matter. During the first few centuries AD, the Straits of Malacca became an important alternative to the better-known Silk Route across the deserts and mountains of central Asia, linking China with India and the Mediterranean World. Located half way along the sea route, Sumatra furnished products such as spices, ivory, rhinoceros horn and incense which were greatly prized in India and China. Control over this trade was worth fighting for.

In the early 7th century there were other ports in Sumatra, each seeking to attract foreign trade. The most important of these was Malayu on the Batang Hari River in the province of Jambi. By AD 700 Srivijaya had forced them all to submit. No foreign traders were allowed to enter the ports without special permission. For the next 300 years, Srivijaya monopolized the rich maritime trade of Asia. Its wealth became proverbial even among the sophisticated courtiers of China and Persia.

Although Srivijaya was a highly cultured center of trade and scholarship, its capital does not seem to have been a densely populated urban area, but a single row of houses which stretched for several kilometers along the banks of the Musi River. Only when the Chinese began to emigrate to Southeast Asia in the late 11th century, did the first Suma-

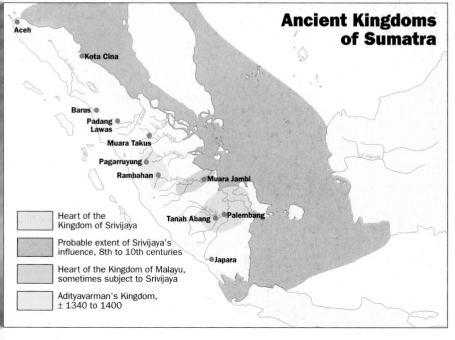

Ancient Kingdoms of Sumatra

Aceh
Kota Cina
Barus
Padang Lawas
Muara Takus
Pagarruyung
Rambahan
Muara Jambi
Tanah Abang
Palembang
Japara

Heart of the Kingdom of Srivijaya

Probable extent of Srivijaya's influence, 8th to 10th centuries

Heart of the Kingdom of Malayu, sometimes subject to Srivijaya

Adityavarman's Kingdom, ± 1340 to 1400

tran towns start to appear.

The rise of Malayu (Jambi)

Srivijaya reached the height of its prosperity around AD 1000. Chinese and Indian sources record that the rulers of Srivijaya sponsored the construction of temples in both these countries, and even densely-populated Java seems to have come under Sumatran influence at this time.

Then disaster struck from an unexpected quarter. In 1025 the mighty Chola kingdom of southern India launched a devastating raid against Srivijaya, from which the kingdom never recovered. An inscription on the wall of a temple at Tanjore in India records that an Indian armada sailed down the straits and

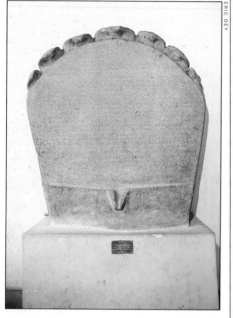

ERIC OEY

subdued one Srivijayan port after another, including the capital itself. The Indian motive for this act—the only such expedition on record in the annals of Indian relations with overseas countries—has never been understood. We can only speculate that Indian merchants traveling this way found Srivijaya's exactions too onerous.

The destruction of Srivijaya brought about important changes in the Sumatran scene. Tamil merchant guilds became active in Sumatra; one set up an inscription in Barus in 1088. Other Sumatran ports—older kingdoms like Malayu as well as several new ones—began to attract international trade. In 1080 Srivijaya's ancient rival Malayu succeeded in reversing their relationship, reducing

Srivijaya to vassal status. Plentiful archaeological remains from Muara Jambi on the Batang Hari testify to Malayu's political and economic domination of Sumatra during the 12th and 13th centuries. By contrast, there are few remains at Palembang from this period.

Malayu's supremacy lasted for 200 years. Few historical sources exist for this period, and we can only assume that Sumatra was peaceful and prosperous, with few disruptions to mar the placid conduct of commerce. This long period of relative stability would have been pleasant to live through, but does not make for interesting history writing.

This extended period of calm ended in the late 13th century. The first blow fell in 1278, when the kingdom of Singhasari in East Java launched a successful expedition against Malayu. According to Javanese sources, a Sumatran princess was taken back to Java, where she married a Javanese prince. In time she gave birth to a son named Adityavarman.

By 1340, this half-Sumatran, half-Javanese noble was living in his mother's ancestral homeland in the Batang Hari lowlands, perhaps sent there to serve as a vassal ruler by the Javanese prime minster Gajah Mada. One of his earliest acts in Sumatra was to set up a statue of monstrous size, depicting himself as a Bhairava, or Tantric Buddhist deity, standing on a pile of human skulls.

Withdrawal to the highlands

Adityavarman broke with tradition by moving his residence into the highlands along Sumatra's west coast, in the area now occupied by the Minangkabau people. Why did he take this radical step? Two theories have been proposed, and both may be correct. First, Adityavarman seems to have severed his ties with Java and set himself up as an independent sovereign. From his home in Sumatra's mountain fastness, he could have defied any Javanese attempt to punish him. Second, the site of his capital is the center of a gold mining region, and in one of his inscriptions he styles himself Kanakamedinindra, "Lord of the Gold Lands." Perhaps he located his palace as near to the mines as possible so as to control this supply of wealth.

Adityavarman left many inscriptions—more than all other rulers of Sumatra put together. These should ensure that his reign would be much better understood than the shadowy ages which preceded him. Unfortunately this is not so. Few of his inscriptions have been transcribed, let alone properly translated and interpreted. One reason for this is that his inscriptions use an odd language combining Old Malay with ungrammatical Sanskrit. This is a marked decline from the standard of composition which prevailed in 7th century Srivijaya, and demonstrates that the ancient traditions of classical learning were on the wane.

The few inscriptions which have been studied do tell us, however, that Adityavarman tried to establish his court in a region which, to our knowledge, had no previous direct contact with the outside world, and no form of government above the level of a federation of neighboring villages. No doubt he struggled hard to recreate the glory of the court life in which he grew up in Java. Fragments of sculpture and architecture remain as mute testimony to his effort, and legends still popular in West Sumatra about contests between champions of autocracy and democracy may echo attempts to superimpose a Javanese-style system of aristocratic rule upon an egalitarian village society.

Adityavarman's last words were inscribed around 1374, when one of his monuments mentions a crown prince, Ananggavarman. After this, a veil of silence descends over West Sumatra, only to lift when Europeans penetrated the area some 300 years later. What happened to this prince? Perhaps he ascended the throne but could not keep alive the traditions his father had tried to transplant. By the 17th century, the West Sumatran political system bore little resemblance to the court system depicted in the classical inscriptions of Srivijaya, Malayu and Java.

A Chinese pirates' nest

Even after its political eclipse in the 11th century, Palembang continued to be an important port. During the 14th century, its Malay subjects chafed under Javanese overlordship. In 1370 Palembang took advantage of the rise of the new Ming dynasty in China by sending a mission to Beijing to request diplomatic recognition. The Ming emperor dispatched envoys to Palembang with documents recognizing Palembang as a Chinese vassal, but the envoys were waylaid and taken to Java, where they were murdered.

In 1392 the ruler of Palembang, a prince whom we know as Parameswara, tried to assert his independence, but a Javanese fleet destroyed the villages on Bangka which constituted his main source of naval strength. He fled to Singapore, where he tried to set up a new Malay stronghold, but he was driven out again in 1397 by an attack by the Siamese. In 1400 Parameswara finally succeeded in establishing a new base at Malacca, which in the 15th century became what Malayu and Palembang had been earlier—the focal point of a triangular trade between the Indonesian archipelago, China and India.

Even then Palembang did not die. According to accounts brought back to China by naval expeditions sent to Southeast Asia in the early 15th century, the Chinese inhabitants of Palembang, several thousand strong, remained behind when Parameswara fled. Left without a local ruler, they chose one from among themselves. Soon his position was usurped by a Chinese ruffian who turned Palembang into a pirates' nest. A Chinese naval expedition attacked Palembang and captured the

ERIC OEY

pirate leader, who was taken back to Beijing and publicly strangled in the marketplace.

After 1430 China turned inward, and contact with Palembang was broken off. When we next glimpse the town, in the early 1500s, it was no longer a Chinese enclave but an important port dominated by Javanese culture. It would be fascinating to know how this transition took place, but unfortunately Sumatra's ancient history resembles less a continuous line than a series of brief dashes separated by broad, gaping spaces.

—John Miksic

Opposite: *A 7th-century Srivijayan inscription.*
Above: *The giant statue of Adityavarman as a Tantric deity standing on a pile of skulls.*

ISLAMIC KINGDOMS

The Rise of Coastal Sultanates

The year AD 1300 saw the beginning of a shift in political and cultural importance from the south to the north of Sumatra, linked with the arrival of a new religion—Islam. Until the 14th century, the great kingdoms of Sumatra had been located at Palembang or Jambi. Now, a number of small Islamic kingdoms began to appear at the mouths of the short, fast-flowing rivers which disgorge into the Straits of Malacca on the northeast coast of the island. It was in these kingdoms that the Malay language, the Islamic religion and a literary tradition using the Arabic script were first elaborated. Yet in the interior of Sumatra, protected by the marshes to the east and the mountains to the west, people continued to speak a dozen mutually unintelligible languages and retained their own religious and cultural traditions.

Along the northern coasts of Sumatra are numerous small rivers where ships from India and the Middle East called for food and water. In the 13th and 14th centuries, trading ports began to appear on the banks of these rivers, and it was in these ports that Islam first gained a foothold in the Indonesian archipelago.

Up to this time, the island of Sumatra had been called "Jawa" or Java Minor by travelers and traders, but now the whole island took on the name of one of the flourishing ports of the northeast, known as Samudra (Sanskrit for "ocean")—or Sumatra.

In 1292, the Venetian traveler Marco Polo sojourned at Samudra for five months waiting for the monsoon to change before continuing his journey back to Europe. His expedition disembarked, and "for fear of these nasty and brutish folk who kill men for food we dug a big trench round our encampment, and within these fortifications we lived for five months." In Marco Polo's time, Samudra was a small kingdom practicing the same shamanistic animism as the peoples of the interior. He reported, however, that the neighboring kingdom of Peurlak (near modern Langsa) had already become Muslim, "owing to contact with Saracen merchants, who continually resort here in their ships."

An Islamic trade network

Ibn Battuta, an Arab traveler, also visited Samudra in 1323. By then it had become a

sophisticated Muslim sultanate, trading with places as distant as south India and China. Many south Indian Muslim traders made their home in the city. Under its preferred Muslim name of Pasai, its rulers issued gold coins, and a system of writing Malay using the Arabic script was developed. Pasai was the earliest center of Islamic scholarship in Southeast Asia. Later sultanates, such as Malacca (on the Malay peninsula), Patani, Aceh and Johor, regarded it as a model of Islamic learning and behaviour.

From Samudra-Pasai, Islam traveled with Muslim traders down the east and west coasts of Sumatra, as well as to the Malay Peninsula and to the trading ports of the north coast of Java. By the 16th century, all the important Sumatran ports were under Islamic authority, and Islam had begun to make inroads in the Minangkabau region, the heavily-populated, gold-producing area in the central mountains where the half-Javanese, half-Sumatran Adityavarman (1356–1375), claiming descent from both Majapahit and Srivijaya, had established his own Tantric Buddhist kingdom.

Sumatran rulers eagerly accepted Islamic legends woven around Alexander the Great, who for Muslims was the world-conquering hero Iskandar Zulkarnain (or "Alexander the two-horned"). Soon after adopting Islam, the kings of Pagarruyung in the Minangkabau highlands elaborated the theory that Alexander had sent his three sons to rule the world—one in China, one in "Rum" (the Roman/Byzantine empire, and its heir in Ottoman Turkey), and the third in Minangkabau.

The Chinese imperial eunuch Cheng Ho (himself a Muslim!) visited Samudra with a huge fleet of ships in the early 15th century, and it may have been the information supplied by him regarding China's needs which prompted Sumatrans to introduce the cultivation of pepper from India. By the late 15th century, Sumatra was the main exporter of pepper to China. Pepper remained Sumatra's principal export until the 19th century, and for much of this period it was the world's major supplier.

The politics of pepper

Samudra-Pasai was just one of the kingdoms on the northern coast of Sumatra. When the Portuguese arrived in Southeast Asia in 1509, there were independent states at Barus, Daya and Lamri (near modern Banda Aceh), Pidië (near Sigli), Pasai and Aru (near Medan). After conquering Malacca and driving out its Muslim merchants, the Portuguese attempted to gain influence in Pasai and Pidië by intervening in their frequent succession disputes. The effect of this was to drive wealthy Muslim merchants to Aceh, where a new and virulently anti-Portuguese sultanate formed at the beginning of the 16th century, on the ruins of the ancient kingdom of Lamri. With the wealth generated through trade, Sultan Ali Mughayat Syah—the first ruler of this new kingdom—was able to conquer Daya, Pidië and Pasai, drive the Portuguese out of northern Sumatra, and begin a century of bitter conflict with the Christian intruders.

Portuguese attacks against Muslim trade, and Aceh's hostile response, introduced an element of holy war into the expansion of Islam in Sumatra. From 1540 to 1630, Aceh launched more than a dozen large expeditions against the Portuguese at Malacca. During one siege in 1547, St. Francis Xavier galvanized Malacca's defenders and was credited with miraculously prophesying the Portuguese naval victory.

The last and greatest of the fleets sent against Malacca contributed to the decline of both powers. In 1629, the Aceh fleet of 19,000 men and several hundred ships was trapped and destroyed by a Portuguese fleet which arrived unexpectedly from Goa in India. Few

LE ROY D'ACHEM.

Left: *An early map of Aceh, whose harbor then supplied half the world's pepper.* **Right:** *The Acehnese sultan seen through European eyes.*

of these ships returned after the fight and the hostile weather encountered on the way. Aceh never fully recovered from this blow.

Aceh's golden age

During the latter half of the 16th and early part of the 17th century, Aceh was supplying Europe with half its pepper. Venetian envoys in Cairo and Constantinople noted with satisfaction—and the Portuguese with dismay—that ships from "Assi" were arriving regularly in Jiddah or Suez laden with pepper. Aceh was then known as the "doorstep to Mecca" (*serambi Mekkah*), because it was from here that Muslim pilgrims from all countries "below the winds" (i.e. Southeast Asia) embarked for their voyage to the Holy Land.

Because of Aceh's abundant pepper, and its known aversion to the Catholic Portuguese, Protestant Europeans made the sultanate their first Asian port of call. The Dutch were welcomed in 1598 and the English in 1600. Mounted on elephants for their official reception at the palace, they were honored with gifts of sarongs and krisses. However, relations between the Dutch and the Acehnese were not always smooth; as an example the first Malay dictionary and phrasebook was written during a year's captivity in Aceh by the Dutch Admiral de Houtman.

Aceh reached its peak of power and wealth under the brilliant but ruthless Sultan Iskandar Muda ("the young Alexander," 1607-1636). Throughout the first half of the 17th century, Aceh's court astonished visitors with its lavish feasts and public rituals. Hundreds of richly-caparisoned elephants and thousands of pikemen accompanied the sultan in the weekly Friday procession from the palace to the great mosque. On the major Islamic feast days and at receptions for foreign guests, the processions were even grander —there were contests between pairs of fighting elephants, buffaloes and rams.

In the early 17th century, Aceh was one of the major powers in Asia. Its effective authority stretched along the coast to Padang in the west and Tanjung Balai (on Karimun Island) in the east. Acehnese viceroys were appointed to rule over the Karo and Simalungun Batak and the Minangkabau. In the Malay peninsula, Aceh ruled Kedah and Perak, and conquered states as far away as Johor and Pahang. Victorious naval expeditions brought back thousands of captives to populate the city, man the war galleys, and carry out heavy construction work in the capital. Three thousand women waited on the sultan in his palace, and meals were served on plates of gold.

Warfare and the impermanence of building materials have left little trace of this former splendor. The city was never walled, a fact which an Acehnese chronicler attributed to the bravery of its people and the ferocity of its war elephants. In 1874, the palace complex was destroyed by the invading Dutch, and the

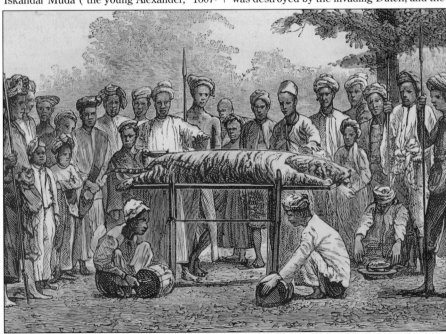

great mosque, which was built of wood, was also destroyed. All that now remains is the curious limestone *gunongan* and *pintu khob*, ornaments built in the 1630s as part of the royal pleasure garden along the banks of the Krueng Daroy, just south of the palace. Today, the style of the perished great mosque can be seen in the mosque of Indrapuri, originally built in the period of Sultan Iskandar Muda, about 20 km upriver from Banda Aceh.

Iskandar Muda's declining years were marked by signs of madness. He killed many of those closest to him, including his own son. His son-in-law, Iskandar Thani, succeeded him in 1636, but died in 1641. A violent succession dispute arose, and the leading men of the kingdom decided to place on the throne Iskandar Muda's daughter (Iskandar Thani's widow), Taj al-Alam ("Crown of the World," 1641-75). During her reign, the stern personal autocracy instituted by her father was relaxed. Traders enjoyed more predictable conditions in the capital, and local lords were able to establish hereditary lineages throughout the country.

Despite being at odds with Islamic law and tradition, the experiment with female rule was deemed so successful that three more queens were successively placed on the throne. As an English visitor explained, "the very name of a kinge is long since become nauseous to them through the Tyrannical Government of their last kinge." Not until 1699, when one of the factions was able to produce a decree from Mecca judging female rule unacceptable to Islam, was a king again on the throne of Aceh.

After the defeat that destroyed its entire fleet at Malacca in 1629, Aceh went into a slow decline. The Dutch were able to prise from Aceh's control both the pepper-growing areas on the west coast of Sumatra and the tin-producing areas on the Malay Peninsula. The major sources of Aceh's continued wealth were then the items that had once been regarded as non-exportable royal treasures—gold and elephants.

Literature and theology

Malay was the language spoken in the cities of Aceh in the 17th century, and it was here that much of the best classical Malay literature was written. The earliest Muslim Malay *syair* (poetry in 4-line verses) still extant is the work of Hamzah Fansuri (Hamzah of Fansur, i.e. Barus) who lived and worked in the late 16th century. Syech Syamsuddin of Pasai, who was the chief *kadi* (Muslim judge) of Aceh until his death in 1630, was influential with Iskandar Muda. Both he and Ham-

zah were adherents of the *wujuddiya* school of mysticism, which in the eyes of its critics so emphasized union with God that it erased the distinction between God and man.

In the reign of Iskandar Thani, a rigidly orthodox current of thought gained the upper hand, the works of Hamzah and Syamsuddin were burned and several of their adherents were executed. This orthodox reaction was led by the most prolific of classical Malay writers, Nuruddin ar-Raniri (of Ranir, in Gujerat), who wrote numerous theological works, and the greatest encyclopedic work of politics and history in Malay, the *Bustan al–Salatin*. He was unpopular with the people of Banda Aceh, and when his patron Iskandar Thani died, ar-Raniri was chased out of Aceh by an angry crowd.

The most influential religious scholar of the second half of the century, Abdur'rauf of Singkel, managed to combine orthodoxy with a tolerant approach to pre-Islamic beliefs and mystical ideas, and today he is revered as the greatest of Acehnese saints. His tomb at the mouth of Aceh river is still honored and he is remembered as Syech Kuala (the Syech of the river mouth). Aceh's state university is named in his honor.

Economic decline

World demand for pepper reached a peak in the middle of the 17th century. From 1650 onwards, the port-states which had dominated Sumatra since the 15th century began to decline along with the trade which had sustained them. Aceh embarked on a long period of internal conflict, and the *uleëbalang* (local chiefs) who controlled the rivermouths of Aceh coast became virtually independent of the capital. Acehnese gradually replaced Malay as the language of literature, and the weight of state authority was lightly felt by the majority of highland Sumatrans.

The lack of any major political authority encouraged adventurers such as the Bugis from South Sulawesi, the Arabs from Hadhramaut, and the Minangkabau from West Sumatra to seize power by warfare, by marrying into the ruling families, or by strategic alliances. Increasingly, European and south Indian merchants were appointed as *shahbandars* or trade officials in the island's ports. By the 18th century, the Europeans emerged as the biggest economic powers while Sumatra was an economic backwater.

—*Anthony Reid*

Opposite: *A royal tiger hunt.*

IMPACT OF THE WEST

Gunboats, Garrisons and Guerrillas

By the 18th century, the decline in world demand for pepper had deprived the rulers of ports such as Aceh and Palembang of the means to dominate their hinterlands. The biggest economic powers in Sumatra were now European—the Dutch established their headquarters at Padang in 1663, and the British at Bengkulu in 1685. Each became a center of rival networks of trade along the west coast, but they were militarily vulnerable. Local Sumatrans drove the British out in 1719 and held Bengkulu for many years. These lonely European outposts also attracted the attention of the French. Admiral Comte d'Estaing occupied Bengkulu for several months in 1760; Admiral Linois pillaged the fort and town in 1803. Dutch Padang was equally vulnerable, falling to the British in 1781-1784 and 1795-1816, and to a French privateer for two months in 1793. During this period Dutch influence was virtually eliminated from Sumatra.

British officials of the Bengkulu administration were the first to give detailed accounts of the Batak interior of northern Sumatra (Holloway and Miller, 1772), and the island of Nias (Jack and Prince, 1819). Raffles himself visited the Minangkabau capital of Pagarruyung in 1818. A great opponent of slavery, Raffles was nevertheless enthusiastic about Nias—"the finest people, without exception, that I have yet met with in the East." He was outraged that the island was a major supplier of slaves to Aceh, the Dutch and the French colonies, and even to the British settlements in Bengkulu and Penang. Raffles proclaimed British sovereignty over the island in 1820, but this was disallowed by London.

Pepper, coffee and tin

A new phase of commercial expansion affected Sumatra from about 1780. British and Tamil traders came from India, British and Chinese traders arrived from the new British port at Penang (founded 1786), and Americans from Salem, Providence and New London. The Americans found willing pepper suppliers in local chiefs on the west coast between Sibolga and Meulaboh, a frontier region beyond the reach of Acehnese authority in the north and the English Company in the south. More than 5,000 tons a year were exported from this region alone in the early

19th century, primarily by Americans. In the Minangkabau area, cassia (a substitute for cinnamon), gambir (used for tanning leather), and from 1790, coffee, became attractive new crops. At the beginning of the 18th century, Chinese miners began to exploit the tin deposits in Bangka.

With the decline of authority, first of the Sumatran rulers, then of the Dutch Company, Sumatra became once again an economic frontier, as colonists from settled areas flocked to new regions to grow export crops. The absence of major powers suited foreign traders, but when commercial disputes escalated into violence they appealed for vengeance to their respective navies. The Americans began this gunboat diplomacy by destroying coastal Acehnese villages in 1826 and 1838, and then French fleets did the same in 1839 and 1840.

The Dutch had to start almost from scratch when their prewar possessions were returned by Britain after the Napoleonic Wars in 1816. Economically on their knees and militarily tied down by the Java War (1825–1830), the Dutch were obliged to accept that others would dominate Sumatra's trade. Meanwhile, they moved slowly, using their limited military force to annex one river port a time, trying to ensure that no other Europeans staked a political claim to any part of the island. Sumatrans did not accept the extension of Dutch authority without a fight.

Anglo-Dutch squabbling over their respective rights following the founding of Singapore was temporarily resolved in 1824, when the British withdrew all claims to Sumatra, in return for the Dutch doing the same on the Malay Peninsula. In 1825, the Dutch seized control of Palembang and the tin-bearing islands of Bangka and Belitung. The Dutch also inherited a British conflict with a militant Islamic movement known as "Paderi" in the Minangkabau highlands, a conflict which dragged on until 1837, when the Paderi's leader, Imam Bonjol was finally killed. (See "History" in WEST SUMATRA.)

Dutch conquests

The Paderi movement disturbed the Batak as well as the Minangkabau areas. A conquest of the southern Batak areas in the 1820s was carried out from the Paderi commercial stronghold of Bonjol in northern Minangkabau. The key leader of the holy war to the north was Tuanku Rao, a Batak who had converted to militant Islam. He led a Paderi force forcing most of the Mandailing and Angkola areas of South Tapanuli to accept Islam. Tuanku Rao appears to have taken his troops even farther north, and tried unsuccessfully to convert the Bataks around Lake Toba.

Opposite and below: *Dutch forces under Colonel van Heutsz finally managed to defeat the Acehnese only after 30 years of bitter fighting.*

ERIC OEY

There is a story that Tuanku Rao invited the tenth Singamangaraja (a Toba Batak priest-king who lived west of the lake) to meet him in the market place at Butar, and there killed him. Other Batak stories say that Tuanku Rao enjoyed extraordinary military success because he was the abandoned nephew of the magical Singamangaraja. European attempts to Christianize the Batak were less successful. It was not until the mid 19th century that any real progress was made. (See "The Batak" in NORTH SUMATRA).

Over two decades, from 1820 to 1841, the Dutch gradually conquered the Minangkabau area and built a series of strategic forts in the highlands. This made the most densely-populated region of Sumatra also the principal Dutch stronghold. The expenses of the garrisons were met by the forced delivery of coffee at fixed prices. There was however enough land to enable the enterprising Minangkabau to take advantage of improving communications and expanding markets to grow their own coffee, tobacco, sugar, cassia and gambir, giving rise to a prosperous, commercially-oriented middle class.

The same group responded enthusiastically to the token efforts the Dutch made to provide modern secular schools for Indonesians. In the 1840s they began funding their own district schools. By 1872 there were almost 1,200 Minangkabau children in school —a proportion several times higher than in Java, where education was limited to the aristocracy. This first generation to be literate both in Jawi (Malay-Arabic) and Latin script provided Sumatra—and the rest of Indonesia—with a large number of its clerks, schoolteachers, journalists and political activists in the 20th century.

Dutch progress on the east coast of Sumatra was hampered by constant protests by British merchants in Singapore and Penang. A Dutch expedition was sent to Siak in 1858 to throw out an English adventurer, and another to the small northern states of Langkat, Deli, Serdang and Asahan in 1865, to establish Dutch rights against claims of Acehnese suzerainty and British commerce.

These small states proved a rich prize, thanks to the volcanic soil which proved ideal for growing tobacco. The pioneer Dutch planter, Jacobus Nienhuys, had moved to Deli (the region around Medan) ahead of Dutch troops, in 1863, and within a decade had established its reputation for growing the world's finest cigar wrapper-leaf. British objections were overcome by opportunities to provision this growing plantation economy.

In the 1870s and 1880s, 20,000 Chinese laborers were brought in each year to cut down the forests and tend the tobacco plantations. Later, the planters turned to cheaper and more tractable Javanese labor. In the 1920s, just before the system of indentured labor was ended, partly due to American pressure, a total of 260,000 Javanese worked on the plantations. Prosperous new towns grew up at Medan, Binjai, Pematang Siantar and Tanjung Balai. The insignificant coastal rajas who controlled the river mouths became enormously wealthy on the royalties from plantation land and (in Langkat after 1890) from oil.

The Aceh wars

The biggest challenge to Dutch colonialism in Sumatra was Aceh, which never signed unequal treaties with the Dutch. It had wealth, arms and foreign contacts from its pepper and betelnut trade. Aceh also had a treaty of mutual defence with the British, arranged by Raffles in 1819, and a guarantee of Aceh's independence was incorporated in the 1824 Anglo-Dutch Treaty, which divided the Malay-speaking world into two halves. It was only in 1871 that British objections were overcome, clearing the way for a more vigorous Dutch approach.

The first Dutch attack was ill-prepared, brought on hastily by energetic Acehnese

attempts to form defensive alliances with Turkey, France and the United States. The US Consul in Singapore agreed to forward a draft Aceh-US Treaty to Washington, though it received no support from the State Department. A Dutch force of 3,000 men attacked the Acehnese capital in April 1873, but withdrew three weeks later having lost its commander and 80 men. Humiliated, the Dutch recruited the largest force they had ever assembled in the Indies, and landed 10,000 men the following December. The Acehnese citadel was taken six weeks later amidst a cholera epidemic that wiped out at least a thousand on each side. This was, however, only the first chapter in a war which was to last until 1903, tying up Dutch resources, men and money, and sapping morale for 20 years, leaving a legacy of bitterness in Aceh.

By the mid-1880s, the leadership of Acehnese resistance passed to the *ulama* (religious scholars) who preached the necessity of a holy war at any cost. The Dutch graveyard in Banda Aceh is a monument to more than 10,000 soldiers who died of wounds or disease on the Dutch side. For the Acehnese, who lost at least 5 times as many, their enduring monument is the memory of countless dead heroes, some now officially recognized as Indonesia's national heroes. Among these are the west coast *uleëbalang* (district chief) Teuku Umar, who defected in 1896 after acting as the principal Dutch ally. Others include

Teuku Umar's gallant wife Cut Nyak Dien and *ulama* leader Cik di Tiro, who defiantly called on the Dutch governor to embrace Islam if he wished to avoid the inevitable destruction awaiting the infidels. Right to the end of Dutch rule, Aceh remained an occupied province. At the approach of the Japanese in 1942, the province rebelled and drove out the remaining Dutch forces.

On the Dutch side, the eventual success was credited to two men in particular. Colonel J.B. van Heutsz, military governor of Aceh from 1898 to 1904, adopted an uncompromising policy of relentless pursuit, and was rewarded by being named governor-general (1904-9). His invaluable key adviser was the Islamic specialist Christiaan Snouck Hurgronje, author of a Dutch strategy of tolerating or even encouraging Islam in what was held to be the religious domain, but resolutely crushing any sign of Islamic political assertion. After 1904 the policies of these two men were extended throughout the Indies. Dutch troops penetrated every corner of Sumatra, and by 1910 the whole island was for the first time under a single authority; but one that did not enjoy much love from its people.

—*Anthony Reid*

Opposite: Oil was discovered in northern Sumatra in the 1890s. **Above:** A plantation economy based on coolie labor made Sumatra the most profitable region in the Indies in the early 20th century.

MODERN HISTORY

Nationalism, Revolution & Independence

The Dutch conquest resulted in the development of a common education and administrative system throughout Sumatra. Together with Islam, this laid the foundation for the emergence of common national sentiment. This first made itself felt through the mass Muslim organization Sarekat Islam, which tapped the suppressed resentment at alien domination. Jambi witnessed a small rebellion in 1916. Aceh was disturbed by riots in 1918–1919, and the Minangkabau developed a radical Islamic movement in the same years. In 1926, the Indonesian Communist Party launched a quixotic revolution; paradoxically, it was some of the relatively commercialized Muslims of Minangkabau who fought hardest for it.

In 1917 the first generation of Sumatrans to have enjoyed Dutch education formed the Young Sumatran League. Support came from Minangkabau clerks, teachers and traders all over Sumatra. Toba Batak students established their own organization in the 1920s, and by 1926 these groups had been incorporated into the National League of Indonesian Students. Sumatran figures such as Mohammad Hatta (later Vice-President) and Soetan Sjahrir (Indonesia's first prime minister) contributed greatly to developing Indonesia's national consciousness.

Sumatra's role in developing a national literature was even more important. Malay had always been the principal written language for most Sumatrans, and its adoption as Bahasa Indonesia, the language of nationalism, involved no linguistic conflict as it did for Javanese and Sundanese. Hence the first writers to adopt Malay to modern literary uses were virtually all Sumatran. In the early twenties, the political activists Mohammad Yamin, Sanusi Pane, and Mohammad Hatta were the first to write Malay poetry in a modern spirit, while the Langkat prince Amir Hamzah and the revolutionary Chairil Anwar wrote the finest Indonesian poetry of the 1930s and 1940s. The development of the modern Indonesian novel in the 1920s and 1930s was almost entirely a Minangkabau affair.

It is not surprising, considering this strong contribution to Indonesian nationalism, that Sumatra rejected all attempts to separate it from Java in the turbulent 1940s. The Japanese invasion in March 1942 caused greater upheaval than in Java. In Aceh the Japanese were assisted by an armed rebellion against the retreating Dutch, whose leaders wanted to end the dominance of the *uleëbalang* (district chiefs). The Japanese initially suppressed all these movements, and forbade any nationalist activity. However, the Japanese gave the nationalists access to the state-controlled media in order to mobilize the population for war purposes. When the war ended, two rival elites—nationalist and traditionalist—eyed each other with mistrust.

The Japanese belatedly fostered the idea of an independent Sumatra in 1945, establishing a powerless consultative council and a secretariat in Bukittinggi. In 1947, the returning Dutch set up federal states in the areas they controlled in East Sumatra and South Sumatra. The following year they encouraged a Sumatran umbrella organization for these and other states, but the idea gained little interest. Sumatrans had already decided in the 1920s that they could only bring together their diverse ethnic groups at a national level.

Independence was declared in Jakarta three days after Hiroshima, but the revolution in Sumatra did not begin until October, when allied troops arrived to accept the Japanese surrender. Young activists, some with Japanese military training, fought against the defeated Japanese for arms, then against the British who occupied parts of Medan, Padang, and Palembang, and finally against the Dutch forces which replaced the British at the end of 1946.

Most of the violence was internal. In Aceh the *uleëbalang* were overthrown by a Muslim-led coalition in December 1945, at the conclusion of a bloody civil war. Three months later, the east coast Malay sultans and Simalungun rajas were overthrown in what was dubbed a "social revolution." These spontaneous movements led to a breakdown in central authority, especially in East Sumatra, where semi-military groups of young men, formed to fight the Japanese and Dutch, became a law unto themselves, funding themselves by sell-

Right: *The oil boom of the 1970s and 1980s has made Sumatra a major world producer.*

ing the produce of the plantations they controlled to Singapore merchants. When the Dutch occupied the plantation area around Medan, and the oil installations of Palembang in mid-1947, these armed groups fought among themselves in Tapanuli.

The vast island was far from integrated politically or economically when the revolution ended with transfer of full sovereignty to Indonesia in 1950. Each former residency had its own battle-hardened military force reluctant to return to civilian life, and each felt it had earned the right to play a part in the Republic on its own terms. Moreover, the rewards of the smuggling trade to Singapore, which had seemed patriotic during both the Japanese occupation and the revolution, were not easy to give up to an impoverished central government in Jakarta which had little to offer in return.

The first post-independence crisis occurred in Aceh, when Muslims objected to being incorporated with Christian Bataks into the province of North Sumatra, and to the failure of the government to declare Indonesia a Muslim state. In 1953, Aceh revolted against Jakarta, and declared Aceh part of Dar al-Islam (the Islamic world). Troops sent from Java quickly re-occupied the Acehnese towns, but the hinterland remained largely in rebel hands until peace was eventually negotiated in 1959. Aceh was then granted autonomous status. Meanwhile Toba Batak

and Minangkabau military leaders joined national politicians dissatisfied with the centralism, corruption and pro-communist policies of the central government, to form the Revolutionary Government of the Republic of Indonesia (PRRI) in February 1958. The central government reacted by bombing Padang and Bukittinggi and sending a large force from Java. The fighting was over within six months, but it left West Sumatra feeling like an occupied province in which locals were no longer trusted with high military or civilian office. If Sumatrans had been over-represented in national leadership before these events, they were under-represented thereafter.

Under President Suharto's New Order government which took power in 1966, regional discontents have eased. Firstly, the government's anti-communist and free-market policies are those which the PRRI had advocated. Secondly, the central government has provided roads, electricity, schools, hospitals and other infrastructural facilities, which have helped transform the economy. Large multi-ethnic provinces were broken up until all except North Sumatra (pre-war East Sumatra plus Tapanuli) were back to the boundaries of the old Dutch residencies, and the army's presence became less obvious. If one still hears grumbles about the *pusat* (center), these are now no different from those heard in every Indonesian province.

—*Anthony Reid*

PEOPLES OF SUMATRA

A Mélange of Ethnic Groups and Religions

More than 40 million people live in Sumatra —one-fifth of Indonesia's huge population— making this the second most populous island in the archipelago, after Java. Four large ethnic groups—the Malay, the Minangkabau, the Acehnese and the Batak—form the vast majority of the island's indigenous population, but over a dozen smaller ethnic groups are also represented, each speaking a different language and possessing a distinct history and culture.

In recent centuries, there has been a significant influx of outsiders to Sumatra as well. The Javanese, who came by the thousands as plantation workers at the beginning of this century, continue to arrive through Indonesia's ambitious transmigration program. The Chinese, who first came as debt-bonded plantation coolies and tin miners in the 19th century, now dominate the wholesale and merchandising sectors of all major Sumatran towns. And a smattering of peoples from other islands of Indonesia and abroad now live and work on the island as civil servants and in the booming oil industry.

Islamic strongholds

Sumatra is among the most thoroughly Islamic regions in the archipelago. History states that Islam first came to Southeast Asia at a town on Sumatra's northeast coast, variously referred to as Samudra or Pasai. From here, the religion spread around both coasts of Sumatra and across to neighboring islands and the Malay Peninsula—largely through an Islamic trading network established by Malay merchants at Malacca in the 15th century. For many centuries the term "Malay" was indeed synonymous throughout Indonesia with "Muslim."

The Malays have a long and illustrious history dating back to the days when the Buddhist Malay kingdom of Srivijaya dominated the straits from a base at what is now Palembang, in South Sumatra, from the late 7th until the 11th centuries. For many centuries thereafter, the figure of the Malay raja embodied the highest cultural ideals of gentility, grace, eloquence, learning and Muslim piety throughout the Malay World. While fishermen and farmers could never match the raja's refinement, they modelled their best behavior on the ideals he represented.

Today the Malays are Sumatra's largest ethnic group, numbering more than 13 million people and inhabiting most of the southern and eastern coasts and lowlands of the main island, as well as the smaller islands offshore. Another 8 million people in neighboring Malaysia also consider themselves to be Malay—though many are descendants of Minangkabau, Cham and Javanese migrants. Even in Sumatra itself, many people of Batak descent call themselves "Malay," so that in fact a tremendous linguisitic and cultural variety is encompassed by this ethnonym.

The second largest ethnic group in Sumatra, and the one most closely related to the Malays in terms of language and culture, are the Minangkabau of the western central highlands. They now number about 5 million, and are known as staunch Muslims, while at the same time retaining vestiges of an unusual matrilineal kinship system that predates their conversion to Islam. This means that the traditional Minangkabau longhouses, fertile ricelands, and positions of leadership within the clan are all transmitted to the next generation through women. While men hold public positions of leadership, they inherit these through their mothers—and when they retire they are replaced by their sisters' sons.

A third major Islamic group inhabits Sumatra's strategic northern coast. The Acehnese, who number about 3 million today, also speak a language related to Malay, and are best known for their fierce resistance against the Dutch during a 30-year *jihad* (holy war) from 1873 to 1903. Long before this, in the 17th century, Aceh was in fact the most powerful Islamic kingdom in the region. Today, Islam still rules the hearts of the Acehnese, and on Fridays the faithful fill Banda Aceh's stately Grand Mosque while the town's shops are shuttered tight. Just as among the Minangkabau, and despite Islam's favoring of males, Acehnese village life revolves around women. Upon marriage, a man usually moves to his wife's village, where her family provides them a house.

Overleaf: *A Karo Batak festival ca. 1920. Photo courtesy of Antiquariaat Acanthus, Utrecht.*

In the highlands of central Aceh live the Gayo, all of whom are Muslim. Their language, like that of the Acehnese, is remarkable for its many borrowings from Mon-Khmer, a language group of mainland Southeast Asia. Unlike the Acehnese, however, the Gayo are patrilineal, and in the majority of cases, a bride moves to her hudband's village. Gayo who live around the edges of Lake Tawar harvest carp and a minnow-like fish called *depik* from the lake; coffee and tea are other major products from this region.

The Gayo fight with words. Poetic duels, *didong*, were once performed at weddings between pairs of speakers representing the families of bride and groom. Later, *didong* helped defuse hostilities between villages, and more recently men have turned this verbal art into a competition between clubs or teams composed of lead singers supported by an encircling chorus.

Christian converts

While the coastal and urban areas of the island are predominantly Muslim, large areas of Sumatra are now mainly Christian, and in fact more Christians live on this island than any other in Indonesia. German Lutheran missionaries working with the Toba Batak enjoyed early and widespread success. Today, the Toba Batak church is the largest Christian body in Indonesia.

In contrast, the Dutch Reformed missionaries who worked in the nearby Karo Batak region met decades of resistance. As a result, the Christian Karo have become a majority only since the 1950s, when an indigenous church emerged. The Simalungun Batak, once part of the Toba church, have separated into their own ethnic denomination.

The hymns and the liturgy in all these ethnic Batak churches are in the vernacular languages, but just as throughout Indonesia, these ethnic churches face competition from Catholic and Pentecostal denominations which operate through the medium of Indonesian, and whose congregations are ethnically mixed.

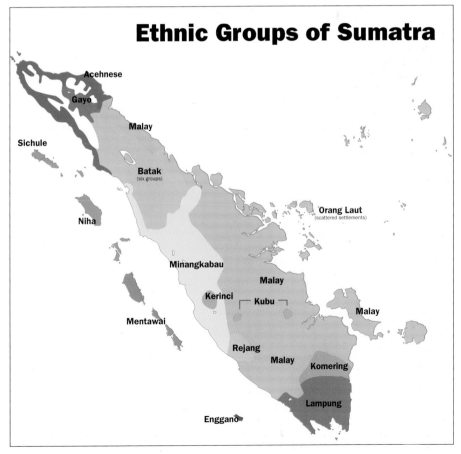

Ethnic Groups of Sumatra

Acehnese
Gayo
Malay
Sichule
Batak
(six groups)
Niha
Orang Laut
(scattered settlements)
Minangkabau
Malay
Kerinci
Kubu
Mentawai
Malay
Rejang
Malay
Komering
Lampung
Enggano

About 10 percent of the Angkola Batak who live to the south of the Toba are also Christian, but the majority, like the Mandailing Batak to the south in South Tapanuli, are Muslim. Other pockets of Christianity include the islands of Nias and Mentawai off the west coast, and some of the original inhabitants of the island of Enggano.

A patchwork of peoples

While most of Sumatra's people live as farmers, small groups such as the Kubu of Jambi Province and the Sakai of the Riau Islands live mainly by fishing and hunting along swampy southern rivers. Another group, the Orang Laut—literally "sea people" but often called sea gypsies or even sea pirates—live in boats among the hundreds of small islands in the Riau Archipelago.

Lake Kerinci, surrounded by wet rice terraces in the highlands of western Jambi Province, is home to the Kerinci people. Lacustrine fishing and tea cultivation supplement a rice economy. Like the Minangkabau, the Kerinci are matrilineal and construct longhouses for matrilineally extended families, but their longhouses are unique in the archipelago for having no communal passage or gallery linking the family apartments. While a man attaches himself to his wife's family, he retains membership in his natal family and lives partly at his own longhouse, where he helps to manage his lineage property and the affairs of his sister's children.

Bengkulu Province is home to the Rejang, who call themselves "We the People of Jang." Their mythical ancestor, Jang, was reputed to be of the royal family of Java's Majapahit kingdom. He is said to have settled in Sumatra in the 14th century, and had four sons who became the ancestors of the four patrilineal clans that today constitute Rejang society, a people numbering around 200,000. The Rejang region spans a diverse terrain, from the coast up gentle foothills to highland peaks covered in tropical rainforest.

Rejang was one of the last regions in Sumatra to accept Islam, so the pre-Islamic focus on ancestor spirits remains strong. Each of Rejang's clans claims dominion over its own territory. The oldest village in each of these territories contains a sacred shrine associated with its founding ancestor. Villages and lineages also have their ancestral shrines, so pilgrimage to the principal clan shrine occur only for extremely important purposes.

To the west of Palembang, near the town of Lahat, the Pasemah Highlands contain megalithic remains dated to AD 100. This statuary, the most extensive of its kind in the archipelago, consists of many animal and human figures as well as dolmens, menhirs and stone cist graves. Although the Pasemah people converted to Islam in the early 20th century, they continue to visit these shrines, and others on Mt. Dempo, to redeem ancestral

ALAIN COMPOST

vows. Although similar to the Rejang in their social organization and even their founding mythology, the Pasemah were bitter enemies of the Rejang, and the lowland Malays as well, in the precolonial era.

The Lampung region at Sumatra's southern tip contains several ethnic groups with different cultural histories, including many Javanese who have migrated here in large numbers, both spontaneously and through the government's transmigration programs. One of the most numerous indigenous peoples of this region, the Abung, say they originated in the mountains to the west where, in the 15th century, they maintained a megalithic culture similar to that of Nias. Headhunting and human sacrifice brought them into conflict with neighboring peoples, especially lowland Malays, who finally drove them into their current setting around 1450.

Abung society is composed of numerous patrilineal clans. Each clan maintains a separate house, occupied most of the time by only a few elderly people. Villages contain as many as 3,000 people and 120 clan houses, but working adults and children spend most of their time in small seasonal settlements outside the village, maintaining their swidden gardens. They return to the village for initiation ceremonies or other special events. Initiations usher men into a series of ranks that indicate their wealth. Formerly, headhunting was a precondition for the highest rank, and initiates to this rank were enthroned on a dolmen of stone.

Although the Dutch attempted to stop their headhunting and human sacrifices, the Abung continued these practices surreptitiously into the 19th century. Like all their neighbors in the region, the Abung are now Muslims. In their modern version of initiation rites, called *papadon*, dancing substitutes for headhunting, and a buffalo is sacrificed instead of a human.

Into the modern world

In the last 20 years, Sumatra's natural resources—particularly oil and natural gas—have helped fuel Indonesia's rapid economic growth. This growth has resulted in a new emphasis on education and on highway construction, which together with newspapers, films and television are increasingly drawing the peoples of Sumatra into a national community and into the world economy. Signs of this emphasis—from the newly-completed Trans-Sumatra Highway running the length of the island, to the puffing gas and oil refineries of Lhokseumawe and Palembang—are everywhere to be seen.

— *Rita Smith Kipp*

Opposite: *A couple in Palembang display the traditional Malay wedding costume, imitating the style of ancient Srivijayan Malay royalty.*
Below: *A wedding celebration in Lampung.*

JILL GOCHER

ARCHITECTURE

The House with Horns and a Tail

The island of Sumatra contains some of Indonesia's richest and most fascinating traditions of vernacular, or domestic, architecture. Even the most casual observer can hardly fail to be impressed by the imposing scale of these buildings, by their ingenious nail-free construction and by the vigor and delicacy of their carved and painted decorations.

The diversity of traditional house styles found on the island is truly astounding. Around Lake Toba alone, for example, are to be found several distinctive styles belonging to the Toba, Karo and Simalungun Batak peoples—while the houses of the Mandailing Batak to the south are different again. The traditional homes of the Minangkabau of West Sumatra are equally unique—renowned for their beautiful floral carving and elegant, soaring eaves.

The Gayo people to the north of Lake Toba formerly dwelt in large multifamily houses holding up to 60 people. Each family had an apartment in the center of the house, with a men's gallery at the front and a women's gallery at the back. Acehnese houses, found along the island's north coast, are airy and well-ventilated, with large shuttered windows and elaborate woodcarving.

But perhaps the most breathtaking Sumatran architecture is found on the island of Nias. Houses stand in rows beside long, stone-paved streets, dominated—as in the famous village of Bawömataluo—by a massive chief's house resting on vertical and diagonal pillars fashioned from the trunks of giant ironwood trees.

Ancient origins

The observer of this astonishing architectural heritage will ask why so many of these houses—particularly the Batak and the Minangkabau—appear stylistically related, not only to each other but to the houses of other Indonesian peoples, such as the Toraja of Sulawesi. The most notable shared features are the pile foundations, the extended or saddle-shaped roof ridge, and the decorative, horn-shaped gable finials. What ancient historical link explains the origin and spread of this remarkable style?

The earliest surviving images of pile-built structures with saddle roofs are engraved on bronze drums found in the area of Dongson

in what is now northern Vietnam. The culture associated with these drums dates from ca. 500 BC–AD 100, and Dongson drums were traded throughout the archipelago as prestige items. Early theories about "waves" of Dongson migration into Indonesia have now been discounted, however, and it is unlikely that an architectural style could have been spread simply by pictures on drums. Much more probable is that the style was already old when the drums were cast, and that the images are simply its earliest surviving representations.

House styles ancestral to those you see today in Sumatra were probably developed in ancient times by Austronesian-speaking migrants. The Austronesians—ancestors of most modern-day Indonesians—originated from a homeland somewhere in southern China and began to migrate into these islands from Taiwan and the Philippines 6,000 years ago. Subsequently, they colonized the islands of the Pacific, and reached as far as Madagascar by AD 400, bringing with them their distinctive building style. Pile buildings with saddle roofs are found as far east as Micronesia, an area settled by Austronesians some time after 2000 BC, and saddle roofs, often of impressive proportions, are a feature of men's houses in New Guinea.

The survival of this ancient style of architecture seems to rest on its aesthetic or symbolic appeal, rather than a commitment to a particular mode of construction. Minangkabau and Batak houses, for example, both have pointed eaves and extended ridge lines, but these are produced by quite different building techniques.

In the Toba Batak house, the living space is essentially created by the roof, which rests on top of very low walls. The rafters are angled outward to produce the projecting gable, and strengthened by means of diagonal ties. In the Minangkabau house, on the other hand, the living space is formed by the walls, which are much taller in proportion to the roof than in Batak houses. The roof sits on top of this space, supported by a truss and crossbeam structure and built up into tall points by means of many small rafters and battens.

Symbolic Acehnese houses

Acehnese homeowners are women. If they can afford it, the parents provide each of their daughters with a house when she marries—otherwise they simply present their own house to a married daughter and move into the kitchen. During the day the house is the woman's domain. Men spend most of their time in public places, or migrate (*merantau*) to earn a living through trade, re-

Opposite: *The elegant, upward-sweeping eaves of a traditional Minangkabau house in Pandai Sikat.*
Below: *Toba Batak houses on Samosir Island.*

turning home only at long intervals.

Though subdued in their outward form, Acehnese houses are rich in cosmological and symbolic significance. The front verandah is the most public and formal part. Here men sit. The rear is private, containing the kitchen and the women's entrance. Male and female are symbolically united in the central room, which has the highest floor level, and contains the two main house posts—called "prince" and "princess"—against which the bride and the groom are seated on their wedding day. This is also where the newly-married couple sleeps. At the top of the house, beneath the gable, is a platform for storing family valuables and heirlooms. Outside at floor level runs a skirting-board, often elaborately decorated. The wall separating the verandah from the inner part of the house may also be decorated with intricate woodcarving.

Monumental Nias villages

South Nias has produced some of Indonesia's most astonishing architecture. In the 19th century, the area was ruled by a warlike aristocracy which enriched itself by raiding outlying districts for slaves. The nobles staged elaborate feasts by which they raised their status on the social ladder. The greatest of such feasts entitled a chief to construct a great house (omo sebua).

A stunning example dating from 1863 survives today in Bawömataluo village in South Nias. It is 22.7 m tall, and is ornamented inside with carved ebony wall panels depicting ancestral thrones, male and female ornaments, animals and birds, and even a Dutch steamship mounted with cannons.

South Nias villages are remarkably large, with up to 6,000 inhabitants, as slave-raiding and headhunting made smaller communities too vulnerable. Most villages have a single main street paved with stone, sometimes crossed by a shorter street at the top forming a giant "T." Some settlements are approached by huge flights of stone stairs. The bowed fronts of the houses—reminiscent of Dutch galleons—form a continuous line on both sides. Stone monuments, commemorating past feasts and important funerals, stand before the houses of the nobility.

A distinctive feature of the houses are the massive ironwood foundation pillars, both vertical and diagonal. The diagonal pillars give added stability to the tall house structure in this earthquake-prone region. The flexibility of the house in tremors is enhanced by the fact that the piles rest on top of their foundation stones, a feature also found elsewhere in the archipelago.

The founding ancestors of South Nias communities originally came from central Nias. Here can be seen houses of an older and plainer style, without the projecting curved front, as well as different kinds of worked stone monuments. You will need the help of a guide to visit this remote area, and you should check on the weather—rivers become impassable in the rainy season.

Houses of North Nias are unusual in having an oval plan. They are less monumental in scale, but share certain features such as the use of diagonal piles, and the cutting of flaps in the roof, which can be propped open to serve as windows. Graves, now Christian in style, continue to be located next to the houses in the traditional manner.

Batak houses

The countryside around lake Toba is dotted with traditional Toba, Karo and Simalungun Batak villages as well as elaborate concrete tombs in the form of houses. The tombs are built with great ceremony and expense to house the remains of the deceased ancestors of a particular family. This traditional concern for the dead remains of great importance to the Toba, and has been integrated with Christian practice. Older sarcophagi of carved stone may also be seen on Samosir Island in Lake Toba.

COEN PEPPLINKHUIZEN

Toba houses stand on foundations of piles braced with cross-beams, forming a space beneath the house where buffaloes were once stalled. The walls are covered with graceful flowing and spiral decorations—unbroken lines are thought to provide protection to the occupants. Friezes with figures may also be seen, and three-dimensional carved protective "monsters" are found at the corners and top of the facade.

On the northeastern shore of the lake stands Pematang Purba, site of the palace of the former rajas of the Simalungun Batak, now a museum. The impressively long house has a realistically modelled buffalo-head on the front gable-end, and a tail made of the tough black fibre of the sugar-palm at the rear. Inside is the raja's private apartment, and ten separate hearths, each formerly the domain of one of his wives. Nearby is a council house with an elaborately carved central pillar, against which the ruler used to sit while giving judgement.

The Karo people living on the north of the lake developed an interesting variation on the extended ridge line, with multiple decorative gables topped by realistically-modelled buffalo heads which protected the occupants from harm. Some fine examples survive in villages around Berastagi, such as Lingga. Traditionally, houses were occupied by four or eight related families, each with its own hearth. A distinctive structure is the *geriten* or "head-house," a miniature house to store the skulls of revered ancestors.

The Minangkabau house

The Minangkabau people are well-known for their matrilineal kinship system. This means that houses and rice fields are passed down from mother to daughter. A typical Minangkabau compound will consist of an older, original house surrounded by others that have been added by married sisters and daughters of the parent family.

The elegant, sweeping eaves of traditional houses are a common sight amidst the lush green Minangkabau landscape. These pointed eaves, locals say, remind them of the legendary "victorious buffalo" (*menang kerbau*) from which their name is said to derive. On larger buildings the roof is tiered to form a series of four or six points, often with an additional peak over a porch set at right angles to the main structure. In the past, huge *rumah gadang* or "great houses" accommodated up to 100 people related to a single female ancestor. Inside was an open gallery with separate sleeping apartments off it. A surviving example—64 m long!—can be visited at the hilltop village of Sulitair, near Lake Singkarak.

Minangkabau rice barns and council houses (*balairung* or *balai adat*) are also built with pointed eaves. The ancestral village of Pariangan in the Tanahdatar valley, contains some very old examples, as does nearby Pagarruyung—site of the former palace of the Minangkabau rajas. The original palace was unfortunately destroyed by fire in 1976, but it has now been rebuilt (on a somewhat enlarged scale) as a museum.

—*Roxana Waterson*

Left: The chief's house in Bawömataluo, South Nias (1863). **Above:** A carved panel from the same house, depicting animals and a Dutch warship. **Right:** A Karo Batak house, with its pointed eaves, low walls and outwardly angled rafters.

LANGUAGE & LITERATURE

Court Malay to Bahasa Indonesia

Sumatra's great size and cultural diversity is reflected in its wealth of languages, which range from the elegant and elaborate court Malay still spoken in the former palace centers of Palembang and Riau, to the rapidly vanishing dialects spoken by a few coastal, boat-dwelling *orang laut* (sea nomads). Most of Sumatra's languages are closely related, and belong to the huge family of Austronesian languages which stretches in a great island arc from Madagascar on the African coast to Easter Island in the eastern Pacific.

Northern Sumatra is dominated by the 1.5 million speakers of Acehnese, who surround a much smaller pocket of Gayo speakers. To the south, around Lake Toba, lie the Batak heartlands, with their many Batak dialects, some so different as almost to constitute separate languages. The most widely-spoken dialect is Toba Batak, followed by Karo, Ang-

BODLEIAN LIBRARY, OXFORD

kola, Mandailing, Dairi, Simalungun and Alas. Four million Minangkabau speakers—the second largest linguistic group on the island—are found in the fertile highlands of West Sumatra, while moving farther south, the provinces of Riau, Jambi and South Sumatra are home to numerous dialects of Malay. Rejang is spoken in parts of Bengkulu, and Lampung is spoken on the southern tip of the island. Several distinct languages are found in the four island groups along the west coast of Sumatra—Simuelue, Nias, Mentawai and Enggano.

Attached like a single-hued lining to this linguistic coat of many colors is the Malay language—for centuries the *lingua franca* of the archipelago, and forerunner of the national language, Bahasa Indonesia. Spoken as a mother tongue by about 11 million Sumatrans, Malay is indigenous to the east of the island but has spread throughout the archipelago as the language of trade and Islam, superseding local languages as a literary and courtly medium in the kingdoms of Aceh, West Sumatra and Riau.

When Sultan Iskandar Muda of Aceh corresponded with King James I of England in 1615, he wrote in Malay, not Acehnese. At the other end of the social scale, Malay has long served as the language of the market place in Sumatra's cosmopolitan port cities. The first Malay phrasebook for foreign merchants, printed in Amsterdam in 1603, contains sample conversations for purchasing provisions, weighing pepper and extracting funds from a recalcitrant debtor, as well as colorful phrases for driving a hard bargain.

Traditional literature

Traditional Sumatran scripts can be divided into two types—those that trace their origin to a South Indian script, and those that derive from a Persian-Arabic script. The earliest example of the latter is an Old Malay stone inscription from 7th century Srivijaya (Palembang). The ravages of the tropical climate have left no traces of texts on more perishable materials from this period, but the Batak and Lampung scripts also belong to this Indic group, and are still in occasional use. The arrival of Islam led to the development of a modified form of the Arabic script known as Jawi—used to write Malay, Acehnese and Minangkabau until the early decades of this century.

Manuscripts from Sumatra come in all shapes and sizes, and use bamboo, tree-bark, palm leaf and bone as well as paper. Sumatra's most important literature is written in the Malay language. Prose works include histories and romances; tales of the Prophet and Muslim heroes, like Alexander the Great (known in Malay as Iskandar Zulkarnain, the "two horned"); and theological, legal, moral treatises. The *Hikayat Raja-raja Pasai*, which relates the coming of Islam to the north coast of Sumatra in the 13th century, is the oldest known Malay history.

The two main genres of Malay poetry are the narrative *syair* and the *pantun*. The four-line stanzas of the *syair* with their a-a-a-a end-rhyme are believed to be the creation of Hamzah Fansuri, a mystic poet who lived in Barus in the 16th century. The *pantun* is a quatrain with an a-b-a-b rhyme in which the first couplet contains a veiled allusion, the meaning of which is usually elaborated in the final couplet. Written literatures also exist in Acehnese—in prose (*haba*) and poetry (*hikayat*)—and in Minangkabau, where the most important epic is the *Kaba Cindur Mata*.

In Sumatra, as in many parts of Indonesia, the dividing line between written and oral literature is blurred, for in semi-literate societies texts were usually composed and written down to be recited to an audience. Professional Sijobang singers in West Sumatra are still in demand at weddings, circumcision ceremonies and other feasts, where recitations of the adventures of Prince Anggun Nan Tungga last all night. (Sijobang performances are now also marketed on cassettes.) Sumatran peoples have a rich stock of folklore, including proverbs, mantras and animal fables—the mousedeer being the hero.

One of the most intriguing written traditions of Sumatra are *pustaha*, the bark books of the Batak. These concertina-shaped books are concerned solely with magic, divination and medicine, and were used as *aide-mem-oires* by apprentice sorcerers during their period of study with a Batak priest or *dato*. Amongst their contents might be oracles for reading the entrails of a chicken, or for divining the portents of the time of day of a child's birth ("a boy-child born at a certain moment will die in war or of smallpox; if it is a girl, she may die of suicide," etc.), as well as recipes for love philtres and poisons.

Modern literature

By the beginning of the 20th century, increasing Western influence manifested itself in a growing popular literature in Malay. Medan became a center for the publishing of "penny dreadfuls," the melodramatic romances, adventures and detective booklets owing much to the stories of Jules Verne and Arthur Conan Doyle.

In the 1920s, when Balai Pustaka—the Dutch colonial government publishing house in Batavia—began to issue novels in Malay, the earliest works were by Minangkabau writers. Many novels centered on the cultural clash between the modernizing influence of Western education and the strictures and arranged marriages of traditional Minang society. Both in the period before Independence and afterwards, Sumatran writers have been in the forefront of modern Indonesian literature.

Armijn Pane's *Belenggu* (Shackles), published in 1940, has been hailed as the first Indonesian psychological novel, and poets like Chairil Anwar and Rivai Apin were influenced by T.S. Eliot and W.H. Auden. Yet the homeland of Sumatran writers often shines through their work—from the forests of Mochtar Lubis's childhood, which form the backdrop to his novel *Harimau* (Tiger), to the images of Lake Toba which permeate the existentialist poetry of Sitor Situmorang.

—*Annabel Teh Gallop*

BRITISH MUSEUM, LONDON

Opposite: A letter from Sultan Iskandar Muda of Aceh to King James I of England, one of the earliest extant examples (1615) of Malay written with the use of Arabic script. **Left:** *A* Batak *dato priest consults his* pustaha *bark books.*

FOOD

The Art of Sumatran Cooking

As the 17th century traveler Sir John Chardin noted, religion—as well as history and geography—has always played an important role in determining a people's diet. And so it is in Sumatra. Pork is the major dietary barrier separating the island's Muslim majority from the Christian minority. Christian Bataks around Lake Toba and elsewhere in North Sumatra eat pork (sometimes also dog), and in their village settlements they often keep pigs. For Muslims, however, the pig is ritually unclean, and may only be eaten if one is faced with starvation.

Muslims nevertheless enjoy many other meats—including the flesh of buffaloes, goats, ducks, lambs, chickens and fish—as well as eggs, fruits and vegetables. Since the 1970s, however, many Sumatran Muslims have developed an additional concern for whether or not the meat they are served is *halal*—slaughtered according to Islamic law by cutting the animal's throat while uttering the name of Allah.

History and geography are also important, of course. After centuries of trading contacts, Sumatran cooking now reflects influences from all around the archipelago (Java, Manado, Bali) as well as from abroad (India, Middle East, China, Holland). In the North Sumatran capital of Medan, for example, you will find several dishes that show a distinct Indian and Arab influence alongside the usual Indonesian dishes. This can be seen in the use of dried seeds and aromatic spices such as coriander, cumin, fennel, cardamom and cinnamon in the preparation of goat dishes. *Gulai kumah* and *gulai bagar* are two goat curries which are rich in flavor, but unlike native Sumatran dishes not particularly spicy.

Near the coasts, seafood features prominently on most restaurant menus. One of the most popular dishes in Palembang, South Sumatra, is *empek-empek*—a fish dumpling (sometimes also stuffed with egg) served hot with a bowl of spicy sauce made of chilli, garlic, dried prawns, palm sugar, soya sauce and vinegar. In addition, Palembang is known throughout Indonesia for the quality of its *kerupuk* (deep-fried tapioca crackers flavored with seafood and spices), since the *kerupuk* made here have a higher proportion of fish or prawn than those produced elsewhere in the archipelago.

Some like it hot!

Sumatra has many regional cooking styles, however the best-known is undoubtedly *masakan padang*—the fiery-hot cuisine of the Minangkabau of West Sumatra, named after the provincial capital of Padang. Padang-style restaurants are found throughout Indonesia, and a number of Padang dishes have achieved national and even international popularity. Today, the famous meat dish known as *rendang* is served in restaurants as far afield as Tokyo, New York and London, and can be found in almost every Dutch town.

Rendang is usually made with beef, cut up into cubes and cooked in coconut cream with a spice mixture of garlic, shallots, chillies, turmeric, galangal, green ginger (all finely ground), lemon grass, kaffir lime leaves, turmeric leaves and salt. Special care and attention are required during cooking so the mixture does not curdle or the pieces of meat disintegrate. Once the coconut cream reaches boiling point, the heat is reduced and the cooking continues until the mixture thickens. When finished, the *rendang* sauce turns to a rich, dark brown residue, but the pieces of meat should still be intact and slightly crisp on the outside.

The prolonged cooking and the spices, especially the chillies, preserve the meat, and it is common for *rendang* to be taken along on long journeys, such the pilgrimage to Mecca. *Rendang* is then both a reminder of home and a handy dish that saves time—as no cooking is needed apart from boiling the rice to eat with it! Solicitous Sumatran mothers cook, pack and send it to their children studying or working in the outer islands. If you eat *rendang*—and you should be sure not to miss it—be warned not to put a whole piece in your mouth at once. It is far too rich and spicy to be eaten whole. Break off a small part, then fold it into a spoonful of rice if you want to enjoy it. One should treat all spicy meat dishes with similar respect.

Padang restaurants, wherever you find them, have a unique way of serving their dishes which never fails to intrigue visitors from abroad. There is no need to order— soon after you sit down, the waiter arrives at your table with an array of small dishes precariously poised along both arms, and deposits them all on the table. You eat whatever you fancy from among these many dishes—sampling the curried eggs, fish, vegetables, chicken and meat, knowing you will only be charged for the number of pieces of egg, fish, chicken or meat that you eat. The sauce is free, and there are stories of skinflints who take a spoonful of sauce from each dish to flavor their rice to have a cheap meal!

Opposite: *Chilli paste, an important ingredient in most Sumatran food.* **Below:** *Spicey Padang food sold at an open-air* lepau *in Bukittinggi.*

DANA IRFAN

Experienced Padang restaurant-goers know exactly which dishes go well together, and make their choices accordingly. Those who are less experienced may find they end up with a plate full of clashing flavors. If in doubt, ask the proprietor for a *nasi rames*. This is a plate of white rice with several bits of meat and vegetable on top, sprinkled with gravy and *serundeng* (grated coconut, roasted with peanuts) and topped off with a *kerupuk*. It generally ends up being cheaper than getting the whole smorgasboard.

As is the custom throughout Indonesia, you eat with your right hand by compressing a bit of rice, meat and curry together with the tips of your fingers and pushing it into your mouth. Forks and spoons are also often provided now, but it is very bad form to stick the spoon you use for eating into the dishes of curry. Use a separate spoon for this!

The normal evening meal for a middle class family consists of four or five dishes and rice. These may include one or two meat dishes—say *gulai ayam* (curried chicken soup) and *dendeng* (sun-dried spicy beef)—as well as a vegetable dish, such as cucumber salad, and a selection of condiments such as *sambal* (chilli paste), pickles (*acar*) and *kerupuk*. The rice supplies the bulk of the meal, and its blandness is ideal for absorbing and combining the flavors of the various dishes.

Of course not all Padang cooking is hot. Try *opor ayam* (chicken simmered in corian-der and coconut cream), *ayam goreng* (crisp fried chicken), or—a dish that all foreigners like—*pergedel* (meat and potato croquettes). Other dishes are prepared with only small amounts of chilli, such as *gado-gado* (vegetable salad with peanut sauce), and *sate*. The latter is found all over Indonesia and consists of pieces of meat marinated in spices and placed on bamboo skewers, then grilled over a bed of charcoal and served with sweet-spicy ground peanut sauce.

A special type of *sate* prepared in Padang needs a chapter all by itself. It consists of pieces of heart, tongue and tripe boiled in finely ground spices—coriander, cumin, galangal, turmeric, ginger, garlic, chilli and shallots—plus kaffir lemon leaf, lemon grass and salt. The meat is then cut into small pieces and threaded onto skewers. The broth of the meat is thickened with rice flour to make a pale yellow sauce. Sprinkled with fried onions, *sate padang* is a feast for the eyes as well as the stomach!

Vegetarians will delight in the variety of *tempe* dishes found in West Sumatra. *Tempe* is a kind of soybean cake prepared from boiled beans which are allowed to ferment, a process that takes three days. The finished product is firm and compact—the beans tightly bound together and covered evenly with a light coating of white mold, with an aroma reminiscent of fresh mushrooms. *Tempe* is a very cheap source of high-quality protein and is crunchy and tasty when fried. It may also be curried or stir–fried with vegetables, potatoes and chilies.

Drinks and snacks

Beer goes very well with most Sumatran dishes—the high-quality Bir Bintang and Anker produced in Indonesia is brewed according to traditional Dutch methods. The religious prohibition against imbibing alcoholic beverages does not command universal observance in Sumatra, and foreigners drinking beer generally do not cause offense. Locals, however, usually prefer to drink weak plain tea or iced water with their meals.

There is, incidentally, one locally produced food which is mildly alcoholic. Sumatrans are very fond of between-meal snacks, and one of the favorites is *tapai*, sometimes spelled *tapé*. Sumatran *tapai* is prepared from boiled or steamed black glutinous rice. Once the rice is cooled, it is sprinkled with a special yeast called *ragi tapé*; two tablets are needed for each kilo of rice. The rice then is placed in a basin with a lid, and wrapped in cloth and left in a warm place for three or four days to ferment.

When it is ready, the mixture is slightly effervescent and has a port-like fragrance. It is usually served with *lemang*—white glutinous rice cooked in a bamboo container lined with young banana leaves in thick, salted coconut cream. (Surprisingly, *tapai* also goes very well with vanilla ice cream!). It is available everyday in central Sumatra, but is especially popular during the fasting month, and around Idul Fitri (the festive celebration of the end of the fasting month).

Another popular snack specific to the region is *dadih* (buffalo yoghurt). It is sold in a small bamboo container and served with *emping*—glutinous rice flakes rinsed with boiling water to soften them—topped with freshly grated coconut and brown palm sugar. It is a very filling meal. *Dadih* is sold in almost every *kedai* or *lepau* (foodstall) all over the island.

On the road

When you travel by bus in Sumatra, foodsellers swarm around at every stop and bus terminal, calling out their wares. In their baskets are hard-boiled, salted duck eggs, tasty maize fritters, crispy fried banana slices (*rakik*), pieces of chopped sugarcane, and a variety of sweetmeats in banana leaves.

Practically every bus stop in Sumatra has one or two local specialities, and the same goes for train stations. Local women who are traveling on the buses will often buy a selection of these as gifts (*oleh–oleh*). When they visit relatives, it is unthinkable to arrive at a house empty-handed—one must have something to "open the door," as they say. There are always children around, and small gifts for them are always warmly welcomed.

The all-purpose banana leaf

Banana leaves, which can be found in abundance everywhere throughout the archipelago, are indispensable in all kinds of situations. They are tough, but when heated, are pliable and easily folded. They are mostly used to wrap food for steaming or cooking over charcoal, and as a wrapper for take-away food bought at a *kedai* or *lepau*. Small items and vegetables bought at the local market, such as *tapai*, bean sprouts or chillies, are usually wrapped up in banana leaves.

At a local *lepau* or *kedai* (foodstall), banana leaves may also serve as disposable plates or plate covers. They meet many needs for which we in the West use cling-wrap or aluminium foil. May they never give way to plastic which cannot be disposed of easily. Banana leaves are bio-degradable and a renewable resource!

—*Yohanni Johns*

Opposite: *Padang waiters showing off their skills.*
Above: *A woman selling snacks sold in her* kedai.

TRANS-SUMATRA HIGHWAY

The Great Traveling Road Show

The recently-completed Trans-Sumatra Highway runs the length of one of the world's largest islands—a distance of over 2,500 km. The journey from Bakauheni in the south to Banda Aceh in the north is truly one of Indonesia's great travel experiences, both for the stunning scenery you pass through and for the people you meet along the way.

However, the trip can equally become a nightmare of frustrations and uncomfortable conditions. Much depends on careful preparation, on having enough time, and on your response to the inevitable delays and minor irritations which all travelers experience in Indonesia. Patience and tolerance are invaluable qualities when traveling here, and will help ensure that your journey through some of the wildest and the least populated regions of the country will be an experience long remembered.

Only as a test of endurance should you take the highway straight through all the way from Jakarta to Banda Aceh. It is possible to do this—the journey takes about 60 hours and costs only $50. The old days of untold delays caused by collapsed bridges and washed-out roads are over. Today, the highway is paved, though your journey could come to a screeching halt if a landslide occurs, especially during the rainy season. But you will not be delayed for long. Maintenance crews show up promptly, as the highway is too important to the national economy for it to be closed more than a few hours.

Setting off: Lampung

Setting off from the south, the first leg of the Trans-Sumatra Highway runs 99 km from the Java-Sumatra ferry landing at Bakauheni, on the island's southeastern tip, up to Bandar Lampung—the capital of Lampung Province. Leaving the ferry landing, the road climbs up around Mt. Rajabasa, giving fine views of island-strewn Lampung Bay. Strands of clove trees line the hillsides, distinctive clumps of conical light green foliage.

A little over 60 km from Bakauheni, the road drops down to the coast, giving a tantalizing glimpse of Lampung Bay, its bright blue surface broken by several steep-sided islands and fishing platforms hovering over the water like giant water-spiders. Houses on stilts line the water's edge, separated from

the road by a thin strip of mangrove swamp. A rail head heralds your entry into the provincial capital, and in a short while you find yourself among huge warehouses and docks.

The next stage of your Trans-Sumatra journey northward takes you 385 km in 9 hours to Muaraenim, through foothill plains skirting the eastern edge of the Bukit Barisan mountain range. The road cuts through rubber and oil palm plantations and fields of corn. There are lots of river crossings—all rivers flow eastward from the Bukit Barisan to the sea.

Stunning emerald-green *sawah* by the roadside are dotted with huts where watchmen stay to keep wild animals at bay. Your bus might have to make several stops to let long "coal trains" by. The red-tiled raised wooden houses, some sitting on ironwood logs two meters off the ground, are traditional Lampung or South Sumatra *rumah limas*, formerly fastened with ropes, not nails.

South Sumatra and Jambi

The highway continues northwest out of Muaraenim, crossing the Lematang River several times before reaching Lahat. Just after Muaraenim, you get a panoramic view of the Lematang River against a backdrop of a primary forest. In the early morning and late afternoon, herds of water buffalo and cattle compete for road space with buses and trucks. Look for an unusually shaped mountain, Bukit Serelo—a bare, finger-like projection on top of a steep-sided hill, standing apart from the foothills of the Bukit Barisan.

Lahat is the place to get off to explore the Pasemah Highlands. However, if you get off the bus here, getting a good seat for the next stage of your journey is a matter of luck. The highway north of Lahat offers plenty of swaying curves and, if the weather is clear, glimpses of the Bukit Barisan range to the west. This is landslide country during the rainy season, but bulldozers quickly clear the road. Coffee is grown on the steep hills and a rubber plantation stretches for several kilometers by the roadside. The next town is Tebingtinggi ("high embankment"), which sits above the Musi River—one of the largest and most important rivers in Sumatra.

The highway then straightens out, and you speed along to Lubuklinggau, on the junction of the main road west to Bengkulu. The tin-roofed houses whiz by your bus window with monotonous regularity for the next 248 km until you cross a bridge over the Merangin River, just outside Bangko. You are now in Jambi Province, and a sideroad to the west from Bangko leads you into the dense jungle and tea plantations of the Kerinci-Seblat National Park around Lake Kerinci.

The next stage, 92 km from Bangko to Muarabungo, seems to take no time at all. Muarabungo is the jumping-off point for Jambi, a long 212 km to the east.

Outside Muarabungo, the bridge over the Tebo River at Telukpanjang offers a view of a riverside mosque. Fifty km further on, the wide Batang Hari River provides irrigation for extensive *sawah* and you are now in West Sumatra. Along the roadside, you begin to see your first Minangkabau style roofs.

West Sumatra

After Kiliranjao the scenery at last improves as the highway winds up into the Bukit Barisan mountains. Here are stunning limestone formations (called "karst towers") and *sawah* which go right up to the edge of the jungle. The tall, white trunks of the primary forest match the pale white outcroppings of limestone. In places, the vegetation grows right from a vertical cliff! The first of the karst towers, small but impressive, rears up on your right at Sungai Langsat. There are five larger

GOTTFRIED ROELCKE

Opposite: *Road conditions have improved considerably since this photo was taken, ca. 1920, but most roads were first built in the colonial period.*
Right: *A winding stretch of road near Bukittinggi.*

ones ahead—awesome oval, dome and stupa-shaped freaks of nature. During the rainy season there are frequent landslides, and your vehicle might have to stop for a couple of hours while bulldozers clear the way.

Having passed through the mountains, you enter a more hospitable landscape of rice fields, small Minang houses and hillsides covered in ferns, before entering a gorge leading into the busy commercial town of Solok.

The next stretch, 53 km from Solok to Padangpanjang, follows the banks of the Sumani River north to Lake Singkarak, a huge and immensely scenic crater lake. The highway hugs the eastern lakeshore all the way to a bridge over the Umbilin River, which drains Lake Singkarak.

At the northern end of the lake, the highway rises to offer some good views before cutting north and east through fertile rice fields to Pandangpanjang. To your right is Mt. Marapi, an active volcano which sometimes emits puffs of smoke, and Mt. Singgalang. Both are about the same height —just a bit under 2,900 m.

Break your journey at Bukittinggi; this is the place to spend a few days recuperating. It's about halfway up or down the island, and there are lots of good hotels, restaurants and pleasant sidetrips to be made in the area (see WEST SUMATRA).

After Bukittinggi, the next leg of the Trans-Sumatra Highway is a grueling 500-km run up to Prapat—the gateway to Lake Toba and Samosir Island, in North Sumatra. It's a long trip, about 15 hours, and if you can afford the time, it is better to break the journey in Padangsidempuan or Sibolga, so as to cross over the Bukit Barisan mountains again in daylight.

The road is paved all the way, but it's narrow and there are lots of curves. Even with a good driver, the crossing can be hair-raising, as you twist and wind up the mountain pass, barely missing oncoming lorries and coaches. Fortunately, there's not much traffic on the road and the coach can't go much faster than 40 km per hour.

Try to be awake at the town of Bonjol, home of the famous Muslim leader of the Padri wars, Imam Bonjol. There's a large, sabre-wielding statue of him in town on a horse—look to the right. Just out of Bonjol, there's a monument marking the equator.

From Bonjol the road climbs up to Lubuksikaping, then descends into a long river valley with rice fields to the right. There are no more steep descents but plenty of jungle-clad

gorges as you wind your way down to Muara-sipongi and Kotanopan, where your eyes are soothed by rice fields dotted with neat little huts and bridges by the river. You are now in North Sumatra.

North Sumatra

From Muarasipongi, the road follows the Batang Gadis River past Kotanopan. The Purba Baru village area here is the center of a huge *pesantren* or Islamic koranic school, the largest in Indonesia, with students from all over the country. Hundreds of tiny huts house boys, aged six to twelve, who spend their primary school years here.

Traditional Minangkabau houses are very few now since you are in Batakland. The people of this region are Mandailing Bataks, forcefully converted to Islam more than one and a half centuries ago.

Panyabungan is a crowded market town which bustles with activity on Monday, market day. Gaudy *becak*s, vegetable-laden housewives, and motorized *becak mesin* all add noise and color to the market scene. As you leave Panyabungan, you see tranquil white mosques set in the middle of rice fields. A stretch of brick factories follows, then the large town of Padangsidempuan greets you by nightfall. This is a good place for an overnight stay, or a change of bus for the one and a half hour drive to Sibolga.

Aside from a few hair-raising bends, the

next stage, to Prapat and Lake Toba, is a pleasant 5-hour ride. The first part, to Tarutung, takes about 3 hours, past roadside markets and denuded hills with isolated stands of pine. After an hour or so, a pass below Mt. Sibualbuali (with a large hotel) marks the division between the Muslim and Christian Bataklands, and churches begin to replace mosques along the roadside.

It's a short half-hour hop on a straight road from Tarutung to the busy market town of Siborongborong. A little way further on

you start winding down to Lake Toba past spectacular rice fields and impressive graves crowned with figures of wide-eyed men on white stallions, elders in *adat* costume, and traditional Toba Batak houses—including one almost big enough to live in. The massive sepulchre on the right, a short way off the road past Balige, is that of the Batak ruler Raja Tano. From here the road winds around lakeside hills to emerge at Prapat.

From Prapat to Medan, the journey takes 4-5 hours. As the road climbs up from Prapat, there are magnificent views of Lake Toba. Then the road winds down through the mountains on a long, gentle slope to the sea via Pematangsiantar and Tebingtinggi. Lush rice fields and estates of rubber and oil palm line the road, while churches are gradually replaced again by mosques.

The final leg: Aceh

The long, 600-km ride from Medan to Banda Aceh takes 14 hours. There's plenty of good scenery, but the only logical place to break up the journey is at Bireuen, about two-thirds of the way up, for a side trip up to Lake Tawar. At Sabat, 17 km out of Medan, the road crosses a wide river and the traffic starts to thin. The road now passes large oil palm plantations and ageing rubber estates. Keep an eye out for a superb mosque on the left just before Tanjungpura. The scenery alternates between broad rice fields (some

stretching two km from the road), coconut groves, single and triple domed mosques, large rivers, bridges over estuaries overgrown with mangroves and nipah palms. Canoes, small boats and houses perched on stilts crowd around the estuary bridges. Further ahead are the grass-covered foothills of the hazy Bukit Barisan range.

The town of Lhokseumawe, which is set a couple of kilometers off the highway, boasts huge banks, government buildings, shopping centers, satellite dishes and five-star hotels and restaurants alongside a small, prosperous "downstream" area of small open shops. Back on the highway heading out of town, you can see several large LNG storage tanks, and flares from oil wells.

Traveling further into the province of Aceh, you will see more the girls wearing the *kerudung* or *jilbab*, the Muslim head scarf which leaves only the face exposed. These girls attend Islamic schools. Mosques here are often roofed with ironwood shingles.

Throughout much of Aceh, the Trans-Sumatra Highway follows the tracks of a long-abandoned Dutch railway. Though much of the tracks remain, most of the bridges have fallen into the river.

On the last leg of the highway, the road leaves the rice fields and coastal towns to cut across the northernmost section of the Bukit Barisan mountains. There are lots of curves as you ride over hills covered with grass, scrub; and later you pass through tall, deserted pine forests. Then, mercifully, the bus stops swaying as the road straightens out to follow the river and fertile rice valley which leads to Banda Aceh at the northernmost tip of Sumatra.

—*Kal Muller*

Opposite: *The equator marker in Bonjol, West Sumatra.* **Above, left:** *A heavily-laden intercity bus squeezes under a low-lying railway bridge.* **Above, right:** *At a crossroads in West Sumatra.*

PART II

Introducing Medan

Medan, the provincial capital of North Sumatra, is a cosmopolitan city of over 2 million inhabitants and a booming commercial center for the region's huge oil and agro-businesses. As a result of major international investments in plantation agriculture from the 1870s onward, it grew from a tiny village to a prosperous colonial city of some 60,000 people by 1943. Following independence, the population exploded at an even more rapid rate, with a dramatic influx of various Batak and other groups from all over Sumatra and Indonesia. Today it is by far the largest city on Sumatra, and the fourth largest in the nation—after Jakarta, Surabaya and Bandung.

Medan's inhabitants are notoriously forward and commercially astute, and physically the city has little to recommend it. Although numerous improvements have been effected in recent years, it has been difficult to sustain an adequate infrastructure to support such a large and growing urban population. Medan, like Topsy, "just growed"—and there have been major problems with electricity, water, drainage and pollution, many currently being tackled by the city's administration and all requiring urgent attention. Lower-lying parts of the city are increasingly subject to flooding due, at least in part, to the deforestation of the hinterland.

Early trading settlements

Some 10,000 years ago, neolithic hunters and gatherers of the "Hoabinhian" stone tool complex settled in the swampy estuarine areas around what is now Medan, accumulating enormous mounds of discarded shells from the seafood they consumed. These shell middens provide us with one of the few tantalizing glimpses of neolithic habitation in western Indonesia, but sadly they have been all but destroyed by commercial lime burners.

By the early second millennium AD—but probably much earlier—Arab, Indian and Chinese traders arrived on these coasts in search of valuable aromatic tree resins from the valleys and slopes of the Bukit Barisan —resins such as camphor (*kapur barus*) and benzoin (*kemenyan*) that were much in demand by the peoples of Asia for medicinal and ritual purposes. Traces of an early trading settlement has been found at Kota Cina near Belawan, the port north of Medan.

In subsequent centuries, riverine communities of traders and seafarers established themselves along the coast under the leadership of Islamic Malay rulers, to take advantage of an increasingly profitable international trade. By the early 16th century, a struggle for the rich resources of the hinterland (especially pepper) ensued between the rulers of Aru—a Malay kingdom based at Deli Tua, near modern-day Medan—and the kingdom of Aceh at Sumatra's northern tip.

The Acehnese attacked and subdued Aru in 1536, and a Portuguese adventurer by the name of Pinto tells of the attack and the struggle of Aru's queen against Aceh. This may also be reflected in the Malay (and Karo) legend of Puteri Hijau, the "Green Princess." Aru was finally conquered by Aceh in the early 17th century, and Aceh thereafter controlled the coasts of both eastern and western Sumatra until the early 19th century.

The wealth and independence of Deli and other Malay polities in the area increased dramatically during the 19th century with the development of a lucrative pepper trade with the British, even though the authority of their rulers was largely confined to areas immediately around the river mouths. The Sultan of Deli, for example, controlled an area extending along the lower reaches of the Deli River, from its mouth to Deli Tua, and only "as far as a cannon shot on either side."

The hinterland areas, by contrast, were at

Overleaf: *Medan's Royal Mosque. Photo by Kal Muller.* **Opposite:** *The Sultan of Deli's ceremonial palace umbrella. Photo by Peter Bruechman.*

this time peopled almost exclusively by Karo Bataks. The Karo lived under their own independent chiefs in the four *urung* (village federations) of Sunggal (Serbanyaman), Hamperan Perak, Senembah and Sukapiring. Due to the influence of the increasingly prosperous Malay rulers of Deli, several chiefs converted to Islam in the early 19th century, and by about 1870 many Karo villagers living in the coastal area had also adopted Islam and Malay culture (*masuk Melayu*).

The plantation boom

The modern history of the Medan area begins in 1862 when a Dutch entrepreneur, Jacob Nienhuys, recognised the potential of the rich volcanic soils of the area and per-

PETER BRUECHMAN

suaded the Sultan of Deli to grant a concession for the growing of tobacco. Deli wrapper leaf for cigars rapidly became world famous, and from the late 19th century onward, foreign capital flooded into the area.

Thus began the dramatic transformation of a region that was at this time still largely virgin rainforest—rich in elephants, deer, wild pigs, tigers, flying squirrels, monkeys and a host of other creatures. Access to the hinterland was quite arduous in those days —involving travel upriver by *perahu* then on foot along narrow jungle tracks up into the foothills and across a series of passes onto the Karo plateau and the Simalungun Batak areas to the southeast.

Approached by a steady stream of Euro-

pean entrepreneurs, the Sultan of Deli proceeded to grant concessions of land to which he had no traditional right, consequently alienating the predominantly Karo inhabitants of the area. This highhanded action led to the Sunggal War of 1872-1897, but with Dutch military help the Karo were put down.

Here too, were the beginnings of the modern Indonesian oil industry. In 1883, following observations of surface oil seepages, a certain Mr. Zijlker was granted an exploratory concession in the Sungai Lipan area by the Sultan of Langkat. This venture was so successful that in 1890 the Koninklijke Nederlandsche Maatschappij tot het Exploiteeren van Petroleum—precursor to Royal Dutch Shell—was formed with a capital of Dfl. 1.1 million, a considerable sum in those days.

International investments were much larger here than in any other area of the archipelago in the pre-war period, as capital for plantation and other development poured in from the United States, Britain, Belgium, Germany, Scandinavia, Switzerland, Japan and Holland. As the indigenous inhabitants were few in number and had no wish to work for European masters, thousands of immigrant laborers were brought in to work the plantations, initially from China and India, but later from Java and Madura. The population of the so-called Cultuurgebied plantation area around Medan subsequently rose ten-fold, from 120,000 in 1880 to 1.2 million in 1920.

The cultivation of tobacco reached boom proportions by 1890, and was followed in turn by rubber, oil palms, sisal and tea. By 1925, over a million hectares of jungle had been cleared and cultivated. The east coast sultans of Deli, Langkat, Serdang and Asahan waxed fat on the incomes of their leased concessions in this period—their splendid courts rivaling those of the Malay Peninsula and Java. This ended abruptly in 1946 with a "cultural revolution" instigated by young rebels, in which many of the Malay aristocracy, including the brilliant Malay poet Tengku Amir Hamzah, were brutally murdered.

Events following Independence upset the status quo in the east coast areas. A rapid influx of Batak settlers into the rich plantation areas caused major demographic changes. From then on the population was no longer predominently Malay, Javanese and Chinese, but was dominated by Batak peoples from the highlands.

— *E. Edwards McKinnon*

Above: *The Sultan of Deli and his consort.*

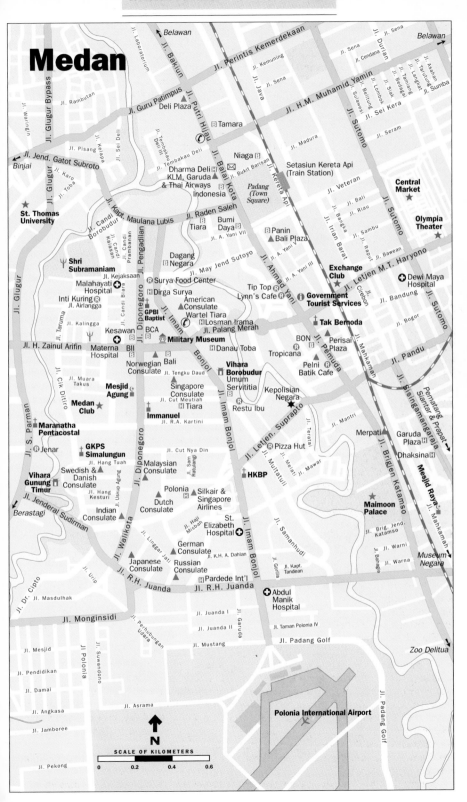

Medan

Belawan

Jl. Laboratorium
Jl. Baklun
Jl. Perintis Kemerdekaan
Belawan

Jl. Rambutan
Jl. Guru Patimpus
Jl. Putri Hijau
Jl. Kemuning
Jl. Java
Jl. Sena
Jl. Sena
Jl. Sena
Jl. Cendana
Jl. Asahan
Jl. Tanjung
Jl. Langkat
Jl. Tamiang
Jl. Bedagai
Jl. Sumba

Jl. Glugur Bypass
Jl. Waringin
Jl. Glugur
Jl. Pisang
Jl. Kelapa
Jl. Sei Deli
Deli Plaza
Jl. H.M. Muhamid Yamin
Jl. Belitung
Jl. Sulawesi
Jl. Siak
Jl. Lombok
Jl. Sei Kera
Jl. Seram

Jl. Karo
Jl. Toba
Jl. Tembakau Deli
Tamara
Jl. Sutomo

Jl. Jend. Gatot Subroto
Binjai
Niaga
Setasiun Kereta Api
(Train Station)
Central Market

Dharma Deli
KLM, Garuda & Thai Airways
Indonesia
Padang (Town Square)
Jl. Madura
Jl. Veteran
Olympia Theater

St. Thomas University
Jl. Kapt. Maulana Lubis
Jl. Candi Borobudur
Jl. Candi Kalasan
Jl. Candi Prambanan
Jl. Raden Saleh
Tiara
Bumi Daya
Jl. A. Yani VII
Panin
Bali Plaza
Jl. Bali
Jl. Riau
Jl. Bangka
Jl. Sambu
Jl. Irian Barat
Jl. Rapul
Jl. Bawean
Jl. Sutomo

Shri Subramaniam
Jl. Kejaksaan
Dagang Negara
Jl. May Jend Sutoyo
Jl. A. Yani V
Jl. A. Yani
Jl. A. Yani III
Exchange Club
Jl. Letjen M.T. Haryono

Malahayati Hospital
Jl. Candi Biara
Surya Food Center
Dirga Surya
American Consulate
Tip Top
Lynn's Cafe
Government Tourist Services
Jl. Cirebon
Dewi Maya Hospital
Jl. Bandung

Inti Kuring
Jl. Airlangga
Jl. Kalingga
Kesawan
BCA
GPBI Baptist
Wartel Tiara
Losman Irama
Jl. Palang Merah
Tak Bernoda
Jl. Bogor

Jl. Taruma
Materna Hospital
BII
Military Museum
Danau Toba
BON
Perisai Plaza
Jl. Pemuda
Jl. Pandu

Jl. H. Zainul Arifin
Norwegian Consulate
Bali
Tropicana
Pelni
Batik Cafe

Jl. Cik Ditiro
Jl. Muara Takus
Jl. Tengku Daud
Singapore Consulate
Jl. Cut Meutiah
Vihara Borobudur
Umum Servititia
Kepolisian Negara
Pematang Prapat Siantar & Sibolangit

Mesjid Agung
Tiara
Jl. Imam Bonjol
Restu Ibu

Medan Club
Immanuel
Jl. R.A. Kartini
Jl. Mantri

Maranatha Pentacostal
Jenar
GKPS Simalungun
Jl. Hang Tuah
Jl. Cut Nya Din
Jl. Sam Ratulangi
Jl. Letjen. Suprapto
Pizza Hut
Jl. Teratai
Jl. Melati
Jl. Mawar
Merpati
Garuda Plaza
Dhaksina

Vihara Gunung Timur
Swedish & Danish Consulate
Jl. Hang Kesturi
Malaysian Consulate
HKBP

Jl. S. Parman
Jl. Jenderal Sudirman
Berastagi
Indian Consulate
Polonia
Dutch Consulate
Silkair & Singapore Airlines
St. Elizabeth Hospital
Maimoon Palace

Jl. Uskup Agung
Jl. Haji Misbah
German Consulate
Jl. K.H.A. Dahlan
Jl. Samanhudi
Jl. Brig. Jend. Katamso
Jl. Warni
Museum Negara

Jl. Dr. Cipto
Jl. Masdulhak
Jl. Urip
Jl. Linggar Jati
Japanese Consulate
Russian Consulate
Jl. Gonila
Jl. Kapt. Tandean
Jl. Warna
Jl. Bahagia

Jl. Monginsidi
Jl. Wallkota
Jl. Diponegoro
Jl. R.H. Juanda
Pardede Int'l
Jl. R.H. Juanda
Abdul Manik Hospital

Jl. Mesjid
Jl. Perhubungan Utara
Jl. Juanda I
Jl. Juanda II
Jl. Garuda
Jl. Taman Polonia IV
Zoo Delitua

Jl. Pendidikan
Jl. Polonia
Jl. Suwandono
Jl. Mustang
Jl. Padang Golf

Jl. Damai
Jl. Asrama

Jl. Angkasa
N

Jl. Jamboree
Polonia International Airport

SCALE OF KILOMETERS

Jl. Pekong
0   0.2   0.4   0.6

MEDAN SIGHTS

Vestiges of a Plantation Boomtown

Medan has changed considerably over the past several decades. Before the war this was a small but fabulously wealthy plantation city with some 60,000 inhabitants. Today it is a sprawling and bustling metropolis—its busy streets are lined with new office and shopping blocks and thronged with minibuses and noisy motorised *becak* that produce voluminous clouds of thick, acrid smoke. The pre-independence population of Chinese, Indians, Javanese and Europeans has been swamped by an influx of indigenous Sumatrans—predominantly Bataks, but also Acehnese, Malays and Minangkabau.

Medan, like Jakarta, is a hot and crowded city, and most visitors rush straight through on the way to the cooler and more scenic highlands. It is in fact quite a shock to land here, especially if you are visiting Indonesia for the first time. On the other hand, Medan has pleasant hotels and well-preserved colonial buildings, a lovely palace and mosque, and numerous fascinating temples, markets and ethnic quarters. A day or two can profitably be spent sightseeing; the best way to get around is to hire a car or motorised *becak* (see "Medan Practicalities").

The old planters' town

Most visitors arrive by air at Polonia International Airport, once the city's racetrack and before that a Polish-owned tobacco plantation. The Deli River flows past the northern end of the runway, marked by a line of coconut trees, with the dome-shaped roof of the Sultan of Deli's palace visible in the distance. Polonia was the fashionable colonial residential neighborhood, and lavish villas still line its broad, shady boulevards.

The colonial period main street, **Jalan Jenderal Ahmad Yani**, with its many European style buildings, is still known locally as Kesawan, the road to the *sawah* or rice fields. Here, behind an iron grill fence alongside numerous Chinese shops, is the mansion of the former millionaire Kapitan Cina or head of the Chinese community, Tjong A Fie, who made and lost a fortune in the booming plantation world of the 1920s and '30s. Opposite his house is the Cafe Tip Top, once a favorite haunt of Medan's colonial society and still in almost original condition—where one can sit beside the sidewalk sipping iced Vienna cof-

fee and nibbling on some of their Dutch-style *koekjes* as the world goes by.

At the northern end of Jl. Ahmad Yani are the offices of London-based Harrisons and Crosfield Ltd., built of Aberdeen granite imported as ballast during the 1920s, and now occupied by P.T. London Sumatra, the British Consulate and the British Council Library. Just behind the London Sumatra building, at the junction of Jl. Kesenian and Jl. Hindu, is a plaque laid by Baron MacKay, former *burgemeester* (mayor) of Medan, in 1926. East on the opposite side of Jl. Hindu, at Gang Bengkok, is a small mosque with an ancient well—reputedly the oldest in Medan—possibly that mentioned by Anderson in 1823.

Around the *padang* or town square to the north of Jl. Ahmad Yani are several colonial buildings, notably the old town hall, the Bank of Indonesia building (formerly the Javaasche Bank), the Bank Negara (formerly the exclusive Witte Societeit club, built in 1879), and the Hotel Dharma Deli, which incorporates the old Hotel DeBoer—made famous by the Ladislao Székely novel, *Tropic Fever*, which describes the experiences of a young European planter in Sumatra in the early years of this century. The old train station has gone, but the *jembatan gantung*, the original suspension bridge over the railway, remains.

On the corner of Jl. Puteri Hijau, the colonial era Post Office stands virtually unchanged, with the Nienhuys fountain just outside—dedicated to the man responsible for the Medan area plantation boom. Just around the corner on Jl. H.M. Yamin (formerly Jl. Serdang), one may walk against the flow of one-way traffic to see the former DSM (Deli Spoorweg Maatschappij) railway office adjacent to a one-meter gauge railway that still carries the bulk of North Sumatra's plantation produce, linking the harbor of Belawan-Deli with Pematang Siantar and Rantau Prapat to the south. On nearby Jl. Tembakau Deli is the former VDM (Vereenigde Deli Maatschappij) building built by Nienhuys in 1869, now headquarters of PTP IX, a state-owned plantation company.

One block from the southern end of Jl. Ahmad Yani is the former AVROS (Algemeene Vereeniging van Rubberplanters ter Oostkust van Sumatra) building, now the Sumatra Planters' Association, with its green-tiled dome and dark teak-panelled boardroom.

Maimoon Palace

Directly to the south is Istana Maimoon, the ceremonial palace of the sultans of Deli, with its yellow trim (yellow is the color of Malay royalty) and typical east coast Malay architecture. It was actually designed by an Italian architect and completed in 1888. The audience hall, with portraits of the Deli royal fam-

Opposite: *The former VDM building, constructed by Nienhuys in 1869.* **Below:** *Maimoon Palace.*

STEVE TEO

STEVE TEO

ily, old Dutch furniture and a few weapons, is open to the public. It has patterned tiles and elegant moorish archways supported by large pillars covered in floral patterns. Malay dance performances, accompanied by traditional music, are held here to accompany weddings and other festivities. The sultan now lives in Jakarta, where he is a member of parliament; the palace living quarters are occupied by the sultan's brother.

During the late 19th and early 20th century, Malay royalty lived with great pomp in splendid style. With the establishment of Dutch suzerainty and the completion of the new palace in Medan they left their old timber-built home at Labuan Deli. Malays conceptualized riches in political terms; a rich ruler was one with many subjects, whose duties were primarily ceremonial. The revenue from plantations enabled the sultans to support a large retinue of followers, to make trips to Europe, and to send their children to Dutch or British schools.

The Deli sultans are reputedly descended from Mohammed Dalek Sri Paduka Gocah Pahlawan, a nobleman of Indian descent, appointed governor and first ruler of the state of Deli by the Sultan of Aceh around 1630. Deli was then conquered by Siak in 1770. In 1814, Mangidar Alam, the Raja of Deli, was awarded the full title of Sultan Panglima Mangidar Alam Syah ("Sultan Warrior who Encircles the World") by the Sultan of Siak.

The Deli family is related by marriage to Malay royal houses in Malaysia.

Beside the Istana is a Karo Batak style *balai* or open pavilion, built to house the *meriam puntung*—the stub of an ancient iron cannon. This is associated with the legendary Puteri Hijau, the "Green Princess," heroine of Deli's wars against Aceh in the 16th century. She is said to have come from Siberaya in the Karo Highlands and thus reflects Deli's close association with the Karo Batak. The cannon is named Indera Sakti and is said to have been one of the princess's two brothers—the other was a *naga* or snake of enormous proportions ("*naga yang mengamuk*") who assisted her in the fight against the Acehnese. This legend may have its origin through Tamil contacts with the Madras area of South India, where there is a similar tale of a Green Goddess.

One block to the east across the single track railway, on Jl. Sisingamangaraja (named after the powerful Batak priest-king killed by the Dutch in 1907), is the **Mesjid Raya** or Great Mosque, with its imposing tiled archway, royal burial ground and adjacent *kolam* or tank across the road. From here, looking back along Jl. Sisingamangaraja one may see also the tall water tower adopted as a symbol of the municipality of Medan.

The Polonia area

A walk from the AVROS building westwards along Jl. Suprapto into the Polonia area adjacent to the airport will give an impression of what the colonial Medan lifestyle was like in the '20s and '30s. This walk leads over the Deli River past the former HVA (Handels Vereeniging Amsterdam) building, now used as a police headquarters, and past St. Elizabeth Hospital. Broad, tree-lined avenues with their tall, red-flowered spathodeas and bungalow-style houses set well back from the road in colorful shrub-lined gardens imparts a feeling of security and affluence. Most of the Medan expatriate population still live here, though as in the rest of the town, changes are visible and numerous architectural alterations have been undertaken to suit modern Indonesian taste.

At the corner of Jl. Imam Bonjol and Jl. Sukamulia, in the courtyard of the Danau Toba Hotel, with its traditional Batak-style entrance, is the former Dutch Assistant Resident's house, now part of the modern hotel complex. Next door on Jl. Imam Bonjol is the Buddhist Vihara Borobudur temple.

Further west on Jl. Diponegoro is the Provincial Governor's office, a single-storey shut-

tered colonial structure with neo-classical pillars, originally the Deli Tabaksproefstation. Immediately behind this, the Medan Club, with its fine timber pillars and open design, was built by Allied prisoners-of-war as a Shinto temple for use by officers during the Japanese occupation.

To the south, overlooking the Babura River, is the **Vihara Gunung Timur**. This is the largest Chinese temple in Medan, perhaps in Indonesia. Nearby is the Immanuel Protestant Church, built in 1921—a fine example of art-deco colonial architecture.

To the north along Jl. Imam Bonjol is another square dominated by the modern Batak-style Provincial Assembly building, the Benteng Restaurant and Convention Hall built on the site of the original military barracks, and the Dirga Surya Hotel, with a line of evening foodstalls in front.

Nearby **Kampung Keling** (Jl. Zainul Arifin), a busy commercial center, is, as its name implies, the original center of Medan's Indian community. Its high-walled Sri Mariamman temple devoted to the goddess Kali was built in 1884; the entrance is topped by a small *gopuram* or ornamental pyramidal gateway. The Medan Indian community are mainly descendents of South Indians who came to work on plantations in the late 19th and early 20th centuries. A second though less impressive Sri Mariamman temple on Bekala Estate, off the road to Pancurbatu some 11 km south of Medan near the Sepit River, was established in 1876 and is the site of the Hindu Theemithi fire-walking ceremony during the annual Thaipusam festival—one of the few places where it is still held.

Medan's Chinatown

East of the railway, centered on Jl. Sutomo, is Medan's Chinatown, the heart of North Sumatra's wholesale trade—with shops selling everything from heavy machinery to toiletries. Here are Medan's two main markets, Pasar Hongkong and Pasar Sentral—havens for local pickpockets. This area has changed dramatically in recent years as the streets have been widened for ease of access. Unfortunately, most of the old shopfronts have been cut off as a result, though you can still see many shops and small Chinese restaurants run in the traditional manner.

During the durian season, heaps of fruit are offered for sale throughout the area (bargain hard!). Here too, in the evening, you will find colorful Chinese and seafood stalls lining Jl. Selat Panjang. Medan can offer a wide variety of delicious food, from roadside foodstalls serving basic Padang or Chinese meals, to plush, air-conditioned restaurants serving expensive Chinese and European banquets.

— *E. Edwards McKinnon*

Opposite: *Mesjid Raya, the Great Mosque.*
Above: *Vihara Gunung Timur Buddhist temple.*

MEDAN SIDETRIPS

Historic Sites Along the Deli River

A number of day excursions may be made to places around Medan. All main roads in the area are in quite good condition, but many secondary (*kabupaten*) roads, although asphalted, are still rough and uneven. Off the beaten track it is advisable to use a jeep-type vehicle with rugged suspension. Organized tours with a car and guide are available to any of these places through agents in Medan (see "Medan Practicalities").

Old Deli

Deli Tua or Old Deli (also known as Benteng Puteri Hijau, the "Fortress of the Green Princess") is the ancient site of the Aru court, overlooking the west bank of the Deli River (Lau Petani) about 10 km upstream from Medan, opposite Pasar Deli Tua. The area may be reached by going south from the Maimoon Palace (Jl. Brigjen Katamso) toward Namorambe. Along the way you can stop at the Research Institute of the Sumatra Planters' Association (RISPA) at Kampung Baru—a good example of prewar colonial architechture—and at **Taman Margasatwa**, Medan's zoo, to see the Sumatran tigers and a range of birds and other animals.

Just before Deli Tua, a small road to the right leads across the river, and further south are tracks leading to two sets of ramparts overlooking the Deli River—one site occupied by the modern Karo village of Deli Tua Lama, the rest given over to the cultivation of cassava gardens. This was once the seat of the piratical kings of Aru who harassed Malacca during the late 15th and early 16th centuries. It is closely associated with the legend of the "green princess" from Siberaya, in Tiga Panah district on the Karo Plateau. Despite Portuguese assistance, Deli Tua was destroyed by the Acehnese in 1536.

According to one version of the story, the Acehnese fired cannon loaded with thousands of small gold coins called *dirham* into the bamboo *pagar* defences, and then withdrew. When the men of Aru cut down the bamboo to recover the gold, the Acehnese attacked, causing a rout.

Belawan and Kota Cina

Medan's port of Belawan, the third largest in Indonesia, is situated in the opposite direction, downstream from Medan, on a man-

grove-lined estuary at the confluence of the Belawan and Deli rivers. Extensive cargo and passenger terminals and palm oil storage facilities have been completed in the past decade to ease what had become a major bottleneck in Indonesia's effort to increase exports. Here also is the giant Ivomas palm oil refinery and oleo-chemical plant, and the nearby archaeological site of Kota Cina.

Belawan is some 25 km north of the city. Most of Medan's new industrial development is sited along the old Belawan road, which was built in the late 19th century and follows the course of the Deli River. Along the way it passes through Pulau Brayan (Tanjung Mulia area), once known as Kota Jawa—where vestiges of a 14th century earthen rampart are visible in a graveyard to the left of the road —then through Kota Bangun and Labuhan. The latter was Medan's first port and consists of a ramshackle street of wooden buildings, now bypassed by the road and by time.

The opening of the Belawan-Medan-Tanjung Muara toll road to the east of the old road means that much of the heavier traffic can now bypass the Belawan town center. The name Belawan derives either from the name of a type of tree found here (*Terminalia citrina*, Roxb.), or from the Karo *dusun* word *erbulawan*, meaning to make an agreement on oath—as here an ancient shrine is associated with the "Green Princess" of Karo legend, and oaths were once made.

There are several good evening seafood restaurants and a flourishing market for modern Chinese-style ceramics. Passenger connections are available to Jakarta, Bintan Island opposite Singapore, Padang and by ferry to Penang. Elaborate bamboo fishtraps line the channel to the sea, and long elevated walkways lead to rows of Malay houses perched on stilts above the water.

Nearby **Kota Cina** is the site of an 11th to 14th century South Indian and Chinese trading settlement, with its adjacent harbor of Paya Pasir. It may be reached from the old Belawan road by turning left at Titipapan (km 16), past the jail on the left and over the Deli River, proceeding about 2 km toward Hamparan Perak and turning right along a track to Rengaspulau and Kota Cina, two typical Malay villages. A caretaker, whose house is adjacent to the village primary school, is usually present.

Evidence suggests that Kota Cina was linked with places as far afield as Java, south China, Sri Lanka, India and the Persian Gulf through a complex web of regional and international trade routes in ancient times. At Paya Pasir, the wrecks of ten ancient ships constructed with the Southeast Asian lash lug technique were discovered by accident when sand was being dug for the construction of the Belawan-Medan toll road. This former harbor site is now, unfortunately, almost totally destroyed due to commercial sand exploitation, and only limited excavation work could be undertaken. Buddha and Vaisnavite images from a brick Buddhist *asrama* and other artifacts from Kota Cina are now in the North Sumatra Provincial Museum in Medan.

Bukit Lawang (Bohorok)

The Bukit Lawang Orangutan Rehabilitation Station, established in 1973 (see following article for more details), is some some 76 km and 3 hour's drive west of Medan (4 hours by bus). About 6 km out of town, you may or may not want to stop at the **Crocodile Farm** at Sunggal—the largest in Indonesia, with some 1,500 reptiles packed in like sardines. From here, the road leads west through Binjai to Belarang—famous for its juicy, grapefruit-like pomelos (*jeruk bali*)—and on to Kuala, railhead for the one-meter gauge North Sumatra railway system. Along the way you pass through vast rubber and oil palm plantations, now obscured by roadside development.

Bohorok was the former seat of the Malayized Kejuruan Langkat, and formed the upper limit of Malay cultural influence on the Wampu River. The Langkat Ulu (upper Langkat) area is, however, essentially a Karo *dusun* area with a sizeable number of Javanese settlers who originally came to work on the plantations. The last stretch along the Bohorok River to Bukit Lawang leads through a lovely irrigated rice area.

At **Bukit Lawang** there are basic bamboo chalets for those who wish to stay overnight by the river at the edge of the forest. Although the elevation, is not high—only about 90 m above sea level—the evenings can be quite cool. Good *durian* and *rambutan* are available in season and Tertiary limestone caves are found in the immediate vicinity, with a pre-Tertiary carboniferous formation around Bohorok. A sidetrip from Bohorok for the fit and adventurous leads to **Pintu Angin**, the "door of the wind"—a hole in the limestone walls near the village of Batukatak, about 5 km upstream from Bohorok. An underground river flows nearby.

— *E. Edwards McKinnon*

Opposite: *Malay villages on stilts at Belawan.*

GUNUNG LEUSER PARK

A School For Orphaned Orangutans

Gunung Leuser, established in 1980, is one of Indonesia's oldest national parks. It straddles the border between Aceh and North Sumatra, covering an area of some 8,000 sq km and encompassing some of the most spectacular montane and equatorial forests in Asia. Its wildlife includes most of Sumatra's extensive range of mammals—including elephants, rhinos, tigers, sun bears, gibbons, macaques, tapirs, squirrels, clouded leopards and orangutans. Also found are about 500 bird species, notably the hornbills and argus pheasant.

As with any Southeast Asian rainforest, the principal difficulty in Gunung Leuser is in finding a way to get in and out without slogging uncomfortably for hours through damp, leech-ridden jungle. The other problem, of course, is to see something once you are there. Fortunately, this park is easily accessible at the Orangutan Rehabilitation Station at **Bukit Lawang**, 9 km past Bohorok and about 76 km west of Medan. Here, young orphaned orangutans are trained to live in the wild, and since its establishment in 1973 over 150 have been returned to the forest.

Visiting the park

A 3-hour journey from Medan (see "Medan Sidetrips") brings you to the village of Bukit Lawang, where permits to visit the center can be obtained upon showing your passport. From here, a rocky 2-km path leads to the banks of the Landat River past cacao plantations and a limestone cave.

The path ends at a bend in the river and one has to cross over here to reach the station, which discourages too many people from entering. In order to cross you have to attract the attention of the park wardens, who ferry you in a cable-and-pulley driven dugout canoe. Make sure you find out the current feeding times in Bukit Lawang before walking to the station, because the wardens are very strict about not letting people cross at other times. Normal feeding times are in the early morning and afternoon, but they are periodically stopped to encourage the orangutans to become more independent.

Once across the river, a steep muddy trail through the forest leads to a platform above the station where the young orangutans are fed their twice-daily ration of bananas and milk. Some of these animals have been deliberately orphaned by hunters who illegally shot their mothers in order to sell them as pets, while others became homeless when their habitat was destroyed by loggers.

New arrivals are kept in quarantine for 3 to 4 months to reduce the risk of passing infections to the wild population. During this period, they are introduced to some of the things every young orangutan should know: how to eat leaves and fruit and how to build a comfortable sleeping nest by bending branches together.

The next stage is to introduce the young orangutans gradually to life in the wild. Park wardens carry the apes piggy-back up to the feeding platform, so they can practice clambering about the branches and make the acquaintance of the other orangutans. After a couple of weeks, they are left at the feeding platform to begin to fend for themselves. Some, pining for human company, return to the station, but most quickly learn the pathways through the forest, and the places to find wild fruits.

The steady diet of bananas at the station is deliberately monotonous to encourage the animals to forage for themselves and find more interesting food. Gradually, the orangutans return less frequently to be fed, and after six months or so they disappear into the vast forests of Gunung Leuser. Most are never seen again, but occasionally one will be spotted in the forest, sometimes with her own baby—a sign of the program's success.

Adventurous types might like to try the speedy route back to Bukit Lawang by hiring an inflated inner tube in the village and riding the rapids downriver from the end of the path opposite the orangutan station. Once back at Bukit Lawang, good food and accommodation are available and there is an excellent visitors' center with displays and slide-shows about the wildlife and ecology of the park.

It is difficult and dangerous for the uninitiated traveler to head off alone into the forest from here because of the dense vegetation, steep terrain and absence of clearly-marked trails, and it is therefore a good idea to join

Right: *Feeding time at the Bukit Lawang station.*

one of the hikes organized by the staff at the visitors' center. These can range from a few hours to several days, depending on the visitors' inclination. One option is to walk right through the national park across the mountains to Kutacane, which takes 3 or 4 days.

The Alas River valley

Bohorok and its immediate hinterland lie in the province of North Sumatra, but most of Gunung Leuser lies in the province of Aceh. The park's administrative center is here, at **Kutacane** (pronounced: KU-ta-CHA-nay) in the Alas River valley, a 6-8 hour drive from Medan. Permits can be obtained for entry into the park on production of photocopies of your passport, but once again, the difficulty is in finding an interesting route into the jungle. One solution is simply to walk along the road running northwest from Kutacane to Blangkejeren. This road bisects the park, and although the area is inhabited it also passes through dense forest. Without the worry of path-finding or attacks from wild tigers, it is possible to concentrate on observing the birds and other wildlife from the road. It is even possible to walk to Blangkejeren in a couple of days, sleeping in villages along the way. There is little traffic, but you may be passed by the occasional minibus which will pick you up if you are tired of walking.

Not far from Kutacane the road passes the scientific research center at Ketambe, but the scientists do not welcome casual visitors and travelers should definitely not plan on staying there. The road to Blangkejeren runs for part of its length along the Alas River, which offers another excellent way to travel through the park, by taking a white-water rafting trip (see "Medan Practicalities" and "Western Aceh" for more details).

Alternatively, you can set out through the jungle with guides and porters hired at Kotacane. The danger from tigers here is probably exaggerated, but be careful; it is said that women squatting in the forest at night are particularly vulnerable. Fieldworkers, however, consider themselves fortunate to catch the merest glimpse of one fleeing from them. Hikers are much more likely to see a wild orangutan or other primates. The graceful dark grey and cream Thomas's leaf-monkey and the more prosaic long-tailed macaques are frequently encountered—a crashing in the branches often indicates the presence of a troop of one of these species.

One of the most exciting experiences of the forest is to see and hear a family of white-handed gibbons or the larger black siamangs, as their whooping calls ring out across the hills and valleys. The white-handed gibbons call in a series of high yells, while the siamangs have a deeper, bubbling whoop backed by a booming sound made by their inflatable throat pouches.

— *Janet Cochrane*

PART III

Introducing North Sumatra

North Sumatra, with its colorful and ethnically mixed population, is Indonesia's most populous province outside of Java. It now has a total of over 11 million inhabitants—more than the entire population of Kalimantan or all the islands of Nusa Tenggara. Dynamic Bataks, Malays, Javanese, Indians and Chinese have created a fascinating kaleidoscope of modern and traditional Indonesian culture. The economy, long established on the basis of plantation agriculture, now supplemented by the huge Asahan aluminum project and various service industries, is one of the strongest in the nation. Tourism, based on the scenic beauties of Lake Toba and the Karo Highlands, is next only to Bali and Yogyakarta.

There are two major ecological zones in the province—a fertile, swamp-fringed eastern plain largely given over to plantations, and a central volcanic core—the Bukit Barisan—formed 70 million years ago by tectonic movements. There is in addition a narrow coastal plain to the west, and a chain of sparsely-inhabited islands lying 125 km off the western coast, of which Nias is the best known.

The jewel of northern Sumatra, Lake Toba, was initially formed some 75,000 years ago in one of the most violent volcanic eruptions ever known—a cataclysm which created volcanic deposits over 600 m thick and hurled ash as far as the Bay of Bengal. A second series of eruptions some 30,000 years ago built up a new volcano inside the older one, and the depression formed by these convulsions now measures about 120 km long by 45 km wide. By comparsion, the much publicized eruption of Mount St. Helens in Washington State left a crater only 2 km in diameter.

The Toba explosion also resulted in the formation of a zoogeographical boundary in the Toba area. Species such as the orangutan, the white-handed gibbon, Thomas' leaf monkey and 17 types of birds are found only to the north of this region—while the tapir, tarsier, Sumatran rabbit, banded leaf monkey and 10 species of birds are found only to the south of it. It seems that the eruption created a vast, desolate region that many wildlife species were unable to cross.

The Bataklands

It is not known when the first humans came into the area but the Batak who dominate the highlands probably arrived from the Philippines and Borneo between 3,000 and 4,000 years ago. Si Raja Batak, the mythical ancestor of all Batak peoples (according to Toba legends), is said to have descended at Mt. Pusuk Buhit (1,981 m), a volcano on the western shores of Lake Toba. There are now six contiguous Batak groups, each with its own language and customs (see "The Batak").

European knowledge of the huge lake in these highlands came quite late. Marsden, who spent 8 years in Bengkulu in the late 18th century, heard rumors of its existence. Two British missionaries, Burton and Ward, entered the Silindung Valley from Sibolga in 1824, but appear to have been carefully restrained from reaching Toba, then considered sacred by the inhabitants. The first European to actually see the lake was the eccentric Dutch linguist, H. N. van der Tuuk, in 1853. Two Boston missionaries, Lyman and Munsen, were less lucky. In the early 1860s they accidentally shot and killed a Batak woman whilst out hunting and were unceremoniously eaten for their pains.

The Batak hinterland came under Dutch control only in the early years of this century, and direct European influence in this area was consequently very brief—coming to an end with the Japanese occupation in 1943. It has commonly been assumed that prior to this time the Batak were an extremely primitive and isolated people. Shocking accounts in the early literature paint them as savage

Overleaf: *The ceremonial* tortor *dance on Samosir.*
Opposite: *A Toba Batak. Photos by Kal Muller.*

headhunters, cannibals and warriors. This image is rather misleading. The Batak not only possessed their own system of writing and a highly developed culture, but seemed to have had early and prolonged trading links with each other and with the outside world.

The Dairi country just to the west of Toba around Sidikalang, for example, was once rich in benzoin—a form of incense that from time immemorial has been in great demand for ritual purposes all over the East. It has long been an important trade item and is still exported from Tarutung to Java. Rotan from the mountains was also important, and Samosir, formerly known for its weavings, also supplied markets around the lake with distinctive earthenware cooking pots known as *hudon*.

Early foreign contacts

Relatively little is known of the early history of the Batak homelands, as tangible archaeological evidence has been difficult to come by. Sherds of Song, Yuan and Ming stonewares nevertheless indicate that several Karo villages, such as Siberaya near Tiga Panah, were in contact with foreign traders by the end of the second millennium AD. Karo folktales suggest that there were well-armed Indian traders here centuries ago, and a small bronze Krisna image in Tamil style was found at Ajibuhara on the Karo Plateau in 1925.

Then there are the Dravidian connections of the Sembiring Sinyombak—Karo Batak septs who formerly set adrift the remains of their dead at the great Pe'kualuh ceremony held at Siberaya. The Sinyombak are forbidden to eat dog meat, though the reason for this is not entirely clear. According to folklore, it is because a Sinyombak ancestor was saved by his dog. There is, however, a more likely reason—an erstwhile association with Tamil traders from South India who came here seeking camphor and benzoin.

The Sinyombak Karo have an interesting group of family names—Berahmana, Culia, Depari, Keling, Meliyala, Pandya, Tekang and Mukham—which relate mainly to South Indian dynasties or castes, and probably originated from an association with a South Indian trading guild, the Ayyavole, who appeared in northern Sumatra in the 11th century AD. The Ayyavole were one of several Indian trading groups who had their own temples, priests and armies, and operated across political boundaries—supplying rulers and aristocrats with valuable textiles, incense, medicinal and ritual items. An Ayyavole inscription dating from AD 1088 has been discovered on the west coast of North Sumatra near Barus.

Other evidence of South Indian presence is reflected in Karo place names such as Lingga, Cingkem and Kubuculia. A small Batak group to the south of here, the Pardembanan, appear to have also exhibited strong Indianized traits. They lived between the Silau and Asahan rivers but have now been completely absorbed by the Simalungun Batak.

In the Padang Lawas area 200 km south of Medan, moreover, there are some impressive remains of the Hindu-Buddhist Panai culture. The most important of these is the brick *biaro* at Bahal near Gunung Tua, erected between the 10th and 14th centuries. Here too is evidence of external trade with northwest India and China—a village named Senamandala, after the ruling dynasty of Bengal, and a *marga* or clan named Daulay, after a locality in the northeast Indian district of Orissa.

Magic seems to have played an important role among the Batak in these earlier times, for there are many tales of the *orang jadi-jadian*, men who could transform themselves at will into majestic tigers—tales which fit in well with the evidence of Tantric Buddhist practices from the archaeological remains.

Conversions and migrations

Prior to Indonesian independence, the various Batak groups largely remained within their ancestral homelands. The Dutch finally annexed the Karolands at the turn of the century and built the first road into the plateau in 1908. The Karo are now largely converted to Christianity and to a lesser degree to Islam, though a number still maintain their ancient *pebegu* animistic religion.

The Toba were converted to Christianity by German and Dutch missionaries in the late 19th century, while the Mandailing and Angkola groups were largely converted to Islam by fanatical Paderis from Minangkabau during the Paderi Wars of 1816-1832. Today, however, Christians and Muslims live peaceably here in a land dotted with mosques and churches, united by the strong bonds of *adat*, strongly influenced by old kinship ties.

The breakdown of law and order at the end of the Japanese occupation occasioned a mass exodus from these uplands to the vastly more fertile and largely empty east coast plains, and many Batak have now spread all across Indonesia as teachers, civil servants and businessmen—enjoying vast new economic opportunities that were previously undreamed of.

— *E. Edwards McKinnon*

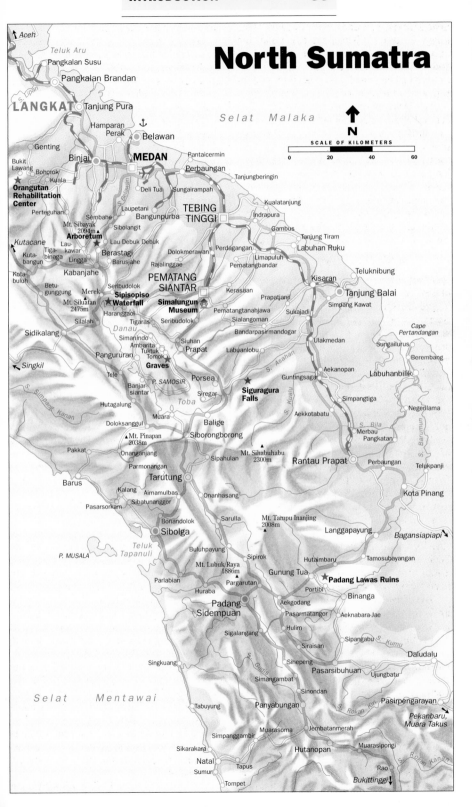

North Sumatra

THE BATAK

Flamboyant Peoples of the Highlands

The colorful but notoriously forthright and aggressive Batak peoples inhabit a cluster of spectacularly beautiful and fertile volcanic basins at the northern end of the Bukit Barisan range—focusing around Lake Toba, with the huge island of Samosir at its center.

The term Batak is probably an abusive nickname given to them by coastal Muslims. It seems once to have been used widely in insular Southeast Asia to vilify pagan, upland peoples; a mountain tribe in the Philippines, totally unrelated to the Sumatran group, shares the same name, and a highland people in Malaysia is called Batek. Because it connotes heathen, pig-eater, cannibal and bumpkin, some Batak eschew the appellation altogether. One Batak group, however—the Toba Batak—have reclaimed the old moniker as an ethnic badge. Batak they are, and proud of it!

Today there are about six million Batak,

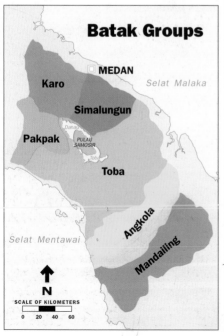

Batak Groups

MEDAN

Karo

Selat Malaka

Simalungun

Danau

Pakpak

PULAU SAMOSIR

Toba

Toba

Angkola

Selat Mentawai

Mandailing

N

SCALE OF KILOMETERS

0   20   40   60

more than half of whom live in the highlands surrounding Lake Toba. They are divided into quite a number of distinct Batak societies, each with its own language, style of ceremonial dress and traditions, and these are generally grouped under six separate ethnonyms (see diagram below). The various languages fall into three distinct sub-groups—with the Toba, Angkola and Mandailing in one, the Karo and the Pakpak in another, and the Simalungun by themselves in a third.

A Toba creation myth portrays Si Raja Batak as the founding patriarch of all Batak peoples, and a mountain to the west of Lake Toba known as Pusuk Buhit ("Central Hill"), as their point of origin. The linguistic pattern does not clearly confirm this, but the Toba Batak who now live in the area around the mountain are indeed the most numerous and visible group.

Nobles, commoners and slaves

Simalungun and Toba societies were divided into three ranks: nobles, commoners and slaves. Rank was acquired from one's parents and had little to do with wealth or achievement. The Toba raja was identified by his elaborate tunic and armband made from the shell of the giant mussel *Tridacna gigas*. (The pre-Islamic Bugis of South Sulawesi and the chiefs of Nias also wore such armbands.)

In the southern Batak regions, the raja held dominion over several genealogically-related villages. Only married men had a say, though the opinions of older female shamans were greatly respected. Among the Simalungun, slaves were the absolute property of their masters and could be crippled or killed at will. In the south, slaves were protected by *adat* (customary law), and in Karo society slaves were not a significant category at all, comprising· only those who had fallen into debt. Neither among the Karo nor the Pakpak was there any nobility, nor any effective political leaders above that of village chiefs.

All Batak peoples are patrilineal, and their societies are segmented into clans who can theoretically trace their ancestry to a single male through a succession of male descendants. The Simalungun have only four clans, the Karo five, but the other Batak societies have 50 or more. Batak clans are exogamous; that is, marriage is fobidden within the clan, even if no blood relation can be found. A man may have more than one wife, and in the past

Right: *The famous royal tomb at Tomok, on Samosir Island, as it looked ca. 1920.*

powerful leaders often had several.

The preferred marriage for a man is in fact with his mother's brother's daughter. The family of the bride is revered as a source of fertility and prosperity. (The Karo call them "the visible god.") A substantial brideprice has to be paid to the bride's family, which occupies an honored place at the wedding and subsequent ceremonies. Complex networks of bride-givers and bride-takers, built up over many generations, provide a sense of identity for the individual. Despite changes brought on by the spread of education and improved communication since independence, such traditional networks are still very important.

Trade and Indian influence

Despite their geographic isolation, the Batak had regular contact with the outside world. Salt, cloth and iron were brought into the highlands in exchange for gold, rice, cassia —an inferior kind of cinnamon—and valuable tree resins such as camphor and benzoin. Horses were also bred and exported. *Ulos*, woven shawls that convey fertility and blessing when presented by bride-givers at weddings, radiated out from the Toba region to the surrounding Batak areas.

Trade between the highlands and the coast was on a large scale. Marsden mentions that at the end of the 18th century, 100,000 bamboo measures of salt were being imported annually to the Tapanuli region. Along

these trade routes came Indian influence. The Toba language contains about 175 words of Sanskrit origin, especially calendrical terms, and the vocabulary of magic and divination. Batak writing, chess, spinning, religious ideas and even many clan names are of Indian origin. A modified Indian script was used to produce books about magic and curing written on bark and folded accordion style.

The first clear historical reference to the Batak comes in the 13th century, when the Chinese geographer Zhau Rugua mentions the name Ba'ta, a location on the northeast coast of Sumatra. The first account of the Batak in English was by Charles Miller, the East India Company botanist at Bengkulu, who visited the Batak countries in 1772 in the company of another Englishman, Giles Holloway. He wrote: "They have no king, but live in villages absolutely independent of each other, and perpetually at war with one another: their villages they fortify very strongly with double fences of camphor plank pointed, and placed with their points projecting outward, and between their fences they put pieces of bamboo, hardened by fire and concealed by the grass, which will quickly run through a man's foot."

In his detailed account of the Batak published in 1783, William Marsden astounded his readers with the paradox of a cannibalistic people who possessed a system of writing. Warfare was endemic and hostilities were for-

mally declared. "The first act of defiance is firing, without ball, into the kampong of their enemies. Three days are then allowed for the party fired upon to propose terms of accommodation, and if this is not done, war is then fully declared."

Attacks took place usually around midnight. Captured enemy were put in stocks, unable to stand or to sit, some of them for years—their legs withering from lack of use. If a village was captured, its inhabitants were enslaved and (in Toba) the village was burned.

Public cannibalism

Frequently mentioned in such accounts was the Batak habit of eating people. An Arab text from the 9th century mentions that Sumatra's

inhabitants ate human flesh. Marco Polo alluded to the same rumor, as did a series of Portuguese travelers in the 16th century, none of whom actually set foot in Batak territory. Among the Batak, public cannibalism was actually an infrequent form of capital punishment. During one and a half years spent among the Toba Batak (1840-1), the geographer Junghun witnessed only three cases. He left a vivid account of one:

"The captive is bound to a stake in an upright position. A number of fires are lighted, the musical instruments are struck. Then the chief draws his knife, steps forward and addresses the people. It is explained that the victim is an utter scoundrel, not a human being at all, but a *begu* ("ghost") in human

form, and the time has come for him to atone for his misdeeds. All draw their knives. The raja cuts off the first piece, being either a slice of the forearm or the cheek, if this be fat enough. He holds up the flesh and drinks with gusto some of the blood streaming from it. Then he hastens to the fire to roast the meat before devouring it. Now all the remaining men fall upon the bloody sacrifice, tear the flesh from the bones and roast and eat it. Some eat the meat raw, or half raw to show off their bravery. The cries of the victim do not spoil their appetites. It is usually eight or ten minutes before the wounded man becomes unconscious, and a quarter of an hour before he dies."

Cannibalism may have seemed more endemic than it actually was because of the fact that many Batak keep the bones of their illustrious ancestors, and these family treasures were often misconstrued as grisly trophies. It may have been in their interests, moreover, to cultivate this unsavory reputation. Rumors of Batak cannibalism no doubt contributed to the region's isolation, helping the Batak maintain control of trade routes into the highlands, and discouraging attempts at conquest by lowland kingdoms. Batak men often hired themselves out as mercenaries, too, and in this role blood-thirsty reputations served them well. The various Batak groups were not equally anthropophagous (the Karo deny that they ever ate human flesh), and while the custom may have persisted as late as the 20th century among the Pakpak, Toba and Simalungun, it was probably rare.

The Batak village

Prior to colonial rule, the Toba Batak lived in villages fortified with earthen and bamboo walls. The village consisted of 6 or 7 houses, at least one council house (*sopo*) and a skull house. The *sopo* surpassed even the chief's house in the splendor of its decorations, with rich leaf-and-flower designs carved on its beams. The houses faced one another across a rectangular square. Boys and widowers spent their nights in the *sopo*; in the south, unmarried girls were guarded by the village chief or slept in a separate house, where they were allowed male visitors. Karo houses were larger (holding as many as eight families), and their villages tended to be larger and more irregular in layout.

Batak houses were built on piles above the ground. The interior was open and quite barren of furniture, but at night mats were let down to provide privacy. Open hearths produced a constant fog of smoke, which in the absence of a chimney was forced to find its way out through the thatched roof.

Early Dutch visitors found these living conditions far from ideal. The scholar Neumann describes a Toba house in the mid-19th century thus: "Soot covers the walls and ceiling, the corners are full of cobwebs, the floors are covered with *sirih* chews and chicken excrement. The houses are like caves into which the openings in the walls scarcely admit a ray of light. Centipedes and scorpions wander about freely, ants build their runways, cockroaches fly unmolested, and lice lurk all over. When the houses are filled with smoke, one asks oneself how human beings can spend a night in one of them."

Like the Toraja of Sulawesi, who share the same ancient heritage, the Batak house was divided into three levels symbolizing a threefold division of the cosmos—the underworld, the earth and the upperworld. Animals were kept below the house (where they warned against attacks), people lived in the middle and sacred heirlooms were hung under the eaves. Important items were kept in the *sopo*: the skulls of slain enemy, magical writings incised on bark, and the bronze drum which summoned villagers to feast or council.

Economic life

Every Batak was, and to a large extent still is, a farmer. Rice is the most important crop, followed by maize, potatoes, taro, yams and various vegetables. Coffee, tobacco, cinnamon, coconut and sugar (and earlier indigo) are raised as cash crops. Cattle, buffalo and other livestock are also important. Irrigated land is very valuable because it may be cultivated continuously, but where thick grasses have taken over, dry fields can be worked with deep hoes between long periods of fallowing. Around the lake, women supplement their income with weaving, and throughout the Batak region men and women transport and sell the region's produce. Rural families who farm and trade, or draw a wage as teachers or bus drivers, are often the most well-to-do.

Toba villages and the surrounding lands belong to a patrilineal descent group, and women ideally move to their husband's village. In reality a man often lives in his wife's village if more land is available. Land passes to male heirs, but this legal standard often bends to accommodate women's needs. Women inherit land as widows, for example, and may receive it as gifts from parents or brothers, or be granted the lifetime use of fields.

As the population in rural areas expanded, migration became the solution to land shortages, and families increasingly invested in education. Some who move away maintain ownership of land, leaving it to be worked by relatives. The Toba regard their land as a sacred legacy from the primal ancestor or village founder; it must not be sold to outsiders.

Cosmology and magic

Traditional Batak religious beliefs were influenced by Hindu-Buddhist ideas, but as in Bali these rested on an older Austronesian substratum dating back some 5,000 years.

The Toba universe was divided into three. The upperworld, which had seven levels, was the home of gods, the middle world belonged

KAL MULLER

to humans and the underworld was the home of ghosts and demons. A high god, Mula Jadi Na Bolon—the Creator—was a remote, mythical being who had a fabulous blue chicken for a wife and did not concern himself much with human affairs. Attending more closely were the ancestral spirits, and these remain important for the Toba today.

Ancestors protect and receive honor from meat-sacrificing communities of descendants, called *bius*. Descendants of a village founder constitute a small *bius*; larger ones are made up of several villages tracing their origins to still more distant ancestors. In the past, major

Opposite: *A magical shaman's staff, or* tunggal panaluan. **Above:** *An ancestor figure.*

bius kept their ancestors' bones in hand-hewn stone sarcophagi, some with a stylized *singa* or "lion" head carved on their face. In recent years, these sarcophagi have been replaced by massive concrete structures and statuary.

Batak medical theory focuses on the condition of the soul. The soul of a healthy person is "hard" and remains firmly in place. Illness befalls someone who has been startled, causing the soul to flee the body. By ritual means, a shaman calls the wandering soul home again and thus "cures" the patient.

Karo shamans (*guru*) were both men and women, although male *guru* tended to have a higher status. Women *guru* were often spirit mediums as well as healers. The Toba shaman (*dukun*), usually male, was instrumental in communicating with spirits, both good and evil, and was second only to the village chief in importance. He was consulted before any undertaking, such as war or harvesting.

The shaman had a magic staff (*tunggal panaluan*) carved with ancestral figures and used to produce rain and to protect the village against enemies. This staff possessed a "warrior" spirit, the *pangulubalang*, which was obtained by kidnapping a child from a hostile village. After extracting an oath from the victim, boiling lead was poured down his throat and he died a quick but painful death, thus securing his ghost as an obedient ally. A magical substance made from his entrails was placed in a hole in the center of the staff.

Muslims and Christians

Starting in the early 19th century, the southern Batak began to face increasing pressure from the neighboring Minangkabau areas to convert to Islam. This culminated with the Paderi War (1816-33), when southern Batak succumbed to the burning and looting of West Sumatran Muslims who aimed to spread their faith and control the gold trade.

The war pushed as far north as the Toba region, but not many Toba converted to Islam. All of the Mandailing did, however, and most of the Angkola, and these southern groups began to renounce the name Batak and to dispense with their traditional clan names. Karo who moved to the East Coast similarly converted to Islam and began to consider themselves Malays. In the past, Batak and Muslim were exclusive categories, although today Batak Muslims are better able to reconcile their religious and ethnic identities.

The Batak were an early and obvious target for Christianizing European missions (see "Missionaries") and today the Toba church is the largest in Indonesia. Benefitting early from mission schools, the Toba moved rapidly to fill positions as teachers, medical technicians and office clerks in the post-colonial order. As a result they remain disproportionately represented in government and in careers requiring education.

— Rita Smith Kipp

MISSIONARIES

19th Century Protestant Conversions

Christian traders had visited Sumatran ports as early as the 10th century, and Franciscan monks ministered to the foreign community of Aceh in the late 17th century, but the only real prospects for Sumatran converts during the colonial period were among the more isolated peoples who had firmly resisted Islam —particularly the Batak of the highlands and the Niha (of the western island of Nias).

In the 19th century, several missionaries undertook the dangerous journey into Batak territory. Some were unlucky. In 1824 two members of the English Baptist Mission Society, Burton and Ward, translated some of the Bible into Batak and spent a week in the Silindung Valley, but were discouraged from continuing by Britain's surrender of its Sumatran possessions to the Dutch at this time. The French Catholic mission in Penang attempted to extend its work to Nias in 1832, but the first two priests sent, Vallon and Berard, died within weeks of reaching Gunungsitoli.

Two American protestants, Lyman and Munson, also visited Nias briefly and then traveled from Sibolga into the Silindung Valley, where they were attacked and killed in 1834. A few Dutch missionaries worked in the Dutch-controlled southern Batakland in the 1850s, but since these areas were largely now Islamic, their progress was minimal.

The great Dutch linguist van der Tuuk (himself part Indonesian) was the first European to see Lake Toba. Though employed as a Bible translator, the eccentric scholar had little interest in promoting Christianity, and instead spent his time compiling a dictionary and grammar of the Toba Batak language.

Conversions really got underway with the decision of the German Rhenisch Mission Society (RMG) to work here in 1861, and the arrival the following year of Ludwig Nommensen, who set off for the Bataklands armed only with a Bible and a violin. He was far-sighted enough to distance himself from colonial authorities and helped the Toba Batak as a doctor, mediator and teacher. Beginning in the Silindung Valley, his work spread north to the shores of the lake and beyond, and bore fruit in conversions of whole communities in the 1880s. By 1900 the Toba Batak were predominantly Protestants, and Christianity had begun to seem a part of Batak identity.

Out of the shock of this transition, nevertheless, were born a number of movements attempting to blend Christian, Muslim and traditional beliefs with the messianic figure of Sisingamangaraja. The Parmalim movement flourished at the end of the 19th century to the south and east of Lake Toba, while the militant Parhudamdam movement threatened European plantations during the WW I years.

There were growing pressures against what some saw as the paternalistic control of European missionaries, leading in 1927 to a breakaway independent church, the Huria Kristen Indonesia (HKI). In response, the Rhenisch Mission was reconstituted in 1930 as a self-governing Batak church (HKPB). This helped meld the Toba into a self-conscious group as they began their expansion into commercial and teaching roles all over Indonesia.

In contrast to the somewhat marginal place of Christians in many parts of Asia, the 3 million Toba Batak Christians are aggressive and unapologetic about their status as Indonesian nationalists who played their part in the revolution and now have a significant role in the Republic's army and government.

Christianity made much slower progress among the Karo and Simalungun, partly because it was associated first with Dutch and later with Toba Batak domination. There were only 5,000 Karo converts by 1940. The removal of Dutch missionaries by the Japanese proved a stimulus to the growth of the Karo church, and with the suppression of communism in 1965 there was finally a mass movement of Karo to Christianity, spurred on by the government's distrust of anyone who "did not have a [universal] religion."

In Nias, systematic missionary work began with the Dutch conquest of the island in 1890. By 1915 there were 20,000 Niha Christians and by 1940 a majority of the islanders, some 135,000 people, were converts. Catholics were excluded from evangelizing in the Bataklands until the 1930s by a colonial partition agreement, but thereafter made rapid gains. Today Catholics represent over 10 percent of the total Batak population.

— *Anthony Reid*

Opposite: *Toba Batak dancers at Ambarita.*

BATAK HOUSES

Traditional Communal Dwellings

Highways leading into the Batak highlands mostly date from the Dutch period, and the settlements seen along the roadside here are not traditional ones. Batak villages were formerly sited far from the main roads for reasons of security. In the Karo highlands, for example, they perched high atop ridges surrounded by deep ravines, which made them more easily defensible. To see traditional Batak houses you thus have to venture off the main roads into more remote areas.

There are a great many regional architectural styles, but most Batak houses have certain features in common. All are essentially rectangular wooden structures on piles, with high pointed roofs. The internal space is open and unfurnished, and was traditionally inhabited by several families. Two families normally shared a common hearth. There is often a balcony or verandah at the front for storage and for guests, and domestic animals such as pigs and buffalo live underneath the floor.

All old houses were traditionally thatched with the fibers of the arenga palm, which also provides palm sugar and wine. The walls and pillars were often ornately carved and painted in symbolic motifs. The *boraspati ni tano* or lizard was a favorite—a good luck and fertility symbol of the earth deity, combined in the Toba area in panels with two or four female breasts. The all-important *sopo* or rice barn stood directly in front of the house.

Today much has changed. Modern single-family brick or cement houses built on the ground are the norm, while corrugated metal sheets often replace *ijuk* thatch on the older houses. In most Batak areas in fact the traditional houses have all but disappeared. Here and there, nonetheless, especially in more isolated areas, one can still find fine examples of traditional Batak architecture.

Karo and Simalungun houses

Traditional Karo houses were massive affairs —constructed and occupied by eight related families. Each family had a living space of about five square meters organized around four hearths. Many older houses are still in use, although the residents are not usually related to one another, as the original owners have often now rented out the "apartments."

Old Karo houses can be seen in villages around Kabanjahe. In the village of **Lingga**, for example, often visited now by tourists, the old houses stand grouped in rows one behind the other. Most date from the 1930s, as no new ones have been built since independence, and each year their number dwindles as one or two collapse through disuse and neglect.

An unusual characteristic of Karo houses is their lack of a distinctive front or back, as they have identical entrances on opposite sides with access by means of bamboo platforms. In some very old houses a deep wooden gutter runs down the center of the floor, dividing the house in half. Debris was swept into this gutter and it served an important ritual function during ceremonies.

The only decoration on many old Karo houses is a large triangular top piece made of braided bamboo, with the inauguration date of the house inscribed on it. Other houses have a decoration that is not immediately recognizable—a lizard pattern braided into palm fibers binding the ribs of the walls together. The broad, round house beams are also sometimes decorated with plant motifs, and the house corners may be adorned with interlocking geometric patterns designed to prevent bad influences from entering.

Traditional houses always had a rice barn, but these are no longer in use today, as rice is now kept in plastic bales inside the house. In some rice barns there was an extra sleeping room for the young men of the village, who were not permitted to sleep in the multi-family dwelling after puberty. Nowadays, adolescent boys sleep in empty houses and the rice barns are used to play chess and chat, especially in the warmer western Karo areas.

Old Simalungun Batak houses are very simple, except for a few belonging to the former rajas. These are built like Karo houses— the raja's living quarters are in front, entered via a wooden staircase, and his wives lived at the back, with their own rooms but sharing a collective entrance. Only two authentic Simalungun royal houses remain—one in **Hutaraja**, the other in **Purbatongga**. A third one in nearby Pematang Purba was actually built during the 1930s as a new home for the

Right: *Toba houses at Tomok, on Samosir Island.*

Hutaraja chief. In Hutaraja, particularly, many of the old houses are still intact and a visit to this village—located about 5 km northeast of Pematang Purba along a small track—gives a good impression of Simalungun villages in the days before the plantation boom.

Toba and Mandailing houses

Toba villages are the most traditional of all Batak settlements. They are normally quite small—consisting of 8 to 10 houses facing each other in rows. A broad central avenue between them is used to dry rice and other produce, and is filled with people during annual village festivals, which mostly take place in June and July. Compared with the enormous Karo houses, those of the Toba Batak are modest. Four families formerly lived in one, which is scarcely imagineable today given their small size. Nowadays one family lives in a house that is often furnished with tables and chairs—even a stereo set.

Toba houses have a distinctive front verandah with a wooden staircase. Very old houses had a trapdoor that could be quickly closed in case of hostilities. At the front of the house the roof protrudes further than the back, and underneath it is an open balcony. During festivals the orchestra sits here and plays to accompany ceremonies taking place below.

The houses are often beautifully decorated with elaborate painted carvings—geometric or cosmological motifs like the "tree of life" which supposedly reaches to heaven. Oracle animals are also depicted, as is a striking, stylized face or *singa* (which literally means "lion" but is not really a lion at all). Like the *gaja dompak* or elephant figure, the latter is probably influenced by the Hindu-Buddhist *makara* or elephant-like sea monster that adorns ancient temple portals.

The placement of a *singa* on the ends of the house was formerly accompanied by special ceremonies and feasting, as if to signify that this was the moment the house was brought to life. Human heads are said to have been suspended in grass bundles from the *singa* at this time, imparting their potent life force to the newly-consecrated house.

Typical Mandailing Batak houses are still found in the remote villages of Simpang Banyak Jae and Simpang Banyak Julu around **Kuta Nopan**, at the southern end of the province. These houses resemble Karo Batak ones, but each houses only a single family. Metallic decorations are attached to the top of the roofs like charm bracelets, and through the influence of neighboring Minangkabau houses, some have a gallery attached.

Opposite the village chief's house one can find an assembly building where nine drums used during festivals are suspended. A raised floor serves as a seat for the village chief on special occasions, and the corners of the floor are marked by four lovely wooden statues.

— *Periplus Editions*

BATAK TEXTILES

Professional Weavers from the Toba Area

Woven fabrics (Toba *ulos*, Karo *uis*) play an important role in traditional Batak society. They are used not only as clothing, but as important gifts presented on ritual occasions to symbolize and reinforce the bonds existing between related groups of people. The need to exchange traditional fabrics at ceremonies such as weddings, births and funerals is indeed the main reason such cloths continue to be produced today, though one can also see them being worn by village women as shawls or head coverings.

In many areas, villagers no longer weave their own traditional fabrics but instead purchase reproductions that are machine-made in the larger towns, for example in Pematang Siantar and Balige. Remaining village weaving centers are mostly located in the Toba Batak region, where the main source of livelihood is still rice agriculture and the soils are relatively poor. When not working in the fields, village women here try to earn a bit of extra money by weaving.

Weaving for a living

In some areas, weaving has long been a full-time occupation practiced by village woman who accept commissions from traders and merchants in the towns (themselves also women). One area where such commercial weaving continues to be practiced is along the northwestern shores of Lake Toba, in the so-called *sitelu huta* ("three villages")—namely Tongging, Paropo and Silalahi. These villages were formerly accessible only by boat, and this form of transport still plays a major role here—especially on market days, when boats converge on the market village in the morning and return late in the evening.

Although the women of the *sitelu huta* are themselves Toba Bataks, they do not normally produce traditional Toba textiles. For generations they have instead produced fabrics for Karo Batak clients to the north, who—thanks to more fertile soils and export crops such as citrus and vegetables—had more money to spend on their traditional fabrics and jewelry than the Toba.

To ensure the accurate reproduction of their traditional motifs, Karo women formerly dyed their own yarns and then had them delivered by intermediaries to the *sitelu huta* villages for weaving. This practice continues

today, though one now finds other types of fabrics being woven here alongside the Karo cloths. Some are modern creations employing synthetic dyes; others are traditional Toba patterns produced in quantity for the tourist trade and sold in souvenir shops in Prapat and around Tomok on Samosir.

Earlier in this century, as the trade with the Karo flourished, many Toba weavers from the *sitelu huta* moved to the Karo area so as to have better access to their market. During the 1920s, when Kabanjahe was still a small, prosperous village, the village chief set aside a special area for these Toba weavers. As the village grew into a regional market center, more and more weavers moved here, and one now finds a whole enclave of Toba Batak weavers and dyers living in Kabanjahe.

Weavers here order their dyed yarns from Toba dyers who also live in the town. These dyers plant indigo in their backyard gardens, but this is often insufficient to meet their needs. Once a week additional supplies of concentrated indigo are brought in from one of the three Toba villages in exchange for locally-dyed yarns, and in this way a connection with the area of origin is maintained.

The patterns woven for the Karo depend on orders, but also on the individual preferences of the weaver. Some older weavers refuse to work with synthetically-dyed yarns. Toba weavers in Kabanjahe tend to be older than their counterparts in the homeland villages around the lake, and they tend to produce more traditional patterns. This is encouraged by their clients, as the Karo themselves are quite conservative.

Today, however, many of the fabrics produced here employ non-traditional dark red colors—a style of coloring emanating from the Simalungun area. These colors have been popular among the Karo for some time now, and younger Karo often do not even know that their own traditional fabrics were once exclusively dyed with indigo blue.

The Toba women in Kabanjahe also weave their own traditional *sitelu huta* village patterns. Some of these they sell, others are kept aside for their own use, to be distributed among family members after their death.

The traditional weaving and dyeing industry is severely threatened today by manufactured goods that look similar but are cheaper and also much thinner—produced with synthetic dyes and yarns. Unfortunately, these fabrics are catching on to the point where the younger generation buys them almost exclusively. There is even an increasing demand for machine-woven fabrics that reproduce traditional Karo motifs using gold and silver threads instead of the traditional dyed colors of indigo and red.

— *Beatriz van der Goes*

Opposite: *A young Toba weaver at work.*
Below: *An example of the Toba* ragi idup *cloth.*

ERIC OEY

SIMALUNGUN AREA

Through the Plantation Belt to Toba

The Simalungun or Timur ("Eastern") Batak occupy the highlands between Lake Toba and the east coast—today a key plantation region with huge estates producing palm oil, rubber, cacao and tea. The area is traversed by a 100-km stretch of the Trans-Sumatra Highway leading up to Prapat via Pematang Siantar.

The name comes from an earlier period in the region's history and means "desolate land" though it is in fact quite fertile. The Simalungun area borders the Karo highlands to the north and the Toba Bataklands to the south. On the west it is bounded by a thin string of Toba settlements, such as Tigaras along the eastern shore of Lake Toba, and in the south by the Asahan River which drains Lake Toba.

The land slopes generally south and east down from the Karo Plateau and the Toba rim to low-lying coastal plains, and is cut by deep ravines and several sizable rivers—the largest of which is the restless and unpredictable Bah Bolon ("Great River") which flows through the market town of Perdagangan to the sea at Kuala Tanjung, the new port built for the Asahan aluminium project.

The country was formerly divided into a number of small and sparsely-populated independent states: Silimakuta, Purba, Raya, Pane, Dolok, Siantar, Tanah Jawa and Bandar—each under its own raja, who held considerable power in his domain. Somewhere in this area was also the ancient kingdom of Nagur.

The Simalungun and the Karo have much in common—Indianizing traits in their dialect, religious practices and script, as well as the presence of village federations known as *urung*. The Simalungun were, however, reputedly cannibals, whereas the Karo were not.

The major Simalungun *marga* or clans are distinct from those in the other Batak areas—namely Damanik, Sinaga, Saragih and Purba. Islamic influence is strong in areas adjoining the coastal Malay settlements. By the early years of this century, the rajas of Purba and Raya invited Rhenish missionaries into their territories. In 1907, the rajas signed the Korte Verklaring of submission to the Dutch, and in 1908 a colonial adminstration was established in Pematang Siantar.

Soon after the arrival of the Dutch, Toba migrants began moving into then unoccupied areas, creating vast expanses of irrigated rice fields, a technique quite alien to the Simalung-

un, who practiced only swidden agriculture. More Toba migrants poured in after Independence, and today the Toba comprise a large proportion of the area's population.

Unlike in other Batak areas, Simalungun lands were held not only by the dominant clans but also by the rajas. After the establishment of Dutch rule, this allowed them to dispose of vast tracts of uncultivated land for plantations, which of course afforded them considerable benefits. Consequently much of Pane, Siantar and Tanah Jawa became cov-

ered in large plantations worked by Javanese labor. This is the only Batak homeland area in which plantations were established, and few old Simalungun villages remain.

Medan to Tebing Tinggi

The highway east of Medan through the Deli-Serdang coastal area is broad and fast, passing through endless groves of rubber trees and oil palms. Those wishing to tour the estates can make arrangements at the Tourist Information Office on Jl. A. Yani in Medan.

A turnoff at Perbaungan leads north to **Pantai Cermin** ("Mirror Beach"), a favorite local holiday and weekend picnic spot, 45 km from Medan. Here are casuarina-lined beaches for swimming and fishing, though incomparable to those along the west coast.

About 76 km from Medan you enter the large town of **Tebing Tinggi**, the east coast rail junction where lines link Pematang Siantar with Medan and Rantau Prapat further to the south. In the rail yard here you can watch old steam locomotives being serviced, some of them dating from the turn of the century.

The main road to Pematang Siantar and Toba turns off here and enters the Simalungan area just south of Tebing Tinggi, passing through the enormous government-owned oil palm and cacao estate of Pabatu. Further along the road is the American-owned Dolok Merangir rubber estate, one of the few plantation enterprises still owned by foreign capi-

tal. The famous American botanist and ethnographer, Harley Harris Barlett—author of *The Labors of the Datoe*—worked here in 1918 and again in 1927.

Pematang Siantar

Pematang Siantar, North Sumatra's second largest city, is the administrative and commercial hub of the Simalungun plantation area, founded by the Dutch early in this century. Colonial houses can be seen amidst the urban clutter, and at 400 m above sea level the climate is notably cooler than on the coast.

The pre-war Siantar Hotel on Jl. W.R. Supratman was used as a headquarters by a small contingent of Dutch troops, and was attacked and burnt by revolutionary forces in 1945. It has now been restored and appears to have changed little since colonial times.

The **Simalungun Museum** on Jl. Ahmad Yani has an interesting collection of *pustaha laklak*—the bark books in Indic Batak script used by *datuk* magicians to record their sacred formulae. It also has notable examples of stone *pangulubalang* or Simalungun guardian images collected during the 1930s. The Siantar Zoo offers an interesting collection of Sumatran wildlife, and a wide variety of seasonal fruits such as durian, mangoes, mangosteens, *rambutan* and *salak* are offered for sale in Siantar's market.

From Pematang Siantar the road ascends steadily through palm plantations and a vast patchquilt of irrigated *sawah*. A few traditional houses and tombs appear by the roadside in the broken country around the Toba rim. The first glimpse of the lake is always breathtaking—a shimmering sheet of blue with the verdant cliffs of Samosir rising steeply from it in the distance.

— *E. Edwards McKinnon*

Opposite: *A rubber plantation.* **Above, left:** *The Simalungun Museum in Pematang Siantar.* **Above, right:** *Siantar's distinctive motorized* becaks.

KAROLAND

A Verdant Highland Plateau

Taneh Karo or Karoland—the homeland of the Karo Batak people—is an exceptionally fertile plateau set in the midst of the volcanic Bukit Barisan highlands south of Medan. Its northern edge rises sharply from densely-forested foothills some 50 to 60 km from the coast, while the southern edge just touches the shores of beautiful Lake Toba. With an area of about 5,000 sq km, the plateau is like a gigantic bowl surrounded on all sides by jagged mountain peaks—looking almost as if it has been scooped right out of them.

For some time now this verdant plateau has served as northern Sumatra's green-grocer. With the construction of a road up from the coast in 1908, European crops such as cabbage, corn, carrots and potatoes were introduced, and Karo farmers began to cultivate market gardens to supply a rapidly-growing urban population in the lowlands—for a

time even supplying vegetables across the straits to West Malaysia and Singapore. Dutch-engineered irrigation works have been maintained and expanded since independence, and few agricultural regions of Sumatra are as productive as these highlands. The *marquisa* (passion fruit) juice produced here is particularly famous throughout Indonesia.

The plateau's elevation ranges from 700 to 1,400 m—assuring a delightfully cool climate throughout the year, with temperatures of between 10 and 28 degrees C. The soil is deep and of rich volcanic origin, the whole region being overshadowed by two active volcanoes —Sibayak (2,170 m) to the north, near Berastagi, and Sinabung (2,451 m) to the west, visible from Kabanjahe—both of which continually emit plumes of steam. Although the rugged escarpment separating the plateau from the coasts formerly served as a formidable barrier to travel, the area has nevertheless been a crossroads for the transinsular trade in salt and tree resins since very early times.

The 'first arrivals'

The Karo people, known among themselves as the *merga silima*—the "five clans"—are a distinct cultural entity with their own language, history and traditions. According to their own legends, they were the earliest inhabitants of these highlands; their name in fact means "first arrivals."

Despite the assertions of some early Euro-

pean explorers, the Karo were never cannibals, though they may have had some rather unconventional habits by European standards. The filing and blackening of teeth, which died out only in the early years of this century, combined with the red-stained lips obtained from chewing *sirih* or betelnut, undoubtedly gave them a somewhat bizarre and fearsome appearance.

About 300,000 Karo today inhabit the plateau, but at least as many live in the coastal lowlands to the east, where they have been for centuries. Since the 1950s many Karo have migrated further afield to Medan, Jakarta and other urban centers.

Highland Karo villages are larger than those of the lowlands (larger also than most Toba Batak villages), owing to the greater fertility of the plateau's volcanic soils. Early European travelers reported villages with as many as 3,000 inhabitants, linked through marriage and descent into loose federations known as *urung*. Intervillage skirmishes were common—even between villages within the same federation—and most were sited high up on the edges of ravines and surrounded by ramparts of earth and hedges of thorny bamboo for defensive purposes.

Each highland village was autonomous, with its own hereditary chief. In the 19th century, some lowland Karo lived under the authority of coastal Malay sultans, but the highlanders bowed to no central authority until the area was finally conquered by the Dutch in 1904. Aceh had earlier attempted to exert control here and to convert the Karo to Islam, but with little success.

Distinctive adat houses

Traditional Karo *adat* houses—with their open floorplan in which eight related families live together under a single upswept or rectangular roof of *ijuk* thatch—are a microcosm of traditional Karo society. The most common floorplan has four hearths, each shared by two families. A central walkway runs through the center of the house leading to doors at either end, with two hearths on either side of the walkway. In these large, partitionless spaces domestic life is carried on in full view of one's neighbors. Though related, each family works, cooks and eats as a separate unit, and life is somewhat inevitably shared with dogs, cats, chickens and other livestock.

The distinctive, oversized roofs decorated with triangular dormers and topped with buffalo horns have no clear purpose, but allow space under the eaves for smoke to pool in the absence of chimneys, and also for rats, bats, lizards and a host of insects to collect. Blackened heirlooms, tools and other objects are hung above the hearths and in the rafters.

Smaller structures with the same roof

Opposite: *The Karo plateau is Medan's green-grocer.* **Below:** *The Berastagi fruit market.*

KAL MULLER

design serve as granaries or contain the bones of distinguished ancestors. In the past, each village had a men's house where men gambled, smoked and rested during the day, and where adolescent boys slept at night. Today, most villages also have a *los*—a shelter for ceremonial events.

Unfortunately, few of these traditional houses remain. During the revolution, the Karo burned all villages along the main roads rather than leave anything for the Dutch, and in the post-war period, single-family dwellings have become the fashion. Traditional houses do still exist in more remote villages off the main roads, but are increasingly rare today and falling into decay.

Wife-givers and wife-receivers

Like other Batak peoples, the Karo reckon descent patrilineally, though neither the village nor the multi-family house is the domain of a single descent line. Each person belongs to one of five Karo clans (*merga silima*) from birth. Marriage between persons within the clan is forbidden, even if there is no traceable blood tie between them.

A family's marriage relations are as important as clan relations by descent, and as with other Batak groups, a distinction is made between wife-receivers (*anakberu*, families into which one's daughters marry), and wife-givers (*kalimbubu*, families whose daughters marry into one's own family). The former are one's social inferiors while the latter are one's superiors. Wife-receivers can be called on to assist at ceremonial events, while wife-givers are honored as a protective, supernatural "visible gods" affecting one's fertility, health and prosperity. In order to be complete, a village or traditional household had to be formed of all three kinds of families—the founder, as well as both types of relatives by marriage. The clan composition of Karo villages and houses is therefore very mixed.

The Karo conceive of their society as a community of kinsmen linked by marriage as well as descent. Meeting for the first time, two Karo inevitably ask each other a series of standard questions in order to construct a metaphorical kinship relation. Whether strangers or neighbors, all Karo address one another with kin terms; first names are seldom used except with children—unless intended as an insult! Recognizing no kings and giving deference only to their kinsmen, the Karo are egalitarian and competitive in their social interaction. The subservience and flowery

etiquette of many other Indonesian peoples thus grate on Karo sensibilities.

Religious pluralism

The first Dutch Reformed missionary arrived in Medan in 1890, at the behest of European planters who hoped the Karo could be Christianized. At first, the mission was confined to the foothills around Sibolangit, but with the Dutch annexation of the highlands, it moved to Kabanjahe. The mission was never very successful in either locale, apparently because Christianity was too closely associated with the hated colonial regime; only a handful of Karo had converted by the time of the Japanese occupation. After the Dutch left, however, an independent ethnic church developed and the Karo began to convert in large numbers.

Today, Karo society is religiously plural. About 60 to 70 percent belong to one of several Christian denominations, while as many as half of the remainder are Muslims; the rest still practice the traditional Karo religion. The latter focuses on ancestral spirits residing in unusual natural formations such as volcanoes or hot springs, and on a host of spirits that either protect or bring illness, death and crop failure. After a funeral, at seances lasting

Above, left and right: *Karo inhabitants of the old village of Lingga near Kabanjahe, now a tourist sight.* **Right:** *Traditional female Karo headdress.*

until dawn, female mediums work in consort with their spirit familiars to retrieve the souls of the deceased. At this ceremony, called *erpangir* (literally: "hair-washing"), even ordinary people become possessed, dance ecstatically and demand special foods.

The ancient Karo *pebegu* or spirit religion demanded special respect for the souls and remains of the dead. After initial interment in an earthen grave, the bones of revered ancestors were dug up after a suitable period of time, washed, and ritually placed in *geriten* or skull houses outside the house of the living.

Most ceremonies in Karoland today have a decidedly secular character, however. The religious portions of a funeral, whether Christian, Muslim or traditional, generally occur at the beginning and end—leaving the hours in between for meals, discussions of inheritance and dancing. Weddings follow a similar pattern. A Christian couple may have a church wedding in the morning and in the afternoon host a traditional feast with dancing.

Dancing at such events involves two large groups of men and women facing one another—the sponsors on one side, their kin on the other. Bending their knees and dipping to the beat of a giant gong, the dancers move their arms and hands slowly. At funeral dances, kin groups carry items of clothing that belonged to the deceased to enhance the grief of the survivors—Karo funeral dancers are expected to weep openly. During the dances, stylized forms of sung poetry are used to address the deceased and express one's sorrow.

Weddings and funerals remain important arenas for celebrating kinship and community relations. They reflect a family's wealth, renown and social network, and may be delayed for years so as to marshal the sufficient funds. Until a proper wedding or funeral is held, a family feels itself in debt to the community. A couple may marry in a simple church or civil ceremony—but years later, often with two or three of their own children present, they will sponsor a lavish wedding feast. Similarly, a family may bury a parent in a simple grave, but after some years will retrieve the bones, lovingly clean and reinter them in a splendid cement edifice while sponsoring an elaborate feast and dance.

Since the 1950s, the Karo have placed great emphasis on education. There are today over 2,000 university graduates in a society of no more than 800,000 people, surely one of highest educational levels achieved by any Indonesian ethnic group. Young Karo attend universities throughout the archipelago, then settle in the cities as engineers, nurses, bureaucrats, businessmen and academics. They return to the homeland periodically for funerals and weddings, and provide money to construct the imposing concrete tombs shaped like house or churches that increasingly dot the Karo homeland.

— *Rita Smith Kipp / E. Edwards McKinnon*

BERASTAGI

Scenic Hill Station on the Karo Plateau

The delightfully cool and picturesque town of Berastagi nestles at the northern edge of the Karo Plateau, 68 km south of Medan (about 2 hours away by car). At 1,330 m elevation, the climate is deliciously mild during the day and bracing at night. The town arose during the 1920s as a Dutch hill station, complete with 9-hole golf course and spacious European villas —even a Dutch school. Today it is a popular weekend resort for Medan residents, and it also makes a convenient stopover point on the way up to Lake Toba. There is a large market selling wonderfully fresh fruits, flowers and vegetables, and this is the perfect base for an exploration of the volcanic Karo highlands—with their thick pine forests, soothing hot springs and traditional villages.

The road up from Medan

About 20 km from Medan, the urban heat and traffic are soon left behind as you begin the climb into the forested foothills of the Bukit Barisan. Sharp S-turns provide panoramic views back across the verdant plains to the city. About 40 km from Medan, history buffs may be interested to stop at the town of **Sembahe**, where a pathway behind the shops next to the main bridge leads half a km or so upstream to a rubber estate where the first "Hoabinhian Sumatralith" neolithic stone tool was discovered in 1926. Nearby is the so-called Rumah Umang—a stone burial chamber with rough relief carvings that is several centuries old. In season, good durians may be purchased in Sembahe and along the road up to Sibolangit.

Several km further on, the **Sibolangit Botanical Garden** lies on an escarpment overlooking Sembahe and the lowlands. This pleasant patch of undisturbed rainforest is worth a stop to wander the pathways amidst giant ferns and moss-covered trees. Botanists will find an interesting variety of native flora, while birders will have a field day. Leeches and mosquitoes are a problem in the wet season, however, so bring along your repellant!

Ten km before Berastagi on the right is the turnoff to Daulu and Semangat Gunung —two villages at the base of active Mt. Sibayak (2,094 m). Also here is **Lau Debuk Debuk** ("Bubbling Water"), a hot sulphur spring regarded as the home of friendly forest spirits (notice the offerings of *kretek* cigarettes

left in lengths of split bamboo or palm stems by the edge of the pools), and also a favorite haunt of friendly locals, who like to enjoy a communal bath after sunset, when the cold air contrasts deliciously with the piping-hot, sulphur-laden water. Sip a cold beer or a hot tea while gazing up at the steaming volcano. A traditional masseuse is on hand to iron out tired muscles. Those wishing to climb Mt. Sibayak may continue along the same road to Semangat Gunung.

Seven km before Berastagi, at **Tongkoh,**

is an arboretum originally established in 1916 that has now been renamed "Great Bukit Barisan Forest Park." A project of the local district head (*bupati*), the park has a zoo, modern cabins for weekenders and elephant rides for the children. Unfortunately, a lot of concrete has been used to formalise the park and "enhance" its beauty.

Visiting Berastagi

Berastagi is a center for vegetable, flower and fruit farming—exporting truckloads of produce everyday to Medan. One of the area's most popular products is enormous yellow passion fruits, made into a refreshing cordial to mix with soda or water. The broad main street is lined with souvenir shops, restaurants and hotels, and the central market attracts farmers from the surrounding area. Here you can watch Karo village women in traditional costume grappling with the produce they have come to sell.

Berastagi is dominated immediately to the north by smoking Mt. Sibayak, while further to the west is higher Mt. Sinabung (2,451 m). Each of these volcanoes can be climbed in a day, though you need to be reasonably fit (see "Practicalities"). On the western edge of town, Gundaling Hill (1,496 m) rises some 110 m above the surrounding plateau, and a park at the top provides good views of the volcanoes. This was the former Dutch resort area, and crumbling old bungalows are found

scattered amongst new concrete hotels. It is close enough to walk up and around in an hour or so. At the northern edge of town is the delightful Bukit Kubu Hotel, a relic from the colonial era set amidst a manicured 9-hole golf course.

Traditional Karo villages

There are many old villages around Berastagi, ranging from very good to "not interesting." Visit a few to compare. The better known are Pecaren, Lingga, Cinkes, Dokan, Barusjahe and Juhar. Many are only accessible via hilly tracks or by changing *bemos* several times, so hire a guide at your hotel.

Right on the northern outskirts of Berastagi, the village of **Peceren** has a number of traditional houses interspersed with more modern ones. It is easily accessible; a guide will show you one of the houses where a small shop has been set up. The family sells crude wooden Karo and Minang figures, and the father serenades you with his *kecapi* lute as traditionally-clad grandmothers look on.

The most popular Karo tourist village is **Lingga**—16 kms southwest of Berastagi and about 5 km northwest of Kabanjahe. Situated near the source of the Lau Garut at an altitude of 1200 m, Lingga has a number of *rumah adat*—some reputed to be 250 years old—but is becoming dilapidated as it is more difficult now to build new *adat* houses due to the rising cost of timber and manpower. Guides will happily show you about and explain various facets of Karo life, including the "birthing seat" on a wooden step by the chief's house where some women still give birth, attended by the village *dukun* (medicine man), gripping two handles high above her head. It is possible to stay in the village and if you care to pay, traditional dances will be performed.

— *E. Edwards McKinnon and Jill Gocher*

Opposite: *View of Mt. Sibayak from Berastagi.*
Above, left and right: *The village of Lingga.*

LAKE TOBA

Jewel of the Sumatran Highlands

Lake Toba, with the mystical island of Samosir at its center, forms the very heart of the beautiful but often harsh Toba Bataklands—a huge volcanic depression set high in the treeless mountains of northern Sumatra. The lake was formed some 75,000 years ago as the result of an enormous volcanic explosion—probably the greatest the world has ever known. This is the largest lake in Southeast Asia—measuring 100 km long, north to south, and 31 km across—with a surface area of about 1,145 sq km. The island of Samosir alone, inside the lake, is 530 sq km—about the size of Singapore. This is also the world's deepest lake, over 450 m deep, though accurate surveys of the lake floor have yet to be made.

Remarkably, no important rivers flow into Toba from the sides of the lake. All drainage from the surrounding areas flows down to the coasts, as the thick mantle of tuff from the Toba explosion has formed a steep "collar" around the lake, blocking earlier drainage channels. The lake's surface lies 906 m above sea level, but may once have been 150 m higher. Thousands of years ago, the collecting water overflowed the caldera to the southeast and eroded the soft tuff, cutting its way out through spectacular, steep-walled ravines via the Siguragura, Harimo and Tangga falls to form the Asahan River. The water level has begun to mysteriously subside again in recent years, and no adequate explanation for this has yet been given.

The Toba Batak homeland of which Lake Toba forms the central part actually comprises five regions. The first is the island of Samosir within the lake itself. The second is the Uluan ("Headwaters")—a fertile region along the southeastern lakeshore between Prapat and Porsea, where the Asahan River drains the lake. The third is Habinsaran ("The East" from Toba *binsar* meaning "sunrise")—an extremely broken, mountainous region which lies further to the southeast, at the headwaters of the Kualu River. The fourth is the Silindung Valley to the southwest, and the fifth is the Hombung region west of the lake.

Dotting the countryside throughout the region, wherever there is adequate water, are Toba villages with houses, churches, tombs and verdant rice fields. The volcanic soils are exceptionally fertile and the Toba area has been inhabited for many centuries.

Berastagi to Prapat

The main route up to Toba from Medan passes through Pematang Siantar and the Simalungun Batak areas and has already been described above (see "Simalungun"). Increasingly popular with tour buses and independent travelers, however, is the scenic backroad across the Karo Plateau from Berastagi that skirts the northeastern edge of the Toba caldera. This is a longer but far more exciting route visually, with many interesting stops.

The first town you pass after leaving Berastagi is the district capital of **Kabanjahe** ("Ginger Garden"), 14 km to the south—a bustling town surrounded by rice fields and market gardens in the very heart of Karoland. This is a crossroads where the highway from Aceh's Alas Valley meets the Medan highway (see "Western Aceh").

Twenty-four km south of Kabanjahe, the road touches the northern rim of the Toba basin at Merek, and a sideroad from here winds down to the lakeshore past a spectacular waterfall known as **Sipisopiso** ("Like a Knife"), which shoots out of a cave at the edge of the plateau and plunges 120 meters straight down to a small, gushing stream below. A gazebo provides panoramic views over the village of **Tongging** at the lake's edge.

From Merek, the road to Prapat hugs the high rim of the ancient caldera, skirting the lake and brushing the bare slopes of Mt. Singgalang (1,865 m) just north of the village of **Seribudolok** ("Thousand Peaks"). A turnoff to the left here leads down an old Karo trail to Bangunpurba, in the East Coast plantation belt. Some 15 km down this road, at Tinggi Raja, are a series of terraces and hot springs with sparse but interesting flora.

Back on the Prapat road, some 4 km past Seribudolok, a sideroad to the right winds 10 km down to the lakeshore at **Haranggaol**, a picturesque market village known for its garlic and shallots. A ferry crosses over to Samosir from here on Mondays and Thursdays, and there are small hotels, canoes and speedboats with fishing equipment to while away the time as you wait.

You are now in Simalungun Batak territory, and at **Pematang Purba**, 8 km past Seribudolok, is the wooden palace of the former Simalungun ruler. Built in the style of a traditional *adat* house, it is said to be 200 years old and has been restored as a museum—

Overleaf: *Tuktuk Peninsula, dotted with hotels.*
Left: *Tongging, at the northern end of the lake.*

Toba's Formation

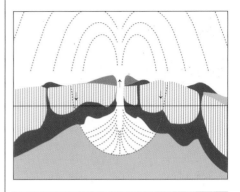

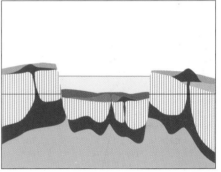

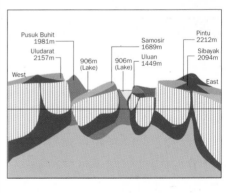

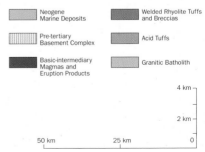

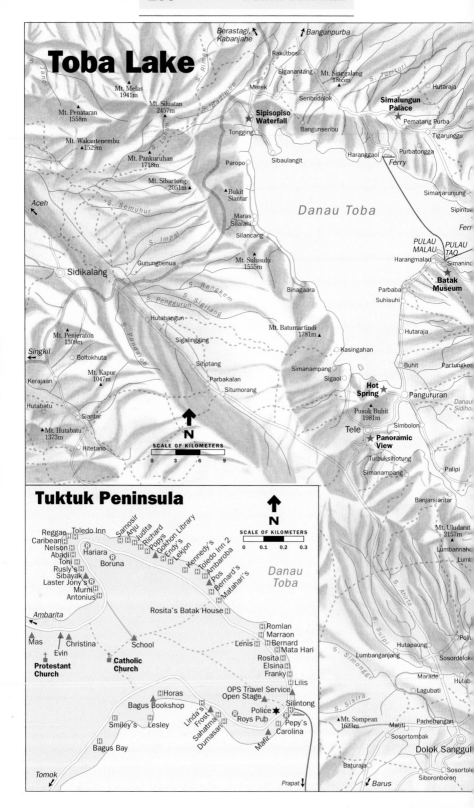

Toba Lake

Berastagi, Kabanjahe
Bangunpurba
Rakutbosi
Siganantang
Mt. Singgalang 1865m
Hutaraja
Mt. Melas 1941m
Merek
Seribudolok
Simalungun Palace
Mt. Siluatan 2457m
Sipisopiso Waterfall
Pematang Purba
Mt. Penataran 1558m
Tongging
Bangunseribu
Tigarunggu
Mt. Wakantenembu ▲1529m
Paropo
Sibaulangit
Purbatongga
Aceh
Mt. Pankuruhan 1718m
Haranggaol
Ferry
Mt. Sibartong 2051m▲
Bukit Siantar
Danau Toba
Simarjarunjung
Sipintu
Maras
Silalahi
Silancang
Ferr
S. Semuhur
S. Impal
PULAU MALAU
PULAU TAO
Harangmalau
Simaninc
Sidikalang
Gunungbenua
Mt. Sulusulu 1555m
Batak Museum
Binagaara
Parbaba
Suhisuhi
Mt. Penjeraton 1309m
Hutabangun
Mt. Batumartindi 1781m▲
Hutaraja
Singkil
Boltokhuta
Sigalingging
Kasingahan
Buhit
Partungkor
Mt. Kapur 1047m
Sihotang
Simanampang
Sigaol
Kerajaan
Parbakalan
Hot Spring
Pangururan
Hutabatu
Situmorang
Pusuk Buhit 1981m
Danau Sidiho
Siantar
Simbolon
Mt. Hutabatu 1373m
Tele
Panoramic View
Hitetano
Turpuksihotung
Palipi
Simanampang

SCALE OF KILOMETERS
0 3 6 9

N

Tuktuk Peninsula

N

SCALE OF KILOMETERS
0 0.1 0.2 0.3

Reggae
Toledo Inn
Samosir
Anju
Judita
Gokhon Library
Caribean
Richard
Nelson
Popys
Endy's
Kennedy's
Abadi
Hariara
Lekjon
Toledo Inn 2
Toni
Boruna
Ambaroba
Rusly's
Pos
Sibayak
Bernard's
Laster Jony's
Matahari's
Murni
Antonius
Danau Toba

Ambarita
Rosita's Batak House

Mas
Christina
Romlan
Evin
School
Marraon
Lenis
Bernard
Protestant Church
Catholic Church
Mata Hari
Rosita
Elsina
Franky
Lilis
OPS Travel Service
Open Stage
Horas
Silintong
Bagus Bookshop
Linda's
Frost
Police
Roys Pub
Pepy's
Smiley's
Lesley
Sahatma
Carolina
Dumasari
Bagus Bay
Mafir

Tomok
Prapat

Mt. Uludarat 2157m
Lumbannahor
Lumi

S. Ahira
Hutapaung
Polh
S. Simongg
Lumbanganjang
Sosordolok
Marade
Hutab
Lagubati
Mt. Sompean 1623m
Matiti
Parhebangan
S. Sisira
Sosortombak
Dolok Sanggul
Baturaja
Sosortole
Siboronboron
Barus

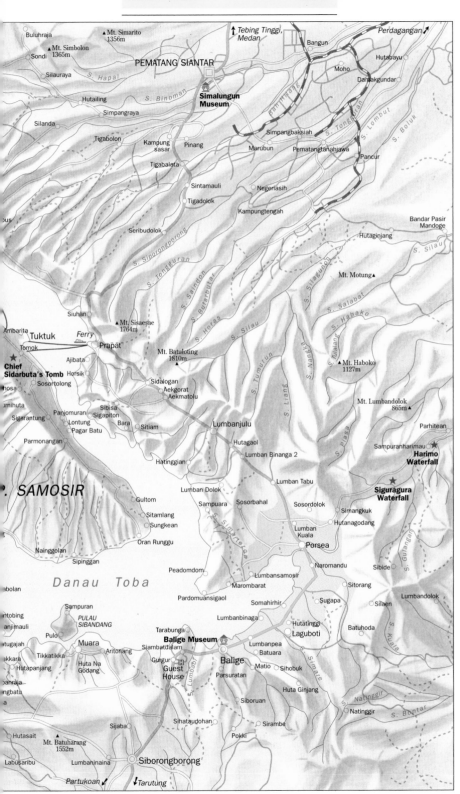

Buluhraja
▲ Mt. Simarito 1356m
↑ Tebing Tinggi, Medan
Bangun
Perdagangan ↗
▲ Mt. Simbolon 1365m
Sondi
Silauraya
Moho
Hutabayu
Damakgundar
S. Hapal
PEMATANG SIANTAR
Hutailing
S. Binoman
Simpangraya
Simalungun Museum
Silanda
Tigabolon
Kampung sasar
Pinang
Simpangbaksiah
Pematangtanahjawa
Pancur
Marubun
Tigabalata
Sintamauli
Negeriasih
Tigadolok
Kampungtengah
Bandar Pasir Mandoge
Seribudolok
Hutaginjang
S. Silau
S. Siporongborong
S. Tongkuran
Mt. Motung ▲
S. Salabat
S. Silagunig
S. Sainton
S. Butarbutar
S. Horas
S. Silau
S. Habako
Siuhan
▲ Mt. Sisaesae 1764m
Ambarita
Tuktuk
Ferry
Prapat
Mt. Batuloting 1810m
▲ Mt. Haboko 1127m
Tomok
Ajibata
Horsik
Mt. Lumbandolok 865m ▲
Parhitean
Chief Sidarbuta's Tomb
Sosortolong
Sidalogan
Aekgorat
Aekmatolu
Sampuranharimau
Harimo Waterfall
hosa
Sibisa
Sigapiton
irnihuta
Sigarantung
Panjomuran
Lontung
Bara
Sitiam
Lumbanjulu
S. Tumurun
S. Liang
S. Piasa
S. Aguen
S. Tulaang
S. Gulangan
Parmonangan
Pagar Batu
Hutagaol
Lumban Binanga 2
Hatinggian
Lumban Tabu
Siguragura Waterfall
SAMOSIR
Lumban Dolok
Gultom
Sampuara
Sosorbahal
Sosordolok
Simangkuk
Sitamlang
Hutanagodang
Sungkean
Lumban Kuala
Nainggolan
Oran Runggu
S. Simare-ca
Porsea
Sibide
Sipinggan
Peadomdom
Naromandu
Danau Toba
Lumbansamosir
Sitorang
abolan
Marombarat
Sugapa
Silaen
Lumbandolok
Pardomuansigaol
Somahirhir
ntobing
Sampuran
Lumbanbinaga
Hutatinggi
Batuhoda
anjimauli
PULAU SIBANDANG
Laguboti
S. Kuala
Pulo
Tarabunga
tugajah
Muara
Aritonang
Balige Museum
Lumbanpea
Batuara
S. Simare
ikkara
Tikkatikka
Siambatdalam
Matio
Sihobuk
Hutapanjang
Huta Na Godang
Gurgur
Balige
Parsuratan
anraja
Guest House
S. Lumbati
Huta Ginjang
S. Natinggir
ngbatu
Siboruan
Natinggir
a
Sihatuodohan
Sirambe
S. Bontar
Hutasait
▲ Mt. Batuharang 1552m
Sijaba
Pokki
Labusaribu
Lumbaninaina
Siborongborong
↙ Partukoan
↓ Tarutung

freshly-painted in the traditional colors of red, black and white. Although the original earthen and bamboo defenses are now gone, the old entrance tunnel can still be seen. The main complex formerly housed the raja and his 12 wives; its dark interior contains royal memorabilia and is well worth a visit. There is an ancient path from here leading down to the lake, and if you have more time, the nearby Perkebunan Marjanji tea estate operates guided tours of their facilities.

At Tigarunggu, 5 km past Pematang Purba, a right-hand turn leads to Prapat via a rough but scenic road that follows a forested ridge overlooking the lake. At a tiny crossroads at Simarjarunjung is a restaurant with a magnificent view. At Sipintuangin, 3 km further on, there is a sideroad to the right leading down to **Tigaras**, another market town on the lakeshore with a ferry service over to Samosir. The main road continues high above the lake through Huta, and rejoins the main Pematang Siantar-Prapat highway near Siuhan. From here, a hard right takes you down through a tunnel and above a sheer cliff at Sibagunding, and after rounding a corner you enter the resort of Prapat.

Prapat

Prapat occupies a small, rocky peninsula jutting into the lake, and has recently expanded southward over a ridge into the adjacent village of Ajibata. A resort since before WW II, the town has boomed in recent years with the opening of many new hotels. The old Prapat Hotel overlooking the harbor was famous throughout the Indies in the colonial period. Indonesia's first president, Soekarno, was imprisoned in Prapat for several months by the Dutch in early 1949, together with Haji Agus Salim and Sutan Syahrir.

Good watersking, speedboat trips, paddlecraft and tennis are all available. Bougainvilleas, poinsettias, honeysuckle and other flowers bloom year round in the equable climate. Shops sell an array of Batak textiles, woodcarvings, ceramics and other goods mixed with the occasional genuine antiques, offered by traders who are aggressive and persistent. Fruits and vegetables are to be found in the market. The local mango, known as *kueini*, has an interesting flavor but is not as good as East Java's *harum manis*.

In the immediate vicinity of Prapat are some interesting geological exposures of granite, fossiliferous sediments, limestone and sandstone. Just to the south, in the Naborsahon River valley, are beautiful terraces indicating the previously much higher levels of the lake.

Samosir Island

Samosir, the huge, arid "Island of the Dead" in the middle of Lake Toba, is a stark remnant of a second powerful explosion that rocked this volcanic cauldron some 30,000

years ago. At this time a subsidiary peak formed but then subsequently split and slumped back into the earlier crater (see diagram). The eastern part now forms the Prapat peninsula and the Uluan shore down to Porsea; the western edge forms Samosir. The island measures 45 km by 20 km, and in fact was originally a peninsula. It became an island only after the arrival of the Dutch in 1906, who dug a canal through the narrow, 200-m isthmus connecting it to the mainland at Pangururan. This action, it is said, caused some considerable consternation among the local inhabitants, as they feared the island would slip into the lake and disappear.

The eastern side of the island rises very steeply up from a narrow strip along the lakeshore to a central plateau towering some 780 m above it. The plateau slopes gently back to the southern and western shores of the island and is dotted with tiny villages that cling precariously to clifftops pierced by deep ravines.

The Samosir plateau is largely barren—with scattered forests, marshes and a small lake. A road of sorts runs all around the edge of the island, but is very rough in places, with some dilapidated and dangerous bridges in the southwest. From Pangururan—the *kecamatan* administrative center on the western side of the island—a road links Samosir to the mainland, climbing up a steep escarpment to dramatic 1,800-m heights at Tele that offer a spendid panorama of the lake, with

Samosir Island spread out down below.

During the northeast monsoon, which blows from September or October through to January, a strong wind known as *alogo bolong*, the "great wind," often springs up at midday from the heights, creating waves of over a meter in height and making it difficult and sometimes dangerous for boats on the lake. Local ferries, often overloaded with people and produce, are occasionally lost in such storms. Formerly, the Batak used enormous dugout canoes known as *solu* cut from a single forest tree, to cross the lake. Today only very small dugouts are seen.

F.M. Schnitger, author of *Forgotten Kingdoms in Sumatra*, visited Samosir in the 1930s and recorded *adat* houses, stone tombs and burial cists in no less than 26 different villages. It seems, however, that since that time many villages have been abandoned, names of others have changed, and some of the enormous stone sarcophagi for which the island is known have been moved from their original resting places so they are not always easy to find. Off the beaten track, time and patience is required to seek out the ancient tombs. But then for many people, a visit to Samosir simply involves an easy ferry ride over to the village of Tomok, where the most famous of all Toba Batak sarcophagi lies just a few minutes' walk from the pier.

Gateway to Samosir

Samosir is accessible by regular ferry from the resort of Prapat, a journey of under an hour—but also by less frequent ferries from Haranggaol and Tigaras on the Simalungun shore to the north. The two main landing points on Samosir are Tomok—a traditional village with beautiful stone tombs and houses—and Tuktuk, where the island's many

Opposite: *The ferry to Samosir.* **Left:** *The famous sarcophagus of the Sidarbuta chief in Tomok.* **Above:** *The chief's wife atop the tomb.*

hotels and restaurants are concentrated. Speedboats can also be rented in Prapat to make a trip around Samosir in 2 to 3 hours.

At **Tomok**, famous for years now as the "gateway to Samosir," the visitor is greeted by a row of stalls selling a bewildering array of Batak handicrafts—traditional *ulos* cloths, carvings, Batak calendars and musical instruments (including the traditional two-string violin, the *harwab*, and the guitar or *hasapi*). Small hotels and restaurants are nearby.

Directly inland, hidden in a bamboo thicket under an ancient banyan tree, is the most famous of the giant Toba sarcophagi. Carved from a single block of stone, the tomb dates from the early 19th century and belongs to a chief of the Sidarbuta clan. In front is an enormous, carved *singa* face—a mythical part buffalo, part elephant-like creature. The saddle-shaped lid is surmounted by the carving of a woman holding a cup or bowl, probably a *paranggiran* used in sacrificial rites. She is said to represent the wife of the dead chief.

There are other modern tombs and stones here, including lichen-covered stone ancestor seats dating from 1950, and a modern sarcophagus made as recently as 1979. The *adat* houses stand in a row opposite, facing away from the lake, with their all-important rice barns in front. They are carved with foliate designs painted in the holy Batak colors of black, white and red—their traditional *ijuk* palm fiber thatched roofs now replaced by

corrugated zinc.

Just to the north of Tomok is the small peninsula of **Tuktuk Ni Asu** ("Dog Peninsula") with its sandy beaches and scores of hotels offering budget accommodation, now a booming resort that is Samosir's answer to Bali's Kuta Beach. Offshore is the tiny island of Pulau Pasir, site of an ancient burial cist.

Four km to the north of Tuktuk along a narrow, paved road is **Ambarita**, an attractive village with ancient stone walls that were once topped with a thick *pagar* or fence of thorny bamboo. Inside are stone seats and modern statuary, the work of a certain Siallagan some 40 years ago. The villagers invent endless stories to explain these attractions to the tourists, for like villagers everywhere they enjoy spinning a good yarn.

Some 19 km further north is **Simanindo**, where the elaborately decorated house of Raja Sidauruk has been declared a museum. Visitors can witness a traditional *tortor* dance and *sigalegale* puppet performance here for a fee, complete with a lively *gondang sabangunan* ensemble. The *sigalegale* traditionally served as a receptacle for the soul of the deceased in Batak funerary rites, though the custom may have originated only about 100 years ago in the Balige area. Just opposite Simanindo is a rocky islet called **Pulau Tao**, with a shallow bay and a small hotel.

About 2 km past Simanindo is **Harangmalau**, the northernmost point on Samosir. At nearby Situngkir and Sialangoan are unusual tombs belonging to the chiefs of Sihaloho. One has a cist decorated with a bull or buffalo head in relief and a lid that is carved into three points. The end above the bull relief is decorated with a *boraspati ni tano*, the sacred lizard that is thought to bring good luck.

Several km further on, past Parbaba, is

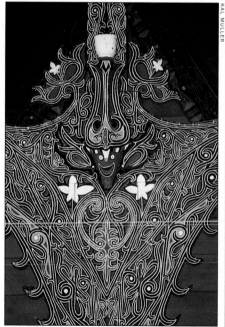

Left: *House decoration (singa) with foliate designs.*
Above and right: *The* tortor *ceremonial dance and* sigalegale *puppet performance at Simanindo.*

Suhisuhi—site of an ancient sarcophagus and a number of modern cement tombs. To the south at **Hutaraja** are five old sarcophogi of the Simarmata clan, including that of Raja Ompu Bontor within the village itself. In front of the chief's house is a miniature dolmen-like monument said to be the spot where a young girl was sacrificed when the house was built. Human sacrifice was apparently once quite common in Toba, used to magically capture and convert the spirit of an unwitting victim into a powerful spirit protector.

A further 5 km on is **Pangururan**, the sub-district administrative center, where a bridge connects Samosir to the mainland. Just over the bridge, a small road to the right leads up to a popular hot spring on the slopes of Mt. Pusuk Buhit (1,981 m), sacred mountain of origin for all Batak peoples. This is where the first ruler—Si Raja Batak—is said to have descended from the heavens. The main road from the bridge winds up to **Tele**, 900 m above the lake, offering panoramic views back across Samosir.

South of Pangururan the road hugs the lakeshore past Simbolon to Nainggolan and Sungkean. Just north of Simbolon, at **Pansur Duggal** (probably the Pancur of Schnitger), is a group of three modern sarcophagi and a number of ancient burial urns. On the rise above Simbolon is the sarcophagus of Raja Ompu Silo Simbolon with an unusual carving of a female figure with raised arms below the

singa. At Huta Godang, near Nainggolan, is the ancient sarcophagus of the Parhusip clan. There are more important sarcophagi at Huta na Bolon and Sipinggan.

South from Tomok

Back on the eastern side of the island, a tiny road leaves the shore just south of Tomok and winds up steeply onto the Samosir plateau (1,689 m), offering wonderful views of the lake. It then follows the crest of the plateau southward. About halfway to the south coast, at the tiny village of **Parmonangan**, a rebuilt replica of the original Situmorang clan house can be seen. On one end it has unusual relief carvings featuring four protruding female breasts and a woman with her arms upraised. The road continues from here down to the south coast at Onan Runggu.

If one has the inclination, however, one can more profitably follow Jean-Paul Barbier, curator of the Barbier-Müller Museum in Geneva, and explore the coasts south of Tomok by boat, putting into shore at will. Along the way you pass lovely coves with white sand beaches and picturesque villages. Around **Panjomuran** and **Pagar Batu**, 8 and 9 km south of Tomok, rows of low stone columns on the shore once supported boathouses storing the huge Situmorang war canoes (*solu*) used to raid neighboring villages. From Pagar Batu, a path leads up to a terrace on the plateau where a village once stood. All that remains

now are a number of tombs and a *lesung batu* or stone mortar. Near the southeastern tip of the island at Sitamiang are elaborate concrete tombs built in the form of miniature Toba-style houses.

Prapat to Porsea

Having explored Samosir, you may want to return to Prapat and travel south to the Uluan region to view a number of fascinating tombs and villages. From Prapat, take the smaller backroad through Ajibata, which winds steeply up a mountain face behind the resort and affords rewarding views back across the lake. Small villages with superbly decorated *adat* houses are set back off the road in clumps of bamboo; unfortunately, most have been pillaged of all removable decorations for the "antique" trade.

To the left of the road, 22 km from Prapat, is the village of **Hutagaol** belonging to the Manurung clan, built in 1935 above an earlier village of the same name. Several km further on is the hamlet of **Lumban Binanga II**, with fine examples of modern Toba house decoration. About 8 km further south, a group of villages on the left—Lumban Na Bolak, Lumban Tabu, Lumban Sibinbin and Lumban Simaria-sonak—have some of the best examples of traditional *adat* buildings in the Uluan style, with animistic and anthropomorphic carvings and friezes. These villages belong to the Sitorus clan; **Luban Tabu** has been declared a

cultural monument under the protection of the Ministry of Education and Culture.

The area south of here around **Porsea** is where the 60-m-wide Asahan River drains Toba to the east. The river is quickly joined by tributaries from the north (Aek Mandosi) and the south (Aek Bolon), and the alluvial plain formed by these rivers is extremely fertile, dotted with properous villages. The road down into the Asahan Valley turns off to the left some 3 km before the town of Porsea. About 1 km along this road on the right is a group of lovely villages, including Lumban Kuala—where there is a fine example of a carved sarcophagus lid belonging to Raja Pabalubis of the Manurung clan.

From here the road descends steeply eastward into the **Asahan Valley**, where the river enters a narrow ravine with vertical walls 250 m high cut from the soft volcanic tuff. This is the site of the Inalum hydroelectric plant—a Japanese-built complex of 3 dams completed in 1975 at a cost of US$2 billion. The largest such plant in Indonesia, it generates 500 Mw of power annually, enabling the plant at Kuala Tanjung on the coast to electrolyze 225,000 tons of aluminium. Access to the road and the falls beyond requires a special permit, obtainable from the Inalum office.

Beyond the plant at **Siguragura** the ravine narrows to a mere cleft in the rocks and the river plunges over a spectacular 200-m falls into another cleft further down known as

KAL MULLER

Sampuran Harimo ("Tiger Falls"), whence it plunges once again into the vale of Tangga, through yet another falls. Formerly, on the south face of the latter, ascent was by means of a series of ladders, hence the name *tangga*—meaning "ladder." From here the road zigzags down into the Asahan plantation belt by the coast, rejoining the north-south Medan road at Bandar Pulo.

The southern lakeshore

Bordering the lake south and west of Porsea

are more fertile *sawah* dotted with villages. **Laguboti**, on the Aek Simare between Porsea and Balige, is known for its woodcarving and statues. At Sigumpar just west of here is the grave of I. L. Nommensen, the German missionary who almost single-handedly converted the entire Toba Batak population to Christianity at the end of the 19th century.

South of Laguboti, a rough trail leads to **Huta Ginjang** and the extensive remains of long-abandoned fortified villages at an altitude of 1,650 m, with earthen walls and tunnel approaches, which to this day are very poorly documented. When the weather is clear, the view from these heights is incomparable, but at this altitude it is often cold and misty.

Balige is an important market town at the southern end of the lake, 65 km from Prapat. The town has a large *pasar* built in the traditional Tapanuli style, and is known for its textile production. There is a monument here to the last Batak priest-king, Sisingamangaraja XII (see below), and to General D. I. Panjaitan, who was murdered in Jakarta in the communist coup of 1965. Two museums are also found here—the Balige Museum and the Sisingamangaraja XII Museum. The latter houses a collection of artifacts relating to this national hero, who is buried at Soposurung.

Various Batak festivals in which local youths engage in traditional sports are now held in Balige. These include the Pesta Horas and Pesta Pantai Lumban Silintong, which in-

cludes a fishing competition. Five km west of Balige a turnoff to the left leads up to the hilltop guesthouse at Adian Nalambok near **Gurgur** offering panoramic views of the road south to Tarutung. At Jonggi ni Huta, just off the main road to the south, is a burial mound and equestrian statue of the Raja Pangalitan of the Nababan clan.

From the town of Siborongborong, about 20 km past Balige, a small road leads north to the southwestern shore of the lake at **Muara**, a small settlement of Malay-type houses dominated by the twin eminences of Dolok Sikke (1,092 m) and Dolok Sitoruna (1,153 m). The town, whose name literally means "estuary," overlooks a bay of the same name and a large island called Pulau Sibandang. Just before entering Muara, at Sosorugan, is an interesting modern tomb in the shape of a traditional house. Just to the south, in the square at Huta na Godang, is the famous equestrian statue, now painted, of the Siregar clan founder, with his wife seated nearby. A number of small fetish shrines are to be seen at other villages in the vicinity, such as Balaian ni Guru and Lumban Tikkatikka.

Past Muara, on an isolated bay encircled by steep hills at the southwestern corner of the lake, is **Bakkara**—the former seat of the mystical Batak priest-kings, the Sisingamangaraja. Around the village are stone walls and other relics of their martial past. The last ruler, Sisingamangaraja XII, was killed in a skirmish with Dutch forces in 1907 following 30 years of guerilla warfare in which he established a god-like reputation among the populace. The Dutch entered the area in 1878, and in the ensuing struggle burned scores of villages, causing the inhabitants to flee.

— *E. Edwards McKinnon*

Opposite: *Steep escarpments line Samosir's eastern edge.* **Above, left:** *Touring the lake by boat.* **Above, right:** *Modern concrete Toba Batak tombs combine traditional and Christian themes.*

TAPANULI

The Rugged Southern Bataklands

North, Central and South Tapanuli districts occupy roughly the southern third of the province, bordering Lake Toba to the north and Riau and West Sumatra to the south. North Tapanuli is inhabited by Toba Bataks, while the areas to the south are home to the Angkola and Mandailing Batak, many of whom converted to Islam under intense pressure from Minang Paderi warriors in the 19th century. For the most part this is a rugged but picturesque country, with longitudinal valleys running north-south in the Bukit Barisan and a broadening coastal plain to the southeast.

Three main roads pass through the area. East of the mountains, the Trans-Sumatra Highway traverses the plantation belt south of Tebing Tinggi to Rantau Prapat and Kota Pinang. It then cuts inland across the arid and undulating Padang Lawas plain past Gunung Tua to Padang Sidempuan—the main market town and administrative center of South Tapanuli, known for its *salak* palm fruits, grown on the slopes of Mt. Lubukraya (1,886 m).

Two roads also lead to Padang Sidempuan from the Toba Highlands via Tarutung. One follows the Batang Toru Valley past Pearaja and Sipirok, joining the east coast route at Pagarutan. Another, more attractive route, drops down to the west coast at Sibolga.

The east coast route

Fifty km east of Tebing Tinggi, an interesting detour from the main highway leads north to the coast at **Tanjung Tiram** ("Oyster Cape"). This village, with its fish market and sandy beach, lies on the river mouth beyond Labuhan Ruku and is the site of an early 19th-century Malay port known as Bogak. For the adventurous, it is possible to hire a boat from here to visit **Pulau Berhala**, a small island 3 hours offshore reputed for its fishing.

Just south of Labuan Ruku at **Limau Laras** is a small, recently-restored palace—seat of the former Malay ruler. In the early 19th century this was an important center for gold-and-silver *songket* weaving, a tradition that continues in one or two isolated villages.

Much further to the south, at Kota Pinang, the highway meets the Barumun River and heads inland across the vast **Padang Lawas** ("Great Plain") region. At the upper reaches of the Barumun lie the mysterious Tantric remains of the ancient Panai Kingdom—made famous by F.M. Schnitger's romantic explorations in the 1930s. This region was an important ancient crossroads, providing access to valuable forest resins in the Bukit Barisan as well as to alluvial gold deposits in the south. Panai, "with water in its bathing ghats," is mentioned in the South Indian Tanjore inscription as having been conquered during the Tamil Chola raid of AD 1018.

Most of the visible remains are concentrated around **Gunung Tua** in a dry rain-shadow area that has a distinctive savannah-like flora. The most impressive remains are three brick *candi* or *biaro* (from the Buddhist term *vihara* meaning monastery) located at Bahal near Portibi, east of Gunung Tua high above the banks of the Barumun River. These *candi* with their eastern Indian and Tantric Buddhist associations are thought to date from between the 10th and 13th centuries. Unfortunately, their sculptors used a soft volcanic tuff, and their work has weathered badly over the centuries. Bahal I, with its sculptured brick panels, has been badly restored in recent years. Other sites are little more than heaps of bricks, though the settings of these remains —associated with orgiastic rites and human sacrifices—are dramatic, especially at sunset.

The Toba Highlands route

South of Siborongborong, **Tarutung** is the administrative center of North Tapanuli district. In the village of Pagaran just to the south lies the unusual sarcophagus of Datu Ompu Panonson Lumban Tobing. According to Barbier, this cist has been moved at least 3 times as it was thought to bring its owners bad luck.

The inland route from Tarutung south to Padang Sidempuan leads past **Sipirok**—a village in the shadow of active Mt. Sibualbuali (1,820 m) known for its weaving and ceramic production. At nearby Padang Matinggi are Dutch redoubts built as a defence against the Paderis in the 1830s. A side road from Sipirok runs northeast to Sipogu past an exposed carbonized forest buried by an eruption of Mt. Sibualbuali. Also in the vicinity, at Tor Sibohi, is a forest reserve with sulphur hot

Right: *Sunset over Sibolga, on the west coast.*

springs reputed for their medicinal properties. A new hotel has been established here.

The west coast

The west coast of North Sumatra, with its narrow plain, steep hills and deepwater bays, is one of the most scenic parts of Sumatra. The 66-km road down to Sibolga from Tarutung follows the sinuous Silindung Valley through deep ravines and dense forests across steep fern-covered slopes—rounding 1,200 hairpin bends that afford magnificent views of Tapanuli Bay as you approach the coast.

The town of **Sibolga** is the administrative center for Central Tapanuli and a major port for steamers and ferries bound for Nias. This is the western gateway to the Batak highlands, overlooking striking Tapanuli Bay, which derives its name from *tapian nauli* meaning "beautiful beach." The town is noted for its seafood, and the bay is dotted with islands—the largest of which is Pulau Mursala, known for its clear waters and bountiful marine life. The British maintained a trading post on Pulau Puncung Kecil, closer to shore, from 1756 to 1824. It was from here that the first Europeans entered the Bataklands in the 1820s.

Good beaches with shady coconut palms await you 11 km south of Sibolga at **Pantai Pandan**, a traditional fishing village where fish are barbecued fresh from the sea. Stalls also sell seashells, coral and gemstones.

Barus, 65 km north of Sibolga, is the site of an ancient port known to the Arabs as Fansur or Pancur since at least the 6th century. Barus had an international reputation as a source of high quality camphor (*kapur barus*) and benzoin brought down from the Dairi region. Numerous Islamic graves dating from about the 14th century also indicate that it was a center of Islamic learning. Earlier there may even have been a Nestorian Christian church here. The Dutch established a trading post in 1668 and there is a well-preserved 19th-century colonial fort, now occupied by the local police.

A Tamil stele dating to AD 1088 was found at the mouth of the Batang Garigis River at **Lobu Tuo** ("Old Village"), north of Barus. The inscription, written in the Tamil Grantha script (often referred to as "Pallawa" in Indonesia), commemorates the activities of a certain Tamil merchant guild known as "the 1500 (swamis of Ayyavole)." It now lies in the National Museum in Jakarta. Remains of a second Tamil inscription, as yet undeciphered, have also been recovered here.

A road climbs up steeply up from Barus to the Dairi (Pakpak) highlands via Pakkat and Dolok Sanggul. Just off this road at **Sijungkang**, overlooking the Sigomot River, is an abandoned village with Islamic Batak gravemarkers painted black, white and red and an unusual carved image of a woman mounted on an elephant.

— *E. Edwards McKinnon*

NIAS ISLAND

Archaic Island of Megaliths

Nias is a small island, 130 km long and 45 km wide (slightly smaller than Bali), lying just 125 km off Sumatra's west coast—close enough that the latter's volcanic peaks can be seen on a clear day. Like the other western islands off Sumatra, however, Nias stands quite apart—the island's rugged terrain, malarial climate and warlike population having served to isolate it from the mainstream of Sumatran culture for many centuries. By contrast, Sumatra was always a fertile land of riches, and early traders and travelers seemed to have preferred it to the hostile environment on Nias.

As a result, Nias never experienced the dramatic influx of Indian, Islamic and European cultural influences to the degree these were felt in other areas. The island's inhabitants have instead followed their own line of development, building on an earlier Austronesian sub-strata of culture which they hold in common with other Indonesian peoples. Today they are best known for their spectacular tribal art and architecture—a unique style that has fascinated generations of scholars and collectors.

Ancient 'megalithic' traditions

Little is known about the island's prehistory, which is a pity since—as any visitor can see—the inhabitants have been working in durable stone and bronze for a very long time. Gold and imported ceramic artifacts form a part of nearly all aristocratic households, and Nias nobles moreover keep meticulous genealogies, some going back 50 generations, noting not only the names of the ancestors but the locations of their villages.

Despite the absence of hard archaeological data, the island's prehistory has nonetheless been the subject of much speculation—much of it intended to portray Nias as a kind of museum for prehistoric Indonesian civilizations. The most prominent theory, put forth by Robert Heine-Geldern in the 1930s, was that the island was populated during the first millenium BC by hill tribes from Assam or Burma, who brought with them a "megalithic" culture characterized by large stone monuments erected during communal feasts to enhance the status of the aristocracy.

This story has been repeated in nearly every account of the island published since the 1930s, yet there is good reason to ques-

COEN PEPPLINKHUIZEN

tion its validity. Recent archaeological evidence from the rest of Indonesia has yet to demonstrate such early dates for "megalithic" cultures elsewhere, and local genealogies seem to indicate that Nias culture acquired many of its distinctive traits no earlier than about AD 750, or around the time that Indian influence was arriving in the archipelago. A more probable line of development is that aristocratic Nias culture developed locally out of a simpler society perhaps akin to that of the Mentawai Islands to the south.

In any event, indigenous oral histories agree on one point—that Nias culture originated in the Gomo River area in the central part of the island. Here the gods descended and begat the human race, and the Nias people today refer to themselves as *ono niha* or "children of the people"—an explicit reference to these founding ancestors. From Central Nias the culture spread north and south, developing local variations but always maintaining explicit symbolic reference to the ritual and artistic homeland in the Gomo area.

Slaves and gold

The association of western Sumatra with the gold trade probably spurred on early explorations of Nias. In the 15th century, Chinese navigators gave the name "Gold Island" to one of the Batu Islands south of Nias. A century later, perhaps dissatisfied with the meager quantities of gold they found in Sumatra, the Portuguese explored Nias, and their presence is still very much alive in local oral histories. Arab traders also arrived at a very early date, but records of their contacts are sketchy. Two identical accounts describe a large patrilineal village in which head-hunting formed part of the marriage ritual; the earliest is dated 851.

In later times, Nias became known as a popular and plentiful source of slaves. From Acehnese sources we learn that there was a European post here in 1626, probably Portuguese, which the Acehnese attacked in order to monopolize the slave trade. The Dutch arrived in 1665, also to buy slaves, and in 1693 signed contracts with the island's district chiefs. In the 1820s, Raffles became intensely interested in the island as a place to buy rice and pigs that were reportedly free of tuberculosis. Between 1819 and 1825, English missions were sent to negotiate an end to the slave trade, and from these contacts we have the first detailed accounts of the island.

The Dutch assumed control of Nias in 1825, at first continuing the slave trade but later outlawing it and enforcing their will through force. Using the slave trade as a pretext, they deposed the independent chiefs of South Nias. In the 1840s they constructed a fort in Lagundri Bay (now a favorite surfing spot with young foreigners), which was later destroyed by an earthquake and tidal wave. In the 1860s, the Dutch launched military invasions that resulted in much suffering and the ravaged several villages. They are still despised for this in parts of South Nias.

Early attempts were made in the 1830s to Christianize the island, with little success. But the arrival in 1865 of German Rhenish missionaries from Barmen marked the beginning of a major change in Nias society. Within a few years the entire northern part of the island had been converted. Central and South Nias later succumbed not to the Bible but to a combination of epidemics and brutal policing. Beginning in 1909, religious art was destroyed or confiscated in large quantities in South Nias.

The island's population today numbers about 500,000 and despite a century of contact and conflict with the outside world, Nias culture remains remarkably intact. The language is a distinctive member of the huge Austronesian language family, and closely related dialects are spoken on the nearby Batu Islands and Simeulue, yet it is surpris-

Overleaf: *A war dance.* **Opposite:** *A North Nias wedding.* **Right:** *A village chief in traditional garb.*

ingly different from all other Indonesian languages, more closely resembling a Polynesian tongue in many ways.

Nias society is strictly hieratic. The nobility (*si'ulu* or *salawa*: "that which is high") do not intermarry with commoners (the *sato* or *sihönö*, literally "the thousands") and have certain special privileges. Slaves (*sawuyu* or *harakana*) were formerly important as servants and as trade items. They were not considered to be human and therefore had to live outside the village areas.

Throughout Nias, two types of traditional dwellings directly expressed the rank and wealth of the inhabitants by the size and complexity of their construction. The traditional *omo hada* could be inhabited by any village citizen, while aristocrats who can afford enormous feasts and sacrifices built special houses called *omo sebua*, or "big houses." Such houses are no longer constructed, due partly to the diminished wealth and influence of the chiefs, but also to the fact that they require the capture and display of human heads for their consecration. While such heads are no longer displayed, they are still under the main pillars of some *omo sebua*.

The island's three culture areas—North, Central and South Nias—now display great differences in language, art and custom. But from a Nias point of view the distinctions are much greater than this, as each region is subdivided into numerous village groups according to their lineages. To the *ono niha*, culture is thus defined on a village level and each village has its own variations in art and custom.

Visiting Nias

The main point of entry to Nias is **Gunungsitoli**, the former Dutch administrative center and base for early German missionaries. It remains the district capital, and aside from a few local architectural embellishments in the town square, looks much like any other Indonesian port town. One notices almost

immediately, however, that nearly all living things seem to be smaller here. The *ono niha* are diminutive people with features quite distinct from their neighbors in Sumatra. Local cats and dogs are small, and one may even be astonished to find chicken eggs the size one would expect of quail eggs.

To see something of the culture one must venture out of the town. In nearby **Hiliana'a** is a fine, rare example of a traditional chief's house, distinguished—like other North Nias houses—by its oval floorplan. In the western

part of North Nias, the village of **Hiligowe** has large village protector figures in stone (*gowe*) that are remarkably intact, though the genitalia have been removed. The nearby village of **Onolimbu** has similar statues in a more blocky style.

Central Nias is extremely inaccessible, yet has some of the island's greatest art treasures. The houses here are rectangular and ornamented with bold geometric sculptures. Villages along the Gomo and Tae rivers are particularly important; **Orahili Idanö Gomo**, **Lahusa Idanö Tae** and **Tundrumbaho** are known for their striking plazas with vertical (*behu*) and horizontal (*harefa*) megaliths. Also found here are round, mushroom-shaped stones called *ni'ogazi* used by women to dance upon—their slapping feet producing musical tones as they imitate the motions of various animals. The so-called *osa'osa* are stone seats of honor with one or three carved monster heads, formerly used by the nobility during large ritual feasts. The village of **Holi** has a unique old *omo sebua* with pyramidal skull tombs in the square in front of it memorializing the great chiefs of old.

The island's most spectacular area, however, is the South—reached by boat from Sibolga or Gunungsitoli. The most important

Above, left: *Spirit mask used in ritual war dance.*
Above, right: *The famous "stone jumping" ritual.*
Right: *The lovely palm-fringed beach at Lagundri.*

village here is **Bawömataluo**, with a massive flight of stairs at the main entrance. It was built in 1888 following the Dutch attacks of 1863; below it stands the newer village of Orahili on the site of the former village destroyed by the Dutch and their allies.

The largest and oldest *omo sebua* in Nias is in this village, still inhabited and owned by the royal family, but run now as a museum (make a small donation at the back). Although the inhabitants claim it is 400 years old, the house actually dates from the founding of the village 100 years ago. Some of the pillars are more than a meter thick and the house is 20 m high. It has exquisite wall carvings that commemorate great ritual feasts held for the smithing of golden head ornaments.

Brackets at the front of the house originally held old Dutch and Chinese plates used by the rulers during feasts. Two small chairs carved in relief inside once held images of the village founders (*adu zatua* or *adu nuwu*). Opposite them is a whimsical relief carving of a steam-powered warship with uniformed Dutch officers aboard. This probably represents a steamer used in the 1863 invasion, but has now become a symbol of man's harnessing of nature, as indicated by the scene of a crocodile being captured below it.

A similar symbolism is displayed by massive megaliths in front of the house. The larger, horizontal stone represents a ship and commemorates the founder of the village, a certain Laowo. On its bow, humans and monkeys capture a shark. A horizontal stone opposite it commemorates the last ruler to hold official titles, a local hero named Saonigeho. The towering vertical stones commemorate feasts to raise the status of the living, while horizontal stones are ships to transport the spirits of the dead.

Bawömataluo literally means "sun-mountain" and in front of the *omo sebua* is a circular flagstone known as the *fusö newali* or "village navel;" close examination reveals a worn circular pattern on it representing the sun.

Smaller but still impressive *omo sebua* can be found in the villages of Onohondro, Hilinawalö and Hilinawalö Mazingö. The first two are not far from Bawömataluo but the third is quite some distance; none should be attempted unless you are in good physical shape.

Onohondro and **Hilinawalö** both played an important role in an ancient renewal ceremony in which a figure of a giant tiger representing the ruler was carried on a high platform and then thrown into the Gomo River. This river, named after the one in Central Nias, is near Onohondro and links the inhabitants to their roots in Central Nias. Afterward, the ruler carried on as usual until the next such ceremony was held, 7 to 14 years later. The ceremony was outlawed by missionaries in 1913, but has recently been revived to celebrate Indonesia's independence day.

— Jerome Feldman

PART IV

Introducing Aceh

Aceh province occupies the northernmost end of Sumatra, its long coastline guarding the entrance to Asia's most important sea lane—the Strait of Malacca. Almost all maritime traffic between East and West passes through these straits, and Aceh was for many centuries the first landfall for Arab and Indian mariners who came to Indonesia in search of spices.

By the end of the 13th century, trading posts and petty kingdoms along Aceh's east coast had developed into Indonesia's first Islamic states. Marco Polo visited Aceh in 1292 on his way back to Venice from China, and wrote of Muslim kingdoms called Ferlac and Samudra. (The name Sumatra probably derives from the latter.) He also claimed to have seen a unicorn, which was probably a Sumatran rhinoceros.

For the next 600 years, foreign merchants and Indonesian traders mingled in Aceh's ports. During a "Golden Age" at the beginning of the 17th century, in the reign of powerful Sultan Iskandar Muda, Aceh became one of Asia's greatest trading emporiums, and in its main port of Kuta Raja (now Banda Aceh) a dozen languages could be heard.

Since the 17th century, Aceh has enjoyed a reputation as the most staunchly Islamic area in Southeast Asia. It has also been proudly independent, resisting domination by a succession of Asian and European powers. Aceh was finally brought under Dutch rule only after a long and bitter struggle against Dutch colonial forces from 1873 to 1903. But the independent spirit of the Acehnese was never completely broken. In 1953, just 3 years after Indonesia's independence was secured, a 10-year rebellion against central government control broke out. As a result, Aceh was declared a *daerah istimewa* or "special region," and granted a degree of autonomy in matters of religion, customary law and education. Only the sultanate of Yogyakarta in central Java has a similar status.

Today, Aceh's economy is booming, despite a population of just 3 million. Following the discovery of huge natural gas fields on the east coast around Lhokseumawe and Lhoksukon, economic growth has been rapid. Most of the gas is exported to Japan in the form of LNG; Aceh also has sizeable reserves of oil, gold, silver, copper and coal. Since 1980, Aceh has contributed between $2 and $3 billion annually to Indonesia's foreign exchange earnings. The province's per capita gross domestic product is one of the highest in the nation.

Despite periodic unrest and the constraints this has placed on the building of roads, schools and hospitals, Aceh's rural economy remains buoyant. For several centuries, Aceh's narrow but fertile coastal strip has produced an annual surplus of rice and cash crops, notably pepper. (In the 17th century, and again in the early 19th, Aceh produced over half of the world's pepper.) Modern fertilizers have boosted rice yields, and the coastal population is well-off by Indonesian standards.

Over half of the province's population live in its coastal region, though there are no large towns. Even the capital, Banda Aceh, has only 80,000 inhabitants. The next largest town is Sabang, on Weh Island, with 25,000 inhabitants. Smaller towns and villages dot the 600 km coastline between Banda Aceh and Medan, connected by an excellent trunk road.

The rugged and isolated interior of Aceh provides a sharp contrast to the fertile coastal plain. Huge mountains rise along both sides of a central valley. This thickly-forested and sparsely-populated region is the home of the Gayo people—an ethnic group who practice syncretic Islam mixed with traces of animism.

Aceh is perfect for travelers who want to avoid the beaten track. A basic knowledge of Indonesian is a must, and a healthy respect for Acehnese religious sensibilities is advised.

— *Kal Muller and Eric Oey*

Overleaf: *The Great Mosque of Banda Aceh.*
Opposite: *An Acehnese couple in traditional costume. Photos by Kal Muller.*

COASTAL TOWNS

Old Islamic Harbors of the North

The northeastern coast of Aceh was the site of Indonesia's earliest Islamic kingdoms. A number of short, fast-flowing rivers descend from the Bukit Barisan mountains to meet the shore here, and for centuries these estuaries provided sheltered anchorages, water and provisions for ships before and after the long voyage across the Indian Ocean. Ports like Samudra-Pasai (Lhokseumawe), Tamiang (Langsa), Peureulak, Samalanga and Pidië (Sigli) developed to service this trade. All of them converted to Islam during the 13th and 14th centuries, then came under the sway of the powerful sultanate based at Banda Aceh (Kotaraja) in the 16th century.

These ancient ports are now somnolent coastal towns connected by a fast asphalt highway running 600 km from Medan up to Banda Aceh. The economy of the region was formerly based on rice, pepper and plantation (rubber and oil palm) agriculture, but is now developing rapidly as the result of an oil and natural gas boom. Oil was discovered here in the 1890s and first developed by the Bataviaasch Petroleum Maatschappij, later to become Royal Dutch Shell. In 1971, some of the richest concentrations of natural gas in the whole of Indonesia were discovered here.

Medan to Banda Aceh

The road from Medan to Banda Aceh follows the old narrow gauge Aceh tram railway, built to help pacify the region during the Aceh War in the latter part of the 19th century. The Aceh tram itself has long fallen into disuse, but the track can still be seen along the route northward, crisscrossing the main road from Pangkalan Brandan to Langsa. Old rubber and oil palm plantations line either side of the highway, interrupted by low-roofed traditional houses on high posts.

At **Kuala Simpang**, about 140 km and 3 hours from Medan, the road crosses the Tamiang River. From here onwards, distinctive Chinese Red and Indian Brahman cattle are a common sight along the roadside. Reaching **Peureulak**, the site of a 13th century Islamic state (the Ferlac of Marco Polo), the road crosses the Peureulak River and some distance later passes Kuala Berkah Beach before crossing into North Aceh regency at Pantonlabu, on the Jambuaye River.

Past Lhoksukon a road branches inland to

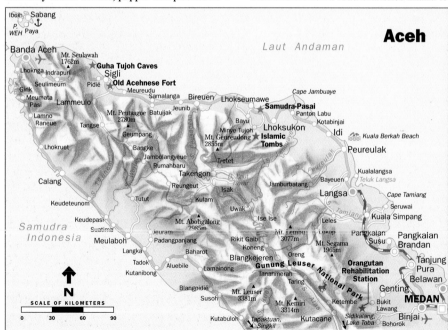

the village of **Minye Tujoh**, Matangkuli, where an unusual early Islamic gravestone or *nisan* is carved in the Majapahit style of 14th century Java and is inscribed in two languages —Arabic and Old Javanese. Such tombstones are a notable feature of the Acehnese landscape and mark the sites of former villages. Indeed, "Aceh stones" (*batu Aceh*), as they are called, were a major export from the 15th to the late 19th centuries, and have been found as far afield as the Malay Peninsula, Brunei, Kalimantan (Banjarmasin) and Java (Banten).

At nearby **Blangme** (*blang* means "cultivated rice field"), some 18 km southeast of Lhokseumawe, are extensive Islamic grave complexes marking the site of the twin cities of Pasai and Samudra, the latter being the port which gave its name to the whole island of Sumatra. In the early 15th century, Samudra-Pasai was a strong rival of Malacca. Formerly sited on both banks of the Krueng Pasai River, it was reputedly the first polity in Sumatra to convert to Islam and was a major entrepôt frequented by all peoples of the east. En route from China to Europe, Marco Polo spent 5 months here waiting for the monsoon to change prior to taking a ship to India in 1292. Both Samudra and Pidië, to the north, were engaged in the lucrative pepper trade.

One of the graves at Blangme is that of Malikul Saleh, first sultan of Pasai, who died in 1297. Here also are tombs of other Pasai royalty made of reworked marble taken from the Hindu temples of Gujerat and decorated with Arabic calligraphy. Best known of these is the grave of Sultanah Bahiyah, who died in 1428. Access to the grave complexes at Blangme is by a track which leaves the main road just east of the bridge at Geudong and leads northeast toward the coast.

The site of the former palace of the sultans is said to be on a high sandy hill named Cot Istana, meaning "palace hill," adjacent to the site of the Royal Mosque at Kota Krueng. This is also near Blangme, reached via a track through the rice fields to the village of Kota Krueng. The story of the founding of Pasai and how Cot Istana was chosen as the palace site was recorded in the *Hikayat Raja-Raja Pasai* or "Chronicle of the Pasai Kings."

Lhokseumawe is the site of several large development projects centering round the oil and gas fields. P.T. Arun is an enormous LNG plant, with a capacity of some 18.8 million metric tons per annum, most of which is exported to Japan. Other large-scale projects in the area are the Asean Aceh Fertilizer plant (capitalized at over US$141 million), a kraft paper factory at Krueng Geukeuh and an LNG plant at Blang Lancang. The town of Lhokseumawe itself is the administrative center for the regency of Aceh Utara (North Aceh), which is also an important rice-grow-

Below: *The tiny, somnolent harbor at Sigli.*

ing area. This, like the other smaller east coast towns has benefitted to some degree from the development of the LNG industry and has a well developed business center and ample accommodations.

The next major town after Lhokseumawe is **Bireuen**, where locally-grown coffee, cinnamon, cloves and tobacco are marketed. A side road forks to the left here and climbs up through thickly-forested hills and coffee plantations into the northern Gayo Highlands—centering around the town of Takengon and scenic Lake Tawar (see "Gayo Highlands").

At **Samalanga**, 35 km past Bireuen, is an elaborately carved *rumah adat* or traditional Acehnese house which belonged to the late Major-General Teuku Hamzah. Ten km on, at **Babah Awe** near Meureudu, are the remains of Kuta Bateë, an Acehnese fortification.

At **Sigli** (Pidië), between the estuaries of the Krueng Baro and the Krueng Tuka, can be seen the remains of another old Acehnese fort—Benteng Kuta Asan—visible to the left of the road. In the 16th century, gold was brought over the hills from Meulaboh on the west coast to the east coast at Pidië, where it was traded to foreign merchants.

Just to the north of here, in the limestone hills above Pidië Point, reached via a side-road from Sigli, is the **Guha Tujoh** or "seven caves" complex, accessible from Menasah Cot via Kayeëkuniet. At **Klibeuet**, 6 kilometers from Sigli, is the grave complex known as

Teungku di Kandang, the tomb of Sultan Ma'arif Syah—the last sultan of Pidië, who died in 1511. A scenic road to the south of Sigli leads up into the highlands to the traditional village of **Tangse**, 52 km away.

Past Sigli, the main highway swings away from the coast and rises up over a pass to the south of Mt. Seulawah (1,806 m), with its twin peaks of Agam (male) and and Inong (female), to meet the Krueng Aceh River at Seulimeum. The road continues down the river 18 km to **Indrapuri**, site of one of the three main mosques of the former kingdom of Aceh Besar (Greater Aceh). The mosque at Indrapuri is said to have been established on the foundations of an earlier Hindu-Buddhist temple. It is set amidst coconut palms on a small hill overlooking the right bank of the river, and can be reached by road via a bridge which crosses the Krueng Aceh just below it. After Indrapuri, the road follows the valley of the Krueng Aceh, past well-irrigated rice fields into Banda Aceh.

Sights of Banda Aceh

This former capital of the fiercely independent sultanate of Aceh is steeped in history. After its conquest by the Dutch it was known as Kutaraja or "king's town" but was renamed Banda Aceh after independence.

The site of the former *dalem* or palace of the Acehnese sultan is marked by the former Dutch Residency, built in 1880 after the

MICHEL GELENINE

palace had been raised by invading Dutch forces. It is now the **Governor's House** (Pendopo Gubernur). The graves of the former sultans, including the great Iskandar Muda, are just to the northeast on the opposite bank of the river, with their gigantic *nisan* or gravestones and other interesting remains.

The **Museum Negeri Aceh** (Aceh State Museum) nearby holds an interesting collection of historical and ethnographic materials. A large bronze bell, the Cakradonia, hangs in front of the museum. It was reputedly presented to the Sultan of Pasai by the Chinese imperial eunuch Zheng He in 1414. It is said to have been seized by Sultan Ali Mughayat Syah (1514–1530), founder of the state of Aceh, when he conquered Pasai in 1524. Another story, however, indicates that it was cast in 1469. In the same complex is a traditional Acehnese house.

Upstream from the palace area, a short distance to the southwest, is the enigmatic stone and plaster *gunongan*—possibly a symbol of authority deriving from the pre-Islamic *meru* or sacred mountain, once part of the **Taman Sari** royal pleasure garden within the palace grounds. It was connected to the palace by a lovely gateway, the *pintu khob* or *pintu aceh* which was used as a symbol of the kingdom and was used to decorate jewelry and coins. This entire complex was reputedly built by Sultan Iskandar Muda (r. 1607-1636) during Aceh's "Golden Age." Nearby is Kandang XII, the

burial place of Sultan Iskandar Thani (r. 1636-1641), where remains of a gold ornamented coffin were excavated some years ago.

The neatly-kept **Kerkhof** or Dutch churchyard to the west of Taman Sari contains some 2,000 graves of Dutch KNIL army soldiers who died during the 19th century wars with Aceh. Many were actually Javanese, Menadonese and Ambonese enlisted men, and more actually died from disease than on the battlefield.

The grand **Baiturrahman Mosque** at the center of Banda Aceh was designed, surprisingly, by an Italian architect and built by the Dutch between 1879-81 to replace the mosque destroyed by their troops during the Aceh wars. The design is Moghul Indian, not traditional Acehnese (as a visit to the older mosque in nearby Indrapuri clearly shows). The market to the north side of the mosque has numerous shops selling Acehnese gold and silver filigree jewelry, among which the *pintu aceh* ("Aceh door") broach design is rightly famous. Other handicrafts, such as the *rencong* or slightly curved traditional dagger worn by both Acehnese men and women, and woven pandan mats and bags, are found.

Sidetrips from Banda Aceh

The beach at **Ujung Bateë**, 17 km northeast of Banda Aceh, and the new harbor with the

Opposite: *An ojek or pedicab in Banda Aceh.*
Above: *The enigmatic gunongan in Taman Sari.*

nearby hot spring at **Krueng Raya**, about 15 km further along the same road, are regular points for weekend outings. The road from Banda Aceh past Peukankrueng and Lamnga follows the coast through coconut plantations littered with ancient gravemarkers and, to the left of the road, past lagoons and fish ponds along the shoreline.

Two old forts on the shore at **Payakameng**, Ladong, known locally as the Benteng Indra Patra and Benteng Iskandar, provide an interesting insight into 17th century Acehnese military architecture. A third fort overlooking the bay at Krueng Raya also dates from the same period.

Extensive modern drainage works are being carried out to curtail the flooding of Krueng Aceh or Aceh River which has threatened Banda Aceh in recent years. The river enters the sea to the north of the town, just east of the village of **Kutalaseumana**, where the famous Islamic scholar Abdulrauf al-Singkel who first translated the Koran into Acehnese is buried. The 5-km road up to Kutalaseumana winds its way through small villages, past fish ponds and mangroves to the beach where there is an interesting raised lookout point.

Kuala Ciangkoi the old Dutch colonial harbor 12 km west of Banda Aceh can be reached by public transport in a quarter of an hour, passing by the beach at the village of **Uleëlheue** along the way. Pulau Weh, the first landmark for sailors crossing the Indian ocean and the erstwhile free port of Sabang, once an important coaling station on the sea route from the Straits of Malacca to Sri Lanka and India, can be seen offshore.

A road leading west through the mangroves from just south of the bridge at Uleëlheue brings one to **Lambaro**, site of the old mosque of Indrapatwa and the ancient harbor once known to Arab and Chinese geographers as Lamri, Lamuri or Ramni. The site has now largely sunk beneath the waters of the Teluk Lambaro bay but local legend has it that the foundations of the old mosque can still be seen at certain times beneath the waves a short distance to the west of the Kuala Pancu. Indeed, the structure was visible on aerial photographs taken during the 1970s. Numerous Islamic gravemarkers, remnants of an earlier settlement, are exposed at low tide when it is possible to reach the beach across the mudflats. Strong currents and murky waters make swimming and diving dangerous. Offshore is the island known as Pulau Tuan or Pulau Angkasa, the site of an Islamic shrine. Portuguese ships may have anchored in the bay between the island and the mainland in the early 16th century, in waters now too shallow for anything other than small fishing boats.

About 8 km southwest of Banda Aceh is the **Museum Rumoh Cut Nyak Dhien**—a replica of the traditional house belonging to a famous Acehnese heroine who fought against the Dutch. As with most Acehnese houses, this one is raised on pillars some 2 meters off the ground and consists of 3 parts: an ornately carved front gallery where guests were received, a central sleeping room, and a rear area reserved exclusively for women. (Well-to-do families often had a separate kitchen built as an extension to the rear of the house, so that smoke from the cooking fire did not enter the living quarters.) As elsewhere in the Malay world, Acehnese domestic construction was generally in timber with the result that very few buildings from earlier periods have survived.

On the main road southwest from Banda Aceh, the casuarina beaches at **Lhoknga** and **Lampueuk** can be reached in about 20 minutes. They provide beautiful unspoiled sands and reefs and are popular weekend picnic spots, with ideal conditions for swimming and walking. This is also the site of a World War II Japanese airfield with bunkers and concrete pillboxes still extant.

— *E. Edwards McKinnon*

AMANDA RICHARDSON

WEH ISLAND

Sabang's Easy Life Evokes the Past

At dusk, as the sun dips behind the western arm of Weh Island just to the north of Banda Aceh, the dominant sounds are the lapping of seawater against the rusting cast-iron legs of a pier, and the chatter of fishermen and strollers. Despite a magnificent deep-water harbor and a strategic location at the entrance to the Strait of Malacca—one of the busiest sea lanes in the world—Sabang, the main town on the island, has sunk into somnolent obscurity.

It wasn't always this way. Thin Phin Sun, portly and genial propietor of a restaurant not far from the waterfront, arrived from China in 1923 with his parents. They had emigrated to join a relative who established a successful business supplying tropical hardwood from the island's forests. "There was much more business then than now," he recalled as customers waited for an order of sweet-and-sour fish, steamed prawns, noodles and mixed vegetables. Pinned to the wall near the table where he does his nightly accounts is a fading black and white panorama of the harbor in 1914. It shows more than a dozen ocean-going passenger liners and freighters anchored offshore or tied to the pier.

As steamers replaced sailing ships in the late 19th century, the Dutch decided to develop Sabang, then a tiny fishing village. They brought coal from mines in Sumatra and stored it in row after row of tin-roofed warehouses that still line the waterfront. A dry-dock for repairing ships and an oil storage depot were built. Fresh water was piped from a lake in the mountains to supply the ships and the Dutch offices, bungalows, clubs and other facilities in the new town. At one point in the early decades of the 20th century, Sabang was a more important port than Singapore. But the transition from steam to diesel power at sea ensured that this ascendency was shortlived.

Japanese military forces quickly entrenched themselves on Weh after overrunning Singapore in 1942. They were only dislodged when Japan surrendered three and a half years later. Visitors to some of the island's beaches swim and sunbathe in the shadow of derelict concrete bunkers and gun emplacements dug into the sides of cliffs and rocky headlands.

War and foreign occupation seem far removed from the tranquil and unhurried life of Weh today. Fishing, coconut and clove plantations provide a subsistence livelihood for many of the 20,000 people who live on the 150 sq km island. In the late March and early April, just after the harvest, the sides of the narrow roads are lined with pungent cloves drying in the sun.

"Life is easy here," said Ismet Harun, who sailed around the world as a merchant seaman for 10 years before coming home to Weh. He has his own small motorised fishing boat. "I can earn enough money working as a tourist guide or as a fisherman," he said.

Weh experienced a second promising burst of business activity after 1970, when the Indonesian government gave Sabang tax-exempt status as a free port. Shipping and trade flourished. Jobs were easy to get and relatively well paid. But in 1986, alarmed at the growth of smuggling to and from the island and anxious to develop Batam, near Singapore, as Indonesia's premier free trade zone, the central government withdrew Sabang's special status. Since then, the population on Weh has declined as people moved to other parts of Indonesia in search of work.

Fishing, a newly established rattan cooperative and tourism seem to offer the best hope of future employment on the island. The crystal clear waters and coral reefs teeming with colorful fish are a natural magnet for tourists. A trickle of tourists, mainly backpackers content to stay with villagers or in several guesthouses in Sabang arrives on the daily ferry from Sumatra. There is no hotel. The nearest thing to nightlife, apart from Mr. Thin's restaurant, are a couple of cinemas.

Sadly, illegal dynamite fishing is slowly destroying some of the best coral, including sections of the splendid undersea garden off Rubiah Island not far from Sabang. Villagers and officials blame unscrupulous fishermen from Sumatra. They say the destruction is difficult to stop because the dynamiters operate at night and use fast boats to carry the loads of stunned fish away.

— *Michael Richardson/Int'l Herald Tribune*

Opposite: *One of Weh's irresistible beaches.*

GAYO HIGHLANDS

Proud People and a Lovely Highland Lake

The Gayo Highlands occupy the mountainous central portion of Aceh—an isolated area cut off from the surrounding coastal plains by the rugged peaks of the Bukit Barisan range. This is the homeland of about 250,000 Gayo people who speak their own language and are known for their dynamism, for the vitality of their traditional arts, and for their high levels of education.

There are four main Gayo regions, each centering around a lake or river valley bordered by high forested ridges. The Lake Tawar region to the north is the most populous, especially the area around the town of Takengon. A good road links Takengon to the north coast at Bireuen, 100 km away. South of Takengon and separated from it by a mountain range is the Isak region, where a number of villages stretch out along the Jambuaye or Isak River.

The road south from Isak winds over a high mountain pass to the southern Gayo region and its main town of Blangkejeren. It is gradually being improved to allow year-round traffic, and from Blangkejeren it is possible to continue southward to Kabanjahe in the Karo Batak area. East of the Isak valley is the Serbejadi region (centered on the village of Lukup), known for its production of *gambir*, the leaf which is distilled into a hard plug and combined with betel, *sirih* and lime for chewing.

Conquest and resistance

In the 17th century these highlands formed part of the Acehnese kingdom ruled by Sultan Iskandar Muda, Aceh's greatest ruler. It was during this period of Acehnese dominance that most of the Gayo converted to Islam.

The Gayo were virtually unknown to Westerners before this century. In 1904, Dutch troops entered the highlands to force the submission of local rulers. The troops met strong resistance along the way and in the Blangkejeren area wiped out several villages that refused to capitulate. The massacres caused a public outcry in the Netherlands.

During the subsequent period of Dutch rule, government and private companies set up coffee, tea and dammar resin-processing enterprises in the Takengon area. The Gayo at this time quickly began growing cash crops, mainly vegetables and coffee, to supplement their staple rice crop.

By the early 1930s, the Gayo began to establish schools to teach secular and religious subjects. Gayo students sought further education outside the region and were quick to obtain advanced degrees in Java. Gayo poets produced religious poetry that taught the essentials of Islam; their poems were written in Gayo using the Arabic script, and one book was even published in Cairo in 1938.

The Gayo strongly supported the Indonesian nationalist cause and fought hard during the revolution, but many Gayo also participated in the Darul Islam rebellion against the central government in the 1950s. As elsewhere in Indonesia, the massacres of 1965 left a deep emotional scar in the highlands.

Gayo pride themselves on their strong kin ties, their attention to traditional social values and the vitality of their poetry and storytelling. They also value their capacity to adapt to the modern world. Unlike in many other

Left: *A Gayo man from the Takengon area.*
Right: *Traditional Gayo* kerawang *embroidery.*

remote areas in Indonesia, the Gayo place great emphasis on schooling, on mastery of the Indonesian language, and on promotion of Islamic values and scholarship.

Rivalries exist between villages and between the two former political domains of Bukit and Ciq near Takengon. These emerge in colorful contests of sung poetry (*didong*) between clubs from different villages. *Didong* contests are team events and last from about nine in the evening until dawn. On these occasions, feelings of resentment and hostility between villages can legitimately be given palpable expression in versified taunts and challenges exchanged by the two teams.

The Takengon area

The Takengon area boasts a cool, dry climate, dense forests and the scenic beauty of Lake Tawar. In 1900 the journey to Takengon from the north coast town of Bireuen had to be made on foot and took up to a week. Today, barring a mudslide or mechanical failure, the bus trip takes about three hours.

The road climbs and winds through pine forests and small stands of coffee. One passes the village of Lampahan, where for many years a plant processed dammar pine sap into resins and turpentine. Since 1989 a logging project has begun to change the face of the landscape, though the hills are still heavily forested. The road finally reaches a high cliff overlooking the smooth surface of Lake Tawar, and then descends into the valley.

Takengon sits at an altitude of 1,200 m on the edge of Lake Tawar, in a caldera formed by the implosion of an ancient volcano. The lake is the headwaters of the Peusangan River which flows northward to the Straits of Malacca. The town was constructed during colonial times, and consists of a central commercial area with rows of shops and a two-story market building, a cluster of government buildings, several schools, a silver-domed mosque built in the 1970s, and several residential neighborhoods. Much of the recent government architecture incorporates the vividly-colored whorls and arabesques of traditional Gayo house designs.

Acehnese, Javanese, Chinese and Minangkabau as well as Gayo live in the town. The Acehnese, mostly bachelors, come here to engage in small-scale trade. Many send money back to their home villages, where they expect to return to marry. Some of the Javanese living in or near the town were brought to Takengon in the 1920s and '30s by the Dutch as laborers on the dammar pine estates. Most live in separate villages where their children learn Javanese and Indonesian. The Chinese remain distinct from the Gayo because of their religion (Buddhist and Christian) and economic ties to Medan and overseas.

A walking tour of Takengon

First climb to the top of **Buntul Kubu**, the

large hill overlooking the town, for a splendid overview of the area. The building on top of the hill was constructed by the Dutch and is now the district office for cultural affairs. Ask here about forthcoming cultural events in the area. Then descend the hill back to the town and visit the "Padang prayer house" (*mersah padang*) next to the river near the new 2-story market building. This prayer house was built by Minang settlers in the late 1920s as a place for their modernist style of worship.

Next to the prayer house a road leads down to the river and a footbridge. From the middle of the bridge, a view of the river and the older houses lining its banks may be enjoyed. On the left bank is the community of **Bale**, with its own reformist prayer house; on the right, further downstream, is the community of **Asir-Asir**, whose prayer house was built by traditionalist Muslims to preserve the older style of congregational worship. All three prayer houses once served as mosques but Friday worship is now only held in the large, silver-domed government mosque. Continue across the river to Bale to visit the new Buddhist temple (a center for Sumatra-wide Buddhist celebrations) and the Catholic church. Caretakers of each are happy to tell the history of the Chinese in the area.

A rich Muslim ritual life characterizes the town, and the Gayo welcome questions from visitors about their religion. Friday is the day of worship at the mosque in town. Men and women then come to town from surrounding villages to shop before and after the noon service. You may be fortunate enough to arrive during the celebration of the *idul adha* feast of sacrifice during the pilgrimage month, or the *idul fitri* feast following Ramadan. Families and entire communities then prepare lavish meals, engage in joyous worship, and visit each other's houses for snacks and to ask forgiveness from each other for any mistakes committed the previous year.

Around Lake Tawar

Lake Tawar is a vital source of livelihood and recreation for the people of Takengon. On three sides of the lake the land rises steeply to peaks of 2,400 to 2,800 m. Several trails lead from the town up these slopes and afford splendid views of the lake.

The village of **Kebayakan** lies by the lake just north of Takengon. The main road to the village takes you through rice fields past the intricately-carved house of the last ruler of the area, Kejurun Zainuddin. Just outside of Kebayakan, and worth a brief stop, is an older style wooden prayer house, once a mosque, with a ball-shaped ornament on the dome. This village is a mosaic of *kampungs*.

A good road also leads south from Takengon across the Peusangan River around the lake's southern shore. Ask at the Hotel Renggali, just outside of town, for a boat and a guide to explore the calm lake from the water. Farther along are small villages, rice terraces and fishing platforms. Inhabitants of these villages use nets suspended from fishing platforms to catch the carp and minnow-like *depek* fish which abound in the lake.

Local Gayo folktales often tell of a particular spot—here is the shore where the Green Princess threw herself into its waters, there the ledge where Syiah Utama rested on his journey to bring Islam to the villagers, and that rock formation is actually a bride who turned to stone as she gazed back on her beloved village as she was leaving.

Hot springs and coffee gardens

A day trip to the north of town should include a visit to the hot springs at Simpangbaleg, a look at the coffee gardens, and a stop at a handicraft shop in the village of Bebesen.

Go first to **Baleatu**, about one km to the north of Takengon, to see the area's open-air morning market (*pasar pagi*). Since the 1930s the highlands have been a center for

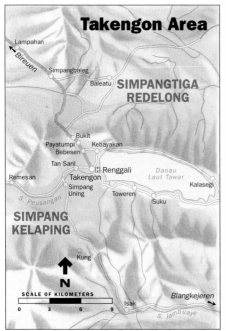

Takengon Area

Lampahan
Bireuen
Simpangbaleg
Baleatu **SIMPANGTIGA REDELONG**
Bukit
Payatumpi   Kebayakan
Bebesen
Tan Saril
Remesan   Renggali   *Danau Laut Tawar*
Takengon
Simpang   Kalasegi
Uning   Toweren
Suku
S. Peusangan

SIMPANG KELAPING

Kung

N

SCALE OF KILOMETERS
0   3   6   9
Isak   *Blangkejeren*
S. Jambuaye

Right: *Lake Tawar in the late afternoon mists.*

fruit and vegetable growing, and for trade in tobacco and coffee. Gayo handicrafts are sold in the market, including large and small ceremonial mats and baskets plaited from dyed reeds. Nested basket sets are used by Gayo women to carry ingredients for betel chewing. Men and women also embroider intricate *kerawang* designs onto cloth.

Next stop is **Simpang Beliq**, 20 km north of Takengon on the main Bireuen road (at km 80), which has a hot spring that is open all year round. The town is also a market center for the coffee grown in this northern Gayo region, whose high altitudes are ideal for producing export-quality Arabica beans. Stop at one of the coffee gardens that line the road to see the trees, and sample the local brew at one of the many small roadside coffee shops.

On the way back to Takengon, stop in **Payatumpi** (km 97) to see one of the distilleries that produces aromatic oils from the patchouli and citronella plants. This is a growing industry here, and the distillery is open to interested visitors. Finally stop at the village of **Bebesen**, just north of Takengon, to visit a *kerawang* cloth embroidery shop.

South to Isak

From the western end of the lake, the Peusangan River flows through broad plains cultivated with rice on its way to the north coast. The main road leading south from Takengon to **Isak** first passes westward for about 10 km through this scenic Peusangan Valley, winding through rice-growing villages with coffee gardens perched on steep slopes to either side. The view from the village of **Tan Saril**, just outside Takengon, is especially beautiful.

These villages along the Isak road afford fascinating glimpses of everyday life in the highlands. Most villagers spend a good deal of the year in their rice fields—preparing the ground for planting (either with horse-drawn ploughs or by driving water buffalo over the earth to loosen it), transplanting seedlings, weeding, harvesting, threshing (usually with the feet) and milling.

The Gayo once lived in multifamily longhouses, but today nearly all families live in smaller dwellings. (A surviving longhouse in **Kung** village, visible from the Isak road, has walls attractively carved in Gayo motifs.) Each village consists of several distinct kin groups. Most members of each group trace their kin ties (through men or women) to each other, and work together to prepare feasts, mourn the dead and hold weddings.

The paved road continues up over the Bur Lintang pass, climbing to 1,800 m before descending into the lush, forested Isak River valley. After lunching at Isak, continue downstream for several kilometers and stop along the river for a dip in its fast-flowing waters. The trip out here and back to Takengon takes a full day.

— John Bowen

WESTERN ACEH

Crashing Surf and a Raging River

The coasts and highlands of western Aceh contain some of Indonesia's most spectacular scenery. Until recently the area was virtually inaccessible, but recent improvements in road conditions have made travel considerably easier, and it is now possible to go down the west coast from Banda Aceh to Tapaktuan thence to Medan or Lake Toba via the town of Sidikalang (or the opposite way, of course). By public bus the entire journey takes about 20 hours.

An incredibly scenic detour leads up the Alas Valley into the huge Gunung Leuser National Park around Kutacane. If arrangements are made beforehand in Medan, you can then raft down the Alas through exciting rapids amidst beautiful mountain scenery.

The west coast

Good beaches and dramatic vistas line Aceh's west coast. Powerful waves crash against the shore, and great caution should be exercised when swimming. Small hotels are found in Meulaboh and Tapaktuan, which make convenient stopover points. Depending on the weather and the time of year, magnificent sunsets blaze out across the Indian Ocean.

Leaving Banda Aceh heading south, the road passes the Andalas cement works by the beach at **Lhoknga**. It then climbs through broken country planted with clove trees, past tiny fishing villages and bays lined with brightly-colored *perahu*. Between Lhong and Seudeu it edges along a precipice, affording spectacular views of the Indian Ocean below and the offshore islands of Pulau Breueh and Pulau Peunasu. The road then descends past a waterfall at Mt. Geureutee to **Lamno**—a small and nondescript market town, some of whose inhabitants are said to have inherited blue eyes from the crew of a Portuguese ship the was wrecked nearby in the 16th century.

Further south, the road hugs the shoreline and one is continually reminded of the wildness of the ocean by the foaming surf and seaspray. Four major rivers here have only been bridged in the past several years. In season, large, juicy pomelos (*jeruk bali*) can be obtained.

Just north of **Calang**, the road turns inland around a sheltered, picturesque bay before heading south past a rocky headland, swamps and sandy beaches to Keudepasi, where it again briefly skirts inland over a new bridge across the Krueng Woila. The road then races past beachside coconut palms and casuarinas to **Meulaboh**, the harbor and administrative center for West Aceh. There is a ferry from here to Simeulue, a remote offshore island known for its clove production.

On the beach just north of town is a monument to Teuku Umar, hero of the Aceh wars who was ambushed and killed by the Dutch in 1899. Also near Meulaboh is a large Indonesian/Belgian oil palm estate and an airstrip. The mountainous hinterland of the region has long been known for its gold production.

South of Meulaboh, the road continues on through Peukankuala and Pantai Seunagan to Kutanibong, where it turns inland, skirting a vast swamp before returning to the coast at Blangpidië. Sixty km further south is **Tapaktuan**, another small port and the administrative center for South Aceh. From Tapaktuan the road again turns inland through mountainous, sparsely-populated country to the North Sumatra border, and the coffee-growing area of the Dairi Batak around Sidikalang.

Rafting the Alas River

The Alas is the longest river on Sumatra's west coast. It starts high up in the central Aceh highlands and flows southward through Gunung Leuser National Park, which boasts the most extensive wildlife of any park in Indonesia—including 520 species of birds, 194 reptiles and 62 kinds of amphibians.

Sobek, the American white water specialists, organize trips down the Alas with experienced guides. The river offers just enough of a challenge for most people—the rapids are classified as class III, halfway between leisurely and impassable. These 4 to 6 day jaunts offer a thrilling combination of white water, unspoiled rainforests and sightings of rare wildlife. Catered comforts includes coolers of beer and meals that border on the gastronomic. And there's always the tantalizing possibility of rounding a bend and startling a herd of elephants, or sneaking up on a red orangutan.

Right: *Rafting the Alas River rapids.*

Most people join the trips in Medan, leaving early in the morning for the 8-hour ride up through Berastagi and Kabanjahe and into the Alas Valley. All gear and passengers are carried in an old Mercedes bus. The first night is spent camping on the banks of the Alas above Kutacane. The guides cook dinner, inflate the boats, and teach everyone to pitch their tents. Tired by these exertions, the crew quickly falls asleep, lulled by the rushing water and a chorus of crickets.

The next morning, after a bright and early breakfast and a quick wash, everyone dons life jackets and piles into two bright yellow inflatable boats. The guides take their positions in the middle, grasping their long oars, and push off from the bank.

Soon you are spinning in the first of the rapids, caught in the embrace of the foaming Alas. The river rushes past majestic trees draped with vines, leaves mingling to form a solid wall of vegetation. Occasionally, you see monkeys swinging through the branches.

By late morning, however, you are drifting through the cultivated Kutacane plain, and the guides have to row hard to keep things moving. The scorching sun beats down mercilessly, and bemused villagers stare as you float past. Friendly waves, shouts of "Da-Da" (hello and goodbye) and the occasional "Hallo Mister" greet you as drift downstream.

At late afternoon, you pitch camp again. This is sometimes in populated areas and attracts the attention of villagers who stand or squat, staring silently; to them it's like watching TV. With the fall of darkness they disappear and the mosquitoes come out; everyone soon heads for the protective tents, quite exhausted by the day's events.

Early the next morning you begin the best part of the trip—three easy days of unspoiled gorges through an astonishing, ever-changing panorama. Vegetation-clad cliffs rise from the swift waters. River and jungle sounds mingle in a natural symphony of the rushing water, the flapping of hornbill wings, the six-note ascending scale of a cuckoo, and the cacophony of cries from siamang gibbons in the treetops.

At the end of the fourth day you camp at the confluence of a cascading tributary. Just upstream, a low branch overhangs the water. Swinging hand over hand along the branch you can hang over the rapids, legs dangling in the rushing water, then let go and be carried into calmer waters below.

On the sixth day, you traverse the river's lower reaches towed by an old river boat. The bus picks you up for the six-hour ride back to Medan, stopping in the afternoon for a coffee and a fresh cob of corn overlooking the northern end of Lake Toba. If you like, however, you can also leave the group here and head up to Banda Aceh, traveling the west coast route described above in reverse.

— *E. Edwards McKinnon and Kal Muller*

PART V

Introducing West Sumatra

After Lake Toba, the fertile valleys and scenic lakes of the West Sumatran highlands are undoubtedly the most memorable—and also the most often visited sights on the island. This is the traditional homeland of the dynamic Minangkabau people who have scattered and settled throughout Indonesia— and who are known far and wide for their canny business sense, their ubiquitous, spicy-hot cuisine and their old matriarchal ways.

West Sumatra is actually composed of three distinct regions—a volcanic highland, a long coastal plain which is swampy in places and cultivated in others, and a string of jungle-clad islands lying about 100 km offshore. The province is dominated by the Bukit Barisan—two parallel ranges of mountain peaks interspersed with broad valleys and several highland lakes. Most of these mountains are still covered in a blanket of pristine montane forest, broken in places by jagged peaks which thrust above the tree line.

The highest peak in West Sumatra is Mt. Kerinci, a dormant volcano standing 3,800 m high (the highest in Indonesia outside of Irian Jaya). A number of others rise above 2,000 m, notable smouldering Mt. Marapi (2,831 m) just to the southeast of Bukittinggi.

The largest and most spectacular lake is Maninjau—17 km long and 8 km across— which snuggles inside an ancient, steep-walled crater just to the west of Bukittinggi. Another crater lake, Singkarak, is similar in size and lies just to the southeast of here. Both are easy to reach, and have accommodations and facilities like waterskiing.

The central and northern highlands of the province contain several valleys which have been intensively cultivated for hundreds, perhaps thousands of years, forming an ancient cultural heartland for the region. Three of these, the *luak nan tigo* ("three valleys"), with a combined area of some 250 square km, are the homeland of the Minangkabau—or, more simply "Minang" people—who have spread from these beautiful mountain valleys throughout the whole of Sumatra to Java and even to the Malay peninsula. This is partly the result of a Minangkabau tradition known as *merantau* (going abroad to seek one's fortune). Minang or Padang restaurants, as they are know, are a familiar sight throughout much of the archipelago, and are even found today in many European and American cities.

The mountainous southeastern portion of the province is still wild—largely covered in jungle and inhabited by elephants, tigers, leopards, tapirs, bears and rhinos. Much of it is included in the huge Kerinci-Seblat National Park, which spills into three neighboring provinces and encompasses several stunning crater lakes—the most spectacular being the one atop Mt. Tujuh). Access to these wildlife areas is not as difficult as one might think, and a number of trekking and wildlife tours are now available in Padang and Bukittinggi.

One hundred km off the coast of West Sumatra lie the Mentawai Islands, which were uplifted when the Indian continental plate collided with the Sunda shelf some 80 million years ago. The island chain consists of four large inhabited islands—Siberut, Sipora, North and South Pagi, and numerous smaller ones. Most are still covered in tropical rainforest, and are fringed by unspoilt coral reefs teeming with marine life.

The large island of Siberut is noted for its exceptionally archaic culture. Until very recently the inhabitants practiced many Stone Age traditions, and even today one can find traditional *uma* or longhouses where tattooing and elaborate rituals designed to please the souls of the community are held.

—*John Miksic and Eric Oey*

Overleaf: *Shimmering West Sumatran rice fields.*
Opposite: *A Minangkabau bride. Minang women are known for their strong character and considerable commercial talents. Photos by Kal Muller.*

THE MINANGKABAU

A Unique Matrilineal Society

West Sumatra is home to about 4 million Minangkabau (often simply called Minang)—an energetic people known throughout Indonesia for their matrilineal kinship, their finely-honed commercial instincts, their fiery cuisine and their strong faith in Islam. They are also famous travelers and migrants, due to the traditional practice of *merantau* (young males going abroad to seek their fortune), and indeed more Minang probably now live outside of West Sumatra than remain. All of them nevertheless consider these beautiful highlands—the *darek*—to be their homeland.

The Minang are among the warmest and friendliest people in Indonesia, and take great pleasure in discussing their unique culture with foreigners. Visitors who make even the slightest attempt to become acquainted with Minangkabau customs and traditions are quickly treated almost as members of the clan rather than aliens from a distant land.

Adat and Islam

The Minangkabau have fascinated generations of anthropologists on account of their unusual combination of a matrilineal family system with a firm adherence to Islam. They are in fact one of the few peoples in the world to have maintained a system of matrilineal kinship into modern times—one in which descent and inheritance are traced through women rather than men. Every Minang thus belongs to his or her mother's descent group, and family houses (*rumah gadang*), as well as paddy fields, are the property of women.

Traditionally the wife remained with her maternal relatives after marriage, and men did not live with their wives but in a special men's house called the *surau*. They also spent a great deal of time in their mother's house, and were more responsible for their sister's children than for their own. This old system has broken down during the 20th century, but in many villages the houses are still arranged in clusters belonging to sisters or otherwise related groups of women.

The Minangkabau are organized into matrilineal clan groups—called *suku*—and in each village a number of *suku* are represented. According to tradition, there were originally only four clans, but they became divided in the course of time and there are now approximately 25, each with its own name.

The *suku* are in turn divided into lineages or *paruik* (lit: "womb"), which consist of all descendants of a single grandmother or great-grandmother. These *suku* and lineages were normally exogamous—which means that members were not permitted to marry someone in their own clan or lineage. This kinship structure is no longer very relevant to young Minang, especially those who have moved to Padang or or other parts of Indonesia, and is now in the process of dying out.

Land, houses and certain valuable goods are owned in common by a lineage, and these possessions may not be sold except under a few conditions. (Nowadays the selling of land is not so rare as it once was, however.) Male representatives of the lineage, such as the *penghulu* or "headman," are responsible for the management of communal property, but it is the women who have the right to use and bequeath it to their offspring. The oldest woman of each household has a plot that she passes on to her daughters after her death, or when she is too old to farm it. Thus the economic position of women is very strong. On the other hand, land no longer has the same value it used to, as population pressures and economic changes have encouraged people to seek alternative sources of income.

Despite the fact that they are devout Muslims, few Minangkabau question the compatibility of such matrilineal traditions with those of Islam. "*Adat* (custom) is based on *syarak*

(Islamic law), and *syarak* is based on the Holy Book (the Koran)," they say. Minang intellectuals and religious leaders, however, have frequently criticized the traditional matrilineal pattern of inheritance as running counter to Islamic law, which states that sons are entitled to two-thirds of their parents' estate, and daughters only to one-third. The outcome of such debates is usually a compromise—that old ancestral property should be divided according to matrilineal custom, while earned property should be inherited according to Islamic law. But this has so far not been put into general practice and houses are still inherited by daughters rather than sons.

Patterns of leadership

One of the most famous Minang legends concerns the struggle between two heroes, Datuk Ketumanggungan and Datuk Pepatih Nan Sebatang, over the proper form of government. In the end, neither won. Some families followed Ketumanggungan, and supported an aristocratic system—they became known as *laras* Koto Piliang and the village of Sungai Tarab in Tanahdatar was their stronghold. Houses of families belonging to this *laras* can be identified by their stepped ends, denoting various levels of superiority. Follow-

Opposite: *A Minang wedding marks the entrance of the husband into the wife's clan.* **Below:** *Silver crafts produced in Koto Gadang, near Bukittinggi.*

ers of Pepatih Nan Sebatang supported an egalitarian form of rule and formed the *laras* Bodi Caniago. Their stronghold was Lima Kaum and extended to cover much of Agam. Their houses have flat floors. Perhaps this legend has a historical basis; it may relate to a cleavage created by the introduction of new concepts by the half-Javanese prince Aditya-varman in the 14th century.

In any case, the system of village government of the two was essentially the same. Although women controlled property, men conducted village affairs (at least in public). There was a council composed of the headmen (*penghulu*) of all lineages in the village (i.e. those with a common female ancestor), and the eldest brothers of the eldest women from each house (*mamak*). Every *suku* in the village also had its own head. Thus the system was rather complicated, with diffused authority and a need for frequent discussion, in conformity with the pan-Indonesian preference for consultation and consensus. The council house or *balai* was an important structure in the village, and many old *balai* are fine examples of traditional Minang architecture.

Life in the longhouse

In former times, each household consisted of three to four generations descended from a single great-grandmother living under one roof. Households had a corporate character; members worked the rice fields together and shared in their yield. The house was the center of social life for the women; the bedrooms were occupied by young married women of the family and their children. On the day of her wedding, a daughter was given the best bedroom at the back of the house, while the older sister or cousin who previously occupied it would have to move to another room. Women past child-bearing age did not have a bedroom of their own; they usually slept near the fireplace. Little children slept with their mothers, and young girls could sleep in the

large open space at the front, which also served as the living area and guest room.

In all respects the house was more of a women's than a men's place. The men spent much of their time outdoors. Young boys spent the night in the *surau*—the Islamic prayer house where they received a religious education. Old men often slept there as well. A married man in the prime of life moved between his mother's and his wife's houses—going at night to his wife's house, then arising to return to his mother's house before dawn. They were therefore referred to as "visiting husbands."

This association of women with the house and of men with public life was combined with restrictions between the sexes. Men and women—particularly unmarried girls—who did not belong to the same household or kin group were not to meet and interact freely. A father could not caress his own daughter, and parents-in-laws were not allowed to sit on the same mat or bench with their children-in-law, or eat from the same banana leaf, lest their fingers touch one another's.

Within the *rumah gadang* there was a complex division of authority. The oldest woman was considered the head of the household with regard to internal affairs. When she became too old, the woman next in seniority was appointed in her stead. She was assisted and advised by a senior male member of the family—the *mamak*, usually translated as "mother's brother"—who was responsible for the well-being and upbringing of his sisters' children, over whom he exercised final authority. External matters were thus firmly in the hands of men.

A man's family role was thus primarily directed towards his mother, his sisters and his sisters' children, and his role as a husband and father was marginal. A man had little authority over his wife and children, and had few obligations towards them. As a result, the conjugal tie was weak, and polygamy and divorce were frequent.

The practice of merantau

The Minangkabau are best known within Indonesia for their exceptional mobility, coupled with a very strong entrepreneurial spirit. Everywhere in Indonesia (now in many foreign cities as well), for example, one can find restaurants serving spicy Minang food—usually referred to as "Padang food."

The mobility of Minang men probably had its roots in the fact that before marriage they slept outside the family longhouse and had few familial obligations. Economic factors also played a role. Because of the matrilineal inheritance system, men had few material interests in the village, as land and inherited wealth were in the hands of women. Trade with harbors on both coasts of the island has been carried on since ancient times—lowland areas referred to by the term *rantau* (which now refers to any place outside the highlands)—and Minang men are particularly known for their trading abilities.

Even prior to the 19th century, it was customary for a young man to leave the village for one or more years to gain experience and seek material wealth in the outside world. When he returned he was prepared to marry, and his worldly ways and possessions made him a much more desirable husband than those who had stayed behind. In former times, migration was thus largely restricted to men, and was temporary.

During the last century, as the population increased and arable land became scarce, this custom became a more general and permanent feature of Minang society. Men in their productive years, whether married or not, moved away to find better jobs. Many took their wives and children with them, and did not return to their village except for short visits. Today some single women are even known to migrate on their own.

This out-migration has had a considerable impact on Minang village life. One thing which invariably strikes the visitor is the large proportion of adult women as compared to men in many rural areas. These days women can join their husbands in the *rantau* if they want to, but then "who will look after the house and the fields?" as many of them say. As a result, many Minang women run households by themselves while the husbands and sons live elsewhere, some of them returning home at regular intervals, others very seldom.

In general, when the men go away to make money, the women tend to see this as profitable arrangement—but it is crucial of course that they keep in touch and send some money back! If there is no news from the husband for a long time, the wife may ask for a divorce. Yet even while very far away from home, most Minang retain a great fondness for their village. As a Minang proverb says: "It may rain gold in the *rantau* and stones in our village, but my love goes to the village."

Successful migrants often contribute to the physical development of their home village, and in villages where the level of migration is high, one sees roads, prayer houses, mosques and elaborate ceremonies that have been financed by wealthy fellow villagers who now live far away.

The performing arts

The Minang have developed a number of unique art forms, including their own *pencak silat*—the combination of dance and martial arts common throughout Indonesia. Traditional dramas called Nalam Sijobang, Randai Simarantang and Bakaba once existed, but are now seldom performed. Graceful women's dances with descriptive names like *tari piring* ("plate dance"), *saputangan* ("kerchief dance"), *kerbau jalang* ("wild buffalo dance") and *tari gelombang* ("wave dance") are similar to those found in other areas of Sumatra.

ERIC OEY

Opposite: *Traditional crafts in Koto Gadang, near Bukittinggi.* **Left:** *A* tari piring *dance performance.*

The Minang are also very fond of versifying in a traditional form known as the *pantun*. Like other Sumatrans, they were skilled in spontaneously composing these rhymed quatrains, especially during courtship—when the ability to create extemporaneous *pantun* was crucial to winning over one's sweetheart.

Into the modern world

The Minangkabau family has undergone significant changes during the past century as a result of demographic, economic and ideological factors. A rapidly growing population has led to a land shortage, and a growing market and money economy now plays an important role in daily life. An increasing number of people, especially men, work outside the agrarian sector. This has meant an ever-increasing exodus of Minangkabau men and their families to towns and cities throughout Indonesia. The strengthening of Islamic values, and the modern ideal of the nuclear family, have also had a considerable impact.

According to Islam and the modern family model, it is the husband, not the uncle or the mother, who is the head of the family. As a result, the *rumah gadang* has lost its function as the center for an extended family, and the modern household has become much smaller. Even in rural areas, many families now consist of just a father, a mother and their children. In such families the father is the head of the household, with authority over (and economic responsibility for) his wife and and his own children. Minang men are no longer "visiting husbands."

Nowadays men tend to become permanent residents in their wife's house, unless they leave their village as migrants. Divorce rates and polygamous unions have decreased sharply. Women have also gained much more access to the public world as a result of new educational and employment opportunities. The worlds of men and women are no longer as separate as they once were.

These changes do not imply that matrilineal kinship is no longer important. Most Minangkabau are proud of their cultural heritage, and traces of the old family structure are still clearly visible. Inheritance still has pronounced matrilineal features, and the matrilineal descent group still plays an important role in people's lives. Closely-related women such as sisters, mothers, daughters and cousins still reside close together. The role of the *mamak* may have been partly replaced by the husband/father, but men still feel responsible for their sisters and their sisters' children. And although men often now reside in their wife's house in rural areas, their place in that house is still rather marginal. The new, one-family dwellings one sees throughout the highlands today do not mean that the matrilineal family system has completely disappeared.

—*Joke van Reenen and John Miksic*

RUMAH GADANG

Distinctive Minangkabau 'Big Houses'

Much of the uniqueness of the Minangkabau is exemplified in their architecture. To understand their houses is also to understand the way the family is run. The Minang themselves explicitly make this connection.

Traditional Minang houses are called *rumah gadang*, literally "big house." They are elongated rectangular structures with gables which rise to peaks at either end. The house normally has only one doorway, in the middle of the longer side, but some older examples have the doorway at the end.

The peaked roofs are often said by the Minangkabau to represent buffalo horns. This is related to a Minang myth and folk etymology regarding a contest between a Javanese buffalo and a Minang calf, which the calf won (see following section, "History").

The Minangkabau house was traditionally constructed with a technique called a stressed ridge beam. The long roof peak was made from a straight piece of wood, upon which the rafters were laid. After a time the middle inevitably began to sag and the ends were pushed upward, thus producing the distinctive saddle shape. The Toraja of Sulawesi have similarly shaped roofs, which they explain as representative of their ancestors' boats. The origin of the technique probably dates back to prehistoric times, for similar houses are depicted on bronze drums found in Vietnam and southwest China. They once existed in Java as well.

The houses are divided into a number of apartments, each occupied by women related to the matriarch of the household. Thus the basic family unit consisted of a grandmother and her children and grandchildren. According to tradition, the number of apartments should always be uneven. One of the largest such houses still in existence, at Sulit Air, is 64 meters long and is divided into 22 dwel-

ling areas (thus an exception to the rule). The largest concentration of traditional houses is in the Payakumbuh area, where almost 2,000 still stand, comprising about 25 percent of all houses in the area.

Although the general shape of the *rumah gadang* is standard, specific types are associated with the three main Minang valleys, and with the division between the Bodi Caniago and Koto Piliang alliances. The Koto Piliang houses (associated with an aristocratic form of government) have a raised floor area called an *anjuang* at either end, whereas the (egalitarian) Bodi Caniago floors are flat.

Traditional houses are decorated by carvings which are often painted. The system of carving is not left to chance, but organized according to a fixed scheme. Certain patterns may be used on window sills, others on the *anjuang*, in the attic, on the rafters, etc. The patterns derive from plant and animal motifs and carry symbolic meanings. For example the pattern called *tangguak lamah* symbolizes humility and courtesy; *jalo taserak* recalls the difference between good and evil; and *jarek takambang* reminds the viewer of the importance of social mores. Thus Minang woodcarvings, like the traditional costumes, are a way of constantly reminding people of the proper way to behave in society, and the house is an advertisement for morality as well as a symbol of Minang social structure.

—*John Miksic*

Left: *Minang girl in traditional costume.* **Right:** *An* old *rumah gadang,* now the Bukittinggi museum.

HISTORY

Fertile Land of Rice, Gold and Pepper

The fertile Minang highlands were settled by Austronesian-speaking peoples several thousand years ago, and this was the first area in Sumatra to develop a culture based on irrigated rice cultivation. Early European visitors like Raffles were astounded by the density of population which they found here.

Very little is known of the history of West Sumatra before AD 1400, though mines in the highlands were probably exporting gold from quite early times—lending the island of Sumatra as a whole the ancient name of Svarnadvipa ("Island of Gold"). The west coast is studded with treacherous reefs, however, and trade goods were formerly carried down the course of the Indragiri River to ports along the eastern coast of the island.

A small bronze Buddha head has been found at Indrapura, in the southern part of the province, and now lies in the Padang museum, but few other antiquities have been discovered. We must presume, therefore, that during the first millennium AD these highlands remained on the fringe of the great east coast civilizations, Srivijaya and Malayu, which derived their wealth from maritime trade.

Seaborne settlers

Minang legends dating from Islamic times trace the ancestry of West Sumatra's inhabitants back to Sri Maharajo Dirajo ("The Glorious King of Kings"), a descendant of Alexander the Great whose ship sailed to Sumatra and lodged atop Mt. Marapi—the volcano southeast of Bukittinggi whose summit was then the only land protruding above the sea. As the waters receded, he and his followers settled at Pariangan ("Abode of the Ancestors"), a village in the Tanahdatar Valley on the volcano's southern slopes. From here they spread to the nearby valleys of Agam and Limapuluh Kota ("Fifty Fortresses").

Another popular story tells of a threatened attack by a huge army from Java. Greatly outnumbered, the Minang proposed a contest between two buffaloes in lieu of a bloody armed conflict. The Javanese agreed, and produced an enormous beast from Java. To their great surprise, the Minang brought forth a tiny calf. What the Javanese did not realize was that the calf had not been fed for days, and had a knife tied to its snout. The calf nuzzled the belly of the startled war buffalo, goring and killing it. The Javanese withdrew, and the Minangkabau have ever since claimed that their name derives from *minang* ("victorious") and *kabau* ("buffalo").

There may be a kernel of historical truth in the story. The Javanese did launch several attacks against Sumatra in the late 13th and 14th centuries, and ancient earthen ramparts with names like Kota Jawa ("Javanese Fort") testify to a Javanese presence. But it seems likely that the story of the buffalo calf is apocryphal, and the name Minangkabau probably derives instead from *pinang kabhu*—an archaic expression meaning "original home."

Conversion to Islam

West Sumatra first appears in the historical record in the 14th century, when a Javanese-Sumatran ruler named Adityavarman issued stone inscriptions in and around Tanahdatar. His rule seems to have had little impact upon the agrarian society of the highlands, however, and after his death (his last dated inscription is 1374) we hear little of his successors.

The momentous conversion to Islam which began around this time seems to have come about as a result of increasing trade with India and influence from Aceh. In the 16th century, large quantities of gold were exported from West Sumatra. Portuguese sources mention that Muslim traders from Gujerat in northwest India called at Pariaman on the west coast to exchange their valuable cloth for gold. In the late 16th century, the sultanate of Aceh claimed sovereignty over Pariaman, and for the next 60 years kept foreign traders out of the Minang areas—channeling West Sumatran products through her port at Banda Aceh.

During the 16th and 17th centuries, West Sumatra became one of the world's premier pepper-growing areas, attracting traders from India, China and Portugal (later also Holland and England). The Dutch ultimately gained control of Padang, in 1663, and established a fortified trading post on the banks of the Batang Arau River, where the West Sumatra

Right: *The mausoleum of Imam Bonjol, the Paderi leader captured by the Dutch in 1837.*

governor's office now stands.

A Portuguese envoy to the Minang court brought back the first description of the highlands in 1683. A triumvirate of rulers apparently controlled each of the three Minang valleys at this time, and their prestige (if not their power) extended to neighboring Batak and Rejang areas, where legends speak of founding rulers sent from the chief Minang court at Pagarruyung in Tanahdatar.

In the late 18th century, the coast came under British rule twice—first during the Anglo-Dutch war of 1781-84. Though Padang was later returned to the Dutch, the British continued to buy pepper and gold at Pariaman. This had the effect of making Bukittinggi and the surrounding Agam area more prosperous than the court center at Tanahdatar. Agam also suffered in one respect—one of the main British imports was opium.

Padang again came under British control between 1795-1819, during the Napoleonic Wars, when Holland's eastern possessions were entrusted to Britain for safekeeping. It was during this period that Thomas Stamford Raffles, lieutenant-governor of Java and later founder of Singapore, visited the Minang area and brought back this glowing report: "As far as the eye could distinctly trace was one continued scene of cultivation, interspersed with innumerable towns and villages, shaded by the coconut and other fruit trees. I may safely say that this view equalled any-

thing I ever saw in Java. The scenery is more majestic and grand, the population equally dense, and the cultivation equally rich."

The Paderi wars

Centralized Minang authority lasted up until the late 18th century. Power rested on royal control of the mines, but by the 1780s the gold was depleted. New sources of income developed—coffee, salt, gambir and textiles —but these were under the control of Muslim traders, whose commercial activity gave rise to an emerging Islamic reform movement.

The reformers were led by the Paderis, puritanical teachers who denounced the lax observance of Islamic law and the matriarchal Minang *adat* which favored female inheritance. Death was the usual penalty for opposing them; most secular leaders, including the royal family, were slaughtered for refusing to accept Paderi dictates.

In 1803, violence broke out in the village of Pandai Sikat in Agam (today a peaceful center for traditional weaving and woodcarving) when a Paderi reformer, frustrated in his attempts to abolish cockfighting, gambling, opium smoking and the drinking of palm toddy, torched the new village council house. Paderi ideas soon took root in poorer villages on the sides of the valleys, where food was scarce, and by 1821 the hills around Agam were mostly under Paderi control. The Limapuluh Kota area also converted, seemingly

without much violence, but there was fierce fighting in Tanahdatar, with no side gaining the upper hand. By the time Raffles visited in 1818, the court at Pagarruyung had been razed three times. The Paderis' religious zeal even extended to the territory of the Tapanuli or southern Batak, who accepted Islam at the point of a sword.

Following the conclusion of the Napoleonic wars, the Dutch returned to Padang to find trade in the highlands badly disrupted by the upheavals. Fearful that the Paderis might challenge their own position, the Dutch made a treaty in 1821 with a nephew of the Raja Alam of Pagarruyung, who had fled the fighting and was living in Padang. He promptly granted them the Tanahdatar valley, and they proceeded to build a fort there and at what is now Bukittinggi (formerly Fort de Kock).

Assisted by local residents, the Dutch used this fort to expand their control over much of Tanahdatar and south Agam, including Pandai Sikat. However, the Paderis put up stiff resistence, halting their advance in 1823. As the war dragged on, the Dutch cut off all trade and applied increasing military pressure. In 1831, new fighting broke out and this time the Dutch were more successful. The war ended in 1837 when the town of Bonjol, home of the most powerful Paderi leader, Imam Bonjol, was finally stormed. By 1832, Paderi power was broken and the Minang highlands were firmly under Dutch control.

The struggle for independence

Throughout the 19th century, debates regarding the proper form of Islam and the permissible degree of accommodation with traditional Minang culture continued. West Sumatrans also played a prominent role in the modernist Muslim movement of the early 20th century, especially in the call for educational reforms, including schools for women. By the 1920s, many educated young Minang become frustrated by a lack of suitable jobs, and in 1926 an armed insurrection broke out, incited by communists. Many who joined it were captured and sent to the dreaded Dutch prison camp at Boven Digul in New Guinea.

After WW II, Padang was the scene of clashes between British forces and young Indonesian revolutionaries. And during the revolution, Bukittinggi was even for a short time the capital of Indonesia. On July 27, 1947 the Dutch launched a "Police Action" on Java and arrested several nationalist leaders. Shortly before his arrest, Soekarno, the first president of the republic, cabled his minister of finance in Bukittinggi and appointed him head of an emergency government. International pressures eventually forced the Dutch to free the republican leaders, and on January 1st, 1950, West Sumatra became a province in the newly independent Republic of Indonesia.

—*John Miksic*

MINANG TEXTILES

Sumptuous Threads of Tradition

Traditional Minangkabau textiles, ornately brocaded with gold and silver threads, play an important role in birth, circumcision, marriage and funeral ceremonies. These shimmering and intricately patterned fabrics, dubbed "gold cloths" by early Western travelers, are material expressions of Minang *adat*—the customary laws which guide one through life from cradle to grave. In the words of a local proverb, "textiles are the skins of *adat*."

Women weave these sumptuous textiles on a base of silk or cotton, onto which a raised pattern of gold or silver threads is added—a process known as *songket*. The most prized threads were thinly coated with gold or silver leaf. More common threads were of fine copper or bronze wire plated in precious metal. Until the beginning of this century, *songket* textiles were woven at four places in the Minang region—Koto Gadang, Padang Panjang, Paya-

kumbuh and Silungkang. Since 1900, however, the ceremonial cloths have been woven only in a few villages and weaving of the famed *kain balapak* has largely been confined to Pandai Sikat, a tiny village 12 km south of Bukittinggi. Today, silk weaving is a thriving cottage industry, and traditional textiles are in great demand both with tourists and with the Jakarta elite.

In the past, the finest silk, gold and silver threads were imported from China, and dyes were obtained from flowers or by grinding rocks. More than a hundred traditional motifs were known, employing plant and animal figures as well as geometric patterns. Unfortunately, after the conversion of the Minangkabau to Islam in the 15th century, the original meanings of most textile motifs were lost.

The most distinctive part of a Minang woman's ceremonial costume is the two-pronged headdress, called a *tanduk* or *tilakuang*. Displaying one's wealth in a spectacular fashion, the *tanduk* indicates the wearer's village by the manner in which it is folded. The headdress is also said to reflect social values; a large, flat triangle of cloth crowning the two-horned red, black and gold headdresses of the village of Tanjung Sungayung, for example, reminds the wearer to treat people from all social classes without preference or prejudice.

—Kunang Helmi Picard

Opposite: *Payakumbuh ca. 1910.* **Below:** *Weaving in the village of Pandai Sikat, south of Bukittinggi.*

DANA IRFAN

PADANG

A Colonial Port and Its Waterfront

Padang is the provincial capital of West Sumatra and the principal gateway to the Minang highlands. The city, which has a population approaching 500,000, has grown at the rate of more than 10 percent a year over the past ten years, and Padang's port, which is 6 km south of the city, is the largest on Sumatra's west coast. Ships call here to load rubber, cinnamon, coffee, tea, nutmeg, plywood, rattan, cement and coal mined at Ombilin in the highlands.

The main attraction in downtown Padang is the **Provincial Museum** (Museum Negeri Adhityawarman) at Jl. Pangeran Diponegoro 10, next to the Hotel Minang. The museum stands in a park and is built in the traditional Minang style known as Gajah Maharam. Collections include prehistoric artifacts, stamps, imported ceramics, manuscripts, modern art, and ethnographic displays of the Minang and

the peoples of the Mentawai Islands, which lies to the west off Padang's coast.

One gallery is devoted to artifacts connected with Minang ceremonies such as weddings, funerals and the investiture of village leaders; another displays implements used in agriculture, crafts, Islamic worship and other daily activities. The **Taman Budaya** cultural center, which is right next door to the museum, holds periodic art and cultural exhibitions.

Historic Padang

It is pleasant just to wander through the older parts of Padang, especially the area around **Kampung Cina** (Chinatown), south of the central business and hotel district, where turn-of-the-century houses line the streets. Start from Jl. Hiligoo and continue south along Jl. Pondok and Jl. Niaga. On these streets, you can find Chinese herbalists and coffee shops with distinctive inlaid tiles, hardwood floors and teak furnishings that serve cool drinks during the heat of the day.

At the southern end of Jl. Niaga, turn right (west) along the river through the **Muara district** (meaning "estuary"), past the old colonial waterfront where small cargo vessels still dock. Stroll by century-old warehouses loaded with fragrant cinnamon and other spices awaiting shipment to Jakarta and Singapore. This wharf saw its glory days in the 1920s, when coffee production reached a peak in the Minang Highlands.

Hand-paddled ferries cross the sluggish Batang Arau River from here, which is full of small boats and a sight in itself. On the other side you can follow a footpath to the Chinese cemetery up on the hillside, where you have a splendid late-afternoon view of the waterfront and the city. The hill, called **Bukit Monyet** ("Monkey Hill") used to be a favorite subject of 19th-century Dutch artists.

To the west of here, standing guard at the mouth of the Batang Arau and overlooking the sea, is a perfectly-formed hill known as **Gunung Padang**. A path leads up to Siti Nurbaya Park at the top (named after the heroine of an early Indonesian novel), where you can find the remains of an old bunker and the Dutch trigonometrical point for all early surveys of West Sumatra. Near the base of the hill is a WW II cannon which still points across the harbor entrance.

Left: *The mouth of the Batang Arau with Gunung Padang in the background.* **Right:** *The facade of a modern bank reflects the roof of the Provincial Museum, built in traditional Minangkabau style.*

Beaches and coral islands

From Padang Hill a path leads south about 4 km and an hour's walk along the coast to the area's most popular beach, **Air Manis** ("Sweet Waters"). The beach can also be reached by direct minibus from the downtown terminal, but avoid it on Sundays, when it is usually crowded. At low tide, wade across to a little islet just offshore. On the beach, Bapak Chili offers basic accommodation and food. A better restaurant has recently opened at the southern end of the beach, and also offers rooms at moderate prices.

The beach borders a fishing village, and is associated with a popular legend about a young man, Malin Kundang, who rose from humble origins to become a rich merchant overseas. When his mother heard that he had come back with his ship, she prepared his favorite food, and wearing her best clothes went to his ship to meet him. However, Malin Kudang felt ashamed of his mother, who was old and toothless by this time, and whose best attire consisted of nothing but a few rags. He pretended not to know her, and ordered his crew to cast her away. His mother's heart broke and she cursed him. As the ship went off, thunder flashed and lightning roared, and the ship sank. Everyone aboard perished, and were turned to stone—a coral outcropping at the beach is said to be their remains.

GOTTFRIED ROELCKE

Bungus is another small village 25 km south of Padang—some 45 minutes by *bemo*. It is situated on a lovely bay with calm water and a good beach, a section of which has been made into a resort. It suffers somewhat from its proximity to a plywood factory, and lack of shade. A small admission is charged.

From Bungus you can hire a small outrigger to visit the coral islands which lie an hour offshore. All the islands have some shade, but at high tide there is often just a narrow fringe of sand left between the water and the rocks. **Sirindah Island**, farthest out to the west, has little shade but is the only one without a rocky core so that you can walk across it. All the islands are ringed by wonderful white sand beaches, sometimes interrupted by rocky outcrops or huge boulders, and all are encircled by colorful coral reefs. The reefs teem with small fish, ranging from 2 to 30 cm in length and displaying an incredible variety of colors ranging from bright blue and green to combinations of yellow, tan, turquoise, pink and brown. The reefs are gradually being destroyed by coral hunters, but the islands are still a minor paradise. Bring snorkeling gear, food and drinks.

Another good beach is **Pasir Jambak**, which lies north of Padang past the airport. To get there, take a direct *bemo*, or watch for the signboard saying "Pasir Jambak" about 2 km past the airport, where you take a left. You will have to walk the last km from the entry gate to the beach, and a small entrance fee is charged.

Cruising

Many of the boats at anchor in Padang harbor are cargo vessels which ply the waters between here and the Mentawai Islands to the west. Because of a lack of regular transport, few travelers ever reach the Mentawais, although cargo boats leave the harbor almost daily for a four- to ten-day swing through the islands, delivering 20th-century goods such as IndoMie (instant noodles) and canned sardines, in exchange for local products and tribal handicrafts.

For those willing to disregard the conventional wisdom about the boatmen, who are widely reputed to be lawless scoundrels, this is a real Indonesian adventure—sleep under the star-filled firmament while afloat on the Indian Ocean, and call on unexplored islands inhabited by fascinating, primitive peoples. Take along some food and leave behind your inhibitions (see "Siberut").

—*J. Miksic, G. Roelcke and J. Goodfriend*

BUKITTINGGI

Delightful Hill Town With Scenic Vistas

The town of Bukittinggi (lit: "High Hill") lies at the center of the Agam valley—one of three valleys which together form the Minang heartland. While Padang is the modern commercial, educational and administrative center of the province, Bukittinggi is the cultural capital of the Minang realm.

The largest city in the highlands, Bukittinggi grew up around a Dutch post, Fort de Kock, built in 1825 during the Paderi conflict. This attractive, bustling town was the birthplace of many Indonesian intellectuals, cabinet ministers and diplomats—including Mohammed Hatta, the nation's first vice-president.

Although less than a degree south of the equator, Bukittinggi has a cool climate due to its elevation—900 meters above sea level. It rains frequently, but many tourists nevertheless find this to be the most hospitable city in Sumatra—everything is within walking distance, food and lodgings are good, there is lots to see and the residents are very friendly.

A walking tour

Bukittinggi's principal landmark is the **Jam Gadang** ("Great Clock")—a clock tower with a miniature Minang house on top overlooking the main square. Visible from many parts of town, it is a good starting point for an exploration on foot. On Saturdays and Sundays, the lively **Pasar Atas** central market next door spills out into the streets. All kinds of fruits, vegetables, spices and meats (except pork) are sold in open-air stands run by assertive Minang ladies. There are sections for everything—brightly colored plastic wares seem to be the main attraction. Bargaining is a popular social activity here rather than a test of wills or an attempt to cheat the unwary traveler. Keep your sense of humor, and bargain hard if you are buying!

From here, walk up Bukittinggi's "mainstreet," **Jalan Ahmad Yani**, which is lined with antique and souvenir shops, restaurants and offices. Two unique stair-streets lead down from here to the right, to Jl. Cinduamato, and are lined with more souvenir shops.

To get a good view of the town and the surrounding area, climb up Jl. Cinduamato to **Taman Bundo Kanduang** park at the top of the hill, where a zoo and a museum are located. The name of the park refers to the legendary "Great Mother" symbolic of the matri-

lineal Minang. The zoo is crowded on Sundays, when it is the principal place in town to see and be seen, but the animals are kept in rather miserable conditions.

The museum in the park is housed in a traditional Minang *rumah gadang* complete with thatched roof and flanking granaries. Inside are examples of wedding costumes and *tanduk* headdresses in the shape of buffalo horns. A small fortune in fine gold jewelry is on display; for several centuries this area was the archipelago's leading producer of the precious metal. The museum also displays old matchlock rifles used against the Dutch, as well as musical instruments.

Breathtaking panoramas

Bukittinggi was formerly called **Fort de Kock**, after the Dutch fortification erected at the edge of a steep-sided ridge here in 1825. Stone ruins and a few cannon are all that is left of the fort, known locally as the *benteng*, but there is a lookout tower that is an excellent spot to watch sunsets and take in a view of Mt. Marapi ("Fire Mountain"), which occasionally vents puffs of smoke. The view alone is worth the walk—to get here, take a path up from Jl. T. Umar, near the corner of Jl. A. Yani.

Another breathtaking panorama is available on the southwestern edge of Bukittinggi, which skirts the lovely **Ngarai Sianok Canyon**. Part of a tectonic rift valley running the entire length of the island, this canyon has sheer walls and a flat bottom, and offers a haunting early-morning spectacle—as dawn caresses the peak of Mt. Singgalang in the background, blankets of mist drift around the canyon's 100-meter cliffs. A river meanders through rice fields below, disappearing in the hazy distance beyond.

A lookout point known as **Panorama Park** overlooks the canyon and is a popular spot with locals who come to stroll in the afternoon air. A path leads down into the canyon, past Japanese-built tunnels under the park. One can explore these tunnels, but a flashlight and guide are essential.

Hike to Kota Gadang

Kota Gadang is a village of silversmiths a few km from Bukittinggi across the Sianok Canyon. Walk one km down into the canyon, turn left and cross a small bridge over the river, and follow the trail up a long flight of steps. From here the village is ten minutes' walk: ask for directions along the way. The speciality here is delicate silver filigree. You can buy pins in the form of ornate flowers, tiny earrings in the shape of Minang houses, and a plethora of exquisite miniature objects. Larger items include model sailing ships, traditional Minang houses and the clock tower.

— John Miksic

Opposite: *Bukittinggi's landmark, the Jam Gadang.*
Below: *Ngarai Sianok Canyon and Mt. Singgalang.*

COEN PEPPLINKHUIZEN

THE MINANG HIGHLANDS

Exploring the Ancestral Homeland

The ancient homeland of the Minangkabau —the *luak nan tigo* or "three valleys" of western central Sumatra—is an incredibly beautiful highland region of lush rice fields, towering volcanoes and spectacular crater lakes. These three valleys roughly define the corners of a triangle centering about sacred Mt. Merapi (2,891 meters), the highest and most active volcano in the area and the spot where, according to local legend, the first Minang ancestors are thought to have settled.

To the south and east of the volcano is the valley known as **Tanahdatar** ("Level Land"), with its focus around the small town of Batusangkar. This is where the royal Minang court was located from the 14th to the 19th centuries. Ancient tombs, inscriptions, palace sites, megalithic stones and other remains dot the area. Tanahdatar was renowned for its gold and iron mines in former times.

The **Agam** valley lies to the north and west of Merapi, centering around the town of Bukittinggi. As we have seen, this area developed rapidly during the last two centuries as a result of contacts with Europeans on the west coast at Pariaman and Padang.

The third and most fertile of the valleys is known as **Limapuluh Kota**; it lies to the east around the large town of Payakumbuh. Megalithic remains abound here, and it is thought that this may in fact have been the earliest of the valleys to have been settled. Access to the east coast is provided by the courses of the mighty Kampar and Indragiri rivers.

Framing these valleys is a tightly-packed cluster of volcanic peaks and two enormous crater lakes, Maninjau and Singkarak. As in the Toba area, these volcanoes have contributed to the fertility of the soils, and as a result the Minang highlands have been relatively densely populated for many centuries.

Although the culture and language in all three valleys is the same, each is unique from the standpoint both of history and of scenic beauty. What follows, therefore, is a series of itineraries using Bukittinggi as a starting point, and working outwards in various directions—first west, then south and then east. While these areas can be visited in a series of day-trips; more time can of course profitably be spent making longer journeys along the scenic backroads that loop around the two lovely crater lakes and over dramatic passes

separating the volcanoes, overnighting in small towns and villages where the facilities may be primitive, but where one experiences a true taste of the justly renowned Minangkabau hospitality.

West to Lake Maninjau

West Sumatra's most famous sight is undoubtedly Lake Maninjau (meaning: "To Look Out Across")—a lake set inside of an ancient crater that is 17 km long and 8 km wide, surrounded on all sides by steep, 600-m jungle-clad walls. Maninjau's spectacular scenery rivals that of Toba, though on a smaller scale.

The lake shimmers on windless days and its transparent waters teem with fish, which swim to the surface at the drop of a crumb. This is the ideal place to relax and enjoy the tranquility of nature. The swimming is good, there are pleasant walks through picturesque villages and dense forests, with adequate facilities that include several hotels, restaurants, boats and even water skiing.

The 2-hour journey to the lake is a wonderful experience in itself. Take the main road south from Bukittinggi for 5 km then turn right (west) at a clearly-marked crossing. This road skirts the foot of Bukit Kapanasan, passes the small town of Matur, then crosses a lush valley before climbing up the crater's rim to **Embun Pagi** ("Morning Dew"). The view from here is breathtaking (elev: 1,097 m) and it is worth asking the bus

driver to stop so you can take photos. There is even a small cottage hotel where you may spend the night. In the early morning, clouds drift below as small children swarm about selling brightly-colored straw handicrafts. From Embun Pagi, the road winds down through 44 hairpin turns to Maninjau village (470 m) at the edge of the lake.

Puncak Lawang is another, higher lookout point north of Embun Pagi. From here you can hike down the crater wall to the lake at Bayur, a village 4 km north of Maninjau. To get there, take the turn-off to the north (right) at Matur to the village of Lawang, a distance of about 5 km; a signboard points the way down to the lake (to the left), just near the toll gate. But before descending, walk another 30 min (or persuade the *bemo* driver to take you) up to Puncak Lawang—the highest point on the crater rim, with a TV relay station and a panoramic view down to the lake and back to Mt. Singgalang.

The steeply descending track down from Lawang passes through forests, coffee plantations and village gardens before meeting the lakeshore road. Allow 2 to 3 hours for the descent. It is an easy walk from here back to Maninjau village.

Small boats leave from Maninjau, ferrying

Opposite: *The Minang Highlands contain some of Sumatra's most fertile and productive rice lands.*
Below: *Spectacularly scenic Lake Maninjau.*

KAL MULLER

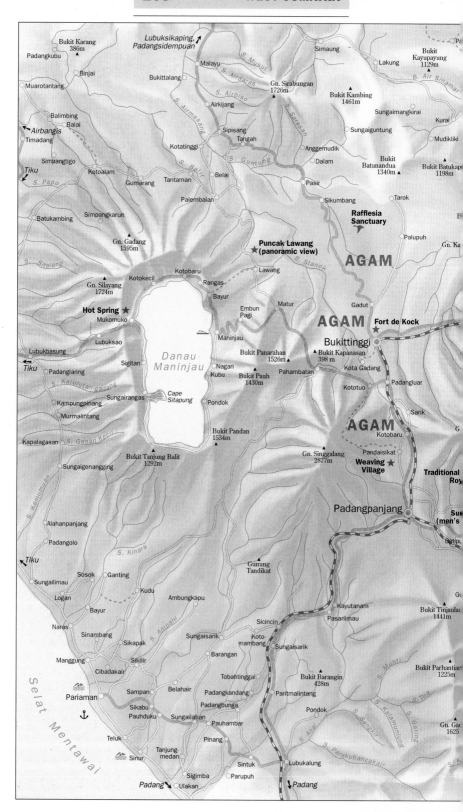

Minang Highlands

↑ Mahat

Bangkinang, ↗
Pekanbaru

↑ N

SCALE OF KILOMETERS

0   3   6   9

Sipinggal
Limbanang

Kotaacik

Gn. Bongsu
1254m

Bukit Sikat
865m ▲

Telaga

Harau Canyon ★

**Old Council
use, Menhirs** ★
Guguk   Pagang

Lamaksari

Tanjung Pati

Parumpang

Parambahan

LIMAPULUH
KOTA

Nankadok

LIMAPULUH
KOTA

Taram

S. Sibayang

Payakumbuh

Padangalai

Kotatengah   Plladang

Limbukan

Tanjungkalin
Pakanarbaa

Sungaipuh

Padangambacang

Labuhgunung   Lingkungan

Bukit Kubanganlado
1022m

Padangbusuh

LIMAPULUH
KOTA

Tanjung Gadang

Mangunaitinggi

oramic
View ★

Tigatanjung
Tabatpatah

Gn. Malintang
2262m

Alangawas

Bukit Gabus
1187m

Salimpaung
Raorao

Situmbuk

Gn. Sago

Batangarang

Gn. Mandiangin
1274m

Bukit Sapan
779m

Sawahgombang

Ladanglawas

S. Pigago

Sungayang

Kawai

Tanjungangsat

Tapiseto

S. Pakis

Bukit Padanglawas
940m

TANAH
DATAR

airung Sari
uncil hall) ★ **Pierced Stone**

Padang Seminyak

Padang Magek

TANAH
DATAR

S. Bulus

ek
imabur

Dusun
Tuo

Limo
Kaum

Pagarruyung

Malayu

Panglan

Tigojangko

Sibiluru

Batusangkar   ★ **Palace**

**Fort Van der
Capellen**

Saruaso

Patamas

Gn. Gedang
747m

Jajaknabi

**Rumah Gadang
(traditional
houses)** ★

Telagagunung

Sawahgalung

Guguksari

pur
tutabal

Balimbing

Bukit Rotan
513m

Kotoalam

Piliang

Sawahpauh

Bukit Ngalautiris
536m ▲

glawas
gek
ungsawah

Umbilin

Bukitkandung

Bukit Sibumbunjantan
990 m

Lurahdalam

Bundung

Danau
Singkarak

Ampang

Telagalawas

Sulit Air

Rawang

Dataralai
Sungaiancing

Kumbayau

Talawi

Kototuo

Padanglawas

air

Gn. Tungku
820m

**Rumah Gadang
(traditional
house)** ★

Kolok

Bukit Kudobarkatuk
633m

Koto
tujuh ↓

Parakgadang

Mandahiling

Sigapung

Tanjung Ampalu

Palaluar

Kudang
Karang

Gn. Papan
957m

Telagogunung

Batugadang
Datar

Muarabungo

Tanjungalai

Muarapinggai

Batugalas

Kabangtiga

S. Umbilin

Pamuatan

Airhilang

Kapalabandar

Bukit Kayugadang
▲ 309m

rapahan   Apa   Berok

Saningbakar
Sumani   Singkarak

Sawahlunto

← Solok

Sijunjung

↓ Solok

villagers around the shores of the lake. This is the best way to sightsee, stopping at various villages along the way. A small road also skirts the northern lakeshore via the villages of Bayur and Kotokecil to **Mukomuko**, on the opposite (western) shore. A river cuts west through the crater wall here and drains the lake; there is a hydroelectric project and a hot spring nearby.

A rough track also leads from Maninjau to Mukomuko around the lake's southern perimeter. From here, the main road continues west down to the Indian Ocean at **Tiku**, whence it is possible to travel down the coast to Pariaman and Padang. For a round-trip, with a full day at the lake, allow 3-4 days.

South to Pandai Sikat

The renowned weaving village of Pandai Sikat (or "Sikek"—the name literally means "weavers") lies just 12 km (about 20 minutes) south of Bukittinggi, at the southern tip of the Agam valley in the saddle between Mts. Singgalang and Merapi. Weaving has been a major occupation in the Agam area since at least the 1780s. Cotton was planted in the western lowlands to supply the industry, but proved insufficient and more thread had to be imported from Surat in India. Today weaving still forms one of the principal sources of livelihood in Pandai Sikat, along with woodcarving, blacksmithing and coppersmithing.

To get there from Bukittinggi, turn off the main road to the right (west) at Kotobaru and follow a small sideroad for 1 km. Young men sit by the side of the street carving decorative murals and furniture, while girls weave the traditional gold-and-silk *songket* on large shuttle looms to supplement the family income. If you have found *songket* cloths expensive in Bukittinggi, take some time out to watch the girls at work—a full day's labor lengthens the fabric by a mere 10 cm or so!

An added bonus for visitors to Pandai Sikat is the exquisitely carved and painted vil-

lage meeting house where marriages are held, the Koran is read and community business is discussed. The village mosque is nearly surrounded by a large artificial pool, whose water is used for bathing and washing clothes. This may reflect the continuation of a pre-Islamic custom of placing religious sanctuaries on man-made islands.

The dormant cone of **Mount Singgalang** (2,877 m) towers to the west of Pandai Sikat. It is an easy 4-hour climb to the top along a well-trodden trail from a TV relay station that

is visible from the village. On a plateau near the summit is a small lake. Get an early start, in order to get to the top while it is (hopefully) still clear. Descend along the same path, or via a track leading north to Kototua, on the Maninjau road. (This takes about twice as long, however.) It is also possible to climb **Mount Merapi** from here (register first at the police station in Kotobaru), however the ascent is treacherous and is better attempted from the southeastern flank (see "West Sumatra Practicalities").

Valley of the ancestors

The **Tanahdatar** plain to the south and east of Mt. Merapi is blanketed by majestic rice terraces and dotted with traditional houses. This is where the ancient Minangkabau kingdom was located for some 500 years before being wiped out by Paderi rebels in the early 1800s (see "History). Most of the main sights may be visited in a single day by walking and hopping on and off local *bemos*.

From Bukittinggi, travel south to Padangpanjang, then turn east (left). The road passes villages with fine examples of traditional architecture. Don't miss the large wooden *surau* or men's house at **Batipuh**, construct-

Above, left: *The crafts of woodcarving are practiced in the village of Pandai Sikat.* **Above:** *Many Minang are staunch muslims.* **Right:** *The mosque at Kotobaru, near Pandai Sikat.*

ed in the aristocratic Koto Piliang style.

Just after Batipuh, turn off to the left (northeast) in the direction of Batusangkar. The road here skirts the southern flanks of Mt. Merapi, and after about 5 km a small track to the left (north) scrambles up the steep volcanic slopes to the traditional village of **Pariangan**, 850 meters above sea level.

Pariangan is set in a picturesque valley with stairways leading to traditional houses, large ponds and a royal tomb. The people here are extremely friendly. Around 4 pm, villagers drift back to their homes from the rice fields as the afternoon sun slowly recedes, casting a warm glow onto the tranquil, green-and-gold landscape. The traditional *surau* or men's house is one of the last of its kind still in use; there is a hot spring outside.

The name Pariangan derives from *para hyangan* meaning "place of the ancestors," and legend has it that this was the first village established by the Minang ancestors who descended from Merapi's peak. Numerous pieces of evidence support the claim that this is indeed one of the oldest villages in West Sumatra. A 14th-century inscription by Adityavarman can be found on a boulder overlooking the hot spring and *surau*. And the local name for this spring is "Raja's Hot Water."

Other important locations in the village include the Medan Nan Bapane ("Hot Field") —an open council ground with stone seats. In the same plot is an artificial mound called a *munggoh*, and an enormous grave over 20 meters long said to be the burial place of Tun Tejo Gerhano, the architect who designed the old council house in Tabek (see below).

A km further up from Pariangan is a field called *sawah gadang setampang baniah*—the "great paddy of the seeds." According to tradition, this was the first cultivated field in West Sumatra, and all rice grown in the area is said to have come from a single sheaf of seedlings. Across the path from here is a hill known as Bukit Seguntang, the same name used for the sacred hill in Palembang where the first Malay ancestors are said to have settled. Nothing remains, but according to tradition a stone structure once stood on the hill, subsequently destroyed by a flood.

On the way back, just before reaching the main road, stop in the village of **Tabek** to see several examples of old Minang architecture. The council hall (Balairung Sari) is believed to be the oldest building in West Sumatra.

Seven km further east you enter the village of **Dusun Tuo** ("Old Village"). Here, on the north (left) side of the road in an enclosure, is the ancient *batu batikam*—a "pierced stone" on an altar-like structure surrounded by stone ancestor seats. According to legend, the stone was pierced in a battle between two powerful Minang chiefs, Datu Ketumanggungan and Datuk Perpatih Nan Sabatang. The site has been faithfully restored. Some anthropologists have suggested that the

pierced stone is a female symbol, and might have been used in religious ceremonies. Nearby are traces of terraces, suggesting that the site once contained more structures.

A further km east is the village of **Limo Kaum** ("Five Clans"). In a low shed here are three large standing stones and several other stone objects—including a mortar and an inscription—collectively known as the Kubu Rajo. The large stones were probably back rests for stone seats. The number three is significant, for it may be connected with the ruling triumvirate of the ancient Minangkabau kingdom, and these may have been thrones for the three kings to use during audiences or ceremonies. The name Kubu Rajo may be interpreted as "Raja's Fort" or "Raja's Grave." The former is probably the correct meaning.

Another section of the site contains a number of stones set up on small terraces. One of them once bore an inscription issued by the 14th-century ruler Adityavarman, in which he compared himself to a heavenly wish-granting tree or *kalpataru*—a motif often sculpted on ancient temples in Java.

Limo Kaum also contains good examples of Minang architecture, all within walking distance. The mosque is especially famous, built in the early Sumatran-Islamic style with a five-storied roof supported by 121 huge wooden pillars, with a large pool beside.

The old royal capital

From Limo Kaum, proceed another 6 km east to **Batusangkar**, the largest town in the Tanahdatar area and the site of an early Dutch fortification, Fort van der Capellen, built in 1821 during the Paderi Wars. The council hall (*balai adat*) at the southeastern corner of the town square is built in traditional Minang style, ornately carved with designs found in local textiles. It was built in 1967.

Little can be seen of the old Dutch fort (now the town's police station), and the most vivid reminder of the colonial presence is the house of the former district chief, now the residence of the *bupati*, across the road from the council hall. In front of the *bupati's* house is a collection of bits and pieces from the past. These include another 14th-century inscription, a spout from a fountain in the form of a woman, now headless, holding her breasts from which water once poured. (Similar spouts have been found at ancient royal bathing places in East Java and Bali.) There is also a curious statue assembled from two broken figures cemented together at the

waist: the lower portion probably belonged to a female deity, while the upper part was male.

Beyond Batusangkar, visitors may make a small circuit of several important historic sites east of the town. Proceeding in a clockwise direction, thus leaving Batusangkar by the northeast, one arrives first at **Pagarruyung** —a small village 3 km away which may be reached on foot, *bemo* or horse-drawn *bendi* ($2 for the return journey). This was the site of the palace of the last Raja Alam of the Minangkabau, Sultan Arifin Muning Alam Syah. In 1815 the extremist Paderi movement attacked the royal family and massacred all but the sultan and one of his grandchildren.

No trace of the palace remains, but visitors may see several 14th-century inscriptions and other stones collected here. The inscriptions are probably from Bukit Gombak, further to the south, where other 14th-century inscriptions have also been found at a place called Batu Basurat (literally "Inscribed Stone").

Following the road south along the banks of the Selo River, the next important village is **Gudam**. A Muslim graveyard here contains unique tombstones with designs featuring a kris in a belt and other more characteristic Minangkabau shapes. According to tradition, the stones mark the burial places of Pagarruyung nobles. In nearby **Padang Magek**, however, similar stones with ornate decoration are said to have marked out a course for traditional horse racing ceremonies. Such races were still held in recent times, and probably date back to the pre-Islamic period. It is quite common for ancient stones to have been incorporated into later Islamic graves.

Further along, at **Padang Siminyak** is the famous Balai Janggo—the recently reconstructed palace of the Minangkabau ruler. A fire destroyed the old palace in 1976, but six years of construction have restored its former magnificence. This enormous rectangular building resembles a traditional *rumah gadang* but on a much larger scale. A long, wooden-pillared central hall, heavily decorated with textiles, greets the visitor. Opposite the entrance is a row of rooms. And at either end of the hall, stairways lead to upper floors where historical objects and Minang handicrafts are displayed. The guard will allow you to climb to the upper floors and can be persuaded to show you the ceramics that were salvaged after the fire. The uppermost floor provides an excellent view of the surrounding countryside.

In front of the palace stand two rice storage barns (*rankiang*). Behind is the royal bathing pool and a path that leads to the royal hunting grounds. The restoration is pleasantly devoid of gaudy coloring, imitation regalia or government propaganda, and the grounds are impeccably well kept. A small admission fee is charged. To avoid the tour groups from Bukittinggi, visit the palace in the morning or late afternoon.

From here the road crosses the Selo River, skirts the foot of Gombak Hill and returns to Batusangkar—thus completing the basic Tanahdatar tour. Rather than retracing the same route back to Bukittinggi, however, follow a scenic backroad over a pass between Mts. Merapi and Malintang, through the traditional villages of **Raorao** and **Tabatpatah**. From atop a ridge after Tabatpatah, on the other side of the pass, one has a sweeping panorama of the entire Limapuluh Kota area on a clear day—including Payakumbuh and the Harau Canyon, with shimmering rice fields and hazy mountains in the distance.

Lake Singkarak

Those with more time to spend will want to go south from Tanahdatar to Lake Singkarak —a crater lake similar in size and scenic beauty to Maninjau. From Batusangkar, a sideroad serviced by *bemos* climbs up over

the low crater wall and down to the lake, passing through the charming hilltop village of **Balimbing** (the name means "starfruit") —a traditional place with several *rumah gadang*, some said to be 300 years old and built without a single nail. The dark wood of the houses lends them an air of antiquity— inside the ceilings have been blackened by countless kitchen fires.

The road meets the shores of the lake at the town of **Umbilin**, where hotels and restaurants provide a convenient stopping-over point. It is not as peaceful as Maninjau, due to the traffic, but boats can be rented and it is still a good place for swimming, hiking and just lazing about.

A highway skirts the lakeshore leading south from Umbilin to the town of Singkarak at the lake's southern tip. Just before Singkarak a turn-off to the left (east) leads up a steep and winding road offering excellent vistas back across the lake (*bemos* go up here several times a day from Umbilin).

The road leads to a remote hilltop village known as **Sulitair**, ("Scarce Water"), where there is a huge, 64-meter *rumah gadang* containing 20 individual apartments, occupied now by just 4 families. Reminiscent of a Dayak longhouse, it is considered by local residents to represent the last material vestige of their ancestral *adat*. Young men returning home from the *rantau* must re-acquaint themselves with local custom by living in the *rumah*

ALAIN COMPOST

gadang prior to marrying one of the village's pretty maidens. The building is reputed to be 100 years old, and is erected on the site of an older house destroyed by fire.

East to Limpuluh Kota

The broad and fertile valley known as Limapuluh Kota (the "Fifty Fortified Villages") spreads out at the northern foot of Mt. Malintang (2,262 m). The largest town here is **Payakumbuh**, an administrative and market center 33 km east of Bukittinggi. The entire valley is intensively cultivated, and is scattered with scores of large megalithic stones that were mysteriously arranged and carved by an unknown prehistoric people. These remains suggest that Limapuluh Kota may have been where the first ancestors of the Minang lived.

More than 20 of these megalithic sites are found within a 20-km radius of Payakumbuh, mainly along the banks of the Sinamar River northwest of the town. A small sideroad follows the river, arriving after 13 km at the village of **Guguk**. On the right side of the road here is the old village council house or *balai adat*, and in an adjacent open space stand a number of megaliths—the tallest measuring 2.75 m. Most are typical West Sumatran menhirs—upright stones with a curving top portion said to resemble the hilt of a *kris* or the head of a bird. The precise meaning of this form is unknown; several of the stones are decorated with vine-like spirals, the symbolism of which is likewise mysterious. One menhir has an elaborate incised design that seems to be a stylized depiction of a vagina. There are 9 vertical stones, as well as 8 flat ones that may have been used as seats.

In addition to the council house site, many more stones are found scattered throughout the village. These include 26 menhirs, an unusual enclosure made of river boulders and 4 stone objects usually referred to as mortars (*lumpang batu*). Similar stones were used in more recent times to pound rice flour. These mortars represent a domestic artifact of great importance, associated with the powerful female sex (since women did the pounding), and have been incorporated into Minang folklore. Legends describe uses other than rice pounding, such as house pillar supports or stepping stones used to mount horses. The wide variety of shapes and sizes of the mortars, and the range of their decoration, indicates that they probably had still other uses.

Many more menhirs and stone objects can be found to the south of Guguk around Kuranji and Sungai Talang, as well as to the northwest in the villages of Balubus (15 km from Payakumbuh), Limbanang (20 km) and Suliki (26 km). The latter three lie along the same road and can be visited in a few hours.

From Limbanang, a track to the right leads up into a remote, bowl-shaped valley known as **Mahat**. The valley is about 5 km in diame-

ter and is ringed by steep-walled mountains where hundreds—if not thousands—of fascinating megaliths are found, including some of the most interesting carved menhirs in West Sumatra. During the colonial period, the Dutch were drawn by the valley's natural beauty and historic interest and built a government rest house here.

Why were these megaliths erected? The valley provides at least a partial clue: archaeologists have discovered skeletons beneath several of them, indicating that the stones were in some cases used as grave markers. But excavations at other sites have produced no evidence of burials. Local stories ascribe to them a role in communal feasts, or even in predicting the weather. Only the most intrepid travelers will want to make the journey to this isolated valley, as it has no accommodations and is only accessible by foot, horseback or jeep during the rainy season.

The road to Riau

Limapuluh Kota's most famous attraction lies 14 km northeast of Payakumbuh, just off the main highway leading to Pekanbaru in neighboring Riau Province. This is the stunning **Harau Canyon**—a broad geological cleft whose 100-m granite walls enclose a lush 315-ha nature reserve where one can trek through dense rainforests, splash around in a delightfully cool waterfall, and spot monkeys, butterflies and birds. The reserve is inhabit-

ed also by tigers, leopards, panthers, tapirs, deer and honey bears—but the most you are likely to see of the latter is a few tracks. There is a museum, however, displaying the animals stuffed, as well as an observation point and trails leading up into the canyon.

To get there, take the main highway from Payakumbuh 11 km north to the village of Lamaksari and turn left; the reserve is 3 km in. Snacks and drinks are sold at stalls, but bring your own food if you want something substantial. There is a small admission fee.

On your way back, detour a further 3 km north on the main road to **Kotobaru**, where excellent Minangkabau *songket* is woven. From here, one can also continue north on a much longer detour (4 hours each way) across the border with Riau to the ancient remains of **Muara Takus**. Here, in a clearing in the jungle, stands the largest ancient brick building in Sumatra—a tall stupa flanked by the ruins of several other brick sanctuaries.

The stupa has the unusual form of a tower rather than the squat bell-shape normally associated with Buddhist architecture. This brick and sandstone stupa, known as Candi Mahligai, was restored in the 1980s and the new exterior completely encases the earlier building. On the west side near the ground, an exposed part shows the visitor what the surface of the older building looked like.

Several other foundations can be seen nearby. To the west is Candi Bungsu, a platform on which stood two more stupas, and to the north is Candi Tua—originally the largest structure of all, with two stairways leading up to yet another stupa. The temples are surrounded by brick walls 74 m long on each side. An earthen rampart more than 2 km long surrounds the complex, but only three sides are distinguishable.

This mysterious site lies in a remote area, yet it must have been important—for the elaborateness of the ruins indicate that a sizeable population once lived here. There is no record of any kingdom in this area, but short inscriptions found among the ruins point to a date in the 11th or 12th century AD. A legend describes the site as the burial place of a Hindu ruler who was turned into an elephant, and wild elephants are said to return to the site on the night of every full moon to dance in homage to their departed lord.

— *John Miksic and Jay Goodfriend*

Opposite: *Lovely Lake Singkarak at sunset.*
Left: *Hundreds of mysterious megaliths lie scattered about the Payakumbuh area.*

RAFFLESIA

World's Most Magnificent Flower

What a wonderful plant is rafflesia! Several of its species have large flowers, but only *Rafflesia arnoldi* opens to a diameter of 90 cm, thus ranking as the largest flower in the world. This species is named after its discoverers, Sir Thomas Stamford Raffles and his botanist friend, Dr. Joseph Arnold, who died shortly after the discovery from a bout of malaria.

Sumatrans call it by various names—the Sun Toadstool, the Stinking Corpse Lily and Devil's Betel Box are some of the more colorful terms ascribed to rafflesia. It is the most specialized of all parasitic plants, having no stem, no leaves and no roots. Apart from the flower, the plant consists only of fungal-like strands within the stem of its host, a wild vine called *Tetrastigma*.

Parts of these strands starts to expand and small orange-brown, cabbage-like flower buds break through the bark of the vine.

These buds take one to two years to blossom; a 15 cm rafflesia bud will take 2 to 3 months to flower. Buds are more frequently seen.

When the bud opens, there issues forth a horrible stench of carrion, irresistible to the flies and beetles which swarm inside, crawling over the hidden sexual parts beneath the spiny plate in the center of the flower. One flower of each sex has to be open in the same area for successful pollination.

The flower stays in bloom only for about a week, then it withers and collapses into an unpleasant, fetid heap, with the fruits buried somewhere near the bottom. Small rodents, insects, deer or pigs, investigating this pile, may inadvertently get the seeds stuck on their feet. It seems incredible that any of these seeds could manage to find their way to the right sort of vine, where they lodge in fissures in the bark.

The Sakai people of southern Sumatra believe that an infusion of the flowers is an aphrodisiac (for men only!). The plant is also used in *jamu*, the traditional Malay herbal cures. An extract from the bud is given to women after childbirth, to shrink the womb and to restore the figure, and is widely believed to confer youth and beauty.

— *Anthony Whitten*

Below: *Inside the rafflesia, where a powerful stench attracts insects necessary for pollination.*
Left: *Tranquil Lake Maninjau.*

ALAIN COMPOST

MENTAWAI ISLANDS

Moile Moile: Be Good to Your Soul!

The Mentawai archipelago forms part of a chain of non-volcanic islands running parallel to Sumatra about 100 km off the west coast. There are four large inhabited islands in the group: Siberut (4,480 sq km), Sipora (845 sq km) and North and South Pagi (together 1,675 sq km). They are covered in dense, tropical rainforest with isolated farming settlements scattered along the river valleys.

Until quite recently, the people who live here retained many Stone Age traditions that were exceptionally archaic but nevertheless remarkably complex. Nowadays most Mentawaians are Christians. Communities which practice the old religion do still exist on Siberut, but the short-term visitor should not expect to get much more than a glimpse of the older culture, especially if he travels only to the main coastal villages on Siberut.

An archaic island culture

The inhabitants of the Mentawai Islands are descended from some of the earliest groups of peoples to have migrated to Indonesia several thousand years ago. They have preserved a neolithic Austronesian culture with some Bronze Age elements, which was virtually unaffected by subsequent Hindu, Buddhist and Islamic cultural influences. Old stone axes are still occasionally found here today (though none is still in use), and nowhere else in Indonesia has this archaic heritage been preserved so well.

The Mentawai people have neither chiefs nor slaves; instead their society is organized into clan groups consisting of about ten families living in large communal houses, called *uma*, built at irregular intervals along the rivers. The inhabitants live off the land, cultivating sago, yams, tubers and bananas. They also raise chickens and pigs and the men go hunting and the women fishing. There is no economic specialization: every man is a canoe builder, a pig farmer, a bow and arrow maker and a vegetable gardener.

The islands' remoteness meant that only at the beginning of this century did external influences begin to seep in. But when they did so, their impact was significant. Under the direction of European missionaries and colonial administrators, head-hunting and traditional religious ceremonies were forbidden.

The pace of change speeded up after Indonesian independence, when the indigenous religion was banned altogether and everyone had to embrace either Islam or Christianity. Punishment for the practice of the old religion was severe, and ritual objects were burned. The government further insisted that communal houses be constructed around a village church and school. Men were forbidden from wearing glass bead decorations and loin cloths, and teeth filing and tattooing were prohibited.

The majority of the Mentawai people became Christians at this time, learned German or Italian church melodies, built simple single-family dwellings, dressed in the modern style, and complemented their subsistence economy with products for trade. But under this veneer of conformity the old beliefs lived on, for example in secluded healing ceremonies, such as the *pangurei* "wedding celebration," in which a sick man is dressed up as a bridegroom to attract his soul back to him.

The harmonious cosmos

Traditional Mentawai beliefs hold that cre-

ation is a harmonious whole. There are spirits everywhere, and objects like trees and rocks have souls. Because they are invisible, man's activities can unwittingly disturb them —for example, a tree that is cut might fall on a forest spirit's dwelling. Before beginning any major activity, therefore, ceremonies are held to entertain and placate the spirits.

Everything—man and beast, plant and rock—has not just a soul, but also a personality. The few implements that the Mentawaians possess are made with special care to match

external form with inner essence. Compatibility is important: a man may possess an excellent hunting bow, but unless it "gets on" with him, he may frequently miss his target. Religious practices are directed at restoring harmony between man and the environment in which he lives.

Siberut Island

The island of Siberut is the largest in the group—an elongated rectangle measuring about 110 by 50 km. Dense tropical rainforest covers more than 90 percent of the island, which is quite hilly—the highest elevation being 384 m. These hills are interrupted by wide valleys, and the eastern slopes facing Sumatra drop gently to the sea. Along the coast, white coral beaches alternate with mangrove swamps, interrupted by muddy rivers. The island's two main administrative centers are here: **Sikabaluan** in the north and **Muara Siberut** in the south. The western shore forms the extreme edge of the Asian continental shelf—dropping steeply beneath a giant surf which rolls across from Africa.

Previously, the inhabitants of Siberut did not live in villages, but in longhouses or *uma* housing 5-10 families related to each other through the male line. Each family had its own section of the *uma*, as well as a field house some distance away where they raised pigs and chickens, cultivated tubers and bananas, gathered sago and fished. Today

only a few of these large communal dwellings remain; most were abandoned as a result of the policy of bringing islanders into the 20th century. In some areas in the south, however, people have built *uma* in new villages; these convey some idea of their former state.

A traditional *uma* is a village under one roof. Floor plan and usage reflect a strong community spirit. A notched trunk serves as a stairway to the front verandah. Skulls of pigs and game (monkeys, deer and wild boars), some of them carved and decorated, hang from the rafters. This verandah is a living room during the day, but at night it becomes a sleeping place for men and guests. The first inner room has a communal hearth used for ceremonial events; here dances are held. Women and children sleep in a second room, which serves in the daytime as a kitchen. To the right of the door on the entry wall of this room, there hangs the main fetish of the community, a bundle of holy plants. Each family has another, smaller field house (*sapou*) for daily activities. People often stay there for weeks to work or just to enjoy some privacy.

Life in the uma

Work is divided evenly between men and women. The men pound the marrow of the sago palm to obtain flour; taro and bananas are cultivated by women, and families own coconut trees planted along the rivers. Coconuts, rattan and other forest products are bartered for axes, bush knives, and material for mosquito nets and loin cloths. The basic diet of sago is supplemented by fish and the occasional pig or chicken. For big feasts, the men hunt game in the forest.

In the traditional *uma*, children grow up freely without constraints or formal educa-

Overleaf: *On Siberut, bodily adornments are considered pleasing to one's soul. Photo by R. Yando Zakaria.* **Opposite:** *Harvesting sago.* **Above, left:** *An* uma *longhouse.* **Above, right:** *Tattooing.*

tion. Boys and girls imitate the activities of adults in their play. Toward the end of puberty, adolescents are tattooed and their incisors chiseled to a point; then the boys start to acquire property of their own. The girls help their mothers, but only when married do they acquire responsibility and possessions.

On Siberut it is forbidden to marry within one's own kingroup. Wives are sought from a neighboring *uma*, and after the wedding the wife moves to the *uma* of her husband. These exogamous marriages are a means of establishing and maintaining relationships with other *umas*. Despite this, rivalries exist, manifesting themselves during religious feasts, when each group strives to outdo its neighbors. In former times, such rivalries often developed into open hostilities.

Help and support for the individual comes from the whole *uma*, and everyone participates equally in celebrations. However, differences do occur. As the group has no chieftain and all have equal rights, only open discussion can sort out problems. If a common solution cannot be found, one faction moves out and establishes another *uma*. This, say the elders, is how Siberut was settled.

A fragile equilibrium

The low population density of Siberut is attributable to an unhealthy climate. However, the people themselves view illness as the result of a person being in disharmony with his or her surroundings. It is their belief that everything has a soul; everything lives. One must be aware of these souls, so as not to disturb the existing equilibrium.

Things are not objects to be used at will; they allow themselves to be used. To obtain their approval one has to communicate, present offerings and adjust to their presence by modifying one's own behavior. If someone brings home a new gong, for example, he must not split coconuts—for otherwise the gong, too, would soon crack. In the house, the soul of the gong will be summoned to familiarize itself with its new home. Joint offerings are made to the gong and its companion objects. This ceremony serves to introduce the new object and placate the souls of the others, lest they feel jealous. Otherwise the souls of the things would turn against their owner and make him sick.

The aim of healing ceremonies is thus to placate and reconcile displeased souls. That is the task of the *kerei*—men skilled in a discourse with souls. The souls of men, the islanders believe, are perpetually in danger.

Souls can detach themselves from the body and wander about freely. Their adventures are the cause of dreams, and during their journeys a soul may encounter unpleasant adventures and flee to seek refuge with the ancestors. Then of course the person dies.

To counter this, the islanders say that a man should lead a life that so pleases his soul that it does not stray. The soul does not like to be hurried. The Mentawai people constantly remind each other of this with the words: *moile, moile!* ("slowly, slowly!"). By the same token, the soul does not like to be intimidated. Children are rarely scolded or forced to do something. The body that houses the soul should also be attractive, and this is one of the main reasons why the Mentawai people are fond of adornments and tattoos.

The great festival

The great *puliajiat* rituals of the *uma* stretch for weeks and are held periodically to reunite the souls of individuals with their bodies, and to purify the *uma* from danger. The house is decorated, and a feast is prepared; there is singing and dancing for several nights. At the climax of the celebrations the *kerei* sits on the front verandah and summons, in long songs, the souls of all the group's members. To entice them hither, carved birds are hung above the entrance to the house. Mentawai people call these *umat simagere*, "toys of the souls."

— *Reimar Schefold*

MENTAWAI WILDLIFE

Beautiful Song of the Bilou

Quite a number of animal species found on the Mentawai Islands are endemic, and many are also relatively archaic. This curious fact reflects an unusual geological history. About 500,000 years ago the islands were connected to Sumatra by a land bridge (via Nias and the Banyak Islands), but since that time they have been separated from the mainland by a 100-km strait of generally calm seas overlaying a 2,000-m deep submarine trench.

Both the contact and the long isolation are significant. The ancient land bridge allowed a considerable in-migration of plant and animal species, while the subsequent isolation has promoted a high degree of evolutionary divergence. By contrast, the other west Sumatran islands have either—like Simeulue—had no land bridges for at least the past 2 million years, and consequently have a very impoverished wildlife, or—like Nias—had much more recent contact so that their wildlife is quite similar to that of Sumatra.

The Mentawai Islands are thus biologically unique. Among the endemic species found here are monkeys, tree squirrels, flying squirrels, civets, frogs and reptiles, as well as an owl and other birds. Best known among them are the four species of primates. In no other part of the world are so many endemic primates found in such a small area.

Endemic primates

The most often seen (or heard) of the primates is the beautiful black gibbon *Hylobates klossii*, known in most areas of Mentawai as the *bilou*. The song of the female *bilou* has been described as "the most beautiful sound made by any land mammal," and is a thrill to hear in the forest on clear mornings. If you are very lucky, you may glimpse a female gibbon and her family hurling themselves

through the branches during the climax of the song. Another endemic, the Mentawai macaque, is superficially similar to the pig-tailed macaque found over much of Southeast Asia. It roams the forests in groups of up to 30 individuals, barking frequently to maintain contact with other individuals foraging on the ground.

The two other endemic monkeys are exceptional in their form of social organization. They are the only monkeys in the Old World to live in monogamous groups (as do gibbons and humans). The long-tailed *joja* (*Presbytis potenziani*), with its shiny black back and tail, white face-ring and throat, and dark brown belly, lives exclusively in such groups and can most often be found by following the sound of its *bagok* alarm calls, which are duets between the male and female—another unique feature.

The pig-tailed langur or *simakobu* (*Simias concolor*) generally lives in monogamous groups, but appears to form normal monkey troops of 7-15 members in the north of Siberut. The *simakobu* can be either a beautiful golden color or a slate grey, and the ratio of the two varies around the island. The species is particularly notable because it is judged to belong to a genus not known elsewhere, although it may be related to the wierd proboscis monkey that inhabits the mangrove swamps of Borneo.

—*Tony Whitten*

Left: *The great* puliajiat *ritual on Siberut, held to reunite the souls of individuals with their bodies.*
Right: *A baby* bilou. *Photo by Tony Whitten.*

PART VI

Introducing Riau

The name "Riau" once applied only to the chain of islands guarding the entrance to the Malacca Strait south and west of Singapore. In 1958, however, the unwieldy province of "Central Sumatra" which had been created during the Indonesian revolution (comprising what are now Jambi, West Sumatra and Riau) was subdivided, and a new Riau Province was created that included not only the neighboring Lingga Archipelago, but also a huge chunk of the Sumatran mainland and a few hundred remote islands lying in the South China Sea to the north of Borneo (the Natuna, Anambas, Serasan and Tambelan groups).

As a province Riau is thus an artificial creation composed of many disparate parts. Its land mass is huge (94,561 sq km—about the size of Hungary) and it comprises not only 3,214 islands and four of Sumatra's largest rivers, but the greatest expanse of tropical rainforest on the island, hundreds of vital sea lanes teeming with fish, and thousands of kilometers of sparsely-inhabited coastline. To top it off, Riau contains the most productive oil fields in Indonesia—pumping half the nation's crude, some 650,000 barrels a day.

The Riau mainland is a densely-jungled lowland formed over many millennia by alluvial deposits brought by the Rokan, Siak, Kampar and Inderagiri rivers—all of which begin high in the western Bukit Barisan range and meander some 300 to 550 km eastward to the coast. The lowlands are poorly drained, however, and are not particularly suitable for agriculture. Only about 2 million people—Malays and migrants from Java and Kalimantan—inhabit small settlements along the rivers. For the traveler this is not a particularly exciting area, as the sights are few and far between and facilities are primitive.

The Riau Islands, on the other hand, are one of Indonesia's best kept travel secrets.

Easy to reach from Singapore on fast and comfortable hydrofoils, the islands of Batam and Bintan have good facilities and beaches. They are jumping-off points, moreover, for romantic excursions by slow passenger ferry, chartered fishing boat or private yacht to a thousand tropical idylls that have changed little since the days of Joseph Conrad. This is the realm of the *orang laut* or "sea people"—former pirates and traders who have settled in villages perched on stilts above the shore.

Change is coming rapidly to some areas. Batam and Bintan are currently the scene of a multi-billion-dollar investment fever that will undoubtedly spill over to nearby islands. One has the feeling, nevertheless, that within this seemingly endless archipelago there will always be more than a few islands that manage to give the modern world the slip.

— *Eric Oey*

Overleaf: *Trikora Beach on Bintan Island.* **Left:** *A Malay woman on Singkep. Photos by Jill Gocher.*

BATAM

Singapore's Neighbor and 'Twin'

Batam is the Indonesian island just opposite Singapore—an island nation and former British colony that has blossomed in recent years to become Southeast Asia's most dynamic and prosperous economy. Batam is so close in fact—just 20 km to the southeast across a narrow strait—that the tips of Singapore's gleaming skyscrapers are visible on the horizon, and the latter's bright lights illuminate the sky at night like some futuristic film set.

Batam is only slightly smaller than Singapore, and would in fact seem to share many of the latter's geographical features—yet this sleepy, half-forgotten island was until recently considered to be of little or no value. Like so many islands in the Riau Archipelago, its porous red-clay soils were covered in thick jungle and ringed with inhospitable mangrove swamps, and its few inhabitants lived in scattered fishing villages around the coast. Many

were descended from fierce *orang laut* sea nomads and pirates who centuries ago served as sailors and fighting men in the navies of Malay kingdoms like Srivijaya and Malacca.

Batam suddenly began to take on a much greater significance in the late 1960s, however, when the head of Indonesia's oil monopoly, Pertamina, decided to develop the island as a base for its massive exploration and supply activities. The advantages of this were clear —Batam's cheap land and labor would reduce costs, while its proximity to Singapore would ensure quick access to the latter's efficient facilities and technical know-how. Following this lead, and watching with considerable envy as Singapore made rapid economic strides during the early 1970s, the Indonesian government at this time decided that Batam should in fact be developed as "another Singapore"—a regional center for industry, shipping and communications that might one day even rival the latter.

The 'Growth Triangle'

For a number of reasons, Batam's development was very slow in getting off the ground. A lack of basic infrastructure meant for many years that most things could be done more easily and cheaply in Singapore. The situation changed dramatically in the late 1980s, however, when Singapore's booming economy in effect outpaced its population growth, and this tiny island republic of 3 million peo-

ple began to experience severe labor short-ages—particularly in the labor-intensive man-ufacturing sector. All of a sudden, companies began to look to Indonesia and Malaysia, and Batam was once again mentioned as a possi-ble site for industrial development.

Much to their credit, it was Singapore's own government which took the lead in con-vincing all parties concerned that Batam could be made viable. In 1989, Singapore's deputy Prime Minister, Goh Chok Tong, pro-posed the linkage of Johor (in southern Mal-aysia), Singapore and the Riau Islands in a synergistic "Growth Triangle"—a free-trade economic zone that would benefit all three areas. In the words of Singapore's Minister for Trade: "Given the right policies and the willingness to work together, all three can prosper much more together than individual-ly." This idea was enthusiastically received and several multi-billion-dollar joint ventures between private Indonesian and government-owned Singaporean concerns were signed within the following months.

These days, Batam's idyllic tranquility is shattered by the incessant buzz of chain saws and the thud of pile-drivers as stretches of virgin jungle are cleared to make way for massive industrial estates, tourist resorts and residential towns. Thousands of Singaporeans make the quick, 25-minute hop across the straits in high-speed hydrofoils every day, and Batam seems destined to become practi-

cally an extension of its better-developed neighbor—as more and more companies move the labor-intensive portion of their operations here.

The immediate plan is that Singapore is to provide expertise and investment to establish basic infrastructure and primary ventures in industry, commerce and tourism that will enable the island to achieve a certain "critical mass" in the eyes of private investors. After that, Batam's natural advantages of cheap land, labor and energy will propel its develop-ment, and will in turn feed back into Singa-pore's own high-tech service economy.

Careful planning, huge investments

The key to Batam's success is seen in careful planning, and much of the island has already been carved up for various projects. The entire east coast is being developed into a modern container facility known as Asia Port that will accommodate ships of up to 150,000 tons. Next to it, Hang Nadim International Airport (named after a 15th-century admiral of Malacca's war fleet who ruled the island) is being expanded to handle jumbo jets.

In the center of the island, a self-contained 500-ha industrial park complete with housing estates for workers is being built—the basic

Opposite: *Batam has a well-developed road network.* **Below:** *Feverish construction work continues around the clock all over the island.*

JILL GOCHER

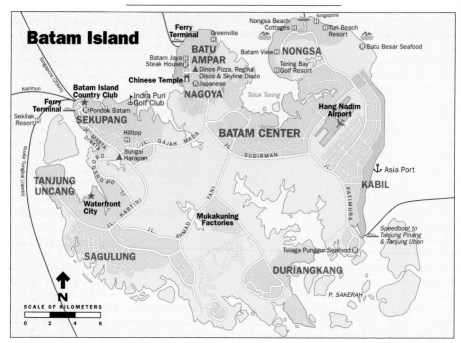

infrastructure of roads, water, sewage, tele-communications and electricity for this project alone is costing US$600 million. So far, 29 corporations, including many Japanese, American and European firms, have already set up manufacturing operations in the park's first phase (50 ha), which is now complete.

Tanjung Uncang peninsula, at the western tip of the island, will serve as a complex for the processing of timber, rubber, palm oil, tin, bauxite, petroleum and other Sumatran resources. Reservoirs and water treatment plants are in place, and an excellent network of roads crisscrosses the island.

Perhaps the jewel in the crown, however, is the planned "New Town" at Batam Centre —an entire city with office blocks, markets, shopping centers and suburban residental neighborhoods that is springing up around the beautiful bay of Teluk Tering, facing across to Singapore. This will be the island's administrative hub, with a polytechnic institute and training center planned.

Indonesian red tape is being slashed for investors, and foreigners commute from Singapore with a minimum of fuss—there are even plans afoot to start a helicopter service. Factory workers, many from the poorer regions of Indonesia such as Java, have started flooding in and live in purpose-built housing a few minutes' walk from their worksite.

Much of the capital needed to realize Batam's ambitious plans will come from abroad, and the Batam Industrial Development Board—an autonomous body that has been given a free hand by Indonesia's President Suharto—is bending over backwards to attract investors. Cash-rich firms plan to use Batam as a manufacturing base in the heart of Southeast Asia, currently the world's fastest growing region economically. A little-advertised attraction is the fact that manufacturers are able to capitalize on the Indonesian Generalized System of Preferences (GSP) allowances for export to the United States, the EEC and Japan. In 1986-7, Indonesia used less than 40 percent of its GSP allocation for the EEC, which allows 10 to 16 percent tax relief on a wide range of products.

Meanwhile, Batam is already becoming a popular tourist getaway. In 1990, more than half a million Singaporeans took the ferry across to Batam to relax, shop, eat and buy duty-free liquor and cigarettes. The island's northeast coast around Nongsa is earmarked as a massive, 350-ha tourist resort that will transform it, along with nearby Bintan, into Singapore's playground. Several luxury hotels, marinas and golf courses are already open, as is a new Singapore ferry terminal. Batam's main attraction is its hotels and resorts, but *kelong*-style seafood restaurants built on stilts over the ocean are also popular.

Batam's best known attraction, however, is Radio Ramako—a pop station whose 24-hour "Amazing Zoo" and "Coast 100" broad-

casts are much beloved by Singaporeans. Their blend of fast music and faster-talking DJs has indeed given Singapore's staid, state-controlled radio station a run for their advertisers' money, and the latter has been forced to counter with a similar 24-hour pop station called "Perfect Ten." More than 100 loyal listeners troop into Radio Ramako every day to meet the DJs and tour the modest facilities.

A day trip to Batam

Apart from the beaches and the seafood restaurants there's really not much to see and do on Batam. It is interesting, nevertheless, to drive through the jungles, visit the coastal Malay *kampungs*, and imagine what these places will all look like in a few years.

A good starting point is the main town of **Nagoya**—formerly known as Lubuk Baja ("Pirates' Waterhole") and today a busy trading centre largely populated by Chinese. It is impossible to get lost here as there are only 3 main streets; have a look around at the busy, duty-free shops and the market, then stop in at Vihara Budhi Bhakti Buddhist temple on the eastern outskirts of town, where busloads of Singaporean worshippers fill the air each day with the pungent smoke of incense.

A few km to the southeast of Nagoya is **Batam Centre**, site of a massive commercial and residential development. A drive around this beautiful bay will give you an idea of the scale of things to come. Continue on to the

northeast coast at **Batu Besar** for a seafood lunch. This is a pleasant Malay fishing village set on a sandy beach, with several seafood restaurants built on long piers out over the water. The food is excellent, though the prices are strictly Singaporean (see "Riau Practicalities"). The airport is close by and jets roar past every few minutes; after lunch, walk down the coast through swaying palms past typical Malay-style houses on stilts.

After lunch, if the weather is fine, head north to **Nongsa** for a swim on the safe, sandy beaches by the new luxury hotels. At Turi Beach Resort you can hire jet scooters, and most of the other resorts rent snorkeling equipment and windsurfers. The waters are clear and there's plenty of shade.

Late in the late afternoon, head for the ferry terminal at **Sekupang** on the northwest coast, or leave from the new Nongsa Pura terminal. If you have time, loop south across the island past the 100-year-old banyan tree just opposite the Batam Industrial Park construction site. Your final stop could be Batam's Radio Ramako station just outside Sekupang, which welcomes visitors—but leave time for Sekupang's excellent duty-free shops, which offer practically everything from Swiss Cherry Brandy at S$45 to dried anchovies (*ikan bilis*) at only S$12 a kilo!

— *Periplus Editions and Julie Heath*

Above: *One of Nongsa's fine beaches.*

BINTAN

Sleepy Island on the Edge of Change

For several centuries Bintan played a pivotal role in Malay history. It was here, in the early 16th century, that the deposed ruler of Malacca took refuge after the Portuguese had driven him from his city. The inhabitants of Bintan at this time were not in fact Malays, but *orang laut* sea nomads who were fiercely loyal to the king. Thereafter the court moved several times—to Johor and to Lingga—but a branch of the royal family eventually returned to settle on Pulau Penyengat, a tiny island just off the southwest coast of Bintan. This was where, at the beginning of the 19th century, Thomas Stamford Raffles sought and received permission to lease the nearby island of Singapore for the British crown.

In the 19th century, Penyengat became an important center for Malay and Islamic scholarship. Imams from faraway Mecca taught in the royal mosque, and over 60 major works of Malay literature were composed here. Even today, something of the royal atmosphere remains in these tiny islands, and it is not difficult to imagine oneself transported back in time a hundred years or more to a slower, more elegant age.

Like neighboring Batam, Bintan is now the focus of multi-billion-dollar development schemes that are designed to drag the island into the 21st century within the next few years. These include a huge industrial park and a mega-resort with luxury hotels and 10 golf courses. Direct ferry services from Singapore to the new ferry terminal on the north coast started in October 1994 when the first of the new tourism developments opened. This cuts traveling time to an hour. Believe it or not, some 7.4 million tourists are projected to visit Bintan by the year 2000! It will be some years before the dream becomes reality, however, although site planning and construction is well under way on the secluded northern beaches. So far, the Bintan you see today is much as it has been for centuries—a rustic and sparsely-inhabited island with a few scattered fishing villages and old Chinese trading settlements on the coast.

Tanjung Pinang

The largest town and main point of entry on Bintan is Tanjung Pinang ("Areca Palm Cape") —a picturesque, predominantly Chinese trading community that spreads across low hills

bordering a sheltered bay on the island's southwestern shore. This is a delightful place to visit, if only on a weekend jaunt from Singapore. You can make a leisurely inspection of the town on foot—starting from the clock tower in the middle of Jl. Merdeka, Tanjung Pinang's main street.

Shipping agents, goldsmiths, restaurants and cassette shops line both sides of this broad and busy avenue. Directly opposite the clock tower is Vihara Bhatra Sasana temple, featuring a statue of Kuan Yin—the Chinese

goddess of mercy—in the central altar. From the temple, walk north along Jl. Pasar past the central market place; villagers come in from the countryside on weekends to sell pots of wild honey here—advertised by cages full of angry, buzzing bees—as well as seasonal fruits and vegetables. Sometimes fire eaters selling patent medicines will put on a show for the crowd.

Duck into a rabbit warren of little alleyways to your right. This is Pasar Baru, the "New Market," where tiny stalls sell clothes and plastic household goods. At the back, next to the water's edge, is a huge fish market where boats unload their daily catch of swordfish, sharks, groupers, squids, prawns, shellfish and dark, plump mangrove crabs.

Heading further north on Jl. Pasar, the street becomes an elevated walkway leading through a maze of wooden houses and shops built on stilts out over the mouth of the Riau River. Little gangways lead off to scores of houses on either side, and at high tide the sea rushes in so that you are standing just above the surface of the water. On both sides are small provision shops and foodstalls selling dried salted fish, prawns, crackers, clothing and steaming bowls of Chinese noodles; at the end of the walkway is Pelantar II pier.

Just before the end, duck down a narrow gangway to your left that leads to a small Chinese temple. Color photographs of visiting trance mediums piercing themselves with

swords and spike balls cover one wall of the temple. Just in front is an open-air theater for Chinese opera performances that perches out over the harbor. Beneath the opera stage you can see brightly-painted dragon boats that are brought out once a year for the midsummer festival races.

At the end of the main pier (Pelantar II), you can catch a sampan or motorboat across the wide mouth of the Riau River to **Senggarang**, visible just opposite. You disembark here at the end of a long jetty in Kampung Cina leading to long walkways that run for several km and connect hundreds of houses built on stilts above the water. Most of the houses are inhabited by Teochew Chinese; you can peek in and see the family altars as you walk gingerly down the long and rotting planks to a number of shops at the end.

Once onto dry land, turn left and follow a concrete pathway to the Aw clan house—the ruins of a 2-story temple whose crumbling walls are completely suspended in mid-air— held there by the aerial roots of an ancient banyan tree. Set directly beneath the ruins is a new concrete box structure that has been erected by a wealthy Aw clansman from Medan to house the ancestral altar.

Continue along this same path past a salt warehouse to Vihara Dharma Sasana, a compex of three temples set side-by-side facing the estuary. The temple in the middle has an ornate roof crowned by a pair of dragons and is said to be 200 years old; unfortunately, its beautiful wooden doors have been crudely repainted during a recent restoration. In the hallway is a tank of live turtles, and a stone tiger leaps out of the wall. The temple has an air of austere serenity, in contrast to the newer and more cluttered temple to its right.

Opposite: *Sunset over Tanjung Pinang harbor.*
Above, left: *Sampans shuttle passengers from Tanjung Pinang to Senggarang and Penyengat.*
Above: *Tanjung Pinang street scene.*

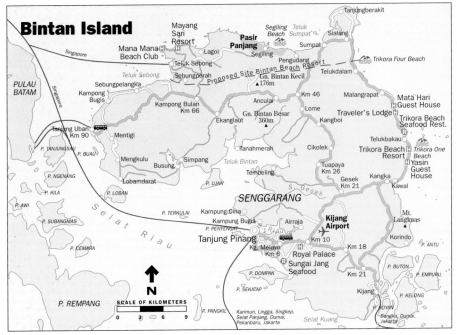

The smallest of the three shrines is dedicated to Toa Pek Kong, the deity of the soil who is synonymous with luck; people come here to make offerings before building a house.

Back in Tanjung Pinang, stroll up to the top of the hill in the late afternoon—to the colonial-style Catholic Church on Jl. Diponegoro. From here, you obtain a splendid view out across the town and over the bay to Penyengat. On the shore just below the hill is Jl. Hang Tuah—a favorite spot for local residents to take in the evening air in a small park with a sculpture of a giant seashell and sea cows (*dugongs*) cast out of concrete. Watch the sun set over Penyengat with a cold drink and *sate* at the peaceful little night market near the harbor.

Touring the island

To the east of Tanjung Pinang town, at **Kampung Melayu** (km 6), stop and pay homage to the grave of Sultan Sulaiman, the first ruler of the restored 18th-century Bugis-Malay kingdom. From here you can walk down to the water's edge and hire a sampan to take you up the **Riau River** ($10 for a half day) to the graves of Daeng Marewah and Daeng Cellak—Bugis brothers from Sulawesi who helped recapture the kingdom from Raja Kecil, a Minangkabau adventurer. The boatmen know all the sites; stop along the way at Kota Piring ("Plate Fort") on a tiny island in midstream—built in the 18th century by the Bugis ruler, Raja Haji. The popular name derives from the many Chinese plates that were once set into the walls; little remains today apart from a few broken embankments. Bring hats, drinks and plenty of sunblock.

About an hour by minibus, 35 km east of Tanjung Pinang on a good, surfaced road are the white sands of **Trikora Beach**. Stretching for 30 km up and down the eastern coast of Bintan, this series of lovely beaches boasts a few simple guesthouses and one more upmarket resort. During the week the beaches are completely deserted; on Saturday afternoons small groups of noisy Singaporeans troop in to the beaches at Trikora Empat (Four), followed on Sunday mornings by the local crowd from Tanjung Pinang. By early Sunday afternoon, however, the crowds disperse and the beach is tranquil again. The other beaches remain quiet.

Trikora actually has four main beaches that are numbered from south to north. Of these, Trikora Four is the last one as you travel up the coast, and it is particularly recommended— that's why it's busy at weekends. After lunching at the Trikora Beach Restaurant (Rumah Makan Pantai Trikora) in **Telukbakau**, continue up the main road until you reach a sweeping, sandy-white shoreline stretching as far as the eye can see—framed by swaying palms and foaming breakers. Wonderfully safe for children, the bottom slopes out very gradually so that 50 feet from

shore you are only in up to your waist, although the water gets deeper the further up the coast you travel.

Kuta Beach has *nothing* on this place. Small stalls by the creek sell fresh coconuts, snacks and fruits, as well as simple meals on weekends. An occasional drawback, though, is sand fleas, which can leave bites lasting for days—but a smelly concoction of coconut oil and onions is said to keep them (and your companions) at bay. With more time on your hands, you can continue along this road to the small village of **Berakit**, or turn off left and head for **Pasir Panjang** on the north coast. This is where the huge, multi-billion-dollar beach resort is currently under construction. This road continues round to the small, busy market town of Tanjung Uban, near the new Singapore ferry terminal. Just along the coast from the new terminal, at **Teluk Tondang**, the first, small new resorts have already opened.

On the way back, cut inland via the main road, which skirts around **Mt. Bintan Besar** —the island's highest point at 371 m. Several historical and legendary figures are believed buried here, including Wan Empok and Wan Malini—two old widows whose rice harvest turned to gold when the first Malay ruler descended atop the hill. Hang Nadim, the famous 15th century Malay admiral, is also said to be buried here. A guide can be hired locally if you want to climb the hill, which is rather overgrown with secondary jungle and has a trail that is difficult to follow. The ascent takes about an hour if you are fit; legend has it that a dragon awaits on the summit. Watch out for leeches.

Offshore islands

From Tanjung Pinang you can catch ferries to the neighboring islands. Rempang and Galang are two sizeable islands to the south and west of Tanjung Pinang. Both were used after WW II as detention centers for Japanese soldiers, who complained bitterly about the Robinson Crusoe-like conditions. Today Galang is an off-limits camp for Vietnamese boat people, administered by the UN. Pulau Mantang, south of Bintan, is home to several hundred *orang laut*, many of whom still lead a semi-nomadic existence. Buton (named after the Sultanate of Buton in southeast Sulawesi), Siulung and Kelong are inhabited by a few Malay-Bugis families who depend on the sea for their livelihood.

After days or even weeks exploring these islands, where things have changed so little over the past century, it is quite a shock to crossover the narrow straits to gleaming, modern Singapore. It's hard to imagine that this too was but another island dotted with tiny fishing villages not very long ago.

— *Periplus Editions and Julie Heath*

Above: *The Chinese temples at Senggarang.*

PULAU PENYENGAT

Tiny Cultural Capital of the Malay World

Pulau Penyengat ("Wasp Island") is a sliver of an island out in the bay just opposite Tanjung Pinang. During the 19th century this tiny island—just 2,500 m by 750 m—was home to about 9,000 people and became for a time the cultural capital of the Malay world. Some 60 literary works were composed here, including the famous *Tuhfat al-Nafis*, a Bugis-Malay history by Raja Ali Haji, and the island's rulers were famed throughout the region for their Islamic piety and learning.

In the late 18th century Penyengat was an outpost in defensive works thrown up around Bintan by a Bugis viceroy known as Raja Haji. In this period the Malay sultanate of Johor was controlled by a line of Bugis rulers who had usurped the throne and were absorbing other Bugis into the Malay elite through marriage and acculturation. In 1804 the Johor ruler, Sultan Mahmud, gave Penyengat to his Bugis wife, Raja Hamidah, as part of her dowry. In doing so, he effectively divided the island realm in two—her son thereafter ruled the Riau Islands from Penyengat, while his half-brother ruled in Lingga to the south.

It was this division between rival brothers in Lingga and Penyengat that was so cleverly exploited by Raffles in 1819. In return for the protection of the British crown and a sizeable stipend, Raffles convinced the Penyengat prince to grant him the island of Singapore in perpetuity. Partly as a result, the period that followed was a "Golden Age" for Penyengat. Ruled by a sophisticated Bugis elite and supported financially and politically by the British, Penyengat drew upon the rich Muslim Malay cultural heritage and attracted scholars from as far away as Mecca.

About 2,000 Malays now live on Penyengat, many of them tracing their ancestry back to the Bugis-Malay nobility of the 18th and 19th centuries. This is a fascinating place to visit—not only to view the lovely mosque and the remains of several 19th-century colonial-style mansions that reflect the prosperity of the island's former rulers, but also to breathe in the relaxed air of aristocratic Malay village life. A network of paved pathways crisscrosses the island, and with a bit of imagination you may think you have stepped into a time warp as you stroll around the island.

Although the main settlements in the 19th century were on the far side of Penyengat,

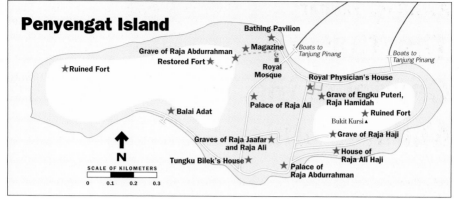

Penyengat Island

Bathing Pavilion

★ Magazine

Boats to Tanjung Pinang

Boats to Tanjung Pinang

Grave of Raja Abdurrahman ★

Restored Fort ★

★ Ruined Fort

Royal Mosque

Royal Physician's House

★ Grave of Engku Puteri, Raja Hamidah

★ Balai Adat

★ Palace of Raja Ali

★ Ruined Fort

Bukit Kursi ▲

★ Grave of Raja Haji

N

SCALE OF KILOMETERS

0   0.1   0.2   0.3

Graves of Raja Jaafar ★ and Raja Ali

Tungku Bilek's House ★

★ House of Raja Ali Haji

★ Palace of Raja Abdurrahman

facing away from Tanjung Pinang, today they face the town and may be reached in 15 minutes by motorized sampan from Tanjung Pinang's main pier. Late afternoon is the best time to visit, as it can be extremely hot at midday. Moreover, the afternoon sun casts a warm, romantic glow over the ruins and the mosque that makes them even more appealing. Start around 3:00 pm and allow several hours to walk around the island.

A walking tour

There are two main piers on Penyengat—ask to be dropped at the one to the left (east). At the end of the pier, a path to the right leads through an attractive *kampung* bordering the shoreline; unfortunately, many of the charming wooden houses are now being replaced by whitewashed concrete ones. A few hundred meters down on the left is a path leading to the covered grave of Engku Puteri, also known as Raja Hamidah—the original Bugis "owner" of Pulau Penyengat. Her grave is considered *keramat* (miracle working) and is visited by people who ask for help or make a wish by tying a yellow cloth over the headstone (yellow is the color of Malay royalty).

Buried outside the mausoleum is the 19th-century scholar and historian, Raja Ali Haji, a grandson of Raja Haji and author of the *Tuhfat al-Nafis* ("The Precious Gift"), a comprehensive history of the Malay world from the 17th to 19th centuries that served to justify the usurpation of the Malay throne by his Bugis ancestors. He is also well-known on Penyengat for his *gurindam duabelas*, 12 short poems of Islamic inspiration.

Return to the main path and continue on past the ruins of the court physician's house (only the outer walls remain). Turn left here onto a path which leads across the island, and left again to climb up Bukit Kursi ("Chair Hill"). On top of the hill is the grave of Raja

Haji, who controlled this area in the 18th century but was killed at Malacca by the Dutch in 1784. His remains were allowed to be brought back for burial in the 19th century, on condition that the grave was not to become a pilgrimage site. The grave of a revered Muslim scholar, Habib Syaik, was therefore placed alongside it so that Raja Haji's grave could be visited without arousing suspicion. Near to the tomb is an authentic 18th-century Bugis gravestone shaped like a huge egg.

Continue on to the southern shore of the island, to have a look at the remains of Raja Abdurrahman's palace. To the east is the former house of Raja Ali Haji, while to the west you will find a 2-story mansion which once belonged to Tungku Bilek ("Lady Room"), so-named because she spent all her time in her room. It stands forlornly in a compound by the sea and looks like an English country home, complete with wrought-iron decoration above the main gate. Further west you pass the new Balai Adat cultural hall used on ceremonial occasions, and a small fishing village. Facing the open sea to the south, this is where the island's 19th century inhabitants lived; at a later date the Dutch compelled the rulers to move to the Tanjung Pinang side, where they could keep a closer eye on them.

Walk back to the north shore from here along the main path which crosses the island past Raja Ali's palace. Make a slight detour along the way to visit the graves of Raja Jaafar and his son, Raja Ali, who is remembered for his strict adherence to Islam. He forbade gambling and cockfighting, the mixing of unmarried men and women, and the wearing of gold and silk. He paid visiting religious scholars to teach at the mosque, and even instituted a dawn watch to ensure that people arose for morning prayers. His covered grave,

Opposite: *Malay houses lining Penyengat's shore.*

painted a pale yellow, has a tranquil atmosphere, with two water tanks outside.

Raja Ali's palace and mosque

The stately palace of Raja Ali further down this path has fallen into ruin and been overgrown by jungle, but is slowly being restored. The southern entrance has a spendid split gate with huge swirls faintly visible on the sides incorporating European, Arabic, Javanese and Indonesian motifs. A canal once lead up here from the sea, but was filled in to prevent mosquitoes. You can climb around the grounds and up the guard tower for a view, but be careful not to fall into the royal loo!

Walk out of the gates and on to the yellow-and-green Royal Mosque at the end of the lane. Completed in 1844, the mosque is supported inside (in the Javanese style) by four huge pillars and has four Moghul minarets, reached by steeply-winding staircases. The roof has 13 cupolas that look like they belong on a European castle, and from a distance the entire complex looks a bit like the palace of Snow White at Disneyland.

Thousands of egg whites were mixed with lime to produce the fine cement that the mosque is constructed of. The magnificently carved cupboards at the entrance contain a valuable library of Islamic books from India, Cairo, Mecca and Medina. A beautiful 17th century Quran is displayed in a glass case; notice the glass chandelier and the intricately carved *mimbar* or pulpit in the main chamber. This mosque was an important center of Muslim Malay learning in the 19th century. (Be modestly dressed when entering—wear long trousers or skirts; no bare arms.)

A small path to the right of the mosque ends at the communal well. To your left here is an attractive, whitewashed stone bathing pavilion. If no one is using it, peep inside to see the well and the stone seats. Then return to the mosque and turn right up a broad, leafy path just after the shops. A hundred meters up on your right you will find an 18th-century powder magazine in whitewashed stone, looking like a small jail. This exquisite building was used to store gunpowder for the island's three forts.

Walk farther up the hill to a large cemetery and look for the tomb of Raja Abdurrahman, the 5th Yamtuan Muda (Bugis viceroy), who originally commissioned the building of the mosque. Continue up the steps on the left hand side of the cemetery and you arrive at an impressive stone fort. This was built in the late 18th century by Raja Haji to fend off a Dutch attack on the Riau River in 1873. Two cannon found during the recent restorations greet the visitor. The fort offers a splendid view of Bintan and the straits to the east. From here it is a short walk back to the pier by the mosque, for the 15-minute boat trip back to Tanjung Pinang.

— Periplus Editions

KARIMUN

Westernmost Island in the Riau Chain

Karimun is a languid, out-of-the-way island with a colorful past. During the Srivijaya period (7th to 13th centuries) and under the later sultanate of Malacca (1400-1511) it was a strategic base occupied by boat-dwelling *orang laut* who helped the Malay ruler control access to the straits. During the 18th and 19th centuries, Karimun was occasionally claimed by those wishing to challenge the authority of Riau's kings. A Minangkabau *lebai* (mosque official) laid claim to it in the latter part of the 18th century, pompously behaving like "an independent sovereign." Sultan Husein of Singapore sent his people here to mine tin in the 1820s, but under the terms of an 1824 treaty between the Dutch and the British, the island reverted to Dutch rule and his men were forced to return home.

Visiting Karimun

Karimun lies about 60 km due west of Batam and is not on any travel itineraries. There's little to do here apart from wandering about the main town of Tanjung Balai, or exploring the lush countryside. Much of the island is hilly and covered in jungle, making a mountain bike one of the most practical and enjoyable ways of getting about. If you don't have a bike, the next best way to get around is on ancient, swaying buses which ply the island's bumpy tracks. The buses cover just the populated southern part of the island; to travel up north means hiring a car and driver.

Tanjung Balai is the main entry point—a pleasant little town on the southeastern tip of the island. Like many other trading towns in the Riau Islands, it is largely populated by Teochew Chinese. The island's main road runs west of here along the coast past a secluded cove to **Meral**, site of an imposing Chinese clan house, now crumbling with age. From Meral, the road continues to **Pantai**

Pelawan, a sandy beach on the west coast, through scattered village settlements and clove gardens set in rolling, forest-clad hills. Carpets of cloves are laid out to dry in the sun by the roadside and their sweet smell hangs in the air. The cloves vary in color from lime green to rust brown, depending on the stage of drying.

As Karimun guards the southern entrance to Asia's most important waterway, it is not surprising that an ancient Sanskrit inscription has been found. The inscription is carved on a large granite outcropping at **Pasir Panjang** on the island's northwest coast, and is unusually cryptic. It simply reads: "The illustrious feet of the illustrious Gautama, the Mahayanist, who set the sphere in motion." This has been taken to refer to an armillary sphere —an instrument used to determine the position of the planets—supposedly given to a local *orang laut* chief named Gautama as a sign of favor by the ruler of Malayu (Jambi) or Srivijaya (Palembang). In fact the inscription is more likely a piece of ancient graffiti left by a passing Buddhist monk, and simply refers to Gautama Buddha, founder of the Buddhist religion. The Buddha's "footsteps" are said to ascend the rock to the left of the inscription in a series of natural, water-worn indentations. Even today the steps are venerated by *orang laut* who bring offerings of food and white flags here.

— *Periplus Editions*

Left: *The royal mosque on Pulau Penyengat.*
Right: *A woman in the Tanjung Balai market.*

LINGGA ARCHIPELAGO

Enchanting Islands to the South

The Lingga Archipelago is a scattered group of islands that straddles the equator some 50 to 150 kilometers south of Batam and Bintan —about 10 hrs from Tanjung Pinang by slow ferry. The two main islands are Lingga and Singkep; to their north lie a number of smaller ones, of which Sebangka and Bakung are the largest. These make the perfect getaway for diehard romantics: few people here speak English and the foreign visitors you meet can be counted on the fingers of one hand.

The boat ride to Dabo on Singkep Island —the main port of call in the Lingga group— is a particularly enchanting one. The ferry leaves Tanjung Pinang in the late morning and never leaves sight of land as it weaves in and out amongst countless isles set in a calm, shallow sea. Isolated *kelongs*—fishing huts on stilts—jut far out into the ocean; beneath them are huge suspended traps. Scattered

houses, often little more than a few planks, cling to the water's edge and break the monotony of an endless series of tiny, sandy coves with gently swaying palms. Late in the afternoon come the first hazy views of Mt. Daik, a large mountain on Lingga Island that has three jagged teeth at its summit, one of which appears to have broken off at the base. Visible from afar, the mountain is immortalized as a symbol of permanency in Malay poetry, and the island of Lingga actually gets its name from Mt. Daik's remarkable profile (*linggam* means phallus in Sanskrit).

As the evening lengthens, the sea turns a deeper steel blue and the setting sun illuminates a sky filled with ragged grey and white clouds. The boat chugs onward past darkening islands with rocky, jungle-clad shores. Small fires glimmer in the fields behind the settlements, and the muezzin's call to prayer drifts faintly across the water. Darkness falls suddenly—you are now just minutes from the equator—and the houses onshore become twinkling islands of indistinct light.

Visiting Singkep and Lingga

Singkep is a small, flat island pockmarked with huge open-cast tin mines that have been worked now for a century and a half and are all but exhausted. The main town of **Dabo** lies at the foot of a steep hill which makes for a pleasant climb in the early morning. The vegetable and fish markets are close to the

harbor and are also best visited early in the morning, when local fishing boats disgorge their catch. Pantai Batu Bedaun, a pretty white-sand beach fringed with palms, is an easy 4-km motorcycle ride south of the town.

The neighboring island of Lingga was the home of Sultan Mahmud, the last effective ruler of the Malay Riau sultanate, who moved his court here in the early 19th century because he feared Dutch retaliation for a pirate attack that he had instigated. The island is lush and spacious, dominated by the towering

and jagged peak of Mt. Daik (1,164 m).

The open-sea crossing in a small boat from Dabo to **Daik** is exhilarating—you are tossed and sprayed by foaming waves. The journey ends in a muddy creek which winds with mysterious intent up through a dense mangrove swamp. The town itself is like something straight out of a Joseph Conrad novel, with little wooden houses that cling precariously to the riverbank.

An hour and a half to the north of Daik on foot are the remains of Sultan Mahmud's palace, which was built a considerable distance from the sea so as to be protected from frequent piratical raids. The island was formerly defended by several earth-and-stone forts bristling with cannon. The best time to visit the palace is the early morning, unless you don't mind the midday heat.

To one side of the *camat* district offices as you leave the town are two huge bronze cannons which date from the late 18th century. The one on the left is *pecah piring* ("the plate breaker") while the one on the right is *padam pelita* ("the lamp extinguisher"). Both names refer to the cannons' fierce reports when fired. A flag in front of the offices flies from a pole set in a cast-iron base bearing the inscription: "W. Macfarlane and Co. Saracen Foundry Glasgow."

Further out of town is Mesjid Jamik, the royal mosque, which is even older than the one on Penyengat. The floor of the mosque is made of cool white marble, and the great drum which hangs at the entrance dates from the 19th century. Inside is a beautifully carved *mimbar* produced by the same craftsman who made the one at Penyengat. The story goes that he was later put to death so that no other ruler could own such a beautiful piece of work. Behind the mosque is the grave of Sultan Mahmud, which is still visited by those seeking his *berkat* (blessings).

The path to the palace crosses a cool mountain stream with a deep pool, just perfect for a midday swim after the long, hot walk from town. Further down the trail on the left is Bukit Cengkeh ("Clove Hill"), on whose serene and tranquil summit lie the graves of later Malay rulers. The path continues along the old road, now barely visible under the undergrowth, to Robat—site of a Bugis nobleman's grave that is surrounded by an iron fence and partly roofed.

After passing through thick undergrowth the trail brings you at last to the palace site at Damnah. The last sultan to inhabit this place, Abdul Rahman, was deposed by the Dutch in 1911 and died in Singapore in 1930. The palace was built entirely of wood, and only the foundations and the elegant circular stone staircases remain. In front of the foundations is the vegetation-clad remains of the *bal-airong*, a pavilion where the ruler received visitors. At the rear is a key-shaped royal squat toilet complete with stone-lined cess pit, and nearby are the foundations of a huge harem the sultan was building at the time of his ouster. According to the Dutch, Abdul Rahman was a "sensual and extravagant" sort; a sign, in Indonesian, simply announces these as the "44 unfinished rooms."

— *Periplus Editions*

Opposite: *Muslim Malay residents of Dabo, on Singkep Island.* **Above, left:** *The enchanting 10-hour ferry ride from Tanjung Pinang to Dabo.* **Above, right:** *The village of Daik on Lingga.*

MAINLAND RIAU

Rainforests, Rivers and Malay Villages

Mainland Riau, with its three great rivers—the Indragiri, Kampar and Siak—is way off the beaten tourist track. Initiative, time and a working knowledge of Indonesian are essential. While there is a fair system of roads (the best link the city to the harbor at Dumai, to Rengat and on to Jambi), the Trans-Sumatran Highway bypasses the province and travel in most areas is still by riverboat. This is a slow process and creature comforts are few, but you get to explore seldom-visited villages offering glimpses of traditional Malay life.

The Siak palace

Riau Province is proud of its historical role in the development of Malay culture. There are many beautiful mosques and important grave sites, but most will interest only Malay visitors. The old royal palace at **Siak Sri Inderapura** is definitely worth a visit. The journey downriver by speedboat takes two hours and the return trip by bus or taxi another three hours; you can also stay overnight here in a small, simple *losmen* built over the river (see "Practicalities").

The palace was built in 1889 by Sultan Abdul Jalil Syafuddin, the 11th of 12 sultans who ruled Siak from 1725 to 1945. Moorish arches and minarets give the palace a strong Indian Moghul look, as was the style in colonial times. The palace was refurbished in 1989, exactly a century after its construction, and the large front lawn and main building are meticulously maintained. Although the gold crown and the sacred *kris* have been removed to Jakarta's national museum, the rest of the furnishings are still there. Life size figures of the sultan and his courtiers sit in the reception area. Large photographs of the last sultans—oriental potentates who formed part of the Dutch establishment—decorate the walls. Much of the decor is European. A big attraction is the large German music player, said to be one of only two left in the world, whose perforated metal disks tinkle Beethoven, Mozart and Strauss tunes which vibrate wonderfully throughout the palace.

West to Bukittinggi

If you are traveling west of Pekanbaru on the main road to Bukittinggi you can stop at **Air Tiris**, near Bangkinang on the Kampar River, to have a look at the Mesjid Jamik mosque.

Built without nails in 1901, this multi-tiered wooden structure has ornate carvings. Sagging with age, it is now reinforced with nails and the original shingled roof has been replaced by corrugated metal sheets. Outside the mosque is a large, mysterious stone that is said to move around under its own power.

Further west, on the border with West Sumatra about 135 km from Pekanbaru, are the ruins of **Muara Takus**. It is said that this ancient city was so large that a cat could wander from roof to roof for three months before

reaching the last house. The ruins, which are scattered across several square kilometers, date from the 11th or 12th century and were surrounded entirely by an earthen wall. The best preserved building is the tall, slender Mahligai stupa, which has been completely restored. The temples of Muara Takus are probably royal graves; it is said that the last ruler was transformed into an elephant, and when the moon is full, his descendants gather to pay homage to their departed ancestor. (See "Minang Highlands" in WEST SUMATRA.)

Jungle wildlife

The vast rainforests of Riau are a haven for animals, though their habitats are increasingly threatened by logging and plantations. It is estimated there are between 1,100 and 1,700 elephants and 100 to 200 tigers, plus a few hundred rare Sumatran rhinos. All of these animals, however, have developed a very healthy fear of humans. Your best chance of seeing elephants in the wild is to visit remote Danau Pulau Besar and Bawah to the south of Siak Sri Inderapura. You can get there during the dry season by chartered jeep. Pulau Berke, a small island at the mouth of the Rokan River opposite Bagansiapiapi, is home to a large variety of birds. You can get to Pulau Berke by road or by boat from Dumai.

It is also possible to see a fair amount of wildlife in the 2,000-ha protected forest of **Bukit Suligi Reserve**, at the western edge

of the province near the source of the Siak River. This is a field-training camp for forestry students from around Sumatra, with dorm-style accommodations for young visitors and rooms for married couples. There is abundant wildlife in the reserve—tapirs, honey bears, deer, boars, civet cats and the odd tiger. More commonly seen are monkeys. In the dense forests it is also possible to see argus pheasants, and on the edges of the swamps, wild pigs and deer come to graze on rattan fruits ripped down by elephants. Birds include hornbills, mynas and jungle fowl. Early mornings and late afternoons are the best times for seeing the animals.

Surfing the Kampar River

Under the pull of the full moon, giant tidal waves sweep 60 to 70 km up the Kampar River, from Ketam Island to Kuala Panduk village. The waves can reach 2 m high, rushing upriver for three hours before running out of steam. (See Somerset Maugham's description of a similar tidal wave in *Borneo Stories*.) Often six or seven consecutive waves appear like a snake slithering up the river. The waves are low near the mouth and rear up as the river narrows. A fearsome roar and misty spray accompanies these *bono* (the local name for the waves), and young men sometimes "surf" them in small canoes, swept along at 10 knots. The *bono* can best be viewed from Teluk Meranti village, about 8 hrs down the Kampar from Pangkalanbaru, 20 km south of Pekanbaru. There is a smaller *bono* on the lower reaches of the Rokan River, up from Bagansiapiapi. This *bono* is considered a weaker female force while the larger one on the Kampar is male: the two are supposed to merge somewhere far inland.

— *Kal Muller*

Opposite: *Logs bound for Pekanbaru's huge plywood mills.* **Above, left:** *A local riverboat.* **Above, right:** *The palace at Siak Sri Inderapura.*

PART VII

Introducing Jambi

The sparsely-inhabited province of Jambi comprises a lowland basin of dense jungles, peat bogs and swamps about the size of Switzerland (53,435 sq km)—all of it drained by a single river system, the mighty Batang Hari and its tributaries. The latter is Sumatra's longest river, "a cruel, whitehot pool of fire" that rises on the slopes of Mt. Rasam (2,585 m) in West Sumatra and snakes eastward for some 800 km to the Straits of Malacca. The river's major tributaries—the Tebo, Tabir, Merangin, Tembesi and Asai—pass through gold-bearing rocks yielding tiny gold granules after heavy rains. People still pan for gold here, and the fabled Svarnabhumi ("Land of Gold") of classical Indian texts may have referred to these upriver regions.

The Batang Hari estuary was the site of an ancient port known as Malayu. Early 7th century Chinese sources indicate that a ruler with 5,000 troops lived here, and by the late 7th century the trade had developed sufficiently to attract the unwelcome attention of nearby Srivijaya (Palembang). In 686, Srivijaya conquered Malayu.

By the early 10th century, a vast complex of Hindu-Buddhist shrines, tanks and canals arose at Muara Jambi, 26 km downstream from the present-day capital. After an Indian attack on Srivijaya in 1025, Malayu reasserted itself for a time, but then came under Javanese domination after 1275. Remnants of the ancient court appear to have moved upriver, to the western highlands, and place names with Buddhist associations are still common in the Kerinci area. The name Malayu itself probably means "hill people" (from the south Indian words *mala* "hill" and *ur* "people"), and Indian influence is evident also in the name of Jambi's greatest river—Hari being an avatar of the Indian god Vishnu.

Islam established itself at Jambi in the 16th century. According to legend, the sultanate was founded by a Turk with the curious Malay title of Paduka Berhala ("His Excellency the Idol"). His son, Orang Kaya Hitam ("The Black Aristocrat"), threw off the yoke of Javanese rule just as Dutch traders appeared on the scene, in the early 1600s.

Dutch relations with Jambi were never very smooth. In 1707 they established a post at the mouth of the Batang Hari to control the pepper trade, but were driven out in 1734. Following the treaty of 1833 this post was reoccupied, but not until 1901 was the area placed under direct Dutch rule, and military action in the hinterland continued until 1916.

Today Jambi's booming economy is based on forestry and plantation agriculture. Products include timber, plywood, rubber, palm oil, copra, coffee and tea. Jambi's 2 million inhabitants are very mixed, concentrated in a few major towns along the rivers. About 1,000 Kubu people inhabit the forests, steadfastly resisting attempts to settle them into permanent communities (see "The Kubu").

Apart from a few fertile highland areas in the far west, Jambi consists of low undulating hills, peaty plains and swamps near the coast. The lowlands are only moderately fertile and receive heavy rainfall throughout the year, making them ill-suited for food crops. Jambi imports much of its rice from Riau and Java.

Jambi's rainforests once abounded in wildlife. Today the bears, deer, elephants, tapirs, tigers and other species are threatened by encroaching forestry concessions, oil palm plantations and transmigration settlements. There are two major reserves: the Kerinci-Seblat National Park in the west (40 percent of which lies in Jambi) and a small, swampy coastal area known as Kuala Berbak, 3 hours downstream from Jambi town. Here, on a branch of the Batang Hari, migrating birds pause to rest between October and December.
— *E. Edwards McKinnon*

Overleaf: *Dense jungle around Lake Kerinci.*
Opposite: *A coconut harvester and his well-trained assistant. Both photos by Alain Compost.*

THE KUBU

Primitives of the Lowland Rainforest

Writing in the 1920s, the Dutch colonial ethnographer Van Eerde noted that he could find no greater cultural contrast in Indonesia than between the highly civilized people of Bali—with their lavish costumes, elegant dances and elaborate religious ceremonies—and the primitive Kubu tribesmen of southern Sumatra, who wandered naked in the jungle, lived in simple huts and foraged for food.

Half a century later, members of these two ethnic groups actually found themselves living next to one another in a Jambi transmigration project. The Balinese had been forced to leave their beloved island because of land shortages, while the Kubu had been compelled by government policies to exchange their "miserable existence in the wilderness" for transmigration settlement houses, plots of farmland and a year's free supply of food.

Much as Van Eerde had predicted, the contrast could not indeed have been greater. While the Balinese were delighted to have the opportunity of building a new future in a new land, the Kubu sullenly and steadfastly refused all assistance. "No, thank you!" they said. "We Kubu prefer the forest. We consider ourselves part of the forest and we prefer to live in freedom. We are not attracted to village life, with its many regulations and officials." Coming from primitive forest dwellers, this is a surprisingly "aristocratic" attitude.

Indigenous hunter-gatherers

The Kubu are southern Sumatra's original inhabitants. As traditional hunters and gatherers, they have inhabited the lowland tropical rainforests of Jambi and South Sumatra provinces for centuries, where they survive by gathering an enormous variety of edible forest products, and by hunting wild game—several species of deer, large lizards, boar, tapirs, honey bears, monkeys, birds and, in the past, even elephants. The one animal they do not hunt is the tiger, due to a special relationship between the Kubu and the tiger.

Apart from this, the Kubu eat wild tubers, fruits, leaves, fish, shellfish and smaller animals such as turtles, snakes and rats.

The Kubu use only a long spear to kill their prey. Dogs are used to chase the quarry and exhaust it so that they can kill it with the spear. Bows and arrows, blowpipes and other weapons are unknown to them, but they do make many types of traps and snares to catch smaller animals.

Such a lifestyle requires a high degree of mobility, which in turn limits the size of Kubu groups. The temporary camps consisting of simple huts which they erect in the forest seldom house more than about eight families. Moreover, the composition of such groups changes rather quickly since its members often move to join other groups or start new groups of their own.

A threatened way of life

Until several decades ago, most of southern Sumatra was still covered in virgin jungle. Villages with surrounding agricultural fields were only to be found on the banks of the large rivers that meander lazily through the lowland swamps, and in the highland valleys. But in recent years the entire landscape has changed dramatically. Logging, mining and plantation agriculture have opened up many lowland areas, while the construction of the Trans-Sumatra Highway has brought a flood of migrants from overpopulated Java, Bali and Madura.

All of these factors have contributed to the destruction of the lowland rainforest environment in which the Kubu live. With the destruction of the forests, many plants and animals essential for their survival are also disappearing, and the process of cultural and physical extinction—predicted already for several decades—seems now to have become irreversible.

Though unable to stop the invading farmers, bulldozers and chainsaws around them, the Kubu have nevertheless managed to adapt their way of life to the deteriorating circumstances. Against their nature they have adopted agriculture on a limited scale—they clear small plots of forest land for the cultivation of upland rice, corn or root crops. Moreover, these fields attract animals such as deer and pigs, which may be hunted with greater efficiency.

Right: *This Kubu man, an indigenous hunter and gatherer by nature, has to work as a daily laborer for village farmers in order to survive.*

Most Kubu now live in close contact with village farmers without becoming or wanting to become village dwellers themselves. They settle on farmers' fields where they can hunt freely, and often they work as daily laborers —assisting at harvest time or cutting trees and opening new fields in the forest. They also gather and trade forest products like honey, rattan and various types of tree resins. Their handicrafts—baskets and fish traps— are increasingly in demand. In exchange, the Kubu receive rice, tobacco, salt, hardware (spearheads, axes, bush knives), medicine and cotton loin cloths (which have long ago replaced their old barkcloth ones). Increasingly, however, the Kubu also request flashlights, guns, radios and other products, and the debris scattered around their forest huts bears silent witness to an increasing contact with the outside world. In addition to the familiar husks, shells and bones of game are now found discarded batteries, empty tins, bottles and plastic trash.

Due to these changed circumstances a kind of economic symbiosis has developed between the Kubu and the farmers, in spite of the fact that both groups remain far apart socially. The villagers—sedentary Muslims with a sense of belonging to a new and developing Indonesia—show little respect or sympathy for the "half naked, omnivorous, uncivilized Kubu" who cling to such an archaic and disorderly way of life.

For their part, the Kubu still consciously reject village life. The heavy work in the fields, the restricted freedom of movement and the numerous obligations and duties imposed on villagers in the form of mandatory schooling, development and political activities, and *gotong royong* (communal exchanges of labor) frighten the Kubu. And so they continually resist the pressures and temptations of the outside world that would force them to become settled villagers.

This explains also why the Kubu never accept houses in transmigration settlement areas and why they soon leave resettlement villages built for their "development and civilization" by the government or by missionary organizations. They prefer the freedom of the forests, living on the margins of civilization as odd-job laborers in nearby farms.

Only when this possibility is taken from them do they appear more openly in the outside world—as beggars in logging camps, at bus terminals or along the roadways. Perhaps one can look upon this as a modified and "modernized" form of hunting and gathering with money, food and cigarettes as its aim, but it is a way of life which the Kubu have not chosen for themselves. What is required is not simply the protection and conservation of their original environment but a fundamental reconsideration of the fate and future of the Kubu people.

— *Gerard Persoon*

GERARD PERSOON

Bustling Tidal Port on the Batang Hari

The modern provincial capital of Jambi combines the old prewar city, seat of the former Jambi sultanate, with a new administrative center at Telanaipura ("city of Prince Telanai") just to the west. It has a total population of some 300,000—a diverse mixture of Malays, Minangkabaus, Arabs, Chinese, Banjarese, Buginese and Javanese. This is a major tidal river port with a booming economy (palm oil, timber, plywood, rubber).

A floating population lives on rafts (similar to those at Palembang) over the Batang Hari at Solok Sipin, just west of the city, and traditional wooden houses stand atop high pillars not far from the modern business center. A new mosque occupies the site of the former Istana—the palace of the sultan overlooking the river. A reconstructed Malay *adat* house, the Mayang Mangurai, has a permanent exhibit of ethnographic materials, including looms.

The Provincial Museum has a small but interesting collection of archaeological artifacts from the Jambi region. There are several bronzes, including an unusual late Chola-style *dipalaksmi* temple lamp recovered from the banks of the lower Batang Hari.

The Muara Jambi remains

Covering over 1,500 ha, the site of the ancient port of Malayu, with its *candi* and *menapo* or brick-built temples and canals, is located some 26 km downstream from the modern capital, on the opposite (north) bank. This is the largest archaeological complex in Sumatra, with a small but interesting site museum—accessible by chartered speedboat or waterbus from Jambi.

The full extent of the site and its associated riverine settlements is not yet known. Restoration of three main structures—Candi Tinggi, Candi Gumpung and Candi Kedaton, the last with an unusual fill of small white river pebbles—has been completed. Among the recoveries at Muara Jambi is an exquisite but headless Prajnaparamita image in East Javanese Singosari style, similar to that in the National Museum in Jakarta, dating from the early 13th century. Exploration, excavation and restoration continue under pressure from the province's expanding agricultural needs in a battle against time.

Muara Jambi is thought to have been attacked and destroyed in about 1377.

According to legend the last ruler of Muara Jambi, Prince Telanai, was fearful of a soothsayer's prediction that his son would bring disaster to himself and his realm. Consequently, on the birth of a son he put the boy with a letter into a chest which was thrown into the sea. The chest was washed up in Siam, where the Sumatran prince was adopted by the ruler and brought up at the royal court. Eventually the young prince returned to Jambi with a great Siamese army, killing his father and sacking the city. Whether there is any truth to this legend is not known but Siamese bronze Buddha images have been found in Jambi and a stone Sukhothai Buddha fragment was found during the course of excavations at Muara Jambi.

Much further downstream, at the mouth of the Kuala Niur, the island of **Pulau Berhala** can be reached by speedboat in about 45 minutes from the village of Nipah Panjang. This tiny island, with its unspoilt white sand beaches, interesting rock formations and simple fishing villages, is reminiscent of the islands of Bangka or Belitung. A 200-m hill dominates the island and has long been used as a navigational landmark by seafarers; it appears on 15th century Chinese sea charts.

Excursions to the hinterland

With the completion of the middle sections of the Trans-Sumatran Highway, including a 210-km feeder road from Muarabungo to the west, and the surfacing of the 260-km oil road from Palembang to the south, the city of Jambi is no longer as isolated from the rest of Sumatra as it once was. Land access to the north is no longer difficult, there's a fast road to Rengat and on to Pekanbaru, both in Riau.

One of Jambi's highlights is a trip to the West. The village of **Rantau Panjang** on the Batang Tabir, 30 km north of Bangko, has a number of traditional houses decorated in tricolor black, white and red motifs. Nearby are a number of early Islamic graves. Just outside the mosque at the town of **Karang Berahi**, on the Batang Merangin some 25 km east of Bangko, is an Old Malay inscription written on stone in the Tamil Grantha script which dates from the year Saka 608 of the Buddhist calendar, or AD 686. The lower part of the stone is carved into a lip where sacred water from ablutions poured over the stone and were collected and drunk by the assembled chiefs. In Malay fashion they "drank" the curse which would kill them if they broke the oath of allegiance to the Datuk or ruler of Srivijaya. Apparently a practical person, the Datuk backed up the magic of the curse with force of arms.

—E. Edwards McKinnon

Opposite: *Butterflies in the jungles of Jambi.*
Below: *A mosque on the Batang Tebo, just to the north of Muarabungo.*

KAL MULLER

KERINCI-SEBLAT

Sumatra's Largest National Park

The highlight of a trip to Jambi province is a visit to the Kerinci Valley in the Bukit Barisan range to the Western edge of Jambi province. Kerinci-Seblat National Park is a particularly beautiful part of this valley, spread across 15,000 sq km and straddling four provinces including Jambi, West Sumatra, Bengkulu and South Sumatra, with its administrative center in Jambi.

The area is overshadowed to the north by an active volcano of the same name. At 3,805 m, Mt. Kerinci is one of Sumatra's highest mountains, and the fourth highest in Indonesia, after those in Irian Jaya. The name may in fact derive from the Tamil word *kurinci*, meaning a hilly tract. Kerinci-Seblat is Sumatra's largest National Park, encompassing a 345-km long strip of mountainous uplands in the Bukit Barisan Range, parallel to the west coast of Sumatra. The scenery is among the most spectacular on the island, dominated by volcanic cones that include Mt. Kerinci.

The area is steeped in history and was once an important source of gold. Megalithic Bronze Age remains have been found here, along with traces of Buddhistic influence and early second millennium imported Chinese ceramics. Village names such as Sanggar Agung may indicate the persistence of Buddhist religious affiliations until fairly recent times. The area was finally subdued by Dutch force of arms in 1903.

Charles Campbell, who visited the area from 'Moko Moko' in 1800, after an arduous climb taking four days, described the inhabitants as "below the common stature of the Malays, with harder visages and higher cheek bones, well knit in their limbs, and active; not deficient in hospitality, but jealous of strangers." They dwelled "in hoards, many families being crowded together in one long building." The longhouse in which Campbell stayed was 230 feet in length and housed 25 families. Such houses have long since disappeared, now replaced by individual Malay-style family dwellings. The people were growing "excellent tobacco, also cotton and indigo," as well as the "potatoe" which had been introduced some years earlier. Kerinci is now an important rice producing area.

Three routes lead into the valley, and to the small town of Sungaipenuh, which is the administrative center and focus of the park.

One road links it with Jambi via the narrow valley of the Batang Merangin from Bangko, a second leads north past Mt Kerinci over the government-owned Kayo Aro tea estate into West Sumatra and a third climbs quickly over the western edge of the Bukit Barisan to the coast via Tapan, also in West Sumatra, from where the road continues on to Muko Muko and Bengkulu.

There are plenty of interesting sights in the Kerinci area. The village of **Pondok Tinggi** has a large, ornately decorated

(carved and painted) timber mosque built in 1874—said to have been constructed without the use of a single iron nail. Here too is an enormous *bedug*, a horizontally-suspended drum used instead of a muezzin to call the faithful to prayer in very old Javanese mosques—a practice that dates to pre-Islamic Hindu-Javanese temples (much like the *kulkul* in Balinese temples).

Important megalithic remains, accessible along tracks suitable only for 4-wheel drive vehicles, are to be found at several locations. At **Desa Kunun**, some 6 km south of Sungai-penuh, is a 1.5-m-long stone known as the Batu Gong. At **Desa Muak** in Gunung Raya district south of the lake, some 30 km south of Sungaipenuh, is the Batu Bergambar or "picture stone"—a stone carved with animal and spiral relief motifs which was moved from its original location to a new site in the village in 1960. Here also is a fallen menhir known as Batu Patah, the "broken stone." At **Desa Pondok** in the same area, 35 km south of Sungaipenuh, is another decorated stone with spiral reliefs 3.85 m in length.

The National Park was set up to preserve the unique habitats to the south of Lake Toba in North Sumatra, in the same way that Gunung Leuser Park preserves a representative portion of habitats north of the lake. The massive volcanic eruption which formed Lake Toba about 100,000 years ago laid waste to such a vast area that a biological barrier was created, separating populations in the northern and southern parts of the island. Today there are significant differences between the wildlife of the two areas: the white-handed gibbon, for instance, only occurs north of Lake Toba, while the dark-handed gibbon is found only to the south. The same applies to many birds: 17 species live only to the north, while 10 are found only south of Toba.

Apart from *orangutan*, which are only found north of the divide, Kerinci-Seblat is home to most of the larger Sumatran mammals—including rhinos, tigers, elephants, sun bears and tapirs, which only live in the south. It also has several endemic mammals, including the Giant Sumatran rat and the Sumatran rabbit. The agile serow, a black mountain goat, lives on forested, inaccessible limestone hills in the park, sometimes quite close to cultivated areas. Persistent stories of short, hairy people known as *orang pendek* exist among local people; it is possible that these tales arose from sightings of sun bears in the poor forest light, or from a folk memory of *orangutan,* which once lived in southern Sumatra.

Visiting the Park

Kerinci-Seblat is best tackled by people with time. Facilities for eco-tourism in the park are improving, and there is simple accommodation and a knowledgeable travel co-operative called Eco-Rural Travel, based in the village of Kersik Tuo, which can help with trekking plans, and can also rent out equipment.

The main town of **Sungaipenuh** lies at the center of a fertile valley watered by the Kerinci River. Paddy fields, tea, clove and coffee plantations are surrounded by the park's

Opposite: *At 3,800 m, Mt. Kerinci is the highest peak in western Indonesia.* **Above, left:** *The rich valley around Lake Kerinci has been settled for centuries.* **Above:** *Rainforest on Mt. Kerinci.*

forested mountains. Maintaining the boundaries of protected areas is difficult here because of the burgeoning human population around them.

In Kerinci-Seblat there are two additional factors which exacerbate the problem: the fact that its territory is administered by four different provinces, and the dense population of the Kerinci Valley within the park itself. This area gives an excellent demonstration of the conflict between the needs of wildlife and human populations, a conflict which is by no means of recent origin. There is evidence that the forests around Kerinci were disturbed by man 7,500 years ago, probably to make it easier to hunt game and also to plant crops. Bronze or Iron Age kettledrums have been found near Lake Kerinci, and standing stones, or megaliths, have been found in Jambi. Living remnants of ancient cultures survive in the Kubu people, hunter-gatherers who still live their traditional existence in forested areas of Kerinci-Seblat and other parts of southern Sumatra (see "The Kubu").

An especially beautiful spot is the lake-filled crater atop Mt. Tujuh, northeast of Sungaipenuh. **Lake Kerinci** is more easily accessible by public transport, however. These lakes, and the forest immediately around them, offer the best places to see the park's rich avifauna, which includes hornbills and jungle fowl; maroon, black and yellow-banded broadbills with their turquoise bills; grey wagtails and chestnut-crowned forktails of the rivers; and the racket-tailed drongos—easily recognized by the illusion they give of a bird being chased by two black butterflies.

Montane forest

Because of the varying altitudes of terrain in Kerinci-Seblat, it contains a great range of habitats, including lowland forests, alpine vegetation and the highest freshwater swamp forests in the western part of the Indonesian archipelago. This type of forest can be seen at Lake Bento, south of Mt. Tujuh, and northwest of Lake Kerinci, where the turbulent action of waves in the lake has prevented the formation of peat.

A climb up Mt. Kerinci or one of the other mountains shows a dramatic change in vegetation from the tall, varied trees of the lower elevations to the stunted, moss-draped montane forests and the sub-alpine heaths and bogs near the summit. A striking plant of Kerinci's upper elevations is the Javanese edelweiss *Anaphalis javanica*, which only occurs on volcanoes. It generally grows to about 4 m high and appears whitish-green all over because of its covering of fine, white hairs. The flowers appear white too, except for a central yellow disc. The volcanic cone itself is bare of vegetation, reflecting its recent activity: it last erupted in 1934. The largest flowers in the world grow in Kerinci-Seblat too, the parasitic *Rafflesia arnoldi* with its monstrous flesh-pink blooms, and the 2 m high spikes of *Amorphophallus titanum*.

Trekking in Kerinci

Local guides can be hired for trips into the park in the small village of **Kersik Tuo** at the foot of Mt. Kerinci. The Eco-Rural group, which has an office in Kersik Tuo, is sponsored by the World Wildlife Fund, and has good maps, and operates treks lasting several days into the remoter, interesting areas of the Park. Picturesque **Lake Kerinci**, 783 m above sea level and some 42 sq km in area, is easy to reach on a day trip by public transport. It is surrounded by mountains. Once plagued with an infestation of water hyacinths (*Eichhornia crassipes*), control methods are now having some positive effect.

Mt. Kerinci, sometimes called Mt. Indrapura, dominates the valley to the north and is accessible by most vehicles. Here too is the 6,000-ha state-owned PTP VIII Kayu Aro tea estate. Kerinci is a popular climb, it takes two days to ascend and descend. There is an overnight camp at about 3,000 m. The summit with its crater lake is best seen for the sunrise. **Danau Gunung Tujuh** is a lake covering some 1,000-ha near the peak of Mt. Tujuh, about 50 km north of Sungaipenuh. At 1,996 m above sea level it has interesting flora and is said to be the highest freshwater lake in Southeast Asia. Temperatures at the nearby resthouse drop to 7 degrees C during the evening. The trail up to the lake starts from the village of Pelompek, 12 km bus ride from Kersik Tuo. The climb to the summit and the lake can be done in a day, but it is also possible to camp, or descend and stay in the simple resthouse. There are other peaks that may be climbed, cross the lake by fishing boat to scale the smaller peaks on the other side. Further north, on the border of West Sumatra's Solok Regency, is the 45-m high **Telun Berasap** waterfall.

—Janet Cochran, E. Edwards McKinnon
and Julie Heath

Right: *The diminutive, shy Sumatran rhino.*

SUMATRAN RHINO

The Elusive, Endangered 'Pocket' Rhino

On the edge of extinction

The two-horned Sumatran rhino (*Dicerorhinus sumatrensis*) is a direct descendant of the prehistoric Woolly Rhinoceros that roamed the earth some 40 million years ago. This "pocket rhino" is the smallest of the world's five rhino species and displays an aptly Asian personality—being far less aggressive than its African counterparts. It is a harmless vegetarian that exhibits a certain charm: the young are known to bleat and squeak like lambs.

The Sumatran rhino is a shy, solitary wanderer—extremely difficult to observe in the field. At least one researcher was obliged to study it almost entirely through plaster casts of the beast's footprints.

Rhinos "speak" through smell—leaving urine squirts and communal dung piles as "notice boards" for other rhinos. For instance different scents indicate to a male whether or not a female is in heat or pregnant.

The Sumatran rhinoceros is on the edge of extinction. Only about 800 survive worldwide, 700 in Sumatra itself. For centuries, the rhino has been hunted for its horn and other body parts prized in Asian folk medicine. In his *History of Sumatra*, Marsden stated that "The horn is esteemed an antidote against poison, and on that account formed into drinking cups." Today it is in demand as a fever tonic in traditional Chinese medicine (not as an aphrodisiac, as commonly believed). The rhino's unfortunate tendency to follow known trails make it vulnerable to pit-trap poaching—the hunter simply sits and waits.

Equally threatening is the steady cutting of the rhino's lowland forest habitat. This has forced most rhinos into rugged upland areas, despite their need for swampy mud-wallows to coat their hides against parasites and dry-cracking. Individuals are now too scattered to form viable breeding populations, and the Sumatran rhino's long-term survival is seriously in question.

In 1985 a captive breeding program was launched. Twelve Sumatran rhinos were distributed amongst zoos in Indonesia, Britain and the United States, and the long wait for offspring is on. Sumatran rhino pregnancies occur only every four years, last 16 months, and result in a single calf.

— *Ilsa Sharp*

ALAIN COMPOST

PART VIII

Introducing South Sumatra

Like the delicate skeleton of a tropical leaf, South Sumatra's enormous network of rivers drains an area the size of Ireland (103,688 sq km). Five mighty rivers, a dozen major tributaries and a thousand small, winding streams link the scattered settlements of this vast and sparsely populated province. At Palembang, most of the larger rivers join the longest and broadest one—the meandering, slow-moving Musi. The story of the Musi is the story of South Sumatra's land and people.

The river rises at the western edge of the province as a small, sparkling stream deep in the jungle-clad Bukit Barisan range near the towering peaks of Mt. Dempo (3,159 m) and Mt. Patah (2,817 m). Leaving the cool uplands, the Musi tumbles and rolls through the foothills past scattered coffee plantations and fields of corn and rice cleared and planted by pioneer settlers. Reaching the plain, it slows to a gentle lope, then to a sluggish crawl—winding across the gently-sloping plain to the steamy marshes of the eastern seaboard. Tiny villages line the banks, where on moonlit nights young Malays row their boats past sleepy waterfront houses.

A thousand years ago, Palembang was the capital of the mighty maritime kingdom of Srivijaya, whose trading network extended to Southern Thailand, the Malay Peninsula and the shores of Java. The town's name derives from *limbang*—to pan for gold—and Palembang's early prosperity was probably founded on river gold. According to ancient travelers' accounts, the ruler's palace contained a pool connected by a narrow canal to the Musi—source of the king's immense wealth. Into this pool every morning he threw bars of gold, which lay shimmering like goldfish beneath the surface of the water. Across the river in the early morning drifted the delicate scent of incense from the monasteries of Palembang, where more than a thousand monks lived and studied Buddhist scriptures.

Today, the river is dominated by Palembang's famous Ampera Bridge. Shortly upstream from it, the Musi is joined by its two main tributaries, the Ogan and the Komering. It then swells to several hundred meters in width; ships up to 10,000 tons regularly make the 100-km journey from the coast to Palembang's Boom Baru harbor. The banks of the Musi are lined with houses on stilts; some stand meters above the water at low tide.

South Sumatra is the homeland of the Malay people and the ancient cradle of Malay culture. The ancestor of all Malay rulers is believed to have descended from the heavens on Bukit Seguntang, a small hill to the north of Palembang. (A second Bukit Seguntang is also found by the village of Pariangan in the Minang Highlands.) Now devout Muslims, the Malays absorbed many Indian beliefs during the first millennium AD, deepening and enriching a native belief system which included the veneration of natural objects such as rocks and trees, and a belief in the existence of spirits which must be propitiated. Several 7th-century inscriptions from Palembang are heavily Sanskritized and much of the ritual and special vocabulary used in later Islamic Malay courts is Indic in origin.

Palembang was the most important center of trade in Southeast Asia for more than three hundred years—from the late 7th to the early 11th centuries. Then, as now, the city spread for many kilometers along the banks of the Musi. While the king lived ashore, his subjects made their homes on the water, manning a huge fleet that provided the basis for Srivijaya's control of the straits. Few relics have survived from this era, but more than 24 archaeological sites have been identified, including the ancient palace, and the future thus promises many exciting discoveries.

— *Ian Caldwell*

Overleaf: *The rocky shoreline of Bangka Island. Photo by Jill Gocher.* **Opposite:** *Girl in traditional Malay* adat *costume. Photo by David Booth.*

PALEMBANG

Bustling City Astride the Musi River

Palembang is a sweltering, bustling industrial and communications center seldom visited by foreigners—that is trying hard these days to upgrade its image. With over a million inhabitants, it is Sumatra's second largest city (after Medan) and the sixth largest in Indonesia (after Semarang). Its booming economy is based on coal mining, plantation agriculture, oil refining and fertilizer production.

Palembang straddles the 600-m wide Musi River at a strategic point just below the confluence of major tributaries providing access to the vast Sumatran hinterland. Despite its new-found oil wealth, Palembang is a city with a 1,300-year history, steeped in Malay culture and site of the ancient Buddhist Srivijayan empire. It still produces some of finest textiles and lacquerwares in Indonesia, and a number of city residents live out over the water—just as they did many centuries ago.

The old palace precincts

The city's main landmark is **Ampera Bridge** —built by the Japanese as a war reparation by order of Soekarno and inaugurated by him with great fanfare in 1964. At the time it was Southeast Asia's longest bridge and the central span between the imposing twin towers neatly hoisted up and down to allow ships to pass. Now, alas, it is stuck.

Running north from the bridge is Jl. Sudirman, Palembang's main street, joining with Jl. Merdeka at a large roundabout in front of the **Mesjid Agung** or Royal Mosque —built by Sultan Machmud Badaruddin I in 1740 and recently restored to its former splendor. This area was the former capital of an Islamic kingdom which warred periodically with the Dutch, until the last sultan— Ahmad Najamuddin—surrendered and was exiled to Banda Neira in 1825.

Start your tour of the city at the **Museum Sultan Machmud Badaruddin II**, facing the Musi River just west of the northern end of the bridge. The museum building, with its imposing semi-circular staircases, is a curious blend of colonial and traditional Malay architecture. It was constructed by the Dutch in 1823 on the site of the former sultan's palace (after the latter had been razed by attacking Dutch forces), and served for many years as the official Dutch Residency. It is presently being refurbished with a traditional

keraton (palace) interior upstairs, complete with royal sleeping and living chambers. Downstairs are restaurants serving Palembang specialities. The Tourist Information Center is at the back, next to a new open-air theater where you can watch traditional Malay dances (see "Palembang Practicalities").

To the rear of the museum is the new **Art Market**, 15 miniature pavilions where you can watch local craftsmen at work on delicate gold or silver *songket* brocades and intricate red-and-black lacquerwares—the latter being

a craft introduced to Palembang from China, perhaps as early as the Srivijayan period. Also produced here are finely woven baskets, *tikar* mats, and seashell souvenirs.

Walk from the museum toward the river and turn right onto Jl. Keraton—through the old fruit market where ladies in batik sarongs and headscarves sit amidst piles of bananas, melons and papayas. The view of Ampera Bridge is impressive, but don't step into the road or you are likely to be run down by an *oplet* or *becak*! About 500 m west of the museum is the old **Benteng Kuto Besak** fortress, surround by a 3-meter high, filthy-grey (previously whitewashed) wall. Built by the sultan in 1797, it is now used by the army and entry is forbidden. From the front gates you can however see the elegant old buildings.

The Musi River

A little further upriver is a boarding point for river taxis that ply the Musi. To experience the true flavor of Palembang, a trip along the river is a must. Head downriver past a group of houseboats lining the opposite bank just before Ampera Bridge. After the bridge, move over to the north bank to see the brisk floating market known as **Pasar 16 Ilir**. River activity peaks at about 11 am, but fortunately there are no traffic jams yet.

One km further downstream, on the left, is Palembang's main harbor, **Boom Baru**. Two km further on is the massive, state-

owned Pusri Fertilizer Plant—said to be the largest in Asia. Immediately past this is **Pulau Kemaro**—a small, untidy island that hosts a large Buddhist temple and the grave of a Chinese princess. The princess is said to have been sent to marry the king of Srivijaya. When she arrived, boats were sent ashore with large ceramic pots. The king expected to find gold and jewels inside, but in the first one he found only preserved vegetables. This made him angry, and he ordered the pots thrown into the river. Seeing this, the princess jumped in too and drowned. But some of the other pots broke open, revealing that they were indeed full of gold. The princess was buried on this island, and the temple erected nearby is considered particularly efficacious in dispensing good fortune.

Traditional rumah limas

The new **Museum of South Sumatra** 5 km north of town has a collection of mysterious megalithic statues from Pasemah, including a famous one depicting an ancient warrior with a bronze drum astride an elephant. There is also a 150-year-old *rumah limas* or traditional Palembang-style house that was transferred here from the city. Unfortunately many of the original furnishings have been transferred to Jakarta's Taman Mini Indonesia, but there is still a fine display of ceremonial clothes, hunting, farming and fishing implements, and traditional coffee preparation. Open Tues-Sat 8-12 am and 1-4 pm; Sun 8-12. Closed Mon.

Two other well-preserved examples of *rumah limas* remain in Palembang—Rumah Hasyim Ning (at Jl. Pulo, 24 Ilir) and Rumah Bayumi (off Jl. Mayor Ruslan), both still occupied. They can be visited if you make arrangements at the tourism office in back of the Sultan Machmud Museum.

—David Booth

Opposite: *Lovely* rumah limas *interior.* **Above, left:** *Life on the Musi.* **Above, right:** *Ampera Bridge.*

PALEMBANG SIDETRIPS

Journey to the Western Highlands

Tourism is in its infancy in South Sumatra, and there are few established routes or facilities outside of Palembang. The province's many natural attractions can nevertheless easily be reached by public transport or by chartering an air-conditioned car or minibus. The highlights are a visit to the Pasemah Plateau—site of mysterious ancient megaliths (see following section)—and to lovely Lake Ranau, a huge crater lake on the border with Lampung. Both are situated in the rugged volcanic highlands at the western edge of the province, which means a full day's drive from Palembang each way on some rather rough roads. Lodgings and food are very basic, but these inconveniences are more than compensated for by the scenery and by a refreshing sense of serendipitous discovery that accompanies you along the way—not to mention the extraordinarily friendly people you meet.

West to Lahat

The winding, potholed main highway leading west of Palembang runs for the first 50 km through a flat, swampy plain past pretty *kampung* villages with wooden houses on stilts. Children wash and swim in the murky water; men fish from small canoes with nets and spears, and women prepare rice or hang their laundry. Padang restaurants by the roadside are open 24 hours for the convenience of passing motorists. From time to time your driver will slam on the brakes, screeching from a breakneck 100 kph to a sedate 10 kph past isolated police checkpoints.

As the terrain gradually rises out of the swampy lowlands, you enter a thickly forested area dotted with charming country villages whose fine wooden houses and fenced gardens are surrounded by flowering bougainvilleas. Ox-drawn carts lumber along and well-fed cows graze by the roadside.

The first large town is **Prabumulih**, about 2 hours and 96 km from Palembang. This is an oil town and rail junction, and lies in the center of a pineapple-growing area—you can buy some of the sweetest pineapples you've ever tasted, for less than ten cents! The road forks here. If you are headed down to Danau Ranau, turn left (south) toward Baturaja. For Pasemah and Sumindo turn right for Muaraenim, a town 85 km west of Prabumulih.

The road west to **Muaraenim** brings you

through dense oil palm groves and pretty villages, with roadside stalls selling pineapples, melons and papayas. After about 40 km you reach a turn-off to the right for **Pendopo**, where the region's oil was first discovered in 1899. Today, the wells in this South Sumatran basin are the most productive in all of Indonesia. The roads around here are very bad, however, so expect slow going.

Muaraenim is the next stop, a quiet town at the confluence of the Enim and Lematang rivers that is a good place to stopover for the night, as it has a reasonable, air-conditioned hotel (Hotel Rene). The road forks again, and you turn to the right (west) for Lahat and Pagaralam, the the left (south) for Baturaja. The nearby town of Tanjung Enim, 13 km south of here, is the site of Indonesia's largest open-cast coal mine.

The road from Muaraenim west to Lahat (43 km) is good, passing from the eastern plains into the foothills of the Bukit Barisan, with sweeping views of paddy fields and the winding Lematang River. Stones are collected from the riverbed in tiny villages here to be sold to contractors; coffee and rice are grown on the fertile hillsides and sun-dried on rattan mats by the roadside. About 11 km before Lahat, stop by the river to admire the view of **Mt. Serelo**, an oval-shaped peak topped by a narrow, finger-like protrusion (also known as Bukit Tunjuk or "Finger Hill"). There is a path leading up from the village of Sukacinta,

and this is a popular outing for local youths.

The medium sized town of **Lahat** is the next stop, a road junction on the Trans-Sumatran Highway that is the jumping-off point for visits to Pagaralam in the Pasemah region (see "Pasemah Plateau"). The road up to **Pagaralam** is especially beautiful—shortly after leaving Lahat, it climbs up to a plateau offering views down across to the Lematang River which wends its way through a valley at the foot of an almost-vertical cliff face. Dramatic mountain vistas unfold after the village of Pulau Pinang—with lofty ridges and peaks in all directions as far as the eye can see.

The Sumindo Highlands

On your way back to Palembang, or if you are heading southward to Lake Ranau or Lampung, you can make a scenic full-day's detour into the Sumindo Highlands—a lush and extremely beautiful region accessed via a winding mountain road south of the main Lahat-Pagaralam highway. This is a sparsely populated, coffee-growing region of tiny highland hamlets. Set off early and allow time for stops to take in the breathtaking scenery. Public transport is unreliable, so charter a

Opposite: *A visit to the Pasemah Plateau around Pagaralam, in the shadow of towering Mt. Dempo, is one of the highpoints of an excursion to the western highlands.* **Below:** *Entrance to the Goa Putri ("Princess") caves west of Baturaja.*

DAVID BOOTH

minibus and pack a picnic lunch, as no restaurants are to be found along the way.

Turn south at Tanjung Tebat, about halfway (30 km) between Lahat and Pagaralam, just near the hairpin bend. The road climbs gently from here to the village of Kota Agung, offering good views of Mt. Serelo to the east. At Kota Agung, turn left to Muaratiga (14 km), then take the right fork in Muaratiga toward Pulau Panggung.

Past Muaratiga the road deteriorates, with potholes the size of bathtubs. Don't be put off by this, because this is where the views start. Steep grades afford superb panoramas of mountain ridges and hillsides thick with durian, some 20 m tall. Fresh durians here cost only 25 cents—the same fruit in Jakarta costs ten times as much. Sculpted rice paddies greet you as you whizz round the bends; villagers laden with bundles of firewood strapped to their backs pass you on the road.

Continue on to **Pulau Panggung**, passing through dense rainforests one minute and emerging the next onto open, green carpets of mature rice waving gently in the breeze beneath rolling hills. After Pulau Panggung, where shops sell drinks and provisions, the road narrows and zigzags round sharp, blind bends. Small patches of forest are being cleared for coffee plantations here and coffee beans lie on large rattan mats. The 1.5 hour drive to Sugihwaras is simply spectacular.

About 2 km before Sugihwaras, the road

descends steeply; keep an eye out to your right for the 80-m-high **Tenang Waterfall**, set against the mountain ridges. A new, 500-m road leads in to a parking lot and you then walk 1 km to a bamboo suspension bridge over the river; another 500 m brings you to the crashing falls, the largest in the province. Back on the main road at Sugihwaras, you can turn left for Muaraenim and Palembang, or right towards Baturaja and Lake Ranau.

Gua Putri caves

If you are heading south, you may want to stop at the Gua Putri caves. The trek through these fascinating caves, at **Padang Bindu** on the main road 35 km west of Baturaja, is not for the faint-hearted. Strong shoes with anti-slip soles are a must, as the rocks are very slippery in places. Guides with lamps and torches will accompany you and provide detailed explanations (in Indonesian) of legends associated with the caves.

The main chamber is about 150 m long and 15-20 m at its widest point. The ceiling is 12 m high in places, and as little as 1.5 m in others. Hundreds of bats hang from the roof; as the light disturbs them, they swish past you like arrows. Underground rivers here feed the Ogan River. To explore very deeply in the caves, you must be slim and supple to squeeze through the gaps between the rocks. Legend tells of a king who formerly had his palace in the cave, and each cavern has its own story. Stalagmites and stalactites with interesting shapes all figure in the tale—here is a waterfall, there a throne surmounted by an umbrella.

Spectacular Lake Ranau

For most people, the highlight of any visit to South Sumatra's western highlands is Lake Ranau—a shimmering crater lake set in the ancient caldera of Mt. Seminung (1,340 m), an active volcano straddling the border with Lampung Province. The lake is 16 km long and 9 km wide, and has a depth of 300 m. The climate in these highlands is deliciously cool, and the remote setting offers lush vegetation, crystal clear waters and delightful excursions to a nearby waterfall, a hot spring and an island in the lake. Although it is popular with locals on the weekends, the lake has not yet been developed for tourism and you thus have the feeling much of the time of having

Left: Tenang ("Tranquility") Waterfall, at the edge of Lake Ranau. Right: A view across the mirror-smooth waters of the lake at sunset.

stumbled into your own "private paradise."

Banding Agung on the northern shore is the main lakeside farming and fishing community, and has several clean, inexpensive *losmen*. The people here are all farmers who raise cash crops like coffee, tobacco and cloves. Some rice is also grown, as well as succulent pineapples, bananas and avocados that are sold locally for only 5 cents a kilo. The lake teems with fish, which are caught and charcoal grilled in small restaurants by the shore. In the early evening, local fishing canoes are reflected on the lake's mirror-like surface against a brilliant golden sunset, with the mountains silhouetted behind.

Kota Batu on the southeastern shore is Ranau's other tiny town, but has no accommodations. Between these two towns lies Wisma Pusri Ranau, a small state-owned hotel. The manager, Pak Suwarso, speaks good English and is an excellent source of information; he is also a superb cook and enjoys meeting foreigners.

There is plenty to do around the lake. A 15-minute walk from Wisma Pusri through a patch of forest and past coffee groves and rice fields leads to Subik Waterfall—a 25-m cascade tucked into a gentle recess in the rocks by the edge of the lake.

Another excursion, this time across the lake by rented motorboat ($5 per hour from Wisma Pusri or Banding Agung), brings you to a hot spring at the foot of Mt. Semuning.

The springs have been walled off from the lake so, unfortunately, the hot and cold waters can no longer mix. The hot water is very hot, lower yourself in carefully. After the dip in the hot pool, a refreshing swim or paddle around in the cooler lake waters is bliss. Be careful of the hot sand by the rockface. Snorkeling here is also a delight, and large rubber inner tubes can be brought along for non-swimmers.

Across from the hot springs is a small islet known as **Pulau Marisa**. According to local legend, the island appeared one night as the failed solution to a love triangle. A pretty young princess named Puteri Aisah had two suitors—Sipahit Lidah ("Bitter Tongue") and Simata Empat ("Four Eyes"). To solve her dilemma, she promised to marry whichever one could manage to build a bridge across the lake, from the hot springs to Banding Agung, in a single night. This island was the only part of the bridge completed by the time the sun arose, so both suitors were rejected. It is just 5 minutes by boat from the hot springs—here you can lunch in the shade of palm trees and catch up on some lost sleep.

If you are in the mood for something more adventuresome, you can organize an expedition to the summit of Mt. Semuning. There is also an elephant training school in the vicinity, and you can hire the elephants for a "safari" through the jungle.

—*David Booth*

DAVID BOOTH

PASEMAH PLATEAU

Mysterious Megalithic Remains

Some of Sumatra's most remarkable megalithic remains are found on the remote Pasemah Plateau at the western edge of South Sumatra—a wide and fertile grassland plain surrounded by an almost impenetrable wall of mountains. The plateau stretches for 70 km in a northwest to southeast direction along a cleft within the Bukit Barisan range, at the foot of dormant Mt. Dempo (3,159 m). In the early centuries of the Christian era, this plateau was the home of a flourishing Bronze Age megalithic culture.

Pasemah's main town is **Pagaralam** (710 m). Scattered around the town are dozens of megaliths—upright stones arranged in neat groups or rows, troughs with carved human heads, terraced platforms, stone mortars, dolmens (stone tables), painted cist graves sunk into the ground and numerous carved stone figures. Many of the better stones have

been moved to museums in Jakarta or Palembang; the most famous Pasemah figure is the magnificent Batu Gajah or Elephant Stone —now in the Museum of South Sumatra in Palembang—which depicts an armed warrior mounting (or perhaps subduing) an elephant. But many more stones still stand where they were originally placed—in the fertile fields and gardens surrounding Mt. Dempo.

Who built these megaliths—and why? Local legends attribute them to a magician known as Lidah Pahit ("Bitter Tongue") who, it is said, could turn people and animals into stone. One of the images at Tinggi Hari is regarded as a petrified princess (Batu Puteri). The story goes that the princess once met Lidah Pahit. He asked her where she was going, but she was too proud to answer, so he turned her into stone.

A more scientific theory is that the megaliths are the work of an ancient people who lived here between AD 0-500. Several carvings depict armed warriors carrying huge Dongson bronze drums, which arrived in the archipelago in the first centuries AD. None shows signs of the Indian influence, which was to lead, in the 7th century, to the rise of great Indianized trading kingdoms such as Malayu and Srivijaya along the courses of the great rivers nearer to the coast. Many of the carvings celebrate military prowess, and point to an unsettled, warlike society.

Often, the carvings are so worn that it is

difficult to know whether they depict men or women. Women are often dressed in a sort of poncho that is tied under the arms. Children wear only a girdle. Men—perhaps engaged in war or hunting—wear a girdle with a loin-cloth over it and on their wrists and ankles are large metal rings or bracelets. Several figures wear broad, flat bands around their necks (similar rings were worn in Nias in the 19th century as a mark of distinction among head-hunters).

Men carry short, broad swords with long

hilts and pommels, and a close fitting head-dress ending in a peak at the back. Van der Hoop, a pioneering Dutch aviator-turned-arch-aeologist who studied these ancient remains in the 1930s, thought they were protective helmets made of bronze or iron. They are also strikingly similar to the Javanese *blankon*—a close fitting cloth cap with a projecting rear knob. Most surprisingly—considering the warlike nature of the carvings—there is no evidence of the use of bows and arrows.

Visiting the megaliths

A megalith depicting a man subduing a head-less elephant can be found next to the Taqwa Mosque on the road between Losman Mirasa and the Pagaralam town center. Next to the elephant is a *lesung batu*, a giant mortar half buried on its side.

Walking in the opposite direction from the Mirasa, a left turn onto Jl. Tanjung Aru before the Hotel Dharmakaya brings you after 2 km to **Kampung Tanjung Aro**. Turn right at house no. 106 and walk 50 m to a pair of cist graves—a bamboo fence encloses the site, now partially filled with water.

On the same street, locate house no. 90 to see another *lesung batu*. Then, with the cist graves to your back, walk 50 m to an amazing set of carved rocks scattered among the rice fields. One has a bas relief of a man wrestling a giant serpent. The setting is spectacular, with Mt. Dempo in the background.

The most impressive group of megaliths and cist graves is found just past the village of **Tegurwangi**, 6 km from Pagaralam. Here, 4 human figures squat on a river bank 50 m from the main road (one has almost fallen in!). The heads are clearly defined—with thick lips, bulging eyes and heavy brows. On their backs they carry large, bulky objects. Originally they stood on a platform with their backs to each other, facing the four cardinal directions. Close by and set in the midst of rice fields are 3 recently-opened cist graves. Inside one is the drawing of a *naga* (dragon) and a human figure with a long, orange nose—now badly faded.

A remarkable 3-m-high figure of a warrior has been carved into a rockface close to Tegurwangi. Walk 100 m back down the road and ask directions to **Batu Balai**. A brisk, 15-minute trek through the rice paddies brings you to a large, rocky outcrop—the carving is on the lower left face. The warrior's plumed headdress is similar to those worn by dancing figures depicted on Dongson bronze drums of the first millennium AD.

Berlubai, 3 km from Pagaralam, has a number of interesting megaliths. Ask at the village chief's house (*kepala desa*) to see the *batu gajah* ("elephant stone"), and hordes of schoolchildren will accompany you through fields cultivated with rice, chili peppers and tomatoes, to an enormous rock carving of a warrior wresting an elephant to the ground. The man is wearing anklets and his right wrist is protected by a small shield. On the return journey, ask to see the three standing figures that are smaller versions of those found at Tegurwangi.

— *Ian Caldwell*

Opposite: *Painting of an owl in a recently-opened cist grave at Kotoraya Lembak.* **Above, left:** *A group of figures on a riverbank, near Tegurwangi.* **Above:** *A warrior astride an elephant near Berlubai.*

BANGKA AND BELITUNG

Magnificent Beaches and Azure Seas

Bangka and Belitung are two verdant islands lying in the placid South China Sea to the east of Sumatra. Geologically they are more closely related to Malaya and Borneo than to Sumatra—forming part of the older, non-volcanic core of the Sunda Shelf. Though seldom visited, they in fact possess some of Southeast Asia's finest beaches, as well as offering refreshing sea breezes and an easy escape (only half an hour by plane) from Palembang's heat and congestion.

Bangka and Belitung are best known as the "tin islands"—part of a rich vein of tin ore running from here up through the Malay Peninsula to southern Thailand, which has historically furnished much of the world's supply of this versatile mineral. As in Malaya and Thailand, the mines here were developed during the 18th and 19th centuries using contract coolie labor imported from China.

Decades of mining have transformed the landscapes of these islands. Densely jungled hills have given way to scrubby forests dotted with small lakes called *kolong*—huge, water-filled cavities where tin has been mined. Despite centuries of large-scale exploitation, the islands are still sparsely populated. Bangka, with 11,615 sq km, has a population of 500,000, while Belitung, with an area of 4,000 sq km, has just 150,000 inhabitants.

Chinese coolie miners

Sea, forest and iron products were the islands' principal exports before tin was discovered on Bangka in 1710. A late 7th century Srivijayan stone inscription found at Kota Kapur testifies to the island's ancient links to Palembang. From the 14th to 17th centuries, the entire area (including Palembang) came under Javanese influence.

When the Dutch East India Company learned of the tin deposits, it cleverly signed contracts with the Sultan of Palembang for deliveries of ore to Batavia (Jakarta)—which was in turn traded to China in exchange for tea, silks and porcelain. Mines in Mentok and along the north and east coast of Bangka were controlled by the sultan through Chinese Muslim agents living on the island.

Tin deposits throughout Southeast Asia usually lie close to the surface, and mining and smelting can be carried out with simple tools and unskilled labor. However, the sultans soon abandoned attempts to work the mines with local recruits and began bringing in coolies from China. Ingenious Chinese mining techniques increased production and the Chinese soon organized themselves into cooperatives (*kongsi*) which developed new mines, managed labor, smelted and sold the ore, and shared in the profits. Although the colonial government took over the island and ran the mines as a state enterprise after 1819, technology and the organization of labor remained in the hands of the Chinese for another century.

The establishment of colonial rule here in fact created serious problems for the Dutch. Colonial bureaucrats were incompetent or corrupt, and between 1819 and 1851 local uprisings repeatedly threatened Dutch rule. When the Dutch extended their control over the *kongsis* after 1850, mortality among the Chinese laborers increased dramatically and they too rose up against their masters.

Bangka thus had two reputations during the 19th century. For the Dutch it represented a lucrative source of income. But for the Chinese, working conditions were notoriously poor and recruitment from China became increasingly difficult. The early coolies were mainly hardy, hard-working Hakkas from a poor and mountainous region of southern China's Guangdong Province. Many stayed on the island and married local women once their contracts were up, and Hakka displaced Malay as the main language in the mining communities. Their descendents, the local-born or *peranakan* Chinese, lived in much the same way as the local people—preferring to farm, fish or clerk for the Dutch rather than work the mines.

In the 1850s a Dutch mining company—the Billiton Maatschappij—opened mines on neighboring Belitung, also importing Chinese labor. By the 1920s, Bangka and Belitung between them had 130,000 Hakka Chinese residents, and by 1930 the Chinese formed nearly half of Bangka's total population and about two-fifths of Belitung's. Dutch-appoint-

Right: *Striking rock formations border pristine white-sand beaches on both Bangka and Belitung.*

ed Chinese officers managed the mines, and were granted in return the lucrative right to sell opium and provide other profitable services. Some became immensely wealthy and erected opulent mansions which may be seen today. Relations between the Chinese and the indigenes have always been good, a fact that all Bangkans are proud of.

Working conditions improved after the mines were mechanized in the 20th century. During the Great Depression, many coolies were laid off and some returned to China. Today only a quarter of Bangka's inhabitants are Chinese; on Belitung only an eighth. The work force in the mines is now made up of local people and Indonesian migrants. The state-owned mining company, Tambang Timah, controls most of the production, although some mines are leased to foreign concerns and local entrepreneurs. While the tin on Belitung has become scarce, mining and pepper continue to dominate the economy of Bangka. Additional income is provided by coconuts, cloves, cocoa, rubber, forestry and fishing. The islands' natural beauty is also being tapped for tourism now, and several large-scale resorts are planned.

Visiting Bangka

Bangka's administrative capital and main port of entry is **Pangkalpinang**, a bustling town of about 100,000 on the island's east coast. Start at the Post Office here and walk south along Jl. Jend. Sudirman to see the city. The mayor's residence, the town square (now a playing field) and many houses date back to the colonial period when the Dutch mining company controlled the island's economy.

There is a small museum belonging to Tambang Timah, the state mining company, near its headquarters at the intersection of Jl. Jend. A. Yani and Jl. Depati Amir, but it is only sporadically open. The Chinese temple on Jl. Mayor Haji Muhidir is in the middle of the business district and was built in the 1830s, when the first mines opened in this part of the island. At that time the town area was a maze of digging sites.

Bangka's best beaches are on the island's northeastern shores (see "Tin Island Practicalities"). The main road to the area leads north of Pangkalpinang through Baturusa to Sungailiat and Belinyu, about 2 hours away by car. Many sideroads to the right along the way end at lovely, white-sandy coves.

Some 10 km north of Pangkalpinang you enter **Baturusa** ("Deer Rock"), and on the right is an early-19th century Chinese temple (*klenteng*)—but alas, it has been extensively renovated. A few houses in this area are still built in the traditional manner, roofed with thatch and walled with bark, but most are of brick and cement. The lakes you pass are the flooded pits of open cut mines.

There is another temple in **Sungailiat** ("Clay River"), 20 km north, with a bell dated

JILL GOCHER

1864 that was cast in China in Foshan, northern Fujian Province. In **Pemali**, just past Sungailiat, is a hot spring and an open pit mine worked with heavy equipment.

From Sungailiat to **Belinyu** is another 50 km, and here a small track to the left leads you to the village of Panji, site of a 200-year-old Chinese temple (although the present building is newer). The grave (dated 1795) of its founder—a tin magnate named Bong Kiung Fu or Kapitan Bong—once lay near the temple, but has been relocated inside the nearby ruins of a *benteng* or fort built in the 18th century for protection against frequent pirate raids. From a nearby stream, now silted up, a magical white crocodile is said to have ruled over the area. With a little urging, the old and nearly toothless caretaker at the fort will provide a story or two about the site.

Bangka's west coast

Mentok on the west coast was Bangka's original capital—strategically facing across the Bangka Strait just opposite the mouth of the Musi River which leads up to Palembang. Mentok is said to have been founded by Chinese in-laws of the Sultan of Palembang at the beginning of the 18th century, just as tin was being discovered here. Tin mining quickly took off, but the mines in the Mentok area gave out a century later, whereupon mining activity shifted to the north and the east. The Dutch used Mentok as the capital until 1913, then moved it to Pangkalpinang.

Mentok is about 120 km (3 hours) from Pangkalpinang. In the town's harbor across from the tin smelting plant stands an old lighthouse that guides vessels through the treacherous Bangka Strait. This and an old fortress at its base are said to have been built by the British during Raffles' tenure in Java, between 1812 and 1817. During WW II, the Japanese used the fort to house Allied prisoners-of-war, many of whom died here.

Mentok's mid-19th century mosque is constructed in the traditional Palembang style; immediately adjacent to it is an even older Chinese temple, probably built in the 1830s. The proximity of the two symbolizes Bangka's history of tolerance. The town's large Rumah Mayor was the luxurious home of two former Chinese officers, a father and a son by the name of Tjoeng. The vast veranda with its imposing columns reflects the family's former wealth, which derived from a traffic in opium and coolies. The interior fittings, especially the family altar, show that money was no object in the attempt to recreate an ostentatious Mandarin lifestyle on Bangka.

Hire a local guide to take you up a hill north of town to see the graves of the Chinese Muslims who founded Mentok, and who came there from Siantan in the South China Sea. Bangkans claiming the titles *abang* (for men) and *yang* (for women) are descended from them. The Tjoeng family erected elabo-

rate tombs decorated with hand-printed tiles.

On nearby **Mt. Menumbing** (445 m) is the guesthouse where President Soekarno, Vice President Hatta and other nationalist leaders were housed after being captured by the Dutch toward the end of the revolution. The place was surrounded by a barbed wire fence until United Nations observers and journalists arrived and began focusing world attention on the plight of the hostages. The guesthouse is open to the public.

Traveling overland after dusk, you will see family altars illuminated by the glow of electric candles in traditional Chinese homes.

Visiting Belitung

For many centuries, Belitung's rock-studded coastline and offshore island with hundreds of tiny coves made it a perfect pirates' nest. The island lay on the fringe of powerful Sumatran and Javanese kingdoms, but was so poor that they rarely, if ever, took any interest. In 1822, five pirate boats captured the Dutch ship *Anna Maria* and sold the captain and navigator to the chief of Sijuk, on the island's north coast. The two men remained for several years as slaves until they were rescued by a Malay nobleman, who paid a ransom of 2 balls of opium. Other Dutchmen were apparently enslaved at Burung Mandi on the east coast. No one knows what became of them, but when the Dutch finally seized control of the island, a Dutch-style building was found there.

Today, most visitors to Belitung come to laze on the island's excellent beaches. The capital and main port of entry is **Tanjung Pandan** ("Pandanus Cape") on the west coast. Next to the tin company (P.T. Timah) offices in the center of town is the house of the former *kapitan* or head of the Chinese community, Ho A Joen. Unfortunately, the building has been renovated, but the Ho family altar still stands inside the house.

Head south from here to the town's Chinese quarter. Three Chinese mansions formerly lined the main street, but only one remains. It houses a small museum with family photos and antiques. The road continues from here past a bustling morning fish market down to the harbor, where Bugis sailing craft load pepper and kaolin for Java. Turn west (right) to the beach; this is where Tanjung Pandan's best houses once stood overlooking the sea. The beach offers a splendid view of Kalmoa Island to the west, and the sunsets here are particularly lovely.

On a hillside south of town is a *benteng* (fort) from which the Depati (native ruler) of Belitung directed his struggle against the Dutch. From the fort you have a view of the mouth of the Berutak River, teeming with crocodiles.

Beaches and pirate coves

Belitung's best beaches are on the northern shore facing the South China Sea—reached via a scenic road that hugs the coast north of the capital. At **Tanjung Kelayang**, 35 km from Tanjung Pandan, glistening white sand beaches are bordered by photogenic rock formations, and the water is as deep blue as the sky. From here you can walk 2 km east along the shore to Tanjung Tinggi—past secluded coves with idyllic beaches where you can swim and sunbathe in absolute privacy. Bring along a picnic lunch.

Boats can be hired to a group of tiny offshore islands where more spectacular beaches await you. A lighthouse and a sea turtle hatchery are found on **Langkuas**, the island farthest from the shore. On the beaches or amongst the trees along the north shore, look for tiny black stones known as Billitonites—said to be bits of fallen meteors.

Other good beaches are found at the southwestern tip of the island on Gembira Bay just south of Membalong, about 60 km from Tanjung Pandan. From here (also from Tanjung Pandan) you can hire a boat to **Mendanau Island**, where pirates are said to have hidden their loot in caves tucked in amongst the coastal rock formations.

On the east coast of Belitung, **Burung Mandi** ("Birdbath") is another former pirate hang-out. An attractive Chinese temple perches on a bluff overlooking the sea here and is dedicated to the Chinese Goddess of Mercy, Guan Yin, who is frequently supplicated for advice and assistance—especially in the hopes of conceiving a son. The beach below the temple is not as white as some but is a wonderful place to watch the sunrise.

Burung Mandi is 90 km east of Tanjung Pandan, north of the town of Manggar. Two roads connect Tanjung Pandan to Manggar, both passing up and over **Mount Tajam**—the highest peak on the island, which has a refreshing spring, waterfall and lake at its summit. Also here is the *kramat* or holy grave of Datuk Gunung Tajam, who is said to have brought Islam to the island from Aceh in the 16th century.

— *Mary Somers Heidhues/Myra Sidharta*

Opposite: *Smoking fish on the island of Bangka.*

PART IX

Introducing Bengkulu

Bengkulu is the smallest and least populated of Sumatra's provinces—with fewer than a million people living in an area of 21,168 sq km—yet its historical and natural charms rival those of any other part of this huge island. The province encompasses a 500-km-long stretch of unspoiled sandy coastline fringed with casuarina trees. From the sea, the land ascends rapidly to the lofty peaks of the Bukit Barisan. Tigers, elephants and rhinos still roam its pristine jungles, where the exotic rafflesia and wild orchids bloom.

For 140 years Bengkulu was Britain's sole colony in Southeast Asia. Established as an alternative source of pepper after the Dutch seized control of Banten in the 17th century, the tiny British outpost on this sparsely-populated coast never amounted to much, as pepper's importance in the world economy soon declined and Bengkulu lay too far off the major trading routes to offer much else. From 1685 to 1825, reports of the East India Company record continual tales of dismal commerce, boredom and early death on this malarial coast, where months could pass without sighting a ship or news from home.

Fort York, the first British base, was built here in 1685, and in 1715, Fort Marlborough was constructed 2 km away. The British found the local Rejang people "indolent" and began punishing their rulers. When William Dampier was at Bengkulu in 1690, he found two local rulers in the stocks "for no other reason but because they had not brought down to the Fort such a quantity of Pepper as the Governour had sent for." Despite the protests of home authorities, similar treatment continued to be meted out during the 18th and early 19th centuries.

Bengkulu was briefly shaken out of its torpor during the governorship of Thomas Stamford Raffles (1818-1824), but in 1825 the colony was surrendered to the Dutch in exchange for undisputed British influence in the Malay Peninsula and Singapore. During his residence in Bengkulu, Raffles undertook the naval explorations which led to the founding of Singapore. The satisfaction he felt on seeing his new colony flourish was tempered by the sad fact that three of his four children died in Bengkulu. The precise whereabouts of their graves is unknown.

British influence was restricted to the narrow coastal plain. The mountainous hinterland was annexed by the Dutch after a series of military campaigns in the 1850s. At the end of the 19th century the Dutch discovered that Bengkulu's mountains contained rich deposits of gold, and Bengkulu rapidly became the largest gold-producing area in the Dutch East Indies.

Bengkulu's people consist of four main groups. The Rejang are mountain dwellers and form the majority. They are subdivided into two populations—the highland Rejang and the Rejang Pesisir who have moved down to the western lowlands. In the south dwell the Serawai, who are related to the Pasemah people who live in the highlands around Pagaralam and Mt. Dempo. Many of the residents of the capital are Malays.

The region has been inhabited since prehistoric times, as is shown by the discovery of stone tools in the northern area, and megalithic structures and ancient drums of Dongson type in the south. The isolated island of Enggano off the south coast was the home of a separate group of people, distantly related to inhabitants of the Mentawai Islands further north. The Engganese, long protected by their remote location, were decimated by smallpox and other diseases introduced by Western visitors in the late 19th century, and soon afterwards their traditional culture was destroyed; the island is now almost deserted.

—*John Miksic*

Overleaf: Rafflesia arnoldi, *the world's largest flower; a meter across. Photo by Alain Compost.*
Opposite: *Bengkulu woman. Photo by Steve Teo.*

BENGKULU SIGHTS

In Search of a Somnolent Colonial Past

Bengkulu is essentially a colonial town—it was founded by the British in 1685 and occupied by them until 1825 (they called it "Bencoolen"), when the Dutch took over, staying up until the Japanese invasion in 1942. It still seems much as it was described then—quiet and tidy. A walking tour is the best way to explore what remains of Bengkulu's colonial past. Start early in the morning, as the heat can be quite unbearable during the day.

Begin at the western end of Jl. Jend. A. Yani, next to the cupola-roofed memorial to Thomas Parr—the unpopular governor of Bengkulu who was stabbed to death and beheaded (probably by Bugis mercenaries) in 1807 while resting at his garden house, 5 km from the fort. Parr had trained in Bengal and was accustomed to unquestioning obedience from a submissive and subjugated people. Once in Bengkulu, he attempted to re-

duce the power of the "Bugis Corps" which had been recruited to supplement the East India Company's forces. After Parr's assasination, a few local rulers who were under suspicion were blown from the guns and several villages were burnt in vengeance. However, relations between the British and Indonesians were not always this bad, and the large Eurasian population led to Bengkulu being dubbed "a regular Batavian colony" by a British critic, meaning that there was "too much mixing of races."

Fort Marlborough

Continue down Jl. A. Yani to Fort Marlborough. The fort was built by the British East India Company between 1713 and 1719, and was carefully restored between 1977 and 1984. Its plan is rectangular, measuring 240 by 170 meters, with projecting bastions on the four corners.

Fort Marlborough was built to replace Fort York. William Dampier, who served as gunner at Fort York, nevertheless declared it to be the most irregular piece of defensive work he had ever seen. "It would moulder away every wet season and the Guns often fall down into the Ditches." And impressive as the fort looked, it fell to the enemy on the only two occasions in which it was attacked— the first time in 1719 by a local uprising, and the second in 1760 by a passing French fleet.

The outer wall is surrounded by a dry

moat. As well as protecting the fort from attack, this moat—according to India Office records—prevented the sentries from sneaking off to the nearby *kampung* to buy toddy, the powerful alcoholic drink made from the sweet sap of palms!

After 1825, Fort Marlborough was used by the Dutch until the Japanese invasion of 1942. After Japan's surrender, it was briefly occupied by the police of the fledgling Republic of Indonesia. The Dutch reoccupied the fort during their attempt to crush the Indo-

nesian revolutionary forces, but in 1950 it was restored to the police, who continued to use it until the mid-1980s. The fort is now open to the public as a museum.

The fort's main entrance faces south, and is protected by a barbican (a double wall). As you enter the outer defenses, you are greeted by the elaborately inscribed tombstones of British officers who served here, including that of Thomas Parr—now worn smooth by the elements. Both the northern and southern entrances were formerly accessed by crossing small wooden bridges. A door on the east side also led out to the Indian soldiers' quarters. There is no rear wall—an earthen rampart defended the fort.

The fort's massive wooden gates open onto a peaceful, manicured courtyard. On one side is the cell in which Soekarno was briefly held in the early days of his exile; on the other is a small museum. Climbing up to the ramparts affords a good view of the town and the sea. A tall tower originally stood over the north gate, but collapsed due to repeated earthquakes. There were no buildings inside the fort; soldiers' quarters, kitchens, offices, guardrooms and stores were all built into the walls. Some of these rooms are now used for displays illustrating the history of the fort, including artifacts discovered during the recent restoration. Poignant graffiti adorn the wall of one room that was used as a prison.

The area around the fort has a brooding

and melancholic air, especially in the evenings—almost as if the sad ghost of Raffles still paces the ramparts, scanning the horizon for the sails of the Fame, a ship which was to deliver him and his ailing wife, Sophia, from Bengkulu. The former **British Residency** is just across from the fort, set back a little from the main road. Now derelict and crumbling, it is surrounded by warehouses and occupied by stray dogs. About 200 m to the north is a point of land called Tapak Paderi, providing beautiful sunset views over the sea. The open square southeast of the fort dates from the time when the British laid out the settlement.

Leaving Fort Marlborough, walk to the old **Chinese quarter** which is located around Jl. D. I. Penjaitan, just behind the British residence and close to the Parr monument. Here, rows of two-storied old wooden shop houses with ornately-carved balconies line both sides of the street. These buildings were all constructed in 1926 after the quarter was destroyed in one of the earthquakes which periodically afflict the province.

The European cemetery

From the fort, a pleasant, 15-minute walk brings you to an obelisk on Jl. Letkol Santoso in the southeastern part of the town, erected over the remains of Captain Robert Hamilton, "who died on the 15th of December 1793 at the Age of 38 Years in Command of the Troops." (Hamilton apparently had an affair with a local girl!)

From here walk a few hundred meters north to the old European cemetery. Most of the British graves date from the late 18th and early 19th century; the later graves are Dutch. During the period of British rule, there were never more than a handful of European wo-

Opposite: *Fort Marlborough, constructed by the British between 1713-19 and now fully restored.*
Above, left: *One of the fort's old cannons.*
Above, right: *Tombstone of a British officer.*

men in Bengkulu and some of the tombstones are affectionately telling: Captain Thomas Tapston's "was erected to his Memory by his much afflicted friend, Nonah Jessminah." Unfortunately, many of the graves have been vandalized. Raffles' three children who died in Bengkulu are possibly buried here, though their gravesites are unknown until this day.

Soekarno's house

A short walk to the east will bring you to the house where Indonesia's first president Soekarno, his first wife, Inggit, and his adopted daughter, Ratna Juami, were exiled by the Dutch from 1938 to 1941. The house is located on Jalan Soekarno-Hatta, in the district called Anggut Atas. On the verandah is the trusty bicycle that Soekarno used while courting his second wife, Fatmawati, then a local Bengkulu belle (Soekarno was in his late thirties at that time). In wooden cabinets are his books, mostly in Dutch, and his clothes. Faded pictures of the family adorn the walls. The house is open 8 am to 2 pm Tues to Thurs, Fri 8-11 and Sat 8-12. There is a small admission charge.

Fort York

Fort York, built in 1685, stood about 2 km north of Marlborough, on the south bank of the Bengkulu River. The area is now called Pasar Bengkulu in memory of the time when the town's main market lay near the fort. No

traces of the old brick fort can be seen, but archaeologists have discovered the foundations of the walls and artifacts used by the fort's inhabitants on the hill where a primary school and slaughterhouse now stand. From the hill you can look down on a landing where local fishing boats sell their catch on the riverbank early in the morning.

The provincial museum

The provincial museum, which is in the southern suburbs of town in an area called Padang Harapan, has extensive collections ranging from prehistoric stones and ancient bronze drums to wooden models of traditional houses. Other displays include traditional Engganese textiles and looms. Of special interest is the batik cloth made in Bengkulu called *kain besuruh*, with designs incorporating Arabic calligraphy and the Majapahit sunburst.

There are also displays of imported ceramics and of *tabut*—towers made of wood and paper used in a local ritual of the same name. Each year on the 10th of Muharram, the first month of the Muslim year, the towers—some as tall as 10 m—are borne in procession through the town in honor of the Prophet Muhammad's grandson, Husein, who fell at the battle of Karbala in Iran in AD 680.

This ceremony is a remnant of earlier Shiite influence, though Bengkulu—like the rest of Indonesia—now follows the Sunni school of Islam. There are two small shrines in the

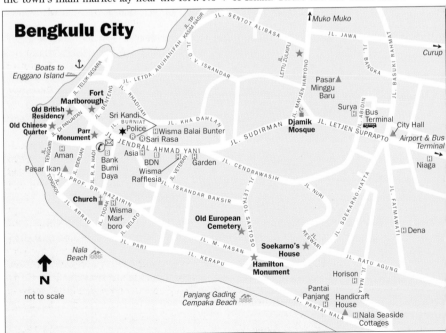

town where those who are to take part in the *tabut* go to burn candles and make requests. If their petitions are granted they will sponsor the construction of a *tabut* tower. The museum is open 8-2 pm Tues to Thurs; 8-11 am on Fri and Sat; closed Mon.

Natural attractions

There are three main places of natural interest on the fringe of Bengkulu town. One is the beautiful, 7-km-long beach which begins at Pantai Nala and continues south, where its name changes to Pantai Panjang Gading Cempaka. Gading Cempaka was a legendary princess whose skin was as fair as ivory (*gading*) and as fragrant as frangipani (*cempaka*). Swimming here is generally safe, but large waves and a strong undertow make it necessary to exercise caution. Signs are erected at the safest swimming spots.

Another spot which attracts nature lovers is a lake called **Danau Dendam Tak Sudah** ("Lake of the Never-Ending Grudge") which lies about 8 km southeast of the town. This lake is surrounded by low hills, above which you can see the peaks of the Barisan mountains in the distance. At the northern edge of the peaty water is a nature reserve where a particular variety of wild water orchid flourishes, the *Vanda hookeriana*.

The small island of **Pulau Tikus** ("Rat Island") lies about 5 km off the coast of Bengkulu. The island measures only 60 by 100 m, and is part of a much bigger coral reef which lies beneath it. In the colonial period, ships anchored in the lee of this reef to be safe from storms raging in the Indian Ocean beyond. Large iron anchors are still set in the reef. Snorkelers and scuba divers report that it is exceptionally rich in marine life.

Bengkulu sidetrips

Bengkulu has many attractions for travelers who wish to see Sumatran nature in its pristine state. Most of these lie in the Barisan Mountains, and can be reached along a winding road which leads, via Kepahiang, to the large town of Curup.

In November the huge *Rafflesia arnoldi* blooms along the banks of streams in the primary forest. The most accessible sites for viewing the world's largest flower are the areas near Taba Penanjung, Bengkulu's official rafflesia reserve on the main Bengkulu-Kepahiang road. Visitors should call at the forestry office in Bengkulu to find out whether any giant flowers are in bloom.

Curup, 85 km northeast of Bengkulu, is an attractive, cool hill town in the Barisan mountains where local agricultural products are sold in the town's market. The town is connected to Bengkulu by a good paved road climbing up through the forests in Barisan mountain and offering spectacular view of Bengkulu city and the Indian Ocean. Major crops are rice, coffee and vegetables such as carrots and cabbage. Rice mills driven by water power can still be seen in many areas of the Tebong Valley around Curup.

A few kilometers outside Curup is a hot spring, **Suban Air Panas**, a popular weekend spot. In ancient times the spring appears to have been a religious site, for on a low rise near it is a base for a statue and a crude Siva *lingga*. A few meters further up the slope is another stone carved into a rectangular shape —connected with a legend about a princess named Puteri Swangka. Another ancient remnant is a large, flat stone called Batu Panco that was possibly used as a meditational spot by religious ascetics. From Curup a road leads north to Muara Aman—center of the gold mining industry during the colonial period. Along the way it passes a lovely mountain lake, **Danau Tes**, famous locally for its scenic beauty and for being the largest lake in Bengkulu.

There are several active volcanoes in the province. Behind Curup towers Bukit Kaba, 1,937 m high, with two main and 12 subsidiary craters emitting sulphurous gases. The most serious eruption occurred in 1845, when 150 people were killed.

Bengkulu also has two major parks. In the north, near Seblat, Mt. Bukit Gedang forms part of the huge **Kerinci-Seblat National Park**. This park, which is Indonesia's largest, is home to rare wildlife such as the Sumatran elephant, rhinoceros and tiger, as well as more common animals like deer, birds and monkeys. (See "Kerinci-Seblat Park" in WEST SUMATRA). In the south, the **Bukit Barisan Selatan National Park** includes the region of Kaur Timur. Besides elephants, tigers and crocodiles, this park contains the Sumatran mountain goat and the slow loris.

In the sub-district of North Bengkulu, 114 km off the coast, lies **Enggano Island**—with its numerous coral sea gardens, sparkling seas and lovely beaches. However, the coastline is swampy and the only way to get there is to take a boat which operates irregularly from Bengkulu. Once you are there, there is no other way of getting around on the 29 by 18 km island except on foot!

— John Miksic

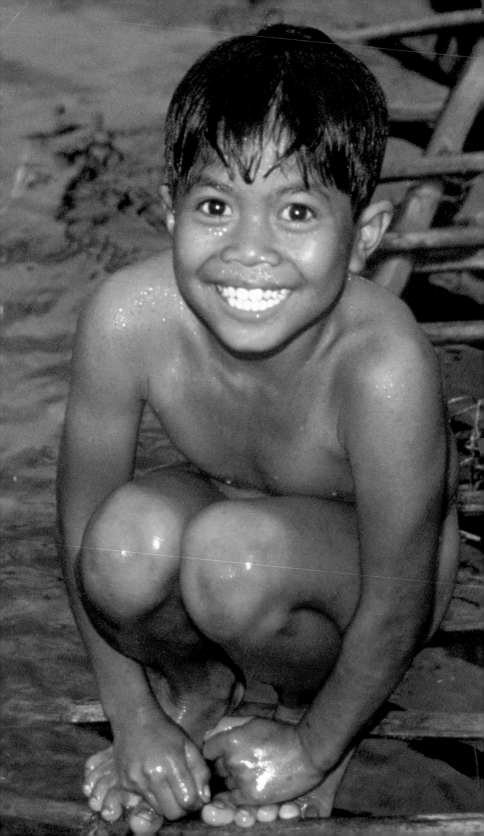

PART X

Introducing Lampung

Lampung is one of the most interesting, and yet least known provinces of Indonesia. It occupies the southernmost tip of Sumatra—separated from Java by the shallow Sunda Straits, that are less than 30 km wide at their narrowest point. Lampung has consequently been the area of Sumatra most influenced, socially and economically, by its densely populated and politically powerful neighbor.

Until the early decades of this century Lampung, like most of Sumatra, was very sparsely populated. Due mainly to a flood of immigrants from Java, it has had one of the highest population growth rates in Indonesia in recent years, and is now the most densely populated (and poorest) province in Sumatra. In the past two decades, the population has grown from 2.5 to over 6 million people living in an area of 33,307 sq km.

Only one in ten of Lampung's present inhabitants is descended from the original population, which comprised three distinct groups: the Orang Abung or mountain people who practiced headhunting and remained in isolation until the 19th century; the Orang Pubian who inhabited the eastern lowlands; and the Orang Peminggir or peoples of the south coasts around Lampung and Semangka Bays, who probably came under the suzerainty of Palembang-based Srivijaya, and were later Islamized through influence from Java.

According to local legends, all these people have a single ancestor, Si Lampung, from whom the province derives its name. Their descendants today speak two closely-related languages, Komering and Lampung, but due to the influx of migrants, even more people here now speak Sundanese or Javanese.

Life in Lampung was probably always unsettled—especially along the coasts, which were susceptible to piratical slave raids. Many early settlements were protected by earthen ramparts and thorny bamboo hedges. Two inscriptions of the mighty Srivijayan empire attest to a direct involvement in the late 7th century, no doubt fostered by Lampung's rich resources of gold and dammar (a valuable tree resin). In the 16th century, the Islamic sultans of Banten in West Java gradually took control of the region, conferring the title of *punggawa* (representative) on Lampung chiefs in return for deliveries of pepper grown in the interior. This made Banten the largest and wealthiest pepper port in the archipelago at the time that the first Europeans arrived. The Dutch eventually took over this trade in the late 17th century.

The traditional culture of Lampung reflects indigenous beliefs overlain by Hindu-Buddhistic and Islamic influences. A strong megalithic tradition continued until fairly recent times; the *pepadon* or ritual throne used by Lampung chiefs appears to have had megalithic origins, and ancient stone sculptures show the ancestors with symbolic motifs that suggest sacrificial rites. The influence of Dongson bronze kettledrums is also apparent in the spirals, curves and stylized human and animal figures of the sacred Lampung "ship cloths." These ubiquitous fabrics played an important role in ritual and marriage ceremonies, and rank among the world's most striking traditional textiles.

Rapid changes have taken place over the past century. Beginning in Dutch times, migrations were encouraged as a means of relieving Java's population problems. This was stepped up in the 1960s and '70s through government transmigration programs (which have now stopped). Today only about 20 percent of Lampung's forests remain—some, like Way Kambas Reserve, now designated as special wildlife areas. Most other areas are cultivated with wet-rice *sawah* or groves of oil palms, rubber, coconut, coffee and cloves.

— *E. E. McKinnon/K. H. Picard*

Overleaf: *Herding wild elephants into the Way Kambas Game Reserve. Photo by Max Lawrence.*
Opposite: *Enjoying a swim. Photo by Jill Gocher.*

SHIP CLOTHS

Rare Ritual Fabrics of Lampung

The three peoples native to Lampung—the Abung in the north, the Pubian in the center and the Peminggir along the southern coast —are all famous for a distinctive form of textile that commonly features geometric ship motifs. These extraordinary fabrics are collectively known as "ship cloths" and are prized the world over by textile collectors.

The production of these striking cloths— usually of cotton but sometimes of silk— dates back to an era when a lucrative pepper trade flourished in Lampung. The collapse of the pepper trade in the last century brought about the demise of many local traditions— including the time-consuming production of these ritual cloths, which have not been woven for over 100 years. Nowadays such fabrics are rare collector's items, costing a small fortune when they can be found at all.

By their form and function, the cloths may be divided into two categories: *tampan* and *palepai*. The former are small and square in shape, measuring no more than a meter across; the latter are long and narrow, averaging 3 meters in length and half a meter in width. The ornamentation of the two is quite different—*tampan* often have very precise, even abstract motifs, whereas *palepai* normally depict solid, easily recognizable objects. The decorative style of both displays a clear affinity with Bronze Age designs found on Dongson kettledrums (see "Prehistory"), especially the stylized double spirals, meanders and hook-and-key motifs on the borders.

Tampan and *palepai* were woven by identical techniques—single-colored supplemental wefts were applied to a plain weave foundation. The biggest job was to count out the threads needed for the intricate patterns before mounting them on the handloom. Peminggir women made *palepai* as well as *tampan*; Pubian and Abung women made *tampan* only.

Ritual uses

The Peminggir are organized in patrilineal descent groups or *suku*. Four or more of these *suku* constitute a so-called *marga*. Their members have a number of titles, of which the Penyimbang, descendants of the founder of a *suku* or *marga*, are the most important— representing an aristocratic class privileged to own *palepai*.

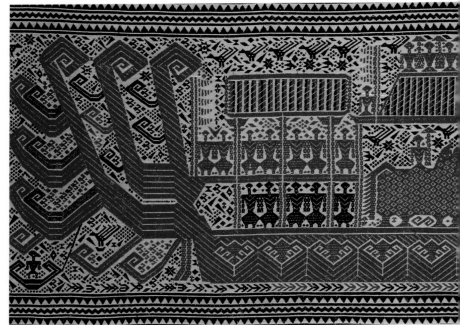

The long *palepai* cloths are employed in all life-cycle rites that a Penyimbang undergoes: birth, circumcision, marriage and death. Apart from this, they are used in rites marking the attainment of higher rankings within the elaborate social hierarchy. During such rites, the *palepai* are hung on a wall inside the house and serve to indicate the family's status within its *marga*. Traditionally there were "strong" and "weak" *suku*—classifications based on the relative age, wealth and size of the descent group.

Tampan cloths are similarly used during life-cycle rites—but unlike *palepai*, they are not the prerogative of any particular group. During such rites the initiate often sits on a *tampan*, and ceremonial gifts of food are also wrapped in them. The quantity is what is most important—the more *tampan* one gives, the more one is respected. Whereas *palepai* remain in the possession of a particular *suku* and symbolize the ruling class, *tampan* circulate among descent groups in all levels of society.

Motifs and symbolism

A number of small, clearly recognizable objects are often depicted on *palepai* standing astride the deck of the ship: people, animals, trees and houses. A distinction is usually made between *palepai* having blue and those having red ships. On very rare *palepai* only rows of human figures are shown whithout any ship at all.

The designs of *tampan* are much more diverse and difficult to categorize. The ship motif is, as on the rare *palepai*, sometimes completely missing—in which case the design may consist of a big bird or various small birds, a tree, or other more abstract motifs. Simple rows of human forms are also found on *tampan*.

The ship motif nevertheless predominates on all these cloths—above all symbolizing transition and movement, a notion appropriate to the life-cycle rituals in which they are used. Apart from this, the ship also expresses social structure. The person undergoing the rite finds himself on the border between two phases in life—a time that is considered unsettling and potentially quite dangerous. He is helped along to the next stage by highly structured rituals, in which the society as a whole is represented as a ship carrying its members along.

During marriage rituals, for instance, the bridal couple is borne in a procession in the shape of a ship, in which all *suku* in the *marga* take up prescribed positions. In this way, the newlyweds are brought from a temporarily insecure position on the fringes of society to a secure and stable position within the social fabric.

— *Toos van Dijk and Nico de Jonge*

Below: *A* palepai *of the red ship type.*

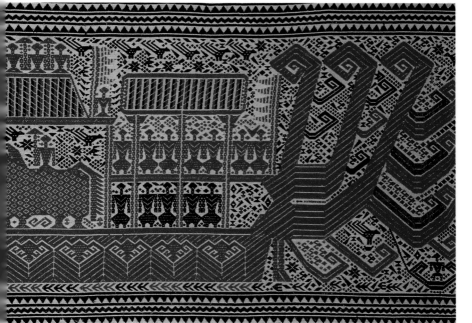

LAMPUNG SIGHTS

Scenic Bays at Sumatra's Southern Tip

Though it is possible to fly to Lampung from Jakarta in under an hour, visitors are encouraged to make the 27-km ferry crossing from Merak, at the northwestern tip of Java, to the new ferry terminal at **Bakauheni** at Sumatra's southeastern extremity. The Sunda Strait separating these two huge islands have a certain grandeur and historical significance, and from the ferry you can sometimes catch ominous glimpses to the south of the infamous Krakatau volcano, which erupted with devastating force in 1883—producing tidal waves that killed 35,000 people on both sides of the straits (see "Krakatau").

From Bakauheni, it is an easy 99 km and 2 hours to Bandar Lampung along a broad, fast road. If you have the time, you can break your journey at **Kalianda**, 38 km from the ferry, to visit the old hot sulfur springs at Way Balirang, 3 km above the town. Constructed by

the Dutch, each of its three pools has a different mineral content. There is a small admission charge. There are also two other hot spring pools in the town itself. Also here are the remains of an old fort from which the Indonesian national hero Raden Intan II (1830-1889) harassed the Dutch. His grave, an object of veneration, lies nearby.

The Kalianda area is dominated by Mt. Rajabasa (1,281 m), a dormant volcano whose slopes are dotted with yellow-green clove trees. A scenic road encircles the volcano to the south of the town, passing along the coast though a series of lovely fishing villages.

From the village of **Canti** you can hop a small ferry to the offshore islands of Sebuku and Sebesi. Boats can also be chartered here for the choppy, 3-hour crossing to Krakatau. From Canti you can also climb up to Mt. Rajabasa's summit in several hours. Book a guide first at the Canti pier, register with the local police and get an early morning start.

North of Kalianda, the main road to Bandar Lampung heads inland, but after 9 km a well-marked sideroad to the left leads to a lovely beach at **Merak Belantung**, a sheltered cove off Lampung Bay. This sandy shore is ideal for swimming and sun-bathing, and there are small cottages here for rent and a restaurant offering meals by the beach.

Other beaches line the road much closer to Bandar Lampung, including **Pasir Putih**, 16 km south of the city, where you have spec-

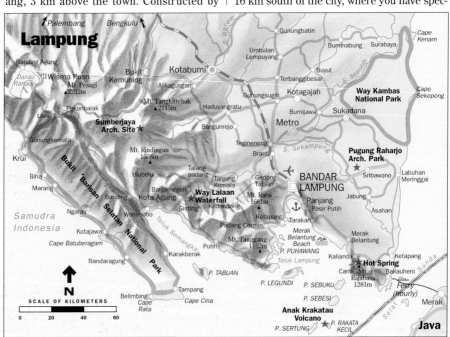

tacular views of Lampung Bay, several small uninhabited offshore islands, and Krakatau in the distance on a clear day. Small boats take you across to a white sand beach on **Condong Island**, which has food kiosks and is only 10 minutes away.

Bandar Lampung

The provincial capital and university town of Bandar Lampung overlooks one of the most scenic bays in the whole of Sumatra. The city was formed recently through an amalgamation of Tanjung Karang, the former colonial administrative center which lies up on a hillside overlooking the bay, and its adjacent port of Teluk Betung down by the water, terminus of the southern Sumatra railway system. Good roads link the capital with all other parts of the province, there are many fine hotels here, and interesting sidetrips can be made using the capital as your base.

The city's main attraction is the **Provincial Museum** on Jl. Teuku Umar, which has a good collection of *kain tapis* embroidered cloth, local musical instruments and wedding costumes. There is also a collection of archaeological finds from Labuan Meringgai (on the east coast) and Sumberjaya (in the northwest), including Dongson bronze drums, Chinese ceramics and carnelian and glass beads—all of which suggest that Lampung was involved in an extensive trading network linking it with eastern Indonesia, India and Indochina some 2,000 years ago.

In the evenings, the **Pasar Mambo** night market near the Teluk Betung harbor has delicious fresh seafood, while the open-air terrace of the **Marcopolo Hotel** up in Tanjung Karang is the perfect place to sit and admire the view as you enjoy a drink.

Eastern Lampung

An excursion to the east of Bandar Lampung leads to the elephant training station and nature reserve at Way Kambas (see "Way Kambas Reserve"), and can be combined with a stop at the fortified prehistoric site of **Pugung Raharjo**, 42 km to the northeast of the city. The latter covers an area of about 30 ha in the midst of pepper, clove and coffee plantations, and has remains dating from at least the 12th to the 17th centuries and probably earlier. Sights here include 13 prehistoric stepped temple mounds (*punden berundak*), a Buddhist statue and the remains of a fortified settlement. Legend has it that water from a spring at the site cures all ills and restores youth, and the area was once considered "haunted." It was uninhabited until transmigrants moved here in the 1950s, which is when the first artifacts were discovered.

To reach the site, take the road northeast from **Panjang** (6 km south of Bandar Lampung). The road climbs away from the bay

Below: *Islets dot the surface of Lampung Bay.*

ALAIN COMPOST

and across a broad plain to the Sekampung River valley. Shortly after crossing the river, a left-hand turn at the Jabung crossroads brings you 2 km north to the small site museum. Displays here include a 7th-century Srivijayan "curse" inscription discovered at the village of Bungkuk, and an unusual *bodhisattva* statue. A further 1 km along a paved road brings you to the archaeological site.

The ancient settlement was defended by an impressive series of ramparts and ditches the remains of which still run for 1,200 m along the eastern perimeter of the site and for 300 m along the west. Inside are a number of megalithic structures, including standing ancestor stones and ancient stepped pyramids which were probably used in pre-Islamic religious ceremonies. Many scholars think that such prehistoric mounds, such as those in India, may have influenced the development of later Buddhist monuments such as Borobudur. Other stones found here include mortars, possibly used in rain-making ceremonies, and several grooved *batu bergores*, the significance of which is unknown. Northeast of the complex is another small megalithic group, known as *batu umpak* (pedestals).

To contine on to Way Kambas, return to the main road and head east across a small range of hills to the coastal plain. Turn left at the T-junction and continue on past Jepara to **Tridatu**. The road to the reserve's elephant school is clearly signposted on the right.

The 16-km road into the park takes you through savannah-like country which is home to around 250 wild elephants. At the training school, which has 30 lumbering "pupils," you can watch the elephants being trained and take a short safari around the park. To visit the nearby Way Kanan River, continue along the main road for another 13.5 km. There, you may hire a *perahu* to take you downriver to the simple guesthouse. Some 280 bird species live along the river, so bring along your binoculars (see "Way Kambas Reserve" for more details).

Western Lampung

Most people just can't wait to hop on a bus to begin the long, arduous and often boring (especially in the south) journey up the Trans-Sumatran Highway to Bukittinggi and Lake Toba. In fact, many interesting sights lie in the vicinity of Bandar Lampung, particularly to the west of the city. Here the Bukit Barisan range meets the Indian Ocean and forms two huge bays—Semangka and Lampung—that create a long and incredibly dramatic coastline. The remote and densely forested mountains at the southwestern "heel" of Sumatra, encompassing much of western Lampung, have recently been declared a national park known as **Bukit Barisan Selatan National Park**. The park covers 3,568 sq km all up and down the west coast and mountains of Lampung province, and is the home of

JILL GOCHER

Sumatran tigers, honey bears, elephants, rhinos, bearded pigs, argus pheasants, rare orchids, rafflesias and the *Amorphophallus titanum*—the world's tallest flower.

A scenic road hugs the rocky western shore of Lampung Bay immediately to the southwest of Bandar Lampung, passing tiny coves and islets on the way to the village of **Padang Cermin**. About 35 minutes out of the city, you arrive at the fishing village of Ketapang, where it is possible to hire motorboats to offshore islands. Be aware that this

is also a top-secret Japanese pearl farming area, and security is tight in some places.

Another road heads due west of the city along the upper reaches of the Sekampung River to the town of **Kota Agung**, located at the head of Semangka Bay, about 2 hours away. After 1.5 hours you can stop at the foot of Mt. Tanggamus (2,102 m), where a concrete stairway constructed during the Dutch times leads 1,100 m down to waterfalls formed by the Way Lalaan River. Beyond the first fall, a second, grander fall awaits the visitor. Bring along your swimsuit!

From Kota Agung, it is possible to take a motorized *perahu* down the west coast of the bay to the village of **Tampang**, located at the southernmost tip of Bukit Barisan Selatan National Park, a journey of about 5 hours. From Tampang you can hike across the peninsula through the jungle along a 32-km trail to **Belimbing**. Of historical interest is a 57-m lighthouse overlooking Belimbing Bay, built in 1879 by the Dutch. From atop the lighthouse you have dramatic views of the Indian Ocean, its powerful surf crashing against the coast, and of a disused airstrip built by the Japanese during WW II. Take a guide and plenty of food and water.

The northwest coast

An alternative route into the park starts at **Bukit Kemuning**, 130 km north of Bandar Lampung on the Trans-Sumatran Highway,

and cuts westward through the mountains to the traditional fishing village of Krui, on the west coast. The road climbs up through the hills, affording magnificent views. At Simpangsari, about 30 km from Bukit Kemuning, turn off left to visit the megalithic complex at **Sumberjaya**, near the headwaters of the Way Besai, a tributary of the mighty Tulangbawang River. Here rows of large upright ancestor stones and dolmens stand facing nearby Mt. Abung. Imported Chinese ceramics from the 8th to 11th centuries (Srivijayan period), which may have been used in ritual ceremonies, have been recovered at Sumberjaya. Other megalithic complexes can be seen in the immediate vicinity.

Further west, you pass several dammar (resin) collecting villages. At **Liwa** a sideroad forks north to beautiful Lake Ranau (see "Palembang Sidetrips" in SOUTH SUMATRA).

From Liwa the road descends steeply through a pass to the coastal village of **Krui**. Pisang Island, visible to the northwest, is where Lampung's famous *kain tapis* are woven and can be reached by boat. Krui is also known for its pepper. During the British occupation of Bengkulu (1685-1824), a tiny outpost was established here.

In the old graveyard at Krui was a tombstone which was once in English but had been reinscribed in the Lampung script. It commemorated one "Bob Brown, son of James Brown Esq." who was Resident of Krui from 1809 to 1814. A translation of the Lampung script reads: "This is the inscription of the grave of Bab Barawan, son of the Resident Masta Barawan Iskanwayar, from a union with a Lampung woman." The dates are illegible but presumably predate Brown's resignation in November of 1814.

— *E. Edwards McKinnon*

Opposite: *Traditional Lampung wedding costumes show a distinctive Srivijayan Malay influence.*
Above, left and right: *Fishing in Lampung Bay.*

WAY KAMBAS RESERVE

Training an Elephant to Play Ball?

Ear-splitting trumpeting echoes across the forest as a young elephant struggles against stout ropes holding it to a wooden frame—and against the pressure of an immense adult elephant. The young wild elephant is undergoing its initiation into Indonesia's first and only elephant training program—designed to transform it within a few years from a wild beast into a tractable, domesticated creature. The elephant training center (Pusat Latihan Gajah) is at **Kandangsari**, in Lampung's Way Kambas Reserve.

Way Kambas is one of the oldest reserves in Indonesia, declared in 1937. It covers a triangle of marshy lowlands along the eastern coast of Lampung, measuring some 1,300 sq km in area. The habitats at Way Kambas are different from those of other Sumatran parks, as they consist largely of freshwater swamps and include one of the few stands of lowland dipterocarp forests in any Sumatran reserve. The coast is lined with mangroves, nipa palms and casuarinas. It was declared a reserve because of its wildlife, and unfortunately most of the forests within the original park boundaries have been cut. Commercial products such as dammar (a tree resin used in making varnish), timber, honey and animals are still being extracted.

The elephant training program was started in the mid 1980s after much deliberation over what to do about southern Sumatra's wild elephant problem. Over the last 20 years the forests of this region have been cleared to make way for plantations and transmigration settlements. Of all the animals displaced, elephants have posed the most persistent nuisance to the new settlers—trampling crops and even attacking their homes. Villagers complained that while elephants had complete freedom to do as they pleased, they were not allowed to do anything to stop them, as elephants are a protected species.

The solution seemed simple enough. In other regions of South and Southeast Asia, elephants are commonly captured and domisticated. In Sumatra, this practice died out hundreds of years ago—but why not revive it? So in 1985, two Thai elephants and their mahouts were brought in to begin a training program, with the aim of taking animals from the wild and training them to become productive members of the tourism industry. Since it

ALAIN COMPOST

began, the program has dramatically raised the profile of the park—from an obscure reserve to a popular place offering "safari" rides on elephant back across the park's flat, open terrain.

In the West, there is a tendency to criticize the use of wild animals to provide amusement and labor for humans. But the alternative for these elephants would probably be a slow death after being caught in a poacher's noose or being poisoned by villagers. They can instead serve a useful purpose in attract-

ing tourists (and their money) to the region, providing jobs and helping to explain to people in concrete terms why there is a need for national parks and reserve areas.

Visiting Way Kambas

The main access to Way Kambas is from the village of **Tridatu**, 10 km north of Jepara. The turn-off to the right is well marked. It takes about 2 hours to drive here from Bandar Lampung, and about 3 hours from the Java-Sumatra ferry terminal at Bakauheni (7 hours altogether from Jakarta). Make sure you arrive during office hours, so that officials at the park office can issue you a permit.

It is estimated there are over 300 wild elephants living in Way Kambas, and this is the best place in Indonesia to see them. After their capture from the wild, the elephants are given twice-daily training classes, at 8 am and again at 3 pm. These classes at the same time provide training for local mahouts, each of whom is assigned his own elephant. It is hoped that looking after an elephant will become a source of pride and income for families in the area, with sons learning to take over from their fathers.

If you intend to stay overnight, there is a simple guesthouse at **Way Kanan**, 13.5 km past the park entrance. The road there is negotiable only by 4-wheel drive vehicles. (If you have no transport of your own, the park wardens will take you to Way Kanan on the

back of motorbikes for a small fee.) The guesthouse at Way Kanan is very basic, and you must bring along all food and eating utensils and to be prepared to cook over an open fire. For most people it is better to make a day trip, timing your visit to coincide with one of the elephant classes at Kandangsari.

Other wildlife abounds in the reserve. Along the road to Way Kanan, agile long-tailed macaques and heavier-set pig-tailed macaques watch you approach before dashing into the bushes, while families of pigs frequently trot across the road right in front of you. In the morning the wild calls of siamangs and dark-handed gibbons ring out in a wonderful morning chorus, adding to the natural concert of a whole host of birds.

From Way Kanan, take a boat downstream to the coast, and ask the driver to turn the motor off so you can drift quietly with the current and see more wildlife. Monitor lizards frequent the river banks, slipping into the river at the slightest disturbance. Giant squirrels and monkeys quickly scamper up trees along the banks, and stork-billed kingfishers with yellow head and red bill take flight in a streak of bright turquoise.

For birders with more time, an alternative route into Way Kambas is via the port of **Labuhan Meringgai**, south of the park. From the port it is a 4-hour boat ride up the coast to the Way Kambas estuary. The river is then navigable for 25 km upstream, and from the boat you can see colonies of herons, storks and waders. During the wet season (Nov to March), higher water levels offer an excellent opportunity to explore swamp areas which are normally inaccessible by canoe.

— Janet Cochrane

Opposite: *The Pusat Latihan Gajah (Elephant Training Center) at Way Kambas has become a popular tourist site. Here, trained elephants play a game of soccer.* **Above, left:** *Nipa palms line the Way Wako.* **Above, right:** *A baby elephant walk.*

KRAKATAU

The Day the World Exploded

Like battered teeth knocked from the mouth of Lampung Bay, the islands of Krakatau lie scattered in the Sunda Straits between Sumatra and Java. Greater eruptions have shaken the island—the one which created Lake Toba is thought to have been the largest the world has ever known—but none is a more powerful symbol of incalculable subterranean energy than the explosion which ripped the old island of Krakatau apart in 1883.

The name comes from an old Sanskrit word, *karkata*, meaning "crab" (perhaps referring to the shape of atolls once formed by the volcano's caldera). It lies in the middle of the Sunda Strait, right on the unstable "elbow" where the range of volcanic mountains forming Sumatra turns abruptly eastward to form Java. Ancient Javanese chronicles tell of a mountain here called Kapi, which in about AD 416 "burst into pieces with a tremendous roar and sank into the depths of the earth, and the water of the sea rose and inundated the land." Whether Kapi was Krakatau we shall never know, but geologists have shown that at least one massive eruption of Krakatau took place in pre-modern times.

Prelude

At the end of the 19th century, Krakatau was a fertile and pleasant island, though one which had been long been deserted by human inhabitants. Tropical jungle clothed the slopes of its three peaks—Rakata (830 m), Danan and Perbuatan. This was the spot where European mariners once filled their larders with giant sea turtles, as well as the occasional supplies of pepper and rice which they purchased from small villages along the shores.

The eruption of Krakatau was not unheralded. Beginning in early June, 1883, tremors shook the town of Anyer on the west coast of Java for several days. By the middle of June, puffs of steam and ash were visible above the cone of Perbuatan. But on an island where the earth regularly trembles and dozens of volcanoes frequently emit smoke, few took special notice.

By the end of June, however, Krakatau presented a fearsome sight. Two columns of steam rose from the island, now blanketed with grey ash, and only the bare trunks of large trees remained of the once-luxuriant jungle. The waters surrounding the island churned and heaved, while here and there floated carpets of pumice so thick a man could walk on them. A party of sightseers from Batavia reported a "fiery purple glow, appearing for a short while every 5 to 10 minutes, from which a fire rain fell."

Climax

This overture to one of nature's greatest known cataclysms lasted for 2 months. Finally, early in the afternoon of August 26th, 1883, Krakatau exploded with a series of roars heard round the world—from Rangoon, Burma to Perth, Australia. A pillar of ash and pumice towered 26 km into the sky. Rock and dust rained over the surrounding region, forming a blanket cloud which turned day into night for 150 km in every direction. Ash from the eruption gradually spread throughout the atmosphere, creating spectacular sunsets across the world for two years.

The finale came the following morning, when a gaping maw in the earth's crust—hollowed out by the expulsion of 18 cubic km of ash and rock—collapsed on itself. The sea rushed in and began to boil immediately upon contact with the molten rock, throwing up tsunamis (tidal waves) 10 meters high. The waves could still be detected a day and a half later when they finally rolled against the coast of France.

The devastation around Krakatau was of incredible proportions. All coastal villages facing the Sunda Straits were obliterated. No one knows the exact toll in human lives, though a common figure cited is 35,000. Eyewitnesses described a wall of water "taller than a palm tree" sweeping away everything in its path. In Teluk Betung (now Bandar Lampung), the funnel effect of the narrow Lampung Bay lifted the waves to a height of 30 meters, carrying a Dutch gunboat more than 2 km inland.

When the waves subsided and the dust dispersed, three quarters of Krakatau was gone. The peak of Rakata was still close to its original height, but its northern half had disappeared—sliced off as if by a knife, leaving a

Right: *An aerial view of Anak Krakatau.*

sheer cliff plunging 300 m to the sea below. Two islands, Panjang and Sertung, had been totally re-shaped, while debris from the eruption merged to form islands farther away.

Krakatau remained in a state of geological flux for some time. The new islands disappeared within a few years, but volcanic activity continued below the surface, and in January, 1928, the rim of a new crater arose close to where the vent of Perbuatan had first erupted. Since then, Anak Krakatau ("Child of Krakatau"), has continued to grow, and now stands 150 m high. This "baby island" gives scientists a fascinating opportunity to observe the colonization of plant and animal species on new soil.

Visiting Krakatau

To see Krakatau you need only travel on the ferry from Java and along the southeastern coasts of Lampung. As long as the air is clear, the old peak of Rakata will be visible on the horizon—a low, symmetrical cone about 50 km offshore. Although most people approach the volcano from Java's west coast, an excursion is also possible from **Canti**, a fishing village not far from the Java-Sumatra ferry, lying along the scenic road that encircles Mt. Rajabasa just south of Kalianda. Choose a sturdy boat and a reliable crew—the return journey can take 6-8 hours and the narrow straits can be dangerous in rough weather (expecially December to April).

Visitors land at the island's southern corner, where pine-like casuarinas, hardy colonizers of the shoreline, offer welcome shade. Walk north along the beach until the vegetation thins out, then strike uphill. The succulent plants of the shore quickly give way to clumps of tough grass, but even these only survive on the first few hundred meters.

The slope looks gentle but the going is tough. The fine, black volcanic sand, hot under the tropical sun, gives way underfoot, causing the trekker to slide backwards with each step. Twenty or thirty minutes brings you to the crest of a ridge—the outer edge of Anak Krakatau's crater. From here the view is spectacular. The smouldering cone is in front and a dark skirt of recent lava flows on either side—while behind you the slope you have just climbed spreads out like a fan, delicately edged with young, green vegetation and fringed with a line of surf. The older islands of Rakata, Sertung and Panjang hover in a circle like ladies-in-waiting.

The truly enthusiastic can venture further, down into a scorchingly hot valley where giant misshapen lumps of lava lie as they fell from the sky, and up a rocky path on the other side past sulphur fumaroles to the edge of the inner crater. The view is no better from here, but there is an awe-inspiring sensation in standing next to a void that leads straight into the underworld.

— Robert Cribb

ALAIN COMPOST

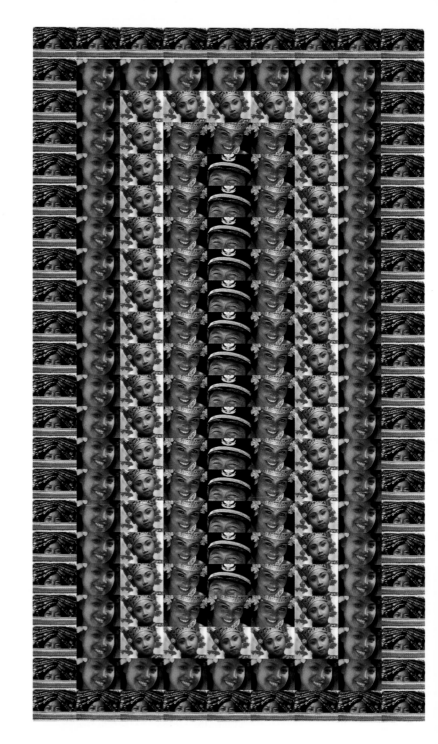

YOU COULD ENCOUNTER THEM in Paris or Vienna, Ambon or Biak. The faces that come from a melting pot of over 300 ethnic groups and 17,508 scattered islands.

OUR FACES NOW SPAN FOUR CONTINENTS AND 300 CULTURES.

The smiles and eyes that light up 34 far-flung cities across four continents and spread to 20 cities in the Indonesian Archipelago.

These are the people that have been hand-picked and trained as our cabin crew. And as they go across the world, they know no foreigners. Because the word 'foreigner' does not exist in our language.

The nearest word that we have is 'tamu'. It means very simply, guest.

Garuda Indonesia
THE AIRLINE OF INDONESIA

1 Medan

2 N. Sumatra

3 Aceh

4 W. Sumatra

5 Riau

6 Jambi

7 S. Sumatra

8 Bengkulu

9 Lampung

Practicalities

KNOW BEFORE YOU GO, TRAVEL ADVISORY, AREA PRACTICALITIES

The following Practicalities sections contain all the practical information you need for your journey. **Know Before You Go** provides background about traveling in Indonesia, from the economy and health precautions to bathroom etiquette. It is followed by a handy language primer. **Travel Advisory** is concerned exclusively with transportation: getting to and traveling around Sumatra.

The **Area Practicalities** sections focus on each destination and contain details on transport, accommodations, dining, the arts, trekking, shopping and services. Most include local street maps. These sections are organized by area and correspond to Parts II to X in the first half of the guide.

PERIPLUS TRAVEL MAPS
Detailed maps of the Asia Pacific region

This five-year program was launched in 1993 with the goal of producing accurate and up-to-date maps of every major city and country in the Asia Pacific region. About 12 new titles are published annually, along with numerous revised editions. Titles in **BOLDFACE** are already available (28 titles at the end of 1995). Titles in *ITALICS* are scheduled for publication in 1996.

INDIVIDUAL COUNTRY TITLES

Australia	ISBN 962-593-046-9
Burma	ISBN 962-593-070-1
Cambodia	ISBN 0-945971-87-7
China	ISBN 962-593-107-4
Hong Kong	ISBN 0-945971-74-5
Indonesia	ISBN 962-593-042-6
Japan	ISBN 962-593-108-2
Malaysia	ISBN 962-593-043-4
Singapore	ISBN 0-945971-41-9
Thailand	ISBN 962-593-044-2
Vietnam	ISBN 0-945971-72-9

AUSTRALIA REGIONAL MAPS

Sydney	ISBN 962-593-087-6
Melbourne	ISBN 962-593-050-7
Cairns	ISBN 962-593-048-5
Brisbane	ISBN 962-593-049-3

CHINA REGIONAL MAPS

Beijing	ISBN 962-593-031-0
Shanghai	ISBN 962-593-032-9

INDONESIA REGIONAL MAPS

Bali	ISBN 0-945971-49-4
Bandung	ISBN 0-945971-43-5
Batam & Bintan	ISBN 0-945971-69-9
Jakarta	ISBN 0-945971-62-1
Java	ISBN 962-593-040-x
Lombok	ISBN 0-945971-46-x
Surabaya	ISBN 0-945971-48-6
Tana Toraja	ISBN 0-945971-44-3
Yogyakarta	ISBN 0-945971-42-7

JAPAN REGIONAL MAPS

Tokyo	ISBN 962-593-109-0
Osaka & Kyoto	ISBN 962-593-110-4

MALAYSIA REGIONAL MAPS

Kuala Lumpur	ISBN 0-945971-75-3
Malacca	ISBN 0-945971-77-x
Johor	ISBN 0-945971-98-2
Penang	ISBN 0-945971-76-1
Peninsular Malaysia	ISBN 962-593-129-5
Sabah	ISBN 0-945971-78-8
Sarawak	ISBN 0-945971-79-6

NEPAL REGIONAL MAPS

Kathmandu	ISBN 962-593-063-9

THAILAND REGIONAL MAPS

Bangkok	ISBN 0-945971-81-8
Chiang Mai	ISBN 0-945971-88-5
Phuket	ISBN 0-945971-82-6
Ko Samui	ISBN 962-593-036-1

Periplus Travel Maps are available at bookshops around the world. If you cannot find them where you live, please write to us for the name of a distributor closest to you:

Periplus (Singapore) Pte. Ltd.
5 Little Road, #08-01, Singapore 536983
Tel: (65) 280 3320 Fax: (65) 280 6290
E-Mail: (65) 280 3095

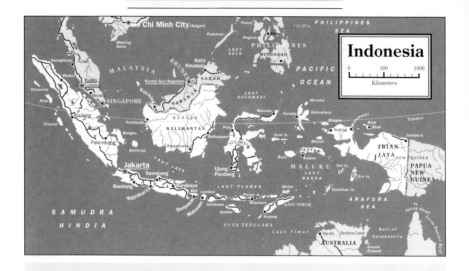

Indonesia at a Glance

The Republic of Indonesia is the world's fourth largest country, with 190 million people. The vast majority (88%) are Muslims, making this the world's largest Islamic country. More than 400 languages are spoken, but Bahasa Indonesia, a variant of Malay, is the national language.

The nation is a republic, headed by a strong President, with a 500-member legislature and a 1,000-member People's Consultative Assembly. There are 27 provinces and special territories. The capital is Jakarta, with 9 million people. The archipelago comprises just over 2 million square km of land. Of 18,508 islands, about 6,000 are named, and 1,000 permanently inhabited.

Indonesia's $175 billion gross national product comes from oil, textiles, lumber, mining, agriculture and manufacturing, and the country's largest trading partner is Japan. Per capita income is $850. Much of the population still makes a living through agriculture, chiefly rice. The unit of currency is the rupiah, which trades at approximately 2,300 to $1 (1996).

Historical overview. The Buddhist Sriwijaya empire, based in southeastern Sumatra, controlled parts of western Indonesia from the 7th to the 13th centuries. The Hindu Majapahit kingdom, based in eastern Java, controlled even more from the 13th to the 16th centuries. Beginning in the mid-13th century, local rulers began converting to Islam.

In the early 17th century the Dutch East India Company (VOC) founded trading settlements and quickly wrested control of the Indies spice trade. The VOC was declared bankrupt in 1799, and a Dutch colonial government was established.

Anti-colonial uprisings began in the the early 20th century, when nationalism movements were founded by various Muslim, communist and student groups. Sukarno, a Dutch-educated nationalist, was jailed by the Dutch in 1930.

Early in 1942, the Dutch Indies were overrun by the Japanese army. Treatment by the occupiers was harsh. When Japan saw her fortunes waning toward the end of the war, Indonesian nationalists were encouraged to organize. On August 17, 1945, Sukarno proclaimed Indonesia's independence.

The Dutch sought a return to colonial rule after the war. Four years of fighting ensued between nationalists and the Dutch, and full independence was achieved in 1949.

During the 1950s and early 1960s, President Sukarno's government moved steadily to the left, alienating western governments. In 1963, Indonesia took control of Irian Jaya and began a period of confrontation with Malaysia.

On September 30, 1965 the army put down an attempted coup attributed to the communist party. Several hundred thousand people were killed as suspected communists.

In the following years, the powers of the presidency gradually shifted away from Sukarno and General Suharto became president in 1968. His administration has been friendly to Western and Japanese investment and the nation has enjoyed three decades of solid economic growth.

Know Before You Go

TRAVELING IN INDONESIA

WHAT TO BRING ALONG

When packing, keep in mind that you will be in the tropics, but that it gets chilly in the higher elevations, and sometimes over the water. Generally, you will want to dress light and wear natural fibers that absorb perspiration. A heavy sweater is also a must, as are sturdy shoes.

Don't bring too much, as you'll be tempted by the great variety of inexpensive clothes available here. Most tourists find a cotton *ikat* or batik shirt more comfortable than what they brought along. If you visit a government office, men should wear long trousers, shoes and a shirt with collar. Women should wear a neat dress, covering knees and shoulders, and shoes.

For those wanting to travel light, a ***sarong*** bought on arrival in Indonesia ($5–$10) is one of the most versatile items you could hope for. It serves as a wrap to get to the *mandi*, a beach towel, required dress for Balinese temples, pajamas, bed sheet, fast drying towel, etc.

Indonesians are renowned for their ability to sleep anytime, anywhere; so they are not likely to understand your desire for peace and quiet at night. Sponge rubber **earplugs**, available from pharmacies in the West, are great for aiding sleep on noisy journeys.

Tiny **padlocks** for use on luggage zippers are a handy deterrent to pilfering hands.

Also bring along some **pre-packaged alcohol towelettes** (swabs). These are handy for disinfecting your hands before eating, or after a trip to the *kamar kecil* (lavatory).

In most Indonesian department stores and supermarkets you can find western **toiletries**. **Contact lens** supplies for hard and soft lenses are available in major cities. Gas permeable lens wearers should come well-stocked.

Dental floss and, sometimes, **tampons** are available in western style grocery stores like Gelael, fast becoming common in cities. **Sanitary napkins** are widely available. *Kondom* (**condoms**) are available at all *apotik* (pharmacies).

On your travels you will meet people who are kind and helpful, yet you may feel too embarrassed to give money. In this kind of situation a small gift (*oleh-oleh*) is appropriate. Fake designer watches from Singapore or Hongkong selling for $5–$10 are a good idea (do tell them it's fake!). Chocolates, biscuits and pens or stationery from your hotel are also appreciated.

CLIMATE

The climate in this archipelago on the equator is tropical. In the lowlands, temperatures average between 21°C and 33°C, but in the mountains it can go as low as 5°C. Humidity varies but is always high, between 60 and 100 percent.

In general, Indonesia experiences two yearly seasons of monsoon winds: the southeast monsoon, bringing dry weather (*musim panas*— dry season), and the northwest monsoon, bringing rain (*musim hujan*—rainy season). Often the changing seasons can bring the time of high waves (*musim ombak*).

The **rainy season** is normally November to April, with a peak around January/February, when it rains for several hours each day. The rain is predictable, however, and always stops for a time, when the sun may come out. Before it rains, the air gets very sticky. Afterwards it is refreshingly cool.

The **dry season**, May to September, is a better time to visit, and especially June to August. This is the time to climb mountains or visit nature reserves. Seasons vary in different areas. Although road transport is improving in Sumatra, during the wet season, especially in southern Sumatra, there may be delays due to poor roads and damaged bridges.

TIME ZONES

Sumatra, Java and West and central Kalimantan are on Western Indonesia Time, which is Greenwich Mean Time +7 hours. This puts Sumatra one hour behind Singapore. Bali, South and East Kalimantan, Sulawesi and Nusa Tenggara are on Central Indonesia Time (GMT +8 hours). Maluku and Irian Jaya are on East Indonesia Time (GMT +9 hours).

MONEY AND BANKING

Prices quoted in this book are intended as a general indication. They are quoted in **US dollars** because the rupiah is being allowed to devalue slowly, so prices stated in US dollars are more likely to remain accurate.

Standard **currency** is the Indonesian rupiah: Notes come in 50,000, 20,000, 10,000, 5,000, 1,000, 500 and 100 denominations. Coins come in denominations of 1,000, 500, 100, 50,

25, 10 and 5 rupiah. Unfortunately, the new coins are very similar in size, so look carefully.

Money changers and banks accepting foreign currency are found in most cities and towns. Banks are generally open 8.30 am to 1 pm, Monday to Friday and 8.30 to 11 am on Saturdays. Some banks however, open until 2 pm on weekdays and close on Saturdays. Gold shops usually bunch together in a specific area of town and change money at competitive rates during hours when banks are closed.

Money changers offer very similar rates and are open longer hours. The bank counters at major airports offer competitive rates. Bank lines in town can be long and slow; the best way around it is to arrive promptly at opening time.

Get a supply of Rp1,000 and Rp500 notes when you change money, as taxi drivers and vendors *never* have change for big bills. When traveling in the countryside, Rp100 notes are also useful.

Carrying **cash** (US$) can be a handy safety precaution as it is still exchangeable should you lose your passport, but it must be carefully stored and not crumpled: Indonesian banks only accept foreign currency that is crisp and clean.

Major **credit cards** are accepted in a variety of more upmarket shops and hotels. But they often add a 3 percent surcharge for the privilege. Most cities have at least one bank at which cash advances can be made—look for Bank Duta, BCA and Danamon. Visa and MasterCard are the most frequently accepted foreign credit cards in Sumatra's larger towns.

There are no exchange controls and excess rupiahs can be freely reconverted at the airport on departure.

TAX, SERVICE AND TIPPING

Most larger hotels charge 21 percent tax and service on top of your bill. The same applies in big restaurants. Tipping is not a custom here, but it is of course appreciated for special services. Rp500 per bag is considered a good tip for roomboys and porters. Taxi drivers will want to round up to the nearest Rp500 or Rp1,000.

When tipping the driver of your rental car or a *pembantu* (housekeeper) of the house in which you've been a guest, fold the money and give it with the right hand only.

OFFICE HOURS

Government offices are officially open 8 am to 3 pm, but if you want to get anything done, be there by 11 am. On Fridays they close at 11.30 am and on Saturdays at 2 pm. In large cities most offices are open 9 am to 5 pm, and shops from 9 am to 9 pm. In smaller towns shops close for a siesta at 1 pm and re-open at 6 pm.

MAIL

Indonesia's postal service is reliable, if not terribly fast. Post Offices (*kantor pos*) are usually busy and it is tedious lining up at one window for weighing, another window for stamps. Hotels normally sell stamps and can post letters for you, or you can use private postal agents (*warpostel*), or freelancers set up outside the bigger offices, to avoid the aggravation.

Kilat express service is only slightly more expensive and much faster than normal mail. International *kilat* service gets postcards and letters to North America or Europe in 7 to 14 days from most cities. *Kilat khusus* (domestic special delivery) will get there overnight.

TELEPHONE AND FAX

Long distance phone calls, both within Indonesia and international, are handled by satellite. Domestic long distance calls can be dialed from most phones. To dial your own international calls, hunt down an IDD phone, otherwise you must go via the operator which is far more expensive.

Smaller hotels often don't allow you to make long distance calls, so you have to go to the main telephone office (*kantor telepon*) or use a private postal and telephone service (*warpostel*). It can be difficult to get through during peak hours but the service in Indonesia now is quite good.

International calls via MCI, Sprint, ATT, and the like can be made from IDD phones using the code for your calling card company. Recently, special telephones have been installed in airports with pre-programmed buttons to connect you via these companies to various countries.

Faxes have become common, and can also be sent (or received) at *warpostel* offices.

ELECTRICITY

Most of Indonesia has converted to 220 volts and 50 cycles, though a few places are still on the old 110 lines. Ask before you plug in if you are uncertain. Power failures are common in smaller cities and towns. Voltage can fluctuate considerably so use a stabilizer for computers and similar equipment. Plugs are of the European two-pronged variety.

TOURIST INFORMATION

The **Directorate General of Tourism** in Jakarta has brochures and maps on all Indonesian provinces: Jl Kramat Raya 81, Jakarta 10450. ☎ (021) 3103117; fax (021) 3101146.

Local government tourism offices, Dinas Pariwisata, are generally only good for basic information. More useful assistance is often available from privately run (but government approved)

Telephone Codes

From outside Indonesia, the following cities may be reached by dialing 62 (the country code for Indonesia) then the city code, then the number. Within Indonesia, the city code must be preceded by a 0 (zero).

Ambon	911	Mataram	364
Balikpapan	542	Maumere	882
Banda Aceh	651	Medan	61
Bandar		Merauke	971
Lampung	721	Metro	725
Bandung	22	Mojokerto	321
Banjarmasin	511	Nusa Dua	361
Banyuwangi	333	Padang	751
Batam	778	Palangkaraya	514
Belawan	61	Palembang	711
Bengkulu	736	Palu	451
Biak	961	Parapat	625
Binjai	61	Pare-Pare	421
Blitar	342	Pasuruan	343
Bogor	251	Pati	295
Bojonegoro	353	Pekalongan	285
Bondowoso	332	Pekanbaru	761
Bukittinggi	752	Pematang-	
Cianjur	263	siantar	622
Cilacap	282	Ponorogo	352
Cipanas	255	Pontianak	561
Cirebon	231	Probolinggo	335
Cisarua	251	Purwakarta	264
Denpasar	361	Purwokerto	281
Gadog	251	Sabang	652
Garut	262	Salatiga	298
Gresik	31	Samarinda	541
Jakarta	21	Semarang	24
Jambi	741	Serang	254
Jember	331	Sibolga	631
Jombang	321	Sidoarjo	31
Kabanjahe	628	Sigli	653
Karawang	267	Situbondo	338
Kebumen	287	Solo	271
Kediri	354	Sorong	951
Kendal	294	Sukabumi	266
Kendari	401	Sumbawa	
Klaten	272	Besar	371
Kota Pinang	624	Sumedang	261
Kotabaru	518	Surabaya	31
Kutacane	629	Tangerang	21
Kuala Simpang	641	Tapak Tuan	656
Kudus	291	Tarakan	551
Kupang	391	Tasikmalaya	265
Lahat	731	Tebingtinggi-	
Lhok Seumawe	645	deli	621
Lumajang	334	Ternate	921
Madiun	351	Tulung Agung	355
Magelang	293	Ujung Pandang	411
Malang	341	Wates	274
Manado	431	Wonosobo	286
Manokwari	962	Yogyakarta	274

Tourist Information Services. Be aware that many offices calling themselves "Tourist Information" are simply travel agents.

Overseas, you can contact the Indonesian embassy or consulate, or one of the following Indonesia Tourist Promotion Board offices:

North America 3457 Wilshire Boulevard, Los Angeles, CA 90010-2203. ☎ (213) 3872078, fax (213) 3804876.

Australia Garuda Indonesia Office, Level 4, 4 Bligh Street, Sydney, NSW 2000. ☎ (61) 2 232-6044, fax (61) 2 2332828.

UK, Ireland, Benelux and Scandinavia Indonesia Tourist Office, 3–4 Hanover Street, London W1R 9HH, UK. ☎ (44) 71 4930030, fax (44) 71 4931747.

The rest of Europe Indonesia Tourist Office, Wiesenhuttenstrasse 17, D-6000 Frankfurt/Main, Germany. ☎ (069) 233677, fax (069) 23-0840.

Southeast Asia 10 Collyer Quay #15-07, Ocean Building, Singapore 0104. ☎ (65) 5342837, 5341795, fax (65) 5334287.

ETIQUETTE

In the areas of Indonesia most frequented by Europeans, many are familiar with the strange ways of westerners. But it is best to be aware of how certain aspects of your behavior will be viewed. You will not be able to count on an Indonesian to set you straight when you commit a *faux pas*. They are much too polite. They will stay silent or even reply *tidak apa apa* (no problem) if you ask if you did something wrong. So here are some points to keep in mind:

☛ The left hand is considered unclean as it is used for cleaning oneself in the bathroom. It is inappropriate to use the left hand to pass food into your mouth, or to give or receive anything with it. When you do accidentally use your left hand it is appropriate to say *"ma'af, tangan kiri"* (please excuse my left hand).

☛ Don't cross your legs exposing the bottom of your foot to anyone.

☛ Don't pat people on the back or head. Go for the elbow instead.

☛ Pointing with the index finger is impolite. Indonesians use their thumbs instead.

☛ If you are having a cigarette, offer one to all the men around you.

☛ Alcohol is frowned upon in Islam, so take a look around you and consider taking it easy.

☛ Hands on hips is a sign of superiority or anger.

☛ It is appropriate to drop your right hand and shoulder when passing closely in front of others.

☛ Blowing your nose in public is likely to disgust everyone within hearing distance.

☛ Take off your shoes when you enter someone's house. Often the host will stop you, but you should go through the motions until he does.

☛ Don't drink or eat until invited to, even after

food and drinks have been placed in front of you. Sip your drink and don't finish it completely. Never take the last morsels from a common plate.

☛ You will often be invited to eat with the words *makan, makan* ("eat, eat") if you pass somebody who is eating. This is not really an invitation, but simply means "Excuse me as I eat."

☛ If someone prepares a meal or drink for you it is most impolite to refuse.

Some things from the west filter through to Indonesia more effectively than others and stories of "*free sek*" (free sex) made a deep and lasting impression in Indonesia. Expect this topic to appear in lists of questions you will be asked in your cultural exchanges. It is best to explain how things have changed since the 1960s and how we now are stuck with "*saf sek.*"

Also remember that Indonesia is predominantly Muslim and it can be startling for Indonesians to see women dress immodestly. Depending on where you are, exposed backs, thighs and shoulders can cause quite a stir.

SECURITY

Indonesia is a relatively safe place to travel and violent crime is almost unheard of, but pay close attention to your belongings, especially in big cities. Be sure that the door and windows of your hotel room are locked at night.

Use a small backpack or moneybelt for valuables: shoulderbags can be snatched. In touristy areas, bags have been snatched from tourists by thieves on motorbikes, so be vigilant.

Big hotels have **safety boxes** for valuables. If your hotel does not have such a facility, it is better to carry all the documents along with you. Make sure you have a photocopy of your passport, return plane ticket and travelers' check numbers and keep them separate from the originals.

Be especially wary on crowded buses and trains; this is where **pick-pockets** lurk and they are very clever at slitting bags and extracting valuables without your noticing anything.

HEALTH

Before You Go

Check with your physician for the latest news on the need for malaria prophylaxis and recommended **vaccinations** before leaving home. Frequently considered vaccines are: Diptheria, Pertusis and Tetanus (DPT); Measles, Mumps and Rubella (MMR); and oral Polio vaccine. Gamma Globulin every four months for Hepatitis A is recommended. For longer stays many doctors recommend vaccination to protect against Hepatitis B requiring a series of shots over the course of 7 months. Vaccinations for smallpox and cholera are no longer required,

except for visitors coming from infected areas. A cholera vaccination may be recommended but it is only 50% effective. **Malaria** is a problem in parts of Indonesia (see below) and you should take prophylactic pills.

Find out the generic names for whatever prescription medications you are likely to need as most are available in Indonesia but not under the same brand names as they are known at home. Get copies of doctors' prescriptions for the medications you bring into Indonesia to avoid questions at the customs desk. Those who wear spectacles should bring along prescriptions.

Check your health insurance before coming, to make sure you are covered. Travel agents should be able to direct you to sources of travel insurance. These typically include coverage of a medical evacuation, if necessary, and a 24-hour worldwide phone number as well as some extras like luggage loss and trip cancellation.

Hygiene

This can be a problem. Very few places have running water or sewers. Most water comes from wells, and raw sewage goes right into the ground or into the rivers. Even treated tap water in the big cities is not potable and must be boiled.

Most cases of stomach complaints are attributable to your system not being used to the strange foods and stray bacteria. To make sure you do not get something more serious, take the following precautions:

☛ Don't drink unboiled water from a well, tap or *mandi* (bath tub). Brush your teeth with boiled or bottled water, not water from a tap or *mandi*.

☛ Plates, glasses and silverware are washed in unboiled water and need to be completely dry before use.

☛ Ice is not made from boiled water. It comes from water frozen in government regulated factories. Locals who are adamant about drinking only boiled water are, in general, not fearful of the purity of ice. However we advise against it.

☛ Fruits and vegetables without skins pose a higher risk of contamination. To avoid contamination by food handlers, buy fruits in the market and peel them yourself.

☛ To *mandi* (bathe) two to three times a day is a great way to stay cool and fresh. But be sure to dry yourself off well and you may wish to apply a medicated body powder such as Purol to avoid the nastiness of skin fungus, especially during the rainy season from October to March.

Diarrhea

A likely traveling companion. In addition to the strange food and unfamiliar micro-fauna, diarrhea is often the result of attempting to accomplish too much in one day. Taking it easy can be an effective prevention. Ask around before leaving about what the latest and greatest of the many remedies are and bring some along. Imodium is locally available as are activated carbon tablets that will absorb the toxins giving you grief.

When it hits, it is usually self-limiting to two or three days. Relax, take it easy and drink lots of fluids, perhaps accompanied by rehydration salts such as Servidrat. Especially helpful is young coconut milk (*air kelapa mudah*) or tea. The former is especially pure and full of nutrients to keep up your strength until you can get back to a regular diet. Get it straight from the coconut without sugar, ice and color added. When you are ready, plain rice or *bubur* (rice porridge) is a good way to start. Avoid fried, spicy or heavy foods and dairy products for a while. After three days without relief, see a doctor.

Intestinal Parasites

It is estimated that 80 to 90 percent of Indonesians have intestinal parasites and these are easily passed on by food handlers. Prevention is difficult, short of fasting, when away from luxury hotel restaurants and even these are no guarantee. It's best to take care of parasites sooner rather than later, by routinely taking a dose of anti-parasite medicine such as Kombatrin (available at all *apotik*) once a month during your stay and again when you get on the plane home.

If you still have problems when you get back, even if only sporadically, have stool and blood tests. Left untreated, parasites can cause serious damage.

Cuts and Scrapes

Your skin will come into contact with more dirt and bacteria than it did back home, so wash your face and hands more often. Untreated bites or cuts can fester very quickly in the tropics, and staph infection is common. Cuts should be taken seriously and cleaned with an antiseptic such as Betadine solution available from any pharmacy (*apotik*). Once clean, antibiotic ointment (also available locally) should be applied and the cut kept covered. Repeat this ritual often. Areas of redness around the cut indicate infection and a doctor should be consulted. At the first sign of swelling it is advisable to take broad spectrum antibiotics to prevent a really nasty infection.

Malaria

Malaria is a problem in parts of Indonesia. This is nothing to be irresponsible about. If you will be in South Sumatra, Riau or Lampung, pay particular attention to this section.

Malaria is caused by a protozoan, Plasmodium, which affects the blood and liver. The vector for the Plasmodium parasite is the Anopheles mosquito. After you contract malaria, it takes a minimum of six days — and up to several weeks — before symptoms appear.

If you are visiting any of the above sites you must take malaria pills. Do not think that pills offer complete protection, however, as they don't. Cases of the more serious strains of malaria have been recorded in Sumatra, and malaria is a real risk to be weighed before traveling there. If you are pregnant, have had a splenectomy or have a weak immune system, or suffer from chronic disease, you should probably not go to risky areas.

Chloroquine phosphate is the traditional malaria prophylactic, but in the past 10–15 years, the effectiveness of the drug has deteriorated. Deciding on an appropriate anti-malarial is now more complicated. There are actually two forms of malaria common in Indonesia: *Plasmodium vivax,* which is unpleasant, but rarely fatal to healthy adults; and *P. falciparum,* which can be quickly fatal. *P. falciparum* is dominant in parts of Indonesia.

Malaria pills. As a prophylactic for travel in the malarial areas of Indonesia, take two tablets of Chloroquine (both on the same day) once a week, and one tablet of Maloprim (pyrimethamine) once a week. Maloprim is a strong drug, and not everybody can tolerate it. If you are planning on taking Maloprim for more than two months, it is recommended that you take a folic acid supplement, 6 mg a day, to guard against anemia. Note: The anti-malarial drugs only work once the protozoan has emerged from the liver, which can be weeks after your return. You should continue on the above regimen for one month after returning.

Another recent drug that has been shown effective against both forms of the parasite is Mefloquine (Larium), although unpleasant side effects have been demonstrated for it as well. Mefloquine is also very expensive, about $3 a tablet. However, it can be a lifesaver in cases of resistant falciparum infection.

These drugs are not available over-the-counter in most western countries (nor, indeed, do most pharmacists stock them), and if you visit a doctor, you may have trouble convincing him of what you need. Doctors in the temperate zones are not usually familiar with tropical diseases, and may even downplay the need to guard against them. Do not be persuaded. Try to find a doctor who has had experience in these matters.

You can also buy Chloroquine and Maloprim over-the-counter in Indonesia, for very little (a few dollars for a month's supply). Maloprim, however, may still be difficult to find. [Note: there is a non–chloroquine based drug sold in Indonesia called Fansidar. This drug is not effective against resistant strains of *P. falciparum.*]

Treatment. Malaria in the early stages is very hard to distinguish from a common cold or flu. A person infected may just suffer from headache and nausea, perhaps accompanied by a slight fever and achiness, for as long as a week until the disease takes hold. When it does, the classic symptoms begin:

1) Feeling of intense cold, sometimes accompanied by shaking. This stage lasts from 30 minutes to two hours.

2) High fever begins, and victim feels hot and dry, and may vomit or even become delirious. This lasts 4–5 hours.

3) Sweating stage begins, during which the victim perspires very heavily, and his body temperature begins to drop.

If you think you have malaria, you should immediately call on professional medical help. A good medical professional is your best first aid. Only if you cannot get help, initiate the following treatment:

1) Take 4 Chloroquine tablets immediately.

2) Six hours later, take 2 more Chloroquine tablets.

3) The next day, take 2 more.

4) The following day, take 2 more.

Note: If the Chloroquine treatment does not cause the fever to break within 24 hours, assume the infection is the very dangerous *P. falciparum* and begin the following treatment immediately:

1) Take 3 tablets (750 mg) of Mefloquine (Larium)

2) Six hours later, take 2 more tablets (500 mg) of Mefloquine.

3) After 12 hours—and only if you weigh 60 kg (130 lbs) or more—take one more tablet (250 mg) of Mefloquine.

Prevention. Malaria is carried by the *Anopheles* mosquito, and if you don't get bitten, you don't get the disease.

☛ While walking around, use a good quality mosquito repellent, and be very generous with it, particularly around your ankles. Wear light-colored, long-sleeved shirts or blouses and long pants.

☛ While eating or relaxing in one spot, burn mosquito coils. These are those green, slightly brittle coils of incense doped with pyrethrin that were banned in the United States some years ago. They are quite effective and you will get used to the smell. (If you are worried about inhaling some of the poison they contain, re-read the classic symptoms of malaria above.) In Indonesia, the ubiquitous coils are called *obat nyamuk bakar*. In places where there is electricity, a repellent with a similar ingredient is inserted into a unit plugged into the wall.

☛ While sleeping, burn *obat nyamuk* and use a mosquito net. Some hotels in affected areas have nets, but not many, and you should bring your own. The *obat nyamuk* coils last 6–8 hours and if you set a couple going when you go to sleep you will be protected. Remember that mosquitos like damp bathrooms—where few people bother to light a mosquito coil.

Other Mosquito-borne Diseases

The other mosquito concern is **dengue fever**, spread by the afternoon-biting *Aedes aegypti*,

especially at the beginning of the rainy season in November. The most effective prevention is not getting bitten (there is no prophylaxis for dengue). Dengue fever symptoms are headache, pain behind the eyes, high fever, muscle and joint pains and rash.

AIDS & Hepatitis B

Surprise! **Safe sex** is also a good idea in Indonesia. AIDS is just beginning to surface with a number of documented HIV positive cases recently. Another consideration is Hepatitis B virus which affects liver function, and is only sometimes curable and can be deadly. The prevalence of Hepatitis B in Indonesia is the basis for international concern over the ominous possibilities for the spread of HIV virus, which is passed on in the same ways.

Medical Treatment

The Indonesian name for pharmacy is *apotik*; and a hospital is called *rumah sakit*. In smaller villages they only have government clinics, called *Puskesmas*, which are not equipped to deal with anything serious.

Fancier hotels often have doctors on call or can recommend one. Misuse of antibiotics is still a concern in Indonesia. They should only be used for bacterial diseases and then for at least 10 to 14 days to prevent developing antibiotic resistant strains of your affliction. Indonesians don't feel they've had their money's worth from a doctor ($5) without getting an injection or antibiotics: Be sure it's necessary. Ensure syringes have never been used before.

Even in the big cities outside of Jakarta, emergency care leaves much to be desired. Your best bet in the event of a life-threatening emergency or accident is to get on the first plane to Jakarta or Singapore. Contact your embassy or consulate by phone for assistance (see below). Medevac airlifts are very expensive ($26,000) and most embassies will recommend that you buy insurance to cover the cost of this when traveling extensively in Indonesia.

ACCOMMODATIONS

Indonesia has an extraordinary range of accommodations, much of it good value for money. Most cities have a number of hotels offering air-conditioned rooms with TV, minibar, hot water, swimming pool and the like costing $100 a night and up. While at the other end of the scale, you can stay in a $2-a-night *losmen* room with communal squat toilet (buy your own toilet paper), a tub of water with ladle for a bath, and a bunk with no towel or clean linen (bring your own). And there's just about everything in between: from decrepit colonial hill stations to luxurious new thatched-roof huts in the rice fields.

A whole hierarchy of lodgings and official terminology have been established by government decree. Theoretically, a "hotel" is an up-market establishment catering for businessmen, middle to upper class travelers and tourists. A star-rating (one to five stars) is applied according to the range of facilities. Smaller places with no stars and basic facilities are not referred to as hotels but as "*losmen*" (from the French "*logement*"), "*wisma*" ("guesthouse") or "*penginapan*" ("accommodation") and cater for budget tourists.

Prices and quality vary enormously. In the major cities that don't have many tourists, such as Jakarta, Surabaya and Medan, there is little choice in the middle ranges and you have to either pay a lot or settle for a room in a *losmen*.

In areas where there are a lot of tourists, such as West and North Sumatra, you can get very comfortable and clean rooms with fan or air-conditioning for less than $20 a night. In small towns and remote areas, you don't have much choice and all accommodations tend to be very basic.

It's common to ask to see the room before checking in. Shop around before deciding, particularly if the hotel offers different rooms at different rates. Avoid carpeted rooms, especially without air-conditioning, as usually they are damp and this makes the room smell.

Advance bookings are necessary during peak tourist seasons (July to August and around Christmas and New Year). Popular resorts near big cities, like the Riau Islands, are always packed on weekends, and prices often double.

In many hotels, discounts of 10%–30% from published rates are to be had for the asking, particularly if you have a business card. Booking in advance through travel agencies can also result in a much lower rate. Larger hotels always add 21% tax and service to the bill.

Bathroom Etiquette

When staying in *losmen*, particularly when using communal facilities, don't climb in or drop your soap into the tub of water (*bak mandi*). This is for storing clean water. Scoop water over yourself with the ladle in your right hand and clean with your left.

If you wish to use the native paper-free cleaning method, after using the toilet, scoop water with your right hand and clean with the left.

This is the reason one only eats with the right hand—the left is regarded as unclean, for obvious reasons. Use soap and a fingernail brush (locals use a rock) for cleaning hands. Or use pre-packaged alcohol towelettes from home. Bring along your own towel and soap (although some places provide these if you ask).

Staying in Villages

Officially, the Indonesian government requires that foreign visitors spending the night report to the local police. This is routinely handled by *losmen* and hotels, who send in a copy of the registration form you fill out when you check in.

Where there are no commercial lodgings, you can often rely on local hospitality. But when staying in a private home, keep in mind the need to inform the local authorities. One popular solution is to stay in the *home* of the local authority, the village head or *kepala desa*.

Carry photocopies of your passport, visa stamp and embarkation card to give to officials when venturing beyond conventional tourist areas. This saves time, and potential hassles, for you and your host.

Villagers in rural Indonesia do not routinely maintain guest rooms. If a cash arrangement has not been prearranged, you should leave a gift appropriate to local needs—biscuits, clothing, cigarettes or D-cell batteries for radios in remote villages. Note down their address and send prints of the photos you took of them.

FINDING YOUR WAY

Westerners are used to finding things using telephone directories, addresses, maps, etc. But in Indonesia, phone books are out-of-date and incomplete, addresses can be confusing and maps little understood. The way to find something, whether you have a specific destination in mind, or want to try to find a good place for *nasi goreng,* is to ask.

To ask for directions, it's better to have the name of a person and the name of the *kampung*. Thus "Bu Herlan, Muara Dua" is a better address for asking directions even though "Jalan Yos Sudarso 14" is the mailing address. Knowing the language helps here but is not essential. Immediately clear answers are not common and you should be patient. You are likely to get a simple indication of direction without distance or specific instructions. The assumption is that you will be asking lots of people along the way.

Maps are useful tools for you, but introducing them into discussions with Indonesians will often confuse rather than clarify. Nevertheless, Indonesians seem to have built-in compasses and can always tell you where north is. If you introduce a map into your discussion, they are likely to insist that the north arrow on the map be oriented to the north before beginning.

FOOD AND DRINK

Pay attention to the quantity of fluids you consume in a day (drinks with alcohol or caffeine count as a minus). Tap water in Indonesia is not potable and it should be brought to a full boil for ten minutes before being considered safe. Use boiled or bottled water to brush your teeth.

Indonesians are themselves very fussy about only drinking clean water, so if you're offered a drink it is almost certainly safe.

Most Indonesians do not feel they have eaten until they have eaten rice. This is accompanied by side dishes, often just a little piece of meat and some vegetables with a spicy sauce. Other common items include *tofu* (*tahu*), *tempe* and salted fish. Crispy fried tapioca crackers flavored with prawns and spices (*krupuk*) usually accompany a meal.

No meal is complete without *sambal*—a fiery paste of ground chili peppers with garlic, shallots, sugar, and various other ingredients.

Cooking styles vary greatly from one region to another. The West Sumatrans are fond of tasty, spicy Padang food, eaten with chili and fermented prawn paste, and served as a variety of side dishes, often as many as 20. You only pay for what you eat, and the rest is kept for next time! This style of food is now popular all over Indonesia. North and South Sumatrans have their own specialities. In the more isolated parts of the archipelago, the food can be quite plain, and frankly, quite dull.

By western standards, food in Indonesia is cheap. For $1, in most places, you can get a meal with bottled drink. On the other hand, Indonesia does not have a banquet tradition and people normally eat in restaurants only out of necessity (when they cannot eat at home). The major exception to this is the Indonesian Chinese, who are fond of restaurant banquets. Most Indonesians eat better at home than outside, and the range of dishes in restaurants is usually not that great.

In most Indonesian restaurants you will find a standard menu consisting of *sate* (skewered barbequed meat), *gado-gado* or *pecel* (boiled vegetables with spicy peanut sauce) and *soto* (vegetable soup with or without meat). Also found are some Chinese dishes like *bakmie goreng* (fried noodles), *bakmie kuah* (noodle soup) and *cap cay* (stir-fried vegetables).

In most larger towns you can also find a number of Chinese restaurants on the main street. Some have menus with Chinese writing, but usually the cuisine is very much assimilated to local tastes. Standard dishes, in addition to the *bakmie* and *cap cay* mentioned above, are sweet and sour whole fish (*gurame asem manis*), beef with Chinese greens (*kailan/caisim ca sapi*), and prawns sauteed in butter (*udang goreng mentega*). Any one of these with a plate of vegetables (*cap cay*) and rice makes a delightful meal.

Indonesian fried chicken (*ayam goreng*) is common and usually very tasty—although the chicken can be a bit more stringy than westerners are used to. Then there is the ubiquitous *nasi goreng* (fried rice), which is often eaten for breakfast with an egg on top.

The beers available in Indonesia are Bintang and Anker, and increasingly, Heineken, Tiger and Chinese Tsing Tao. Most are brewed under Dutch supervision and rather light (perhaps appropriately for the tropics). With electricity such a precious commodity, however, in out-of-the-way places the only way to quaff it cold is to pour it over ice.

Warung (Street Stalls)

Restaurant kitchens do not necessarily have healthier food preparation procedures than roadside *warung*. The important thing at a *warung* is to see what's going on and make a judgement as to whether or not the cooks inspire confidence. *Warung* rarely have a running water supply, so always beware.

The food is laid out on the table and you point to what you want to eat. Your first portion probably won't fill you up, so a second portion is ordered by saying "*Tambah separuh*" (I'll have another half portion, please). But only the price is halved. The amount of food is more like three-quarters. Finish off with a banana and say "*Sudah*" (I've had plenty and would like to pay now please). At this point the seller will total up the prices of what she served you and ask you how many *krupuk* and *tempe*, etc. you added; so keep track. The total will come to between Rp500 and Rp2,500 (30¢ to $1.25).

Vegetarianism

Say "*saya tidak makan daging*" (I don't eat meat) or alter menu items by saying something like *tidak pakai ayam* (without chicken) or *tidak pakai daging* (without meat). Dietary restrictions are very acceptable and common here due to the various religious and spiritual practices involving food. However, finding food that truly has no animal products is a problem. Often meals which appear to be made exclusively of vegetables will have a chunk of beef in them to add that certain oomph.

POLITICAL ORGANIZATION

Sumatra is made up of eight provinces or *propinsi*—Aceh, North Sumatra, West Sumatra, Riau, Jambi, Bengkulu, South Sumatra and Lampung.

Each of these *propinsi*, headed by a *gubernur* ("governor") is further divided into *kabupaten* (districts), headed by a *bupati* (district head); *kecamatan* (subdistricts), headed by a *camat*; villages (*desa*) headed by a *kepala desa* (village head); and *kampung* (hamlets).

It is not quite this simple, of course, as in parts of Indonesia where there are large cities (*kota*), there are also *kotamadya*, ("municipalities"), whose "mayor" has the status of a *bupati*, and *kota administrasi* ("administrative cities") whose "mayor" falls somewhere between a *bupati* and a *camat*. But the basic progression is: *propinsi*, *kabupaten*, *kecamatan*, *desa*, *kampung*.

SPELLING

The Indonesian spelling of geographical features and villages varies considerably as there is no form of standardization that meets with both popular and official approval. In this guide, we have tried to use the most common spellings.

CALENDAR

The Indonesian government sets a certain number of legal holidays every year, both fixed and moveable dates. Most of these holidays are for the major religions practiced in Indonesia. Both the Christian Easter and all the Muslim holidays are based on the moon, so confusion results in attempting to extrapolate several years ahead.

The fixed national holidays on the Gregorian calendar are the Christian New Year, Jan. 1; Independence Day, Aug. 17; and Christmas, Dec. 25. Easter Day, Good Friday and Ascension Day are honored in Indonesia. The Balinese new year, Nyepi, and the Buddhist Waisak New Year are also legal holidays.

Official Muslim holidays in Indonesia (the dates are for 1995):

Idul Fitri. March 3 and 4. The end of the Muslim fasting month of Ramadan; this holiday is also called Lebaran. It is very difficult to travel just before and just after Idul Fitri as just about everyone wants to return to his or her home village to celebrate, then get back to their places of work in the cities.

Idul Adha. May 10. The day of Abraham's sacrifice and the day that the *haji* pilgrims circle the Kaaba in Mecca.

Hijryah. May 31. The Islamic New Year, beginning the month of Muharram, when Muhammad traveled from Mecca to Medina.

Maulud Nabi Muhammad SAW. August 9. Muhammad's birthday.

Isra Mi'raj Nabi Muhammad SAW. December 20. Muhammad ascended on his steed Bouraq. The 12 lunar months of the Muslim calendar are:

Muharram
Safar
Rabiul Awal
Rabiul Ahir
Jumadil Awal
Jumadil Ahir
Rajab
Sa'ban
Ramadan (the fasting month)
Sawal
Kaidah
Zulhijja

Note: The Muslim calendar begins with the Hejira, Muhammad's flight to Medina, in A.D. 622 according to the Gregorian calendar. Early A.D. 1995 corresponds to A.H. 1415. The Muslim calendar is a lunar calendar, and gains 10 or 11 days on the Gregorian calendar each year. Islamic holidays will thus regress 10–11 days a year against to the Gregorian calendar.

SHOPPING

Be extremely cautious when buying antiques, works of art or other expensive objects, especially in the tourist areas. Most are reproductions, though very good ones and cheap to boot!

Handicrafts are produced all over Indonesia, and even if a good selection is available in hotels and tourist areas, it can be fun to seek out craftsmen in the villages (though often it's not cheaper unless you are very good at bargaining).

Bargaining

The secret here is to appear not to care. Some merchants are very up-front about giving fixed prices (*harga pas:* fixed price), but the trader who expects the buyer to bargain is more commonplace. A general rule of thumb is to aim for half the asking price by opening with an offer lower than that. The 50% rule is by no means universal and many sellers will only come down by 20%. On the other hand, in tourist areas, vendors will often ask 10 times or more the selling price.

More often than not the deal is closed in a ritual in which you cheerfully thank the purveyor for their time and take steps towards the next stall or the door as the case may be. At this point keep your ears pricked for the *real* final offer of the seller and either thank them again and move on or return and claim your prize. If your final price is accepted it is a major breach of etiquette not to consummate the purchase.

In any event, staying cheerful and good humored will not only be more fun but can make a huge difference in the price you finally pay (and the success of any important interaction with an Indonesian). This isn't just about money and, yes, you should pay a bit more than an Indonesian would. That's the way it works.

Souvenirs

The best places for souvenir-shopping are West Sumatra's Bukittinggi, Medan and Palembang in South Sumatra. The traveler's problem is how to lug around the goods for the rest of the trip.

PHOTOGRAPHY

Some Fuji and Kodak film is available in Indonesia, including color print film from ASA 100 to 400 and Ektachrome and Fujichrome 100 ASA daylight slide film. In larger towns you can buy Fuji Neopan black and white as well. You can't buy Kodachrome in Indonesia although Fuji Velvia is available in the larger towns. Avoid local processing if you value your negatives or transparencies.

Indonesian Language Primer

Personal pronouns
I *saya*
we *kita* (inclusive), *kami* (exclusive)
you *anda* (formal), *saudara* (brother, sister),
kamu (for friends and children only)
he/she *dia*   they *mereka*

Forms of address
Father/Mr *Bapak* ("*Pak*")
Mother/Mrs *Ibu* ("*Bu*")
Elder brother *Abang* ("*Bang*" or "*Bung*")
              Mas (in Java only)
Elder sister *Mbak*
Younger brother/sister *Adik* ("*Dik*")
Note: These terms are used not just within the
family, but generally in polite speech.

Basic questions
How? *Bagaimana?*
How much/many? *Berapa?*
What? *Apa?*
What's this? *Apa ini?*
Who? *Siapa?*
Who's that? *Siapa itu?*
What is your name? *Siapa namanya ?*
(Literally: Who is your name?)
When? *Kapan?*
Where? *Mana?*
Which? *Yang mana?*
Why? *Kenapa?*

Useful words
yes *ya*   no, not *tidak, bukan*
Note: *Tidak* is used with verbs or adverbs;
bukan with nouns.

and *dan*
with *dengan*
for *untuk*
good *bagus*
fine *baik*
more *lebih*
less *kurang*

better *lebih baik*
worse *kurang baik*
this/these *ini*
that/those *itu*
same *sama*
different *lain*
here *di sini*
there *di sana*

Civilities
Welcome *Selamat datang*
Good morning (7–11am) *Selamat pagi*
Good midday (11am–3pm) *Selamat siang*
Good afternoon (3–7pm) *Selamat sore*
Goodnight (after dark) *Selamat malam*
Goodbye (to one leaving) *Selamat jalan*
Goodbye (to one staying) *Selamat tinggal*
Note: *Selamat* is a word from Arabic meaning
"May your time (or action) be blessed."
How are you? *Apa kabar?*
I am fine. *Kabar baik.*
Thank you. *Terima kasih.*
You're welcome. *Kembali.*
Same to you. *Sama sama.*
Pardon me *Ma'af*
Excuse me *Permisi*
(when leaving a conversation, etc).

Numbers
1	*satu*	6	*enam*
2	*dua*	7	*tujuh*
3	*tiga*	8	*delapan*
4	*empat*	9	*sembilan*
5	*lima*	10	*sepuluh*

Pronunciation and Grammar

Vowels
a   As in father
e   Three forms:
    1) Schwa, like the *the*
    2) Like *é* in touch*é*
    3) Short *è*; as in b*e*t
i   Usually like long e (as
    in Bal**i**); when bounded
    by consonants, like
    short **i** (h**i**t).
o   Long o, like g**o**
u   Long u, like y**ou**
ai Long i, like cr**i**me
au Like **ow** in owl

Consonants
c   Always like **ch** in **ch**urch
g   Always hard, like **g**uard
h   Usually soft, almost un-
     pronounced. It is hard
     between like vowels,
     e.g. *ma**h**al* (expensive).
k   Like **k** in **k**ind; at end of
     word, unvoiced stop.
kh   Like **k**ind, but harder
r   Rolled, like Spanish **r**
ng   Soft, like fli**ng**
ngg Hard, like ti**ngle**
ny   Like **ny** in So**ny**a

Grammar
Grammatically, Indonesian is
in many ways far simpler than
English. There are no articles
(a, an, the).
The verb form "to be" is usually not used. There is no ending for plurals; sometimes the
word is doubled, but often
number comes from context.
And Indonesian verbs are
not conjugated. Tense is com-
municated by context or with
specific words for time.

11	*seblas*	100	*seratus*
12	*dua belas*	600	*enam ratus*
13	*tiga belas*	1,000	*seribu*
20	*dua puluh*	3,000	*tiga ribu*
50	*lima puluh*	10,000	*sepuluh ribu*
73	*tujuh puluh tiga*		

1,000,000 *satu juta*
2,000,000 *dua juta*
half *setengah*

first *pertama*   third *ketiga*
second *kedua*   fourth *ke'empat*

Time

minute	*menit*	Sunday	*Hari Minggu*
hour	*jam*	Monday	*Hari Senin*
(also clock/watch)		Tuesday	*Hari Selasa*
day	*hari*	Wednesday	*Hari Rabu*
week	*minggu*	Thursday	*Hari Kamis*
month	*bulan*	Friday	*Hari Jum'at*
year	*tahun*	Saturday	*Hari Sabtu*
today	*hari ini*	later	*nanti*
tomorrow	*besok*	yesterday	*kemarin*

What time is it? *Jam berapa?*
(It is) eight thirty. *Jam setengah sembilan*
(Literally: "half nine")
How many hours? *Berapa jam?*
When did you arrive? *Kapan datang?*
Four days ago. *Empat hari yang lalu.*
When are you leaving?
 Kapan berangkat?
In a short while. *Sebentar lagi.*

Basic vocabulary

to be, have	*ada*		
to be able, can	*bisa*		
to buy	*beli*	correct	*betul*
to know	*tahu*	wrong	*salah*
to get	*dapat*	big	*besar*
to need	*perlu*	small	*kecil*
to want	*mau*	pretty	*cantik*
to go	*pergi*	slow	*pelan*
to wait	*tunggu*	fast	*cepat*
at	*di*	stop	*berhenti*
to	*ke*	old	*tua, lama*
if	*kalau*	new	*baru*
near	*dekat*	then	*lalu, kemudian*
far	*jauh*	only	*hanya, saja*
empty	*kosong*	crowded, noisy	*ramai*

Small talk

Where are you from? *Dari mana?*
I'm from the US. *Saya dari Amerika.*
How old are you? *Umurnya berapa?*
I'm 31 years old.
 Umur saya tiga pulu satu tahun.
Are you married? *Sudah kawin belum?*
Yes, I am. *Yah, sudah.*   Not yet. *Belum.*
Do you have children? *Sudah punya anak?*
What is your religion? *Agama apa?*
Where are you going? *Mau ke mana?*
I'm just taking a walk. *Jalan-jalan saja.*
Please come in. *Silahkan masuk.*
This food is delicious.
 Makanan ini enak sekali.

You are very hospitable.
 Anda sangat ramah tamah.

Hotels

Where's a *losmen?* *Di mana ada losmen?*
cheap *losmen* *losmen yang murah*
average *losmen* *losmen biasa*
very good hotel *hotel cukup baik*
Please take me to... *Tolong antar saya ke...*
Are there any empty rooms?
 Ada kamar kosong?
Sorry there aren't any. *Ma'af, tidak ada.*
How much for one night?
 Berapa untuk satu malam?
One room for two of us.
 Dua orang, satu kamar.
I'd like to stay for 3 days.
Saya mau tinggal tiga hari.
hot water *air panas*
Here's the key to your room.
 Ini kunci kamar.
Please call a taxi. *Tolong panggil taksi.*
Please wash these clothes.
Tolong cucikan pakaian ini.

Restaurants

Where's a good restaurant?
 Di mana ada rumah makan yang baik?
Let's have lunch. *Mari kita makan siang.*
I want Indonesian food.
 Saya mau makanan Indonesia.
I want coffee, not tea.
 Saya mau kopi, bukan teh.
May I see the menu?
 Boleh saya lihat daftar makanan?
I want to wash my hands.
 Saya mau cuci tangan.
Where is the toilet? *Di mana kamar kecil?*
fish, squid, goat, beef
 ikan, cumi, kambing, sapi
salty, sour, sweet, spicy
 asin, asam, manis, pedas

Shopping

I don't understand. *Saya tidak mengerti.*
I can't speak Indonesian.
 Saya tidak bisa bicara Bahasa Indonesia.
Please, speak slowly.
 Tolong, berbicara lebih pelan.
I want to buy... *Saya mau beli...*
Where can I buy... *Di mana saya bisa beli...*
How much does this cost? *Berapa harga ini?*
2,500 Rupiah. *Dua ribu, lima ratus rupiah.*
That cannot be true! *Masa!*
That's still a bit expensive. *Masih agak mahal.*

Directions

north	*utara*	west	*barat*
south	*selatan*	east	*timur*
right	*kanan*	left	*kiri*
near	*dekat*	far	*jauh*
inside	*di dalam*	outside	*di luar*

I am looking for this address.
 Saya cari alamat ini.
How far is it? *Berapa jauh dari sini?*

Travel Advisory

GETTING AROUND IN INDONESIA

This advisory gives you an overview of the wide range of travel options available during your stay in Indonesia. A comprehensive run-down of travel services enables you to plan your way around the island according to time and budget. More specific details for each area you will be visiting can be found in the relevant Practicalities sections.

Prices are in US dollars, unless otherwise stated. Prices and schedules are given as an indication only as they change frequently according to the season. Check with a travel agent prior to departure for the most up-to-date information.

In many ways, Indonesia is an easy place to get around. Indonesians are as a rule hospitable and good-humored, and will always help a lost or confused traveler. The weather is warm, the pace of life relaxed, and the air is rich with the smells of clove cigarettes, the blessed durian fruit and countless other wonders.

On the other hand, the nation's transportation infrastructure does not move with the kind of speed and efficiency that western travelers expect, which often leads to frustration. It is best to adjust your pace to local conditions. There is nothing more pathetic than a tourist who has traveled halfway around the world just to shout at some poor clerk at the airport counter.

The golden rule is: things will sort themselves out. Eventually. Be persistent, of course, but relax and keep your sense of humor. Before you explode, have a *kretek* cigarette, a cup of sweet coffee, or a cool glass of *kelapa muda* (young coconut water). Things might look different.

GETTING TO INDONESIA

You can fly to Indonesia from just about anywhere. Most people traveling from Europe and the US arrive on direct flights to Jakarta, or perhaps Medan, while those coming from Australia generally go first to Bali. The main international entry points are Sukarno-Hatta airport in Jakarta, Ngurah Rai airport in Bali, and Polonia airport in Medan. There are now also flights between Singapore and Surabaya, in East Java, on Singapore Airlines (direct) and Garuda (via Jakarta). SilkAir, also based in Singapore, flies direct to Manado in North Sulawesi.

Sukarno-Hatta airport is served by many international airlines, with over a dozen flights a day from Singapore alone. A cut-price alternative from Europe or the US may be to get a cheap flight to Singapore, and buy an onward discount ticket to Jakarta from there: the cost of these can be as low as $90 single, $155 return. A return ticket from Singapore to Bali with stops in Jakarta and Yogyakarta, good for a month, is available in Singapore for around $450. Buy through travel agents—check the *Straits Times* for details. Note: you need a return or onward ticket to get a tourist visa on arrival.

Direct flights also connect Jakarta with many major cities in Asia and Europe. Air fares vary depending on the carrier, the season and the type of ticket purchased. A discount RT fare from the US or Europe costs from $850: about half that from Australia or East Asian capitals.

Air tickets from **Batam** and **Bintan** can be less expensive than those from Singapore, unless there's a special offer on, and these Indonesian islands just off the coast of Singapore can be reached via short ferry hops from Singapore's World Trade Centre. Ferry tickets to Batam cost $12 single, $18 return, and to Bintan $35 single, $45 return.

There are several daily jet flights from Batam as well as Tanjung Pinang in Bintan, to most Sumatran cities, and to Jakarta, via Merpati/Garuda and Sempati flights. Contact the **Merpati/Garuda** office in Batam ☎ (0778) 45820. **Sempati** office in Batam ☎ (0778) 411612/453050. **Sempati** in Tanjung Pinang, Bintan ☎ (0771) 21612/25283.

Airport tax for departing passengers is Rp17,000 for international routes and between Rp1,500 and Rp6,000 for domestic flights, depending on the airports.

Having arrived in Indonesia, your choices for onward travel depend, as always, on time and money. Possibilities on Sumatra range from boats, trains, hire cars and chauffeur driven, to both slow and fast buses. Hiring a car or minibus with or without driver is one of the most rewarding ways of getting around.

VISAS

Nationals of the following 36 countries do not need visas, and are granted visa-free entry for 60 days upon arrival (this is non-renewable). For other nationals, visas are required and must be obtained in advance from an Indonesian embassy or consulate.

Argentina	Iceland	Norway
Australia	Ireland	Philippines
Austria	Italy	Singapore
Belgium	Japan	South Korea
Brazil	Liechtenstein	Spain
Canada	Luxemburg	Sweden
Chile	Malaysia	Switzerland
Denmark	Malta	Thailand
Finland	Mexico	United Kingdom
France	Morocco	United States
Germany	Netherlands	Venezuela
Greece	New Zealand	Yugoslavia

Be sure to check your passport before leaving for Indonesia. You must have at least one empty page to be stamped on arrival, and the passport must be valid for at least six months after the date of arrival. For visa-free entry, you must also have proof of onward journey, either a return or through ticket. Employment is strictly forbidden on tourist visas or visa-free entry.

Visa-free entry to Indonesia cannot be extended beyond two months (60 days) and is only given at the following airports: Ambon, Bali, Batam, Biak, Jakarta, Manado, Medan, Padang, Pontianak, Surabaya. Or at the following seaports: Bali, Balikpapan, Batam, Bintan, Jakarta, Kupang, Pontianak, Semarang.

Other Visas

The 2-month, non-extendable **tourist pass** is the only entry permit that comes without a great deal of paperwork.

A **visitor's visa**, usually valid for 28 days, can be extended, every month, for up to 6 months, but is difficult to get. You must have a good reason for spending time in Indonesia (research, relatives, religious study) and you must have a sponsor and supporting letters. Even with a sponsor and the best of reasons, however, you might be denied. The process can take days or weeks, and extensions are at the discretion of the immigration office where you apply.

A **business visa**, valid for 28 days and extendable to 6 months requires a letter from a company stating that you are performing a needed service for a company in Indonesia. This is not intended as an employment visa, but is for investors, consultants, or other business purposes.

Two other types of passes are available: the temporary residence pass (KIM-S) and permanent residence pass (KIM). Both are hard to get.

Customs

Narcotics, firearms and ammunition are strictly prohibited. The standard duty-free allowance is: 2 liters of alcoholic beverages, 200 cigarettes, 50 cigars or 100 grams of tobacco. There is no restriction on import and export of foreign currencies in cash or travelers checks, but there is an export limit of 50,000 Indonesian rupiah.

All narcotics are illegal in Indonesia. The use, sale or purchase of narcotics results in long prison terms and huge fines. Once caught, you are immediately placed in detention until trial, and sentences are stiff, as demonstrated by westerners currently serving sentences as long as 30 years for possession of marijuana.

Keeping Your Cool

At government offices like immigration or police, talking loudly and forcefully doesn't make things easier. Patience and politeness are virtues that open many doors in Indonesia. Good manners and dress are also to your advantage.

TRAVELING IN INDONESIA

Getting around in Indonesia is not—to those used to efficient and punctual transportation—effortless. Bookings are often difficult to make; reservations are mysteriously canceled.

What seems like nerve-wracking inefficiency is really so only if one is in a hurry. If you have to be somewhere at a particular time, allow plenty of time to get there. Check and double-check your bookings. You can't just turn off the archipelago's famous *jam karet*—"rubber time"— when it's time to take an airplane and turn it on again when you want to relax. You will get there.

Peak periods around holidays and during the August tourist season are the most difficult. It is imperative to book well in advance and reconfirm your bookings at every step along the way. Travel during the week of the Islamic Lebaran (Ramadan) holiday (usually around 14 or 15 March) is practically impossible. Check the "Practicalities" sections for more details.

GETTING AROUND SUMATRA

The first thing to realize about Sumatra is that it is huge, and the distances are great. If you want to see even a tiny percentage of what Sumatra has to offer, then you'll probably have to be prepared to fly at least some short hops. The question is how to travel so as to get to where you are going with your energy intact—and hopefully to see something along the way. Trains are found only in the very south, from Lampung up to Palembang, and in the north from Medan to Pematang Siantar (near Toba). Both flying and traveling by bus have their advantages and disadvantages. A third and much better way to go anywhere is to rent an air-conditioned minibus with driver for several days or even weeks (see below). This way you go where you want to when you want to—and at around $50 per day including gas and expenses, this is not expensive when split between a small group.

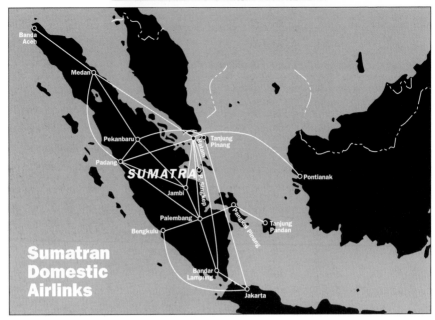

Sumatran
Domestic
Airlinks

Domestic Air Travel

Medan's Polonia Airport is Sumatra's main gateway—but Batam, Padang, and Pekanbaru are also now served by international flights (mainly from Singapore). Keep in mind that Singapore is closer to most Sumatran cities than Jakarta, and that Kuala Lumpur and Penang (in Malaysia) are closer to Medan than Singapore. From many cities in Europe or North America, it is cheaper and easier just to buy a ticket to Singapore or Malaysia and purchase a ticket to Sumatra there. For details of flights to each city, check the respective "Practicalities" sections. Cost of a Singapore-Medan RT ticket, for example, is about $175—check the *Straits Times* classifieds in Singapore or Kuala Lumpur for the best deals. There are also of course daily flights to all major Sumatran cities from Jakarta. From Bali, Yogya and other points in Indonesia you have to travel through Jakarta.

There are also daily flights to all major Sumatran cities from Batam, the Indonesian island just below Singapore. It often costs you less to take the ferry across from Singapore's World Trade Centre ($12), take a taxi to the airport at Batam ($4) and then hop on a plane to your Sumatran destination. The problem is that it can be tricky to book in advance, although the service is improving. Sometimes it can be difficult to get accurate information over the phone about flights and ticket availability. So in practice you risk spending the night in Batam, and hotels there are expensive. The island is served mainly by Merpati and Sempati, both flying jets, but also by SMAC and Bouraq prop planes.

The national air carrier is Garuda, which has a subsidiary called Merpati. All domestic routes have now been turned over to Merpati. In addition, there are four private airlines operating in Sumatra: Sempati, Bouraq, SMAC and Mandala. Only Sempati has jets; the others fly creaky old props with fares that are 10 percent lower. Service on all these airlines is pretty good by Third World standards, but can be pretty awful by Western ones, although it is improving. Note the following important points:

✈ It is difficult to confirm bookings out of a different city than the one you are in. You can buy a ticket and the computer may say you have a booking, but don't believe it until you reconfirm with the airline office in the city of departure.

✈ Always reconfirm directly with the airline in the city of departure between 24 and 72 hours before your flight, particularly during the peak tourist seasons and Indonesian holiday periods. Your seat may be given away if you reconfirm either too early or too late (or not at all).

✈ Make bookings in person, not by phone, or buy a ticket through an agent in your hotel and let them do it. (Reconfirmations can be made by phone, however.) Request written evidence of your booking and jot down the name of the person who makes it in case you are later told you don't have a booking.

✈ Note down the computer booking code, as names have a way of going astray or being wrongly entered. When you change your booking, get a new sticker put on your ticket. Concrete evidence of your booking is essential.

✈ Get to the airport an hour before the flight. As long as you have a sticker, you can often get

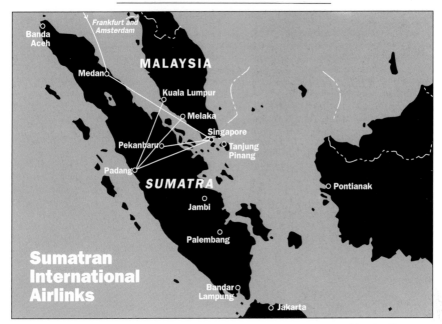

Sumatran International Airlinks

on even if your name isn't in the computer.

➜ If you are told a flight is full, go to the airport anyway two hours before departure and ask that your name be entered on the waiting list. Hang around the desk and be friendly to the staff; 15 minutes before departure you will probably get on. Flights are chronically overbooked but rarely completely full.

➜ Students (10–26 years old) receive a discount of 25% (show an international student ID card), and children between the ages of 2 and 10 pay 50% of the regular fare. Infants not occupying a seat pay 10 per cent of the regular fare.

Sea Travel

To get the real flavor of Sumatra, arrive the way people have for centuries—by sea! There is four times as much sea in Indonesia as land, and for many centuries transportation among the islands has been principally by boat. To travel by boat, you need plenty of time. Think of it as a romantic journey, and don't be in a hurry.

Pelni, the national passenger line, has 10 large ships criss-crossing the archipelago carrying up to 1,500 passengers each. These boats travel on fixed schedules and the first and second class cabins are comfortable. Two such fairly new and comfortable air-conditioned Pelni passenger vessels, the KM Rinjani and Umsini, serve Sumatra, sailing back and forth on alternate weeks between Jakarta and Medan, with stops at Mentok (on Bangka Island) and Kijang (on Bintan Island, just opposite Singapore). The boat leaves Bintan every Sunday morning. There's also a sailing to Dumai on the Riau coast every Friday night. You will need to time your movements to catch these ships, but if you can, it's cheaper and more interesting than flying. Tickets are available only in the port of departure, however, and cannot be ordered in advance. (See "Practicalities" for Medan, Riau and Bangka for boat schedules and prices.) In addition to the Pelni ship, there is also a fast hydrofoil from Penang to Medan.

By ferry from Riau. An even more adventurous way to get to Sumatra is by local ferry boat. All sorts of crafts ply the Straits of Malacca and the South China Sea, radiating out from Batam and Bintan through narrow channels between the scattered islands of the Riau chain, up the Batang Hari and Siak rivers to Jambi, Dumai and Pekanbaru. These are generally slow and cheap, but there are an increasing number of faster and more expensive speedboats with twin 100 Hp outboards, as well as some new hydrofoils. There are daily speedboats from Bintan and Batam to Pekanbaru and Jambi. Given plenty of time, you can island-hop on inter-island ferries from Singapore right down through the Lingga Archipelago to Bangka and Belitung, thence to Palembang or Java. You need plenty of time to do this, and the conditions are not exactly luxurious, but it can be the adventure of a lifetime—like moving back to the romantic days of Joseph Conrad! Check respective "Practicalities."

By ferry from Java. The ferry from Java is fast, comfortable, frequent and cheap. Don't even think of flying to Lampung from Java unless you really don't have the time to go overland. There's also a hydrofoil which operates direct from Jakarta to Lampung. See "Lampung Practicalities" for details.

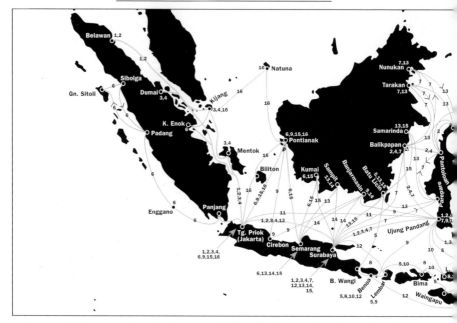

Long-haul Bus Travel

Traveling across Sumatra by bus is one of the island's quintessential experiences, and you've not really "been there" until you have done at least one stretch of the Trans-Sumatra Highway on one of these huge caravans. The highway is now paved along its entire length, and is mostly in good condition, although during the rainy season there could be landslides and fallen trees that bring you to a halt. Once off this main artery, however, road conditions are highly variable. What may look like a major road on the map can be little more than a bone-shaking pot-holed track that has rarely, if ever, been resurfaced since it was first constructed during the Dutch colonial times. On the other hand, road construction crews all over the island are making rapid progress and you can find some excellent stretches of newly-paved and very scenic secondary roads.

A number of companies operate so-called "Non-Ekonomi" or luxury intercity buses on the Trans-Sumatra Highway that are large, new, air-conditioned and mostly in quite good condition. Competition for business is keen. The general consensus is that ANS (for Aman-Nya-man-Sejuk "Safe-Comfortable-Cool") is the best company overall, with connections to all major cities. By local standards their fares are considered a bit expensive: Padang to Jakarta for $25, for example. When you consider that this is a 34-hour ride, though, it isn't that much. Other companies offer similar services, and might charge the same or a bit less. Check them out. Older, non-AC "*Ekonomi*" buses may cost half

the price, but are hot, dirty and crowded, and can add many hours to the journey.

On ANS at least the AC works, the seats are fairly wide and they recline, pillows are provided and there are squat toilets at the back. The latter are only for peeing, however; other calls of nature have to be attended to during the frequent meal stops.

Intercity buses depart more or less on time, but invariably arrive later than scheduled. Schedules are in fact very approximate, and actual travel times vary by hours depending on road conditions and traffic (and how the driver feels). Night buses are faster, but you don't see much.

Bus fares also vary greatly. In theory they are regulated, with increments allowed for certain facilities. In practice, you can pay quite different prices for the same facilities. Western faces, moreover, invite surcharges. Check with several other agents of a given company. Most important of all, know what you are paying for, as buses from the same company have different rates depending on the "extras".

Buses are almost always full. If you are on an overnight journey and can afford it, buying an extra seat may help you sleep better. Onboard entertainment is all the rage now, so you often have to suffer through interminable Indonesian tear-jerkers, or even worse—a karaoke sing-along. Treat it as a cultural experience. Passengers, usually men, who grab the mike to belt out a number—some with remarkably good voices—receive an appreciative round of applause from fellow passengers.

Long-haul bus crews usually consist of two drivers who relay each other, plus a helper who

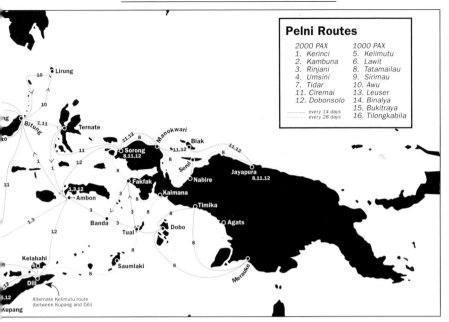

Pelni Routes

2000 PAX	1000 PAX
1. Kerinci	5. Kelimutu
2. Kambuna	6. Lawit
3. Rinjani	8. Tatamailau
4. Umsini	9. Sirimau
7. Tidar	10. Awu
11. Ciremai	13. Leuser
12. Dobonsolo	14. Binalya
	15. Bukitraya
—— every 14 days	16. Tilongkabila
----- every 28 days	

Alternate Kelimutu route
(between Kupang and Dili)

cleans out the bus and washes the windows at every stop. The buses do break down, but drivers carry an impressive array of tools and spares, and you are usually on your way after only a short hiatus.

Health-conscious Westerners will be thankful for the ban on smoking in some AC buses. But the rule is not always enforced, as many drivers are themselves chain smokers. Smokers can have nicotine fits lasting several hours. When the bus finally stops for gasoline, everyone stands around the pumps puffing away madly, oblivious to the "No Smoking" signs posted all around.

The large restaurants where buses stop invariably serve spicy Padang food, with dishes stacked across your table; you pay for what you eat. If you are unaccustomed to spicy food, ask the waiter *Apa yang tidak pedas?* ("What is not hot?") as the food is brought over. You might ask for a spoon and fork (*garpu dan sendok*) if you are not yet used to eating with the right hand only—a messy proposal for many foreigners.

While the best views are from the front row seats, nervous passengers should avoid them. In the mountains, curves are hair-raising and space on the road is at a premium, especially at the center of the highway—the preferred place to be. Most Sumatran bus drivers take a devil-may-care approach to driving. Top speed, pedal-to-the-metal, hand-on-the-horn style. Never touch the brakes unless they are absolutely necessary, and at absolutely the last possible instant. The situation is further aggravated by incessant road works and digging of drainage ditches. Not a few buses end up in them.

The best seats are snapped up where the long-haul buses start, in the provincial capitals. Purchase your ticket a day earlier to get a better seat (front seat or window on the side with better scenery). Seat numbers are not strictly observed, however, and the same number is often sold twice, so there may be someone in yours when you get there. Polite smiles will (usually) get you your rightful place.

The smaller buses making the "local" runs are no fun, but provide an insight into how the common folk travel. Your luggage goes topside or serves as an extra seat inside. It's hot if sunny, wet if rainy. Diesel fumes are wafting everywhere. Just when you thought no more people could possibly get on, three more pile in, with luggage.

Always beware of an empty bus, which like nature abhors a vacuum. It means very long waits, as the bus will definitely not go anywhere apart from the petrol station and back until more people pile in.

Bus stops can turn into a 3-ring circus. As you get further north, men accost you with collection boxes for their mosque or charity. Blind men with begging bowls chant verses from the Koran, led around by young boys. Insistent vendors flog a variety of food or drinks in bags.

Tickets are available at the bus terminals, which are always on the outskirts of town, and there are usually a number of buses going your way at any time. Have a look around, check out the seats or the photos if the buses themselves are not present, to see what you are getting. Try to buy a ticket from a counter, but if they are sold out you may have to buy from a scalper. Check the official rate and allow a 10 percent "premium." In some cases these scalpers and touts can be helpful in getting you and your things on the bus, but follow your instincts in judging the "good" ones from the cheats and pickpockets, and remember to check your tickets very, very carefully.

Local Buses

Usually old rattle-traps, quite different from the sleek intercity buses. These run along major and minor roads, stopping anywhere to pick up and discharge passengers. Only use them if you are going short distances or are looking for a "local experience," as you do get to see quite a cross-section of village society, including the domestic animals. Fares are ridiculously cheap. Flag one down on the roadside.

Express Minibuses

Called *travel* or *transport*, these are 6-, 10- or 14-passenger vans, often AC and quite comfortable, that connect major cities and will deliver you right to your destination. They also sometimes pick you up. Most travel only during the day, though on longer routes they may travel at night like the bus. More expensive than the bus, but much more comfortable and convenient. Also much safer as they tend not to drive as fast.

Local Minibuses

These non-AC vans (*kol* or *bemo*) are the real work-horses of the transport network, going up and down relatively impassable tracks to deliver village farmers and produce. There are no set fares; the conductor, often a small boy, tells you how much, and it isn't much. Flag one down on any roadside. You can also charter them. Just say "charter" and where you want to go, then bargain for the fare in advance.

Car Rentals

Sedans or taxis with drivers are available in major cities but are very expensive, and they don't really like to go long distances. Also, you have to return them to the point of rental. More for daytrips or business clients than for touring. In Medan, self-drive cars are available now (see "Medan Practicalities") but unless you have experience driving in Indonesia, it's not a good idea. You'll need a valid international license.

Chartering a Minibus

Undoubtedly the best way to tour Sumatra is to rent a minibus with driver. This is especially true if you are traveling with a group of 3 to 5 people. The vans can take up to 7, but you need extra space because you'll be in it for hours, so 6 including the driver is generally maximum. Most travel agents can arrange this for you, and will provide driver/guides who speak English and may even be able to tell you what you are seeing. It is a very good idea to hire the van for a trial day around town first.

Set your itinerary. You need to allow the driver time to get back if you are not returning to the starting point, but this usually means an extra day's rental with gas and food money. Rates vary greatly. Bargain and ask around at different places. For a 5-day journey, approximate cost should be around $300 including the driver. You pay for the gasoline (which is cheap). You'll have to pay the full rental amount in advance, before the trip. You also pay for the driver's food and lodging en route, but he usually sleeps in the van and food is cheap. At the end of the trip, fill up the tank, and give him extra money for gas, food and cigarettes along the way. For a good driver, a tip of Rp5,000 is appreciated, as the vehicle owner, not the driver, gets the lion's share of the charter fee.

PLANNING YOUR ITINERARY

Sumatra is so huge, the first thing to realize is that you can never cover the whole island, even if you were to spend several months there. Don't make an impossibly tight schedule, and try not to spend all your time on the road. Better to spend more time in a few places and see them at a leisurely pace than to end up hot and bothered; you'll see more this way, not less. Also realize that the long drives take their toll; budget some time for rest and recuperation.

Top places on your list should be Lake Toba and the Minang Highlands. If you love wildlife and the great outdoors, visit one of the national parks or go hiking in the mountains. All of the volcanoes can be climbed, but you need to be prepared and to hire a guide. Travel agents can help to arrange such trips.

If you like beaches, try the Riau Islands or Bangka and Belitung (South Sumatra) or head for just about any place along the west coast. For something truly exotic, visit the western islands (Mentawai or Nias).

TOURS

While not generally the way to go, there are some great deals from agents in Singapore and Malaysia. For example, a 5-day, 4-night tour of Medan, Berastagi and Toba costs just $300 per person double occupancy including return airfare, hotel and transport. The drawback is that you are stuck with a busload of tourists. But the prices are low, and you do see quite a bit if your time is limited. In Sumatran cities like Medan, Padang and Bukittinggi there are many travel agents offering tours of the region, which can be a timesaver for those trying to squeeze in as many sights and experiences as possible.

1 Medan PRACTICALITIES

INCLUDES GUNUNG LEUSER AND BUKIT LAWANG

North Sumatra, along with Thailand and Malaysia, is putting a tremendous effort into improving infrastructure, hotel and tourist services. For a region with such a diverse cultural heritage, reflected in its mixed population and a wealth of scenic beauty, the potential for this area as a cultural showcase is enormous. Given also the extensive natural resources, primarily oil, natural gas and plantation products, Medan is a rich focal point for tourist activity. Sumatra's largest city, and the fourth largest in Indonesia, Medan is bustling and cosmopolitan, with a high standard of tourism services. But it's also crowded. Telephone code is 061. *See pages 67–77.*

GETTING THERE AND AWAY

By air (international). There are regular flights in from Singapore with Garuda and SilkAir, Singapore Airlines' new subsidiary. Check the main local papers. There are also direct flights from Amsterdam and Frankfurt on Garuda, as well as a planned direct flight in from Thailand via Phuket in tandem with Thai Airlines.
By air (domestic). Garuda flies to and from Jakarta four times a day ($180). Sempati Air also has several flights per day. Some Sempati flights make stopovers in Riau. Mandala is now operating the smaller DC-10 planes previously used by Garuda with American pilots, a real competitive upgrade in service. Local airline offices: **Garuda** Hotel Tiara Convention Hall, Jl Cut Mutia ☎ 53-8527. 515869 also, Dharma Deli Hotel ☎ 51-6400. Ticketing office, Jl Letjen Suprapto 2 ☎ 516066. **Singapore Airlines** and **SilkAir,** Hotel Polonia, Jl Sudirman ☎ 537744, 514488. **Mandala** Jl Brig. Jen. Katamso 37-E ☎ 538183. **Merpati** Jl Brigjen Katamso 72/122, ☎ 514102. **SMAC** Jl Imam Bonjol 59 ☎ 537760. **Sempati** Hotel Tiara Convention Hall ☎ 537800, also Dharma Deli Arcade ☎ 327011. **Thai** Airways, Dharma Deli Hotel, Jl Balai Kota ☎ 514483, 510541.
By sea. Hydrofoil services from **Penang** to the main harbor at **Belawan** are available through most travel agencies. Two companies, **Bahagia Express** and **Perdana Express** ply this route, with one way fares at $35. The state-run shipping company **Pelni** operates two ships on alternate weeks, the *Rinjani* and the *Kambuna*, between Jakarta and Belawan. These ships actually go as far as **Ujung Pandang**, and if you have the time it is a pleasant way to travel down the straits. Fares are $85 first class for a double cabin with attached hot shower, and meals. The fresh air and gentle seas of the Malaccan straits are restful. Other classes are $65 for second (four to a cabin), $45 third class (6 per cabin with a gang shower), $35 for fourth class (8 per cabin), and $25 deck class (usually extremely crowded and spartan). The Pelni office is at Jl Kol. Sugiono 5–7, on the corner with Jl Cakrawati, ☎ 518899, 517474.
By road. With the gradual but inevitable development of the Trans-Sumatra Highway from Aceh all the way to the southern tip of Sumatra, bus travel is gradually becoming a viable alternative for long distance travel. Be advised, however, that the road is still not completely developed along its entire length, and that maintenance, particularly of bridges, can still be problematic, especially in the wet season. This often produces delays. By far, **ALS** is the best bus service to and from Java or southerly points of Sumatra.

GETTING AROUND

Polonia airport is still in the middle of the city, though there is a plan to move it 15 kilometers out in the apparently distant future (witness Medan people's love of racket and incessant din, believed to keep away bad spirits and therefore be soothing rather than disturbing). The city limits of Medan are expanding considerably. There is now a partially finished four-lane bypass road connecting the airport to Jl Berastagi (Letjen Djamin Ginting S). You can actually walk out of the airport's entrance and get straight on local transport. Airport taxis cost about $2.50.
Taxis. Medan now has a large number of metered taxis, the most convenient way to get around the city. Most destinations in the city will be less than $1.50. Hourly rates are negotiated with the cab. You can pick these up along any main thoroughfare or at the Danau Toba, Surya, Tiara, or Polonia Hotels. You can also try calling taxis, though not always successfully, on these numbers: **Metax** ☎ 524659, **Kostar** ☎

611252. Others can be found in the local yellow pages. **Minibuses** ply important routes around the city and average fares are 50 cents. **Motor Becak.** Average fare is 50 cents, plus 50 cents per kilometer.

TRANSPORT OUT OF MEDAN

Taxis. A number of taxi companies have single seats or whole vehicles for travel out of Medan. Try **Inda Taxi**, Jl Brig. Jen. Katamso 61, and **Hotma Taxi**, Jl Tinta 54 ☎ 521789. You can also go directly to **Poltaks** on Jl Brig. Jen. Katamso, near Pacto travel agent, though you will probably have to wait till the car fills up.

Buses. ALS, Jl Amaliun 24 ☎ 718499, 719959 is still the best server of this route, with clean AC buses on dependable schedules. ALS can take you to points further on in Java and even connect out to Bali and beyond. Smaller bus companies for shorter routes operate out of the large station on Jl Sisingamangaraja, and from the station on Jl Veteran behind the Pasar Sentral known as Sambu. **Pribumi** from Sisingamangaraja terminal takes you to **Berastagi**, **Sidikalang** and **Tarutung**. **Makmur**, located on Jl Sindoro 30 ☎ 532812, plies the route to **Aceh**. For short trips by bus, to **Belawan**, **Binjei**, etc, pick up buses at Jl Veteran station.

Trains. There is a service leaving from the main train station at Lapangan Merdeka to **Siantar**, **Rantau Parapat** and **Belawan**. Trains in many cases are pulled by vintage steam engines from the turn of the century, and there is a classic turntable service area in Tebing Tinggi which you shouldn't miss. Tickets run $3.50 to Siantar and Parapat, and $9.50 the end of the line at Rantau Parapat. Binjei is $2. Buy your tickets directly at the *loket* or ticket booths at the Setasiun Kereta Api, Jl Kereta Api, bordering Lapangan Merdeka.

Car rentals. Generally this is not a real choice for newcomers to Medan. Traffic is fierce and aggressive. However, if you have the nerve (or bravado), experience and the cash, National Car Rental ☎ 327011, fax 327153, has an office in the Dharma Deli Complex, Rates range from $55 to $88 per day for four types of automobile, and from $288 to $490 per week. Add $5 per day for insurance, though this turns to a flat rate of $60 for twelve days and over. Add $12 per day if you need to have a driver. There's 10 per cent tax. You can also drop the vehicle in Padang with a drop-charge of $150.

ACCOMMODATIONS

Budget

Deli Raya Hotel (21 rooms), Jl Sisingamangaraja 29 ☎ 712997 and **Lubuk Raya** Hotel, Jl Lubuk Raya 1 ☎ 721071. Two hotels under the same ownership/management. The **Deli Raya**, located next to the Garuda City Hotel, has AC rooms for $15 and $20. The **Lubuk Raya**, just behind Dhaksina Hotel, has good, clean facilities with fans at $9.50 for a double and $11.50 for a triple. Excellent value and conveniently located. Losmen **Irama**, Jl Palang Merah 112S (off Palang Merah on a small side street to the left from the Imam Bonjol/Diponegoro traffic light) is the place for travelers interested in moving on to Nias. Penginapan **Tapiana Naibaru**, Jl Hang Tuah 6 ☎ 512155, is in a beautiful setting next to one of Medan's nicer parks and the Vihara Gunung Timur Chinese temple, one of the biggest and most impressive in Sumatra.

Moderate

Many good possibilities in the mid-range hotels in Medan, which are improving their facilities fast. Choose your hotel for location. **Dhaksina** (40 rooms), Jl Sisingamangaraja 20 ☎ 720000. Dhaksina is currently upgrading its facilities, which probably augurs an upgrade in price as well. For the moment, it is pleasant and clean. $12 and $25. **Garuda City** Hotel (68 rooms), Jl Sisingamangaraja 27–39 ☎ 718553, 717975, fax 714411. Up and coming, newly renovated, brand new wing. The hotel is expanding to compete with Garuda Plaza just of the street. Ranges from $17 to $35. **Elbruba** (48 rooms) Jl Perintis Kemerdekaan (Jl Jati) 19 ☎ 530476, 520119. No frills, good value. The hotel is expanding and will no doubt improve its facilities to keep up with the competition. $27 to $40 with 20 per cent discount. Hotel **Sumatera**, Jl Sisingamangaraja 35 ☎ 718807. Hotel Sumatera is really just on the border of cost for those who want midrange conveniences with low prices. $17 to $25. **Pardede International** (136 rooms), Jl Ir. H Juanda 14 ☎ 543866, fax 553675. Pardede is part of the same chain as Hotel Danau Toba, with a more modest atmosphere and rather notorious night life. $43 and $60, cottages also available at $75. **Sumatra Village** (58 rooms), Jl Djamin Ginting Kilometer 11 ☎ 720-964, is a new chalet type hotel and resort out on the road to Berastagi. While a bit out of town, the surroundings, the quality of the facilities, including a luxurious pool and floating bar, and the price are a real deal. $45, $55, and $95. **Wai Yat** (80 rooms) Jl Asia 44 ☎ 718975, 718575. Still a favorite as one of the oldest Chinese style hotels in Medan. Great value for your money, with a well-known Chinese restaurant known for its Babi Hong (roast pork). $25 to $30. **Wisma Benteng** (24 rooms), Jl Kapt. Maulana Lubis 6 ☎ 518426. A guest house run by the Indonesian army, Wisma Benteng is one of the most pleasant places to stay in Medan. Rooms are modest but pleasantly furnished, with nice gardens and one of the best *halal* Chinese restaurants in Medan. $22, $32 and $75.

Luxury

The three best hotels in Medan below are all centrally located in the city with easy access to the main shopping centers. As with all hotels in Medan, always ask for a discount. You should be able to get 10 to 15 percent at many places. **Danau Toba International** (258 rooms) Jl Imam Bonjol 17 ☎ 557000, fax 530553. The Danau Toba is the most centrally and conveniently located of all of Medan's hotels. It has the best swimming pool, good restaurants, plus the Tavern, a nice afternoon watering hole though the Filipino bands may blow out your eardrums, and the Piano Lounge, which will soothe them afterwards. The Riung Lembur restaurant in the back is a real asset. Recently renovated, $90–$199. **Dharma Deli**, Jl Balai Kota ☎ 327011, fax 327153. Nostalgia is the main thing with the Dharma Deli, as well as its reasonable prices. The adjacent small arcade has a Garuda office and a National Rent-a-Car. $45 to $130. **Dirga Surya** (63 rooms), Jl Imam Bonjol 6 ☎ 321555, fax 513327. Dirga Surya has, with its Xanadu nightclub, one of the hot spots of Medan's nightlife, and besides a good general restaurant on the first floor, you have the Surya food center right next store. $60 to $110. Hotel **Tiara** (182 rooms), Jl Cut Meutiah ☎ 516000, 523000, 538880, fax 510176, 513720. Recently renovated, and remains the chief competitor against the Danau Toba. It has a huge convention hall facility, and the Clark Hatch health club, which is the best in its class. $90 to $145. **Garuda Plaza** (151 rooms) Jl Sisingamangaraja 18 ☎ 716255, 711411, fax 714411. This Minang-styled hotel has improved its facilities several times over the past few years, and is a pleasant place to stay. Has a small but cozy executive lounge with good keyboard music. $55 and $65. Hotel **Polonia** (177 rooms), Jl Sudirman 14 ☎ 542222, 535111, fax 519553. Has one of the best Chinese restaurants in town, a small health club with good squash and handball courts tucked away in back, and a Singapore Airlines office. $60 to $90.

FOOD

Western food. European dining is not well catered for in Medan. The **Ambarita Grill** in the Hotel Tiara and **Hotel Toba Danau Coffee Shop** are the only other real venues for Western food, and with only certain dishes up to par. For cafe dining try **Lynn's Cafe**, Jl A Yani 98 across from the Tjong Afe mansion, though a bit smoke filled. Similar fare though lighter atmosphere at the **Batik Cafe**, Jl Pemuda 14C. **Tip Top** on Jl Yani and the **DeBoer** Restaurant in the Dharma Deli Hotel serve some Western dishes, and Tip Top has good ice creams. Music Cafe in the new Deli Plaza-Yuki Plaza sky cross serves the best grilled Western favorites. The best Western-style restaurant in Medan is in the **Executive Club** at the Uniland building just over the railroad tracks on Jl Palang Merah. Reasonably priced though not cheap, the menu is varied and truly international quality in a superb setting. The club also has a fine bar and cocktail lounge, as well as an excellent Chinese restaurant. Short-term memberships can be arranged.

Chinese food. Medan's real specialty is Chinese food, which can be found on virtually every block. Moderate to expensively priced restaurants with big local reputations to boot are **Asean** Jl Glugur Bypass 5; **Benteng** Restaurant, Jl Kapt. Maulana Lubis 6 (north end of Lapangan Benteng, specializes in Chinese food cooked without any pork; *halal*, first class); **Polonia** Restaurant in the Hotel Polonia; **Jumbo** Restaurant, Jl Balai Kota (across from Deli Plaza); **Sheraton Palace**, Jl Orion (next to Medan Plaza). **Tip Top** Restaurant on Jl Yani offers a classic old Dutch-styled setting and serves good Chinese food.

Indian food. Try **Kohinoor** restaurant on Jl Hindu, the best in town for North Indian style food. Recently opened **Farhan** on Jl Taruma, just up from Royal Holland and Tahiti bakeries, is offering some competition in the North Indian area. The renowned *martabak* of Malaccan straits lore can be found every night on Jl Jenggala and Jl Cik di Tiro in **Kampung Keling**, along with good mutton curries which tend to be hot and zingy. For South Indian cuisine, ask at Kampung Keling.

Indonesian food. For Central Javanese cuisine, a must-try is **Wong Solo**, situated behind the golf course and another, on Jl. Gadjah Mada. The **Ayam Goreng Kalasan**, Jl Iskandar Muda 294, next to Medan Plaza, has the best fried chicken outside of Java. Sundanese/Javanese style fish cooked fresh in characteristic settings can be found at **Ratu Kuring**, Jl S Parman, and the **Lembur Kuring** out around the end of the airport. Lembur Kuring is an interesting setting, with large fish pools around the complex of eating units up on stilts. Padang or Minang style restaurants are in great abundance all over Medan and the food is hot and delicious. The larger ones include **Ambassador**, Jl Palang Merah; Garuda, Jl Gadjah Mada, Jl Gatot Subroto, and Jl Pemuda. If you're in Kampung Keling area, try **Bintang** on Jl Taruma just past Tahiti Bakery.

Japanese food. The **Fuji** restaurant in the Hotel Danau Toba International is the place for Japanese food. Japanese fast food from Iroha, near to Kentucky Fried Chicken on Jl Gadjah Mada.

Seafood. The area of Jl **Selat Panjang** remains a local favorite for all sorts of ocean fish, crabs, lobsters and shellfish. But also try **Waringin**, on Jl Waringin near the intersection of Jl Gatot Subroto and Jl Gereja. Likewise at **Belawan**, with the added attraction of a number of shops near the restaurants selling all sorts of fine ceramics and imported goods.

Korean food. Still the place of choice for Korean food is **Thamrin Hall** on the 5th floor of Thamrin Plaza. Steamboats at $5 and all you can eat.

Budget food. If you're counting the rupiah, the best bet is **Surya Food Center**, next to Dirga Surya Hotel. Similar kind of stalls are located also at the **Seri Deli** across from the Mesjid Agung near the Maimoon on Jl Sisingamangaraja. The Seri Deli Restaurant serves Melayu and Javanese style food at reasonable prices. All of the plazas have fast food shops, mostly selling Indonesian-style fast food items like *nasi goreng*, *sate* and the like. One new spot called **Tamia** on Jl Uskup Agung near the intersection with Jl Sudirman, and rather oddly placed in a residential area, is specializing in both fruit salads and take away fast food of good quality. There are also two **Church's Fried Chicken** outlets (one in Yuki Plaza and one in Thamrin Plaza), two **KFC**'s (one on Jl Gajah Mada and one in Perisai Plaza), **Swensen's Ice Cream**, and also a **Pizza Hut** on Jl Sudirman, on the corner with Jl Rivai.

SHOPPING

Kampung Keling is about the closest thing to instant success for most of the real basics. Next in line are the plazas, notably **Deli**, **Thamrin** and **Medan** plazas for covering just about every other need. **Jl Yani** provides most of the antique shops in close proximity with other places you might want to go to, including the Post Office. And Kampung Keling, Jl Yani, the Post Office and **Deli Plaza** are all easy walking distance of each other.

Antiques

Crispo still commands the scene in the area of antiques. Besides his expanded shop on Jl Arifin, he has also opened up in the Danau Toba Hotel. Also check out **Chang and Chang** on the back side of Yuki Plaza, and **Tanu** on the third floor of Deli Plaza across from the theater. Less true antiques than contemporary kitsch. On Jl Yani you should not miss looking through **ABC Art Gallery**, **Borobudur Art and Curios**, **Toko Arjuna**, **Toko Asli** and **Toko Rufino**, among others. Also **Toko Seni** around the corner on Jl Yani VII/2.

Bakeries

Royal Holland Bakery, **Suan's Bakery** and **Tahiti Bakery** are all next to each other on Jl Taruma. Each has a wealth of international-type breads and cakes, fresh baked daily. Royal Holland and Suan's have excellent wholewheat breads. All also have a selection of ice creams with snack bars attached for light meals Indonesian style. The more modest **Medan Bakery** on Jl Arifin provides basic breads and some simple pastries.

Books

The two largest bookstores are **Gramedia**, located on Jl Gadjah Mada across the street from KFC, and **Gunung Agung** on the fourth floor of Thamrin Plaza. Don't go into these places expecting to come out with many books in English or other European languages.

Cinemas

The cinema remains the average Indonesian's entertainment besides the TV. The best cinemas include **President** theater in the Deli Plaza building and the four theaters atop the Sinar Plaza right next to it. Others include **Thamrin 21** in the Thamrin Plaza, **Plaza** theater in Medan Plaza, and the **Majestik** theater at Petisah turnaround.

Clothing

All the major plazas have clothing shops of all shapes, sizes and price ranges. **Matahari** in Deli Plaza and especially **Thamrin Plaza** are enormous. Vast arrays of tee-shirts and oversize items are relatively sure bets there. There are some new higher-end shops in the walkways connecting Deli Plaza and Yuki Plaza.

Computers

Do not expect the last word in expert technical support and advice. Try **Royal Computer**, Jl Raden Saleh 39 (across from the old Balai Kota building) ☎ 511448 for IBM equipment, and **Computer House**, Jl Raden Saleh 23 ☎ 533900 for Apple and Macintosh items. Personalized attention can be had from Hugo Brevoort, **Euro Computer Consulting**, Jl Sei Bagerpang 12/33 ☎ 517469.

Courier Services

Major courier services are now operating in Medan with a wide range of prices for sending letters and packages inside and outside Indonesia. **DHL** (PT Birotika Semesta), Jl Cakrawati 1A ☎ 519240. **Elteha** International Ltd, Jl Mayjen Sutoyo Siswomihardjo 121 ☎ 513487, 516-164. **Federal Express** (Victory Cargo), Jl Biduk 85 ☎ 522085. **EMS** mail service (Express mail at the main Post Office), Jl Bukit Barisan 1 ☎ 51-740. **UPS** (PT Global Putra), Jl Brigjen Katamso 43M ☎ 510123, 513824. **Skypak** International (TNT Express Worldwide), Jl Juanda Baru 77 ☎ 538584.

Drugstores

In Kampung Keling you have **Apotek Bintang**, Jl Arifin 85 and **Apotek Bandung**, Jl Arifin 182, open seven days a week until 9 pm. **Apotek Kimia Farma** on Jl Palang Merah, near the intersection with Jl Yani, is open 24 hours.

Film Supplies

Try **Toko Solo** (Jl Arifin in Kampung Keling) or **Fuji Image Plaza** on Jl Gatot Subroto across from the Medan Fair for the best selection of both color print and slide film. You can now also regularly get black and white print film in these locations. Precious shots should be developed at home, or in a specialist lab.

Gold and Silver

Medan is still known in the region for some of the best gold prices. There are gold shops in all the major plazas, especially **Deli Plaza** and **Medan Plaza**. You might have a look in there and then try your luck over in the **Petisah** shopping complex, where there are a number of more reasonable shops. In the **Kesawan** area, have a look at **Toko Mas Bangkok**, Jl Yani V/39, **Toko Masa Batu Bara**, Jl Yani 51 and **Toko Mas Kesawan**, Jl Yani 53, among others.

Markets

For browsing and bargain-hunting, markets are the treasure troves of Indonesia. **Pasar Kampung Keling**, behind Jl Muara Takus, offers mostly meat, vegetables and fruit. **Pasar Ikan Lama** on Jl Perniagaan in the Kesawan area is a special place for fabrics of all sorts. **Pasar Peringgan** is the best place in town for fresh fruit and flowers, as well as fine coffee at the best possible local prices in the lane along the market, both in powder and roasted bean form. **Pasar Petisah** has a wide range of clothing and household wares for sale, as well as an interesting bird market. The gold shops just across the street have some of the best prices in all of Asia. For an adventure in the city, take a trip to the **Pasar Sentral**, or central market off Jl Letjen Haryono behind the Olympia shopping center. It is now called the Medan Mall, but do not expect what the name implies.

SERVICES

There are several **money changers** around the city, particularly accessible is the **PT. Gembira City**, Jl Arifin 101 in Kampung Keling. Medan has fine banking facilities. **Bank Kesawan** appears to offer the best rates and has numerous currencies available. Overseas banks such as **Standard Chartered Bank** (Hotel Danau Toba International Complex ☎ 512000), and **Hong Kong Bank**, BII building, Jl Diponegoro 18 ☎ 558806) conduct most business. Private Indonesian commercial banks like **Bank Central Asia** (Jl Diponegoro 15 (corner with Jl Arifin) ☎ 548800, 555800), **LippoBank** (Jl Pemuda 14-AB ☎ 556622, 550322), and **Bank Niaga** (Jl Bukit Barisan 5 ☎ 512256, 520110) handle most transactions. **Credit card** transactions:

American Express has a representative in Pan Indonesia Bank (but if you wish to get cash advances on your card, go to Pacto Travel, Jl Brigjen Katamso 62-A ☎ 513699, 510081). **Diner's Club** is at Balai Kota 2 (Dharma Deli Arcade) ☎ 514480. **Communications** are advanced. There are **Wartels** (private Telkom offices) on every other block. The official **Telkom** center, is just up the street from the Post Office.

TOURS AND INFORMATION

Tours can be arranged at all the big travel agencies. Try **Pacto**, which specializes in tours. Any one of the following recommended tourist agencies can provide you with a wide selection of packages, trips and options. Try **Best Travel**, Jl M Yamin II/5 ☎ 522708, **PT Boraspati Express** Tours and Travel, Jl Dazam Raya 77 ☎ 52-6802, fax 322906 or **Edelweiss**, Jl Irian Barat 49 ☎ 517497. The **Tourist Information Office** on Jl Yani, next to the Tjong Afi mansion (☎ 511-101) is a good source for general information, brochures and specifics.

INTERNATIONAL SHIPPING

Shipping, packing and handling of potentially valuable goods to be sent home is best handled by one of the most experienced companies in Medan, such as **Metrasco International**, Jl Mayang ☎ 520788. Or try **Maersk Lines**, Jl Hang Jebat 2 ☎ 511017, or **Samudra Indonesia**, Jl Pemuda 11 DEF ☎ 511703 or **Trikora Lloyd**, Jl Kol Sugiono 5–7.

SPORTS

Cricket is played at the Medan International School field on the third Sunday of every month. Check **Lynn's Cafe** for information on fixtures. **Golf** is a great pastime in Medan. The **Polonia Golf Course**, run by the Air Force, is on the other side of the airport runway. It has nine holes and reportedly is to be upgraded to 18, and the ground fees and caddie fees for 18 holes will cost you about $10. **Nicotiana**, at the other end of town out past the Pulau Bryan area (accessible most easily via Jl Karya going east), is run by the PTP II plantation (primarily growing tobacco, hence the name). It has a small airstrip right next to the first hole and is the greater challenge to your game. Fees are the same as Polonia. **Tuntungan** is run by the Deli Golf Club, which has an office on Jalan Yani and a driving range near the airport on the city side, it is truly world-class. Eighteen holes, extremely well kept, and much more internationally priced. Expect to spend about $35 to $40 in caddies and green fees as a non-member, and also expect to find it much more crowded than any of the the other more modest courses. The **Tamora** course at PTP II on the road to Parapat, is also interesting. A bit further out, about an hour one way from Medan, is the **Pamitran** course at Batu Karang, PTP V, which is 18 holes and boasts some incredible scenery and equally incredible long par fives. Further on towards Siantar, there is a course at PTP IV just outside of Tebing Tinggi, with an air strip running down it, and further on again, another 9-holer at the **Goodyear Plantation**.

Clark Hatch Fitness at the Hotel Tiara ☎ 516-000 is probably the best fitted out and most complete in its facilities and services, with good squash courts. **Danau Toba Fitness Centre** at the Hotel Danau Toba International and **Polonia Fitness Centre** ☎ 325300, run a close second. **The Exchange Club**, Uniplaza, West Tower 8th floor ☎ 532356 has a small fitness club with good rooftop tennis courts.

Swimming pools can be found at the three top international class hotels—open also to non-guests. The most interesting and luxurious is **Hotel Danau Toba International**. The **Gaperta** pool off Jl Gaperta is Olympic-sized and run by the army. The swimming pool in the **Thamrin Plaza**, top floor, has a modest-sized water slide.

ENTERTAINMENT

Despite being Sumatra's largest city, nightlife in Medan is not all that varied, offering the usual clubs, cinemas and karaoke bars. The hottest disco in town is the **Dynasty** in the Hotel Danau Toba International Complex. Other nightclubs include the **Bali Plaza**, in the Bali Plaza Restaurant on Jl Kumango, and the **Xanadu** in the Dirgha Surya Hotel.

ARTS AND MUSEUMS

Museum Negara, the Government museum on Jl H M Joni off Jl Sisingamangaraja just after the Taman Pahlawan cemetery, is the only real museum of note in Medan. It presents various sorts of ethnological and archaeological items rather poorly.

Bukit Barisan Museum, Jl Arifin, across from the Bank Bali building, is the local Indonesian Armed Forces museum, primarily interesting for its displays on the Sumatran theater of the Indonesian revolution in the 1940s.

Taman Budaya Medan, the arts center, is located on Jl Perintis Kemerdekaan, just after its intersection with Jl Sutomo. Programs include local music and drama groups, as well as art exhibits by local artists. Large billboards display current events.

The PPIA (Indonesian American Friendship Association) on Jl Dr Mansur past the USU campus has an expanding library and multi-media center. Also wide-ranging cultural events. Call ☎ 813197 for details.

Alliance Francaise on Jl Uskup Agung 2 offers language classes and French movies.

The Perpustakaan Negara (main library) is across the road from the Maimoon Palace. It also incorporates the old British Council Library. Not a bad collection.

HEALTH

Outpatient services can be had immediately and in most cases on a 24 hour basis at **Dewi Maya** Hospital, Jl Surakarta 2 ☎ 519291; **St. Elizabeth** Hospital, Jl Imam Bonjol/Jl Haji Misbah ☎ 512455; **Rumah Sakit Herna**, Jl Mojopahit ☎ 510766. There are also several other hospitals in the city, ask at your hotel.

SPORTS EQUIPMENT

Several shops along Jl Yani can serve many of your sporting equipment needs. Golf equipment, tennis equipment and sports shoes can all be found at **Medan Sports**, Jl Yani 101 and **Ratan Sports**, Jl Yani 81. **Hari Bros**, Jl Yani 89, is probably the largest on the street and where you can also get tennis rackets restrung or golf clubs repaired. For fishing enthusiasts, try **Toko Rejeki Nelayan** on Jl Merbabu 6B/C. They are well stocked for rods, reels, line and some assorted lures. Sibolga, on Sumatra's west coast, is one of the best places for fishing.

Gunung Leuser and Bukit Lawang

About 76 km west of Medan, inside the huge Gunung Leuser National Park, is the **Bohorok Orangutan Rehabilitation Station** near Bukit Lawang, one of the most accessible places in the park. To visit the park, get a permit from the **PHPA** (Forestry) Office at **Bukit Lawang** village, donations are appreciated. You can see the animals at feeding times (8 am and 3 pm), with free river crossings by boat. It's about 2 km from the village to the Station, where you will cross the river with the park warders after reporting. There are two **guesthouses** inside the park, and simple food is available over the river just outside the park. There's also a **camping area** with toilets. Guides can be hired for the day from the Station, and walkers trekking in the park must bring a guide along. There's accommodation in Bukit Lawang village at **Wisma Sibayak**, which has 40 reasonable rooms and a restaurant, and also the similar **Wisma Bukit Lawang**. There are daily buses to and from **Medan** and **Berastagi**. Some routes change at **Binjai**, others go direct. Ask at the bus terminal in Bukit Lawang.

Now one of the largest conservation projects in the world, the Gunung Leuser National Park is also a fine ecotourism opportunity. A new set of bungalows has been developed with special tour packages. Contact Ms Nelly in Medan at tel/fax: 555832.   *— Edward Van Ness*

North Sumatra PRACTICALITIES

INCLUDES BERASTAGI, LAKE TOBA, NIAS AND SIBOLGA

North Sumatra's countryside is full of opportunities for trekking and sightseeing in a relatively quiet setting. Highlights of the area are the lovely Lake Toba and its surrounding highlands. While on weekends it can be pretty packed with international and domestic tourists, weekdays generally are quiet. Tourist facilities are well-developed. The climate is temperate and fairly wet all year round. The area's geography is dominated by the Gundaling hill, near the center of Berastagi, and the two large volcanoes, Mt Sibayak and Mt Sinabung. There are plenty of opportunities for hiking, modest freshwater fishing, horse riding, swimming and just plain relaxing. *See pages 81–121.*

Berastagi

Telephone code is 0628.

Berastagi is one of the classic mountain resorts in Indonesia, perched up in the Karo highlands at about 1,200 m. An easy day trip from Medan, and a pleasant place to visit for a few days. The local Karo Batak is a distinct group among the Batak tribes in North Sumatra, in terms of language, customs and traditions. Among other things, the Karo Batak's culture shows many distinct influences from India, though indelibly interwoven with wholly indigenous cultural traits. A friendly people, you will be impressed with their passionate approach to everything, and their distinctive regional dress and handicrafts.

GETTING THERE AND AWAY

By taxi. Taxis to Berastagi can be chartered through all of the taxi companies listed in the *Medan Practicalities* section at $25 for a drop.
By bus. You can get local buses to Berastagi anywhere along Jl Djamin Ginting S, from the intersection with Jl Monginsidi, for about 75 cents. Choose your vehicle well as there are many.
By motorbike. The trip is possible by motorbike, though you should be ready for two sections of pretty hairy hairpin turns. Don't try this on a bicycle unless you expect to hike these sections, and have tons of time.

Be aware that on the way to Berastagi there are a few sites of interest. Several spots along the road up are nice places to stop off and even have a swim. The **Sibolangit** Botanical Garden is a particularly nice place to take a break in your trip, with several converging trails including one along the rim of the mountains with a magnificent view all the way to the sea on clear days. Flora are marked here and there. On week days the garden is quiet.

GETTING AROUND

The best way to get around Berastagi is to **walk**. Many of the major spots of interest are within walking distance, and you will find the mountain air brisk and refreshing. Remember that it often rains as clouds pass over unexpectedly, so take an umbrella along. Renting **bicycles** can be arranged through your hotels at an extremely low price. Sudakos, the ubiquitous reconditioned **pickup trucks** carrying passengers in the back are plentiful. You can rent these by the hour for local travel, at about $4, more for out of town trips.

Berastagi map:
- Sibayak Mountain
- Sinabung Resort
- Football Field
- Sibayak Multinasional Guest House
- Sibayak Int'l
- Swimming Pool
- Medan, Lau Debuk Debuk, Peceran, Tahura National Park, Mutiaka Brastagi Hotel, Rose Garden Hotel, Rud Ang Hotel & Bukit Kubu Hotel
- Danau Toba
- Mosque
- Fruit Market
- Lingga Inn
- Fuji Studio
- Gundaling Cottages
- Police Dept.
- Memorial
- Ginsata
- Gundaling Hill
- Namakan Souvenir Shop
- Timur
- Modesty Souvenir Shop
- Rafflesia Tour
- JL. TRIMURTI
- Losmen Trimurty
- Berastagi Cottages
- Torong Inn
- Asia
- Shangri La Seafood
- Anda
- Traffic Police
- Babi Panggang
- Losmen Pusat
- Public Health Centre
- General Hospital
- Losmen Sibayak
- Rumah Makan Terang
- Eropah
- Bukit Tongging
- Budi Aman
- Losmen Gunung
- Hiba Taxi
- Sistra Bus Station
- JL. MASJID
- Billiards
- Ria Cinema
- Warung
- Jaya Billiards Taxi
- Ore et Labora
- Rumah Makan Sehat
- JL. PERNIAGAAN
- Market
- N
- not to scale
- Kabanjahe Bus Station
- Wisma Dieng
- Sinulingga Souvenir Shop
- **Berastagi**
- Lingga & Lake Kawar
- Wisma Sibayak
- Kabanjahe & Lake Toba
- JL. VETERAN
- JL. GUNDALING
- JL. UDARA

ACCOMMODATIONS

There has recently been a tremendous increase in the number of hotels. All of these are vying for the best views of either Sibayak or Sinabung. Be sure to ask for a discount, which is often easy to get due to the competition.

Budget

Losmen Sibayak (16 rooms) on Jl Veteran 119 ☎ 91122, 91895, has rooms for $3.50 with bathroom attached. This is one of three accommodations in Berastagi owned by the Pelawi family. It sits off the road across the street from the public health center. Also under their ownership, **Wisma Sibayak** (23 rooms), at the fork of Jl Veteran and Jl Udara ☎ 91104, has rooms for $3 per night without bath and dorm rooms for $1.50 per night, which can house up to 6 people. Also in town on or near Jl Veteran are **Ginata**, **Anda** (Jl Trimurti) and **Torong Inn**, Jl Veteran. Up the Gundaling Hill look into **Wisma Ikut** and **Kaliaga Bungalow**, and several places on Jl Pendidikan including **Karo Hill**, **BIB** and **Miranda**, all in the $5 to $10 range.

Moderate

Sibayak Multinasional (7 rooms), Jl Pendidikan 903 ☎ 91031 offers rooms for $12.50 per night with hot water and attached bathroom. Located up at the foot of the Gundaling hill, it's good value and owned by the management of the Losmen Sibayak and Wisma Sibayak in town. **Berastagi Cottages** (76 rooms), on Jl Gundaling ☎ 91345, 91546 (522162 in Medan), offers a fine view of Berastagi to the east. Rooms from $10 to $28. **Rose Garden** Hotel (89 rooms), Jl Picaran ☎ 20099 (518583 in Medan), has standard rooms at $32. **Rudang** Hotel (43 rooms, including cottages) on Jl Sempurna 16 ☎ 20921 (☎ 3425172 in Medan), has rooms from $32, $40 for cottages, and is popular with tour groups. Situated near to the Bukit Kubu, just out of town, it's a bit behind the times, but a viable option.

Luxury

Hotel **Mutiara Berastagi** (115 standard and deluxe rooms) is your first encounter with resort accommodation before entering Berastagi proper. With rooms at $50 and $75, it has a magnificent lobby which looks over a unique swimming pool shaped in two asymmetric globules connected with a bridge and floating bar. ☎ 91555 (☎ 510605 in Medan). **Bukit Kubu**, Jl Sempurna No 2 ☎ 91533, 91524 (☎ 5196-36 at the Medan booking office), is a Dutch period residence with luxurious rolling hills in front, which houses a pleasant nine-hole irons course, tennis courts and lovely pine tree groves.

Rooms in the old building are classic Dutch colonial, with large fireplaces in the dining room and lounge, and wooden floors. For the atmosphere of colonial days and magnificent grounds, it is among the most beautiful hotels in Indonesia. Rooms range from economy $18 to $24, standard $26 to $38, with suites and bungalows at $50 upwards, tax and service included, real value for money. Be advised that it is almost always prebooked, so call through first to reserve. **Sinabung Resort** Hotel (80 rooms), Jl Kolam Renang ☎ 91400, 91401, fax 91300, 525115 in Medan, is located on the way up towards Gundaling. There are several other hotels in the same class, though pricier. Follow the signs after going through the ticket booth on the way up turning right, and you'll find Sinabung definitely has the most impressive view of all the new hotels, with a five hole irons golf course, children's play area complete with a maze, and a big swimming pool. Rates range are standard $55, deluxe $68, with cottages at $75 and up. Hotel **Sibayak** (113 rooms), Jl Merdeka ☎ 91301/8, fax 91307 (☎ 710200 in Medan), is built in Swiss chalet design. It has an excellent heated swimming pool, two restaurants, 24-hour coffee shop, health club and sauna. Rooms range from $68 to $72, and cottages from $80, tax and service included.

FOOD

The best Chinese food is at **Asia** restaurant, Jl Veteran 9–10, just near the entrance to Gundaling market. In spite of being incessantly busy, the service is quick, and the prices moderate. The **Bukit Kubu** restaurant is idyllic, perched atop one of the hills of its little golf course, and offers both Indonesian and Western cuisine, with daily buffets. All of the major hotels have restaurants which offer the same type of fare, moderately to expensively priced. Try the **Hotel Sibayak** guest house for a bit of cozy atmosphere, and **Berastagi Cottage Restaurant** or **Lingga Inn** for Chinese and Padang style food. Other restaurants along Jl Veteran which offer various cuisines and moderate to inexpensive fare are **Rumah Makan Eropah**, **Terang**, **Budiaman**, **Muslimin** and **Sehat**.

PLACES OF INTEREST

A visit to the Government **Tourist Office** ☎ 910-84 at the entrance to Gundaling road, just next to the entrance to the big market, will provide you with a wealth of information and options for tours, jaunts and things to do in the area. The bureau offers several tour packages which are reasonably priced and will take you to most of the major sites of interest in the region. The Sembiring and Tarigan tours include climbing Sibayak and Sinabung, respectively. You can try these yourself, with advice to be careful as there are some dangerous spots, particularly on Sibayak which is the site of frequent accidental falls. Take a guide with you. Sibayak is accessible from the Gundaling hill side. Trek from the village called **Semangat Gunung**. From here you can get out via the Medan road and the **Lau Debuk Debuk** hot springs.

Sinabung has a volcanic lake at its base, which unfortunately is suffering a bit from too many tourists. You can also do this trip from the Medan road. At the **Doulu** junction, turn in towards Sibayak. You can walk in to Sibayak from here. There is a waterfall called Sikulkap, with an approximately 31 m drop, located about 12 km out and about 400 m in off the road towards Medan.

For a relaxing place to sit in the midst of towering pine trees, visit the pleasant **Tahura** park on the right, just out past the Mutiara Hotel. This is really just the entrance to the large Tahura reserve, which extends into the base of Sibayak and beyond. Elephant rides and other attractions are to be found there.

The Karo has unique traditional houses, quite different from the other Batak groups. Though there are many scattered all over the area as you can find from the government tourist map, two *kampung* frequently visited for their distinctive architecture are those at **Peceran**, after the Rudang hotel on the way towards Medan and **Lingga** village. Turn at the bus terminal just outside of Berastagi on the way to **Kabanjahe**, and follow the road past the post office and bear to the right. Both of these are easy bicycle trips and hefty day walking trips. Check the tourist map and with your hotel regarding other *kampung* nearby.

Other trips worth making out of Berastagi include visiting the market in Kabanjahe, 12 km out. Further out again, at about 36 km, is the turn off to **Tongging**, a 92 m waterfall at the tip of lake Toba, and **Haranggaol**, the village at the bottom of a magnificent winding road down to the lakeside. There are a few cheap and spartan accommodations there, and several equally spartan restaurants. The area is good for swimming, with expansive sandy beaches. It is much quieter than Prapat.

SHOPPING

In town, if you've visited the tourist office, you're right next to the famous Berastagi fruit market. The *pasar* is famous for all sorts of fruit, boiled and roasted locally grown corn, and the famous *marquisa* or passion fruit. Don't be shocked at the prices, however, as the place is heavily frequented by tourists. Bargain hard. There are a number of souvenir shops along Jl Veteran, mostly just at the head as you enter on the left. **Crispo**, under the same ownership as that in Medan, is well stocked and reasonable. Try

also **Toko Namaken**, across the street, and **Modesty**, further up the road. Karo is famous for its unique *ulos* cloths, and characteristic wooden items used for offerings and ritual practices. There is also a wealth of interesting baskets from the area. You can also find a wider selection of these in the market behind the bus station and the market at Kabanjahe. Visit any of the traditional *kampung* and you will certainly have people offering you all sorts of items, old and new. It is a good idea to visit one of the established shops before you buy.

KARO CULTURE

Like the other Batak groups, the Karo has its own unique culture. Traditional formal dress includes an impressive head-dress for women folded from the bright reddish Karo *ulos*. Karo music is a sort of miniature of the Batak Gondang ensemble, with a tiny double reed oboe-like instrument and a tiny pair of high-pitched barrel drums played with sticks. You will hear this everywhere on cassette tapes and radio, and it is an important formal ensemble for all major Karo rituals. The Karo *kachapi*, a small plucked lute similar to that found in the Toba area, is an important instrument for traditional healing ceremonies and entertainment. Karo ritual dancing is also remarkable for its extremely limited movements, primarily just the hands and slight undulations up and down from the knees, in contrast to the vigorous style of much Toba Batak dance. The Karo dances at all of their important rituals, as do the other Bataks.

Should you happen to be at a ceremony in progress, you may with all due courtesy and respect, observe what is going on from a distance. Some of the most common rituals are secondary burials, where the remains of several generations are exhumed from their graves at an opportune moment and 'reburied' in monuments built for the purpose. At these events, the descendants will literally dance with the bones of their ancestors, with wailing and lamentation which helps to compose the proper atmosphere. Ask at your hotel or the government Tourist Office for scheduled performances like those at Lingga, held three days a week.

Lake Toba

Lake Toba is one of the awesome natural wonders of the world—a crater lake of such size that there is an island in the middle of it nearly the size of Singapore. Driving around the circumference of the lake would require something like 11 hours. Until now there is no definitive data on how deep it actually is, though 450 m is the usual estimate given. At 500 m above sea level, the climate is refreshingly cool at night and tolerably warm during the day.

There are opportunities for boating and swimming, including aquatic mopeds for hire (unfortunately as yet no water skiing) but facilities are developing a bit slowly. It is difficult to understand why there is no sailing club as yet on the lake, apparently in the Dutch period there were lots of sailboats on the waters. Unfortunately the most populous tourist beaches are disturbed by jet planers using outboard engines whose driver/owners seem to find sport in seeing how close they can get to innocent swimmers. Nonetheless, the lake environment is exhilarating. The absence of any highly developed tourist infrastructure may not suit everyone, but the low cost of accommodation and food, and the area's magnificent natural beauty make a stay at Toba an unforgettable experience.

The Toba Batak are a curious mix of rural, tribal personalities intermixed with some frequently disarming cosmopolitanism. It is not unusual on Samosir for example to find people who outwardly appear to be completely "local" in experience and worldview speaking fluent German or English, due to contacts with missionaries or even study abroad. The Toba Batak are well known for their forthright openness of expression, and don't be surprised if you are asked questions which might seem impertinent, albeit a bit rude, especially coming from strangers. Don't be surprised either at the volume level of normal conversation. This is permanently at full blast and apparently not related to any particular change in mood. A normal conversation differs from an argument in content and not necessarily in tone.

GETTING THERE AND AWAY

Toba is accessible from the south via Padang, from Medan, or via Berastagi. The road from Berastagi is scenic and much improved over the last few years, though there are the inevitable potholed sections. From Medan, the trip takes about 3 hours plus,without stops.

By Taxi. A taxi from a major hotel will cost about $20 per person. Taxis arranged directly by phone (see *Medan Practicalities*), such as Indah Taxi, or Cantik Taxi, cost about $6 per person. You may want to consider buying two seats to get you there a bit more comfortably, especially if you're carrying a lot of gear.

By Bus. Buses run from Medan for the hearty and budget-conscious, fare $1 to $1.50. Be sure to try and get an express bus from one of the terminals to avoid doubling your travel time, try Jl Sisingamangaraja near the Sisingamangaraja monument. It is also possible to get to **Prapat** via **Berastagi**. You will pass through Kabanjahe, then along a road which borders the lake part of the way to **Siantar**, and then to Prapat.

You might want to break your trip at the **Simarjarunjung** restaurant, atop a magnificent view of the lake about mid-way between Berastagi and Siantar. Part of the Siantar Hotel group, there are no overnight facilities there, but the view is one of the most spectacular of all and it's a perfect spot for lunch. Another route from or via Berastagi can bring you on to Samosir from the western bridge via **Sidikalang**, although this route is strictly for the adventurous since road conditions may to be precarious.

Prapat

Telephone code is 0625.

There is no real need for any sort of transport around Prapat itself, since everything is within walking distance. There is very little reason to spend much time here except for eating and souvenir shopping. Most vestiges of traditional culture are best tracked down on Samosir, including the most impressive examples of Toba Batak architecture.

The best Chinese food in Prapat, also good value, is **Asia** restaurant, located just beyond the entrance to Prapat proper on the left side of the road on the road continuing out of Prapat. **Prapat Hotel** has a fine old dining room facing the lake. Other more modest restaurants include **Singgalang**, **Hong Kong** and **Bali**. For souvenirs, there are a collection of stalls on the corner of the road leading down to **Tiga Ras**, the local market and boat slip. Bargain hard. The selection can be better on Samosir or Medan.

ACCOMMODATIONS

In both Prapat and on Samosir, hotel rates in all classes are cheap to intermediate compared to Medan or Siantar, although Prapat is slightly the more expensive of the two. Be sure to book ahead if you are looking to stay in any of the better places on the island. At certain times of year, around big national holidays, the hotels can be overrun with domestic visitors from Medan, and Toba is becoming more popular with vacationers from Malaysia and Singapore. All good establishments on Tuk Tuk have phones, and booking offices in Medan as well, which will save you relatively expensive long distance calls if you book from Medan. Be sure to inquire as to whether a pick-up service is offered in Prapat.

Moderate and Luxury

Hotel **Patra Jasa** ☎ 41796 (in Medan ☎ 323-535), $50 economy, $285 for superior and $280 for a presidential suite. Owned by Pertamina, the national oil company, it's located out on a peninsula about 3 km before you enter Prapat proper. It commands a magnificent view of the lake, has a spring-fed and briskly icy swimming pool and lovely grounds. Be sure to ask for a room up in the main building. As you enter Prapat proper, you'll find Hotel **Siantar Prapat**, one of the first on the way in before the turn into the beachside road. Along the beach, try Hotel **Prapat** ☎ 41048, $38 standard, $44 deluxe, $50 for a suite. It's one of the beautiful old hotels in the area. Next to it is Hotel **Tara Bunga Sibigo** ☎ 41089/41700, $21 to $25, with rooms right down near the water. Up the road on the end of the same peninsula with Hotel Prapat is **Danau Toba Cottages**, ☎ 44172, $22, on the hill facing the lake, part of the Hotel Danau Toba International Group. A similar brand new hotel on the next peninsula up, just past the *pasar* at Tiga Raja and visible from the ferry slip, is **Niagara** Hotel ☎ 521128 in Medan, $55 standard, $65 deluxe. Niagara is set back from the lake and a bit removed from the bustle of Prapat, but has superior facilities. A good choice if you only intend to look at the lake from a distance, but require amenities at your accommodation.

Samosir

Telephone code is 0645.
The near-island in the center of lake Toba is the most popular spot with tourists. Accommodation of all classes and restaurants abound. **Tomok** and **Tuk Tuk** are the favorite areas.

GETTING THERE AND AWAY

By Boat. Flat bottomed boats ply back and forth for about 35 cents per person. Be sure to spec-

ify your destination as either **Tomok** or **Tuk Tuk**; being two separate villages on the island. If you have already made bookings at any of the larger hotels on Samosir, many of them have their own boats so keep your eye out for them. If you have come by **car** or **motorcycle**, you can take your vehicle across at the ferry slip up past Tiga Ras.

After coming in to Prapat, continue along the one-way road through the market, and up the hill. The turn-off to the ferry slip is 100 m up to the left. The ferry runs every three hours back and forth, and costs about $6 for a full car, and $1 with motorcycle.

By speedboat. You can hire speedboats at widely negotiable but expensive rates, usually a minimum of $10 per boat with perhaps a maximum of four passengers. When you consider transport, keep in mind that the micro-climates on a large body of water like Toba can be extreme, with large waves and strong winds coming up during rainstorms. The large boats with their flat bottoms are prone to roll, though apparently rarely capsize. If it is raining heavily, take your time and have a look around Prapat until it passes. The particular conditions around the lake make most storms short-lived.

GETTING AROUND

As yet there is not much public transport, with only occasional **buses** which go around the island. Land transport in large vehicles can often be disrupted due to bridges being out, though recently there have been many improvements

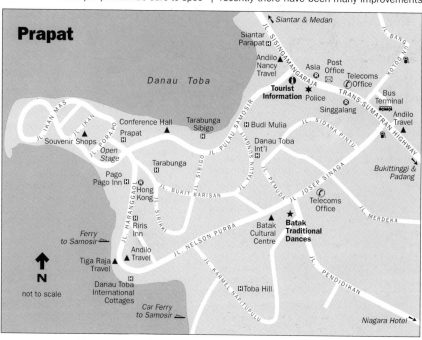

in roads around the main tourist areas at Tomok and Tuk Tuk. You can always pick up **boats** which ply around the coast almost incessantly, (though be aware that nearly everything stops at nightfall) and this is by far the easiest and most pleasant way to get around. Stand on any dock or projection out into the lake and something will come along. Be sure to designate you destination and settle the fare to avoid nasty surprises.

If you bring a **car** over, be sure to fill up at the gas station in Prapat just up beyond the Asia Restaurant as there are no gas stations on the island itself. You can rent **motorcycles** for anywhere from $7.50 to $15 per day, and these can be great fun for getting up into the higher ground or off the main roads. The better hotels can provide vehicles, mostly expensive **minibuses**, but certainly convenient for groups. You will find that if you pay good attention to the maps, most of the areas you probably want to visit around Tuk Tuk are easily walkable.

MONEY

It is best to make any conversions before you get to Prapat since rates are extremely poor anywhere in Prapat or on Samosir. Check the banks recommended in *Medan Practicalities*.

TOURIST INFORMATION

There are several agencies in Prapat proper advertising tourist information. In fact you really don't need much. Try to acquire the government tourist brochure and map in Medan on Jl Yani. Hotels will provide you with all the information about transport and services that you need.

ACCOMMODATIONS

Budget

There are a large number of *losmen* type accommodations on Tuk Tuk, mostly in traditional Toba houses on pilings. **Bagus Bay**, one of the first as you come around the narrow neck of the Tuk Tuk peninsula, is pleasant and ultra reasonable. Dorm accommodations are $1.50 per person. Ten other rooms at the time of writing cost around $5 per room, with the possibility of three in a room with an extra bed. All other budget accommodations can be measured against this one for standards and atmosphere, as well as for facilities such as a good restaurant and bookshop. Try **Abadi** or one of the many others located at various points along the peninsula, and around the turn over on the mainland. All are located on the Tuk Tuk peninsula within easy walking distance of each other. All are more or less similar, with rooms in Batak-styled cottages, few of them actually old buildings, many

facing directly on the beach. Take your time and walk along the peninsula to ask around. The accommodation is generally down by the lake side, and above, at road level, there'll be a small cafe serving cheap local and Western dishes.Tuk Tuk offers so much choice, it's a great place for anyone on a budget.

Moderate and Luxury

The **Tuk Tuk Toledo Inn** ☎ 41181 (☎ 513561 in Medan) is one of the oldest hotels on the island. It has one of the best swimming beaches, and a large, pleasant restaurant. Frequented by large groups coming in from abroad, it is wise to book ahead of time, rates from $32. Hotel **Silintong** ☎ 41345, (☎ 321304 in Medan), $30 to $35, is smaller but in the same class as Toledo. Its restaurant is small but good, and the rock jetties out in the lake in front of the hotel are interesting. A grove of tall pines offers pleasant shade and a restful place to sit and relax down at the lakeside. The Hotel **Toba Beach** ☎ 41275, is located down from Tomok in Parambatan, turn left out of the boat slips in Tomok as opposed to right for Tuk Tuk. Standing more or less by itself about 2 km down the road, the lakeside restaurant is one of the most pleasant spots on the island. Room rates from $30 to $35, economy $10 to $25. **Tuk Tuk Carolina** ☎ (0625) 41520, fax 41521, is indisputably still everyone's favorite on Tuk Tuk, although it's become more expensive over the years. With several types of rooms available, ranging from $17 to $25, including a number of Toba Batak traditional houses, you can't beat the facilities. Several rooms have hot water. The restaurant is certainly among the best on the island, with an open-air pavilion in the style of a Javanese *pendopo* overlooking dazzling views. Top it off with the most pleasant and attentive service anywhere. Remember to book.

FOOD

All the larger hotels have restaurants. **Carolina** perhaps rates among the best for both food, price and location, but try any of the larger hotels for a similar though more varied and costlier cuisine. There is no place which is expensive. Try any one of the numerous restaurants along the road in Tuk Tuk. Generally speaking, food served is mostly **Chinese** style, with some **Malay**-type curries and basic **European/Dutch** styled cuisines. **Toba Batak** food itself is hardly distinguished, but there is a kind of **Ikan Mas**, a large golden carp which is frequently cooked in specific spices. The most distinctive Batak food is **Saksan**, roast pig served with a spicy sauce heavy with ginger which includes the blood of the animal and goes very well with the vigorous mountain air and Batak people. Order in advance at the hotel for this dish.

PLACES TO VISIT

At **Tomok**, directly in front of the main boat slips and about 100 m up from the ferry slip, there is a long road heading towards the center of the island lined with souvenir shops, Tomok's answer to Kuta Beach. Take your time and bargain. As you walk up the road, on the right side is a small enclave of traditional houses, still inhabited, which will give you an insight into the typical *Batak Huta* or nuclear village. You can also have a look at one of the important cultural sites on the islands, the 300-year-old graves of King Sidabutar and his descendants, with famous boat shaped *sarcophagi*.

Ambarita has an archaeologically important meeting place for a king of the *Siallagan marga*, which supposedly served as a kind of hall of justice and, in an adjacent clearing, a place of execution for those condemned. It has some impressive large stone chairs. There are a number of good examples of traditional houses, a few souvenir shops, and a pathway leading up the mountain, good for hiking. **Simanindo**, up at the tip of the island, is the site of some of the best traditional Toba Batak houses, particularly that of King Sidauruk. There is a small museum. In the grounds, and people magically appear at any time of day to present the intriguing *Sigalegale* puppet dance and a staged example of *Tor Tor*, the ritual communal dancing done at all important *pesta* or events.

Tao Island is just off Simanindo, and has a hotel, a small museum and a pleasant setting. **Pulau Tao Cottages** offers about 20 rooms. Booking can be done through PO Box 4, Pematang Siantar. Or you can take a chance and head there by boat from Prapat, or pick up a boat just five minutes away in **Simanindo**. The small boat-building industry on the waterfront in Simanindo is worth seeing. **Pangururan** is a village just to the south of bridge connecting Samosir over to the mainland on the **Dairi** side, and has some hot springs and simple *losmen*. Samosir also has the unique distinction of having a lake up in the mountains, thus a lake within a lake. You can drive up by car, by motorcycle or take a hefty all-day hike up from Tomok. It's about 14 km on a poor road with dazzling scenery, up to **Pasanggrahan** where there is accommodation available. The road continues about 22 km over the top through **Ranggumi** village and down to Pangururan. Another route from Pasanggrahan will bring you to a forest house, from where there's a short cut down to Ambarita.

TREKKING ON SAMOSIR

The most popular trek is the one across the island between **Ambarita** or **Tomok** in the east and **Pangururan** in the west. The climb is easier starting from the west, and the wonderful scenery is in front of you, not behind. The trek and the journey from Tuk Tuk can be done in a day (8 to 9 hours), but there is accommodation in Pangururan and it's better to stop over there and start fresh in the morning rather than traveling round from Tomok and setting off directly. It's also possible to stay at **Ronggurnihuta** village, 16 km along the trail. The descent to Ambarita is steeper than the easier trail down to Tomok. Other tracks branch out from Ronggurnihuta and Tomok for the adventurous, ask the locals in Tomok for details.

CULTURAL PERFORMANCES

Samosir and Toba are the centers of the Toba Batak culture, one of the five great Batak tribes in North Sumatra. Unfortunately most of the music and culture of these peoples tends to appear only in the context of important life rituals, not as performance events for audiences to attend. If you are lucky you may just happen upon a ritual celebration or *pesta* almost anywhere on the island. If you wish to watch, you will certainly be welcome as long as you observe all due propriety in dress and manners.

Two kinds of music ensembles, the **gondang sabangunan**, with a unique combination of five tuned drums and a large double-reed instrument played with circular, continuous breathing. These are used in large outdoor rituals, and the dynamic, rhythmic energy is breathtaking. Participate in dancing only if you are invited to do so, since the **Tor Tor** or ritual dancing is not a social activity but a kind of choreographed enactment of the various relationships between various groups present at the event.

The chamber version of this ensemble, **gondang hasapi**, is played with a wider array of smaller, less penetrating instruments, and may be used indoors or in less formal situations. You will find the plucked stringed instrument *Hasapi* as a nice souvenir in many shops around the island as well. The chief informal music is a repertory of songs in Batak language sung with tremendous gusto and usually self accompanied with guitars. **Lagu Batak**, as they are called, are akin with Spanish *flamenco* and Portuguese *fado* traditions, from which they have developed a lively emotional appeal. Groups can be found in all the major hotels, either at regular scheduled appearances, or on request. You'll also certainly encounter spontaneous music-making on the streets at night.

The Toba Batak are intensely Christian following the work of German Lutheran missionaries in the latter half of the 19th century, and the countryside is dotted with churches. The musical side of Lutheranism found exceptional resonance with the singing Batak, and often over half a congregation will be singing old Lutheran hymns with Batak words in impressive improvised four part harmony. Some of the melodies still sung here have disappeared elsewhere. Each church may have as many as 10 choirs, from children to elderly, which will periodically stand up from their pews and belt away. You can feel free to enter any church on Sunday morning, well attired, please. A great way to experience local life and culture.

Nias Island

Telephone code is 0639.
The island of Nias, off the west coast of Sumatra, is 130 km long and 45 km wide. It is famous for its wood and stone sculptures, stone jumping, traditional village architecture, war dances and beautiful surf beaches. The people of Nias are mainly rice growers and fishermen. Vestiges of the old culture still survive in the war dances and in the sport of stone jumping—the jumper leaps from a small stone about 500 m high and launches himself feet first into the air over a stone column, measuring 2 meters high and half a meter broad.

GETTING THERE AND AWAY

By air. Daily morning flights from Medan to Nias are available on SMAC airlines. The fare is $55 one way and you travel in either a 10 or a 20-seater aircraft. The plane lands on Nias, 22 km from the capital town of **Gunung Sitoli**. Here you are met by the SMAC agent and transported to Gunung Sitoli in a 4-wheel drive, fare $1.50. He'll offer tours of the island and recommend accommodation if you're interested.
By Sea. A ferry service is available from **Sibolga** on the west coast of North Sumatra, to Gunung Sitoli every two days. The *Idapola I* is a car ferry with VIP cabins priced at $11 first class, $7 standard and $4 economy. The trip takes seven hours, compared with the older daily boats which take anything from 10 to 24 hours.

Gunung Sitoli

Located 22 km from the airport, this town is the capital of Nias and is located in the north of the island. There is plenty to see and a number of willing guides, though tourism is still relatively new in this area. *Becaks* are the main form of public transport in the town and rates are very reasonable—Rp 200 is the average price. **Motorbikes** can be hired for longer trips to surrounding villages and beaches. Bargain hard for a good price in advance, the average is about $7 to $10 per day.

ACCOMMODATIONS

Budget and Moderate

Gomo Hotel, located in the center of town, offers standard rooms with fan or AC for $10–$12. The rooms have individual bathrooms with western-style toilets. The **Hawaii** Hotel, also in the center of town, offers rooms with fans or AC, and individual local-style toilets for $12. Excellent service. **Miga Beach** Hotel ☎ 21460, fax 21188. A convenient place to stay for those going to the surf beaches at **Lagundi** by bus, or returning from there. SMAC has an office here and offers free transport to airport. Rooms with fan for $7. **Wisma Solika** is a tourist hotel on the road from the airport. Pleasant and quiet. Standard rooms from $10–$12.

GETTING AROUND

Buses travel daily from Gunung Sitoli to Teluk Dalam. They are small and crowded, so get a seat in the middle two rows for the most comfortable ride. The fare is $3 for a six-hour trip. They leave at 7.30 am so those coming from Medan by plane will need to stay the night in Gunung Sitoli. The scenic road, although bumpy, has improved greatly and bridges are now safe. You can also charter **4-wheel-drive** vehicles (hardtops) from the SMAC office in Gunung Sitoli. A one-way trip from Gunung Sitoli to Teluk Dalam or the other southern beaches will cost

Nias Island

$50–$75. Much more comfortable than the bus! **Minibuses** can also be chartered, as can **motorbikes** with or without drivers. The cautious should be warned that no crash helmets are worn here. However, the driving is usually slow and careful. Negotiate the price for a day charter before you start out.

Teluk Dalam

This is a small bay where passengers from Padang and northern Nias arrive by barge. Accommodation is limited to a *losmen* or a few rooms above a Chinese store. However this store-cum-hotel and restaurant is fairly pleasant, with Chinese and Indonesian meals available.

Bawomataluo

Located about 15 km from Teluk Dalam is the ancient village of Bawomataluo. There are fantastic stone carvings here, some weighing up to 18,300 kg. It is situated at the top of a hill and is reached by a stone stairway. The palace of the tribal chief is impressive, and so is the cultural program presented on Saturdays. This includes stone jumping and war dances. There's a German Mission Hospital here.

Lagundi

Located 12 km from Teluk Dalam, this small village has a good surfing beach and coral lagoon. There are many 50 cents *losmen* along the beach. Most serve good food geared to western tastes. Seafood is plentiful and inexpensive. The **Fanayama** Motel is the only 'hotel' at Lagundi. Facilities are basic, but all rooms are fully mosquito-screened and have private western-style bathrooms. Located close to the beach are the $5-a-night **Harus Damai** cottages.

Sorake Beach

Located about 15 km from Teluk Dalam, this small village has great surfing beaches. There are many basic *losmen*, and the new **Sorake Beach Hotel**, a 3-star hotel with cottage-style rooms from $54. ☎ 0630 21195.

Sibolga

Telephone code is 0631.
Sibolga is a port town on the west coast of North Sumatra. Boats for Nias Island leave from here. It is 88 km northwest of **Padang Sidempuan**, 378 km north of **Bukittinggi**, 174 km southwest of **Prapat** and 73 km south of **Tarutung**. The last 60 km of the road from the north boasts 12,000 bends, through uninhabited infertile hills. Before reaching the town, stop at the national monument and hotel, which offers a spectacular view of Sibolga and the bay. It is not clearly signposted, but is located on the left, at the top of the escarpment, before the coastal descent.

ACCOMMODATIONS

Indah Sari on Jl Jend A Yani 27–29 is clean and serviceable, with reasonable private bathrooms and air-conditioning. **Mutiara Sari** on the same street, opposite Indah Sari Hotel, is also cheap, clean and basic. **Nauli** Hotel on Jl Sutomo 17 ☎ 22326 offers clean, private bathrooms and AC. Also an adequate but unexciting restaurant.

FOOD

There are many seafood stalls along Jl S Parman. Very cheap and good, clean, tasty food. The stalls open from 5 pm until midnight. A few of the better local restaurants are **Bahagia** Restaurant on Jl Imam Bonjol, **Jumbo** on Jl S Parman, and **Teluk Indah** on Jl Jend A Yani.

SIGHTSEEING

Not many people choose to stay in this area, using it mostly as a departure point for Nias. However there are a few interesting sights around, particularly good beaches and pretty islands with seas teeming with marine life, if you'd like to explore further. Most sights can be visited in a day, but simple accommodation can be found in most towns.

Barus is the oldest of Sumatra's West Coast entry port towns, 65 km from Sibolga. Many old graves and relics can be found here. The white sand beaches are ideal for swimming and sunbathing, and the big waves of the Indian Ocean allow for surfing as well. **Boran Dolak**, situated 9 km from Sibolga at 850 m above sea level in the sub-district of Sibolga, overlooks the Tapianauli Bay and offers a beautiful view of the sea. **Pantai Pandan** is a white sandy beach 11 km south of Sibolga on the road to **Padang Sidempuan**. It has shady coconut groves, souvenir shops and restaurants specializing in freshly barbecued seafood—well worth trying. Boats can be hired to visit offshore islands. **Pantai Kalangan** is another white sand beach, slightly further south at 20 km from Sibolga. There are a number of souvenir shops, restaurants and *losmen* here. To reach **Pulau Poncan**, boats can be hired from the seaport at Jl Ade Irma Suryani. It takes 20 minutes to reach this island, which has a beautiful white sand beach. **Pulau Musala** is a sub-district of Sibolga, lying in the Indian Ocean. The trip there takes one hour from Sibolga by boat. Marine life abounds. There are waterfalls, white beaches and good hunting areas.
— *Edward Van Ness*

3 Aceh PRACTICALITIES

INCLUDES WEH ISLAND AND GAYO HIGHLANDS

Aceh's reputation as Indonesia's most Islamic stronghold has not deterred tourists and travelers from making their way to this fascinating province. The magnificent virgin jungles of the Bukit Lawang National Park and the wilderness of the Alas River have become increasingly accessible, while the wild and rugged west coast has recently opened up with newly surfaced roads and strong Australian bridges replacing the rickety tree trunks that once served as main roads. *See pages 125–137.*

Banda Aceh

Telephone code is 0651.
The 'special region' (*daerah istimewa*) of Aceh enjoys virtual autonomy in matters of religion, *adat* law and education. But there is no need for apprehension—visitors who dress conservatively (no short shorts or sleeveless tee-shirts) and treat the locals with respect will find the Acehnese to be friendly and polite.

GETTING THERE AND AWAY

By air. Garuda flies daily to and from Jakarta to Banda Aceh via Medan, with four extra weekly flights. From Medan there are two flights to Banda Aceh daily. **Merpati** Airlines and **SMAC** fly to secondary destinations within the province. From Jakarta, the fare is $185; from Medan $54. The taxi ride from the airport to town costs around $7.50, and taxi is the only means of transport in the afternoon. The main Garuda/Merpati office is on Jl T P Polem ☎ 32523.
By bus. Most visitors take a bus from Medan to Banda Aceh. The 600 km journey takes 8–10 hours, and costs $8–$16 depending on the comfort level. Most of the large bus companies in Medan (telephone code 061) are on Jl Gajah Mada, including **Pelangi** on ☎ 326143, **Melati** on ☎ 552546, **ATRA** on ☎ 521216 and **Flamboyan** at Jl Asia ☎ 710998, 514363. Aceh airline offices: **Pelangi** ☎ 32006, **Melati** ☎ 23520, **ATRA** ☎ 23621, 23502 and **Flamboyan** ☎ 22949. To save wear and tear on the nervous system, it is worth paying extra for a non-stopping bus.
By sea. There is a ferry service from Penang in Malaysia to Lhokseumawe in North Aceh.

GETTING AROUND

The center of Banda Aceh is not large, and the city is easily walked around. Otherwise, take a minibus or *bemo* known as *labi labi* costing from 10 cents. Sidecar motorcycles called *becak mesin* cost from 50 cents. Hone your bargaining skills as prices are highly negotiable. Minibuses are crowded but are a cheap way of getting around. Metered **taxis** can be hired from Cempala Company ☎ 22963.

ACCOMMODATIONS

Hotel prices in Aceh have risen enormously. The good old days of cheap accommodations are over and prices are now more in line with other Sumatran cities.

Budget and Moderate

Losmen **Aceh** was once a beautiful colonial house, but is now horribly decrepit, and looks ghost-ridden if not worse. It is located across from the main mosque. Large rooms from $7 ☎ 21354. Losman **Sri Budaya** is another old colonial house divided into clean cupboard size rooms with a very Islamic staff. From $5, Jl Madjid Ibrahim 111/5E ☎ 21751. Wisma **Lampriet** has eight plain rooms. Jl Nyak Arief 125 ☎ 23-995, Prices from $6 fan, A/C $8.50. Losmen **International** on Jl A Yani, is opposite the night market. Small rooms cost around $3, larger rooms with a bathroom around $4–$5 ☎ 21834. Or try the similar Losmen **Pacific** across the road. **Medan** Hotel has 60 rooms, some with AC, bathroom, hot water, fridge, satellite TV, hotel coffee shop. Prices from $8–$25. On Jl A Yani. On the same street, **Prapat** Hotel has 48 rooms. It's newly renovated and Chinese-run, is clean and offers friendly, no-frills service. Restaurants are located nearby and drinks are available from the hotel ☎ 22159. From $9 for fan and bathroom, $13 AC and TV.

Luxury

Many of the luxury hotels will agree to a discount of up to 20 or 30 percent if you inquire at the

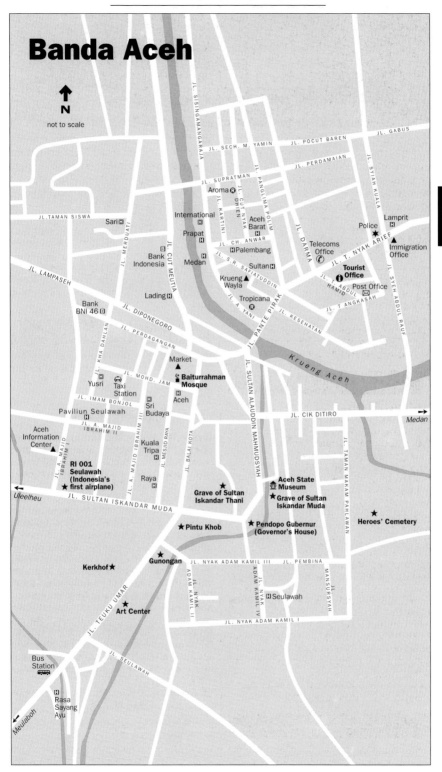

Banda Aceh

N
not to scale

JL. SISINGAMANGARAJA
JL. SECH. M. YAMIN
JL. POCUT BAREN
JL. GABUS
JL. PERDAMAIAN
JL. SYIAH KUALA
JL. SUPRATMAN

Aroma Ⓡ
JL. KARTINI
JL. CUT NYAK DHIEN
JL. PANGLIMA POLIM

International Ⓗ
Aceh Barat Ⓗ
Lamprit Ⓗ
Police ★

JL. TAMAN SISWA
Sari Ⓗ
Prapat Ⓗ
JL. CH. ANWAR
Palembang Ⓗ
JL. DARMA
Telecoms Office
JL. T. NYAK ARIEF
Immigration Office

JL. MERDUATI
Bank Indonesia
Medan Ⓗ
Sultan Ⓗ
JL. S.R. SAFIATUDDIN
Tourist Office ⓘ
JL. T. HAMID ABDUL
Post Office ✉

JL. LAMPASEH
JL. CUT MEUTIA
Lading Ⓗ
Krueng Wayla ▲
Tropicana Ⓡ
JL. KESEHATAN
JL. T ANGKASAH
JL. SYEH ABDUL RAUF

Bank BNI 46 🏦
JL. DIPONEGORO
JL. A. YANI
JL. PANTE PIRAK

JL. PERDAGANGAN
JL. KHA DAHLAN

Market ▲
Krueng Aceh

JL. MOHD. JAM
Ⓢ Baiturrahman Mosque
JL. SULTAN ALAUDDIN MAHMUDSYAH

Yusri Ⓗ
Taxi Station 🚕
Sri Budaya Ⓗ
Aceh Ⓗ
JL. CIK DITIRO
Medan →

JL. IMAM BONJOL
Paviliun Seulawah Ⓗ
JL. A. MAJID IBRAHIM II
JL. A. MAJID IBRAHIM III
JL. MESJID RAYA
JL. BALAI KOTA
JL. TAMAN MAKAM PAHLAWAN

Aceh Information Center ▲
JL. A. MAJID IBRAHIM I
Kuala Tripa Ⓗ

RI 001 Seulawah (Indonesia's ★ first airplane)
Raya Ⓗ

← Uleelheu
JL. SULTAN ISKANDAR MUDA
★ Grave of Sultan Iskandar Thani
Aceh State 🏛 Museum
★ Grave of Sultan Iskandar Muda
★ Heroes' Cemetery

★ Pintu Khob
★ Pendopo Gubernur (Governor's House)

★ Gunongan
JL. NYAK ADAM KAMIL III
JL. PEMBINA
JL. MANSURSYAH

Kerkhof ★
JL. TEUKU UMAR
JL. NYAK ADAM KAMIL II
JL. NYAK ADAM KAMIL IV
JL. NYAK ADAM KAMIL I
Ⓗ Seulawah

Art Center

Bus Station 🚌
JL. SEULAWAH

Ⓗ Rasa Sayang Ayu

← Meulaboh

Aceh 3

front desk. It's always worth a try. **Kuala Tripa** (40 rooms) Jl Mesjid Raya. The best in town with a Chinese and European restaurant and floating expat population. The only bar and disco in town, *and* a swimming pool. Located in a quiet street with a garden food center opposite. It is close to the main mosque and a good kilometer from the central shopping area ☎ 21455, 21879, 33337. Prices from $65–$200. **Sultan** Hotel on Jl Panglima Polim is well run and reasonably comfortable. It is the most popular hotel in town with tour groups and individual visitors. The restaurant serves a variety of Chinese, European, Japanese and Indonesian dishes ☎ 22469, 22479, 31443, 32753, fax 31770. Prices from $35 to $150. **Pavilion Seulawah** is on Jl Mesjid Ibrahim 11/3, Banda Aceh. It's a small and well-run place in an old Dutch complex. Prices from $30–$90. Hotel **Cakradonya** on Jl Khairil Anwar 10–12 ☎ 23735, 23879 offers 68 rooms. A small, basic hotel with friendly staff. Rooms cost from $10–$40. Hotel **Rasa Sayang Ayu** is on Jl Teuku Umar 439. Near the bus station, it offers AC rooms from $16 to $30 ☎ 21379, 21983.

FOOD

Banda Aceh may have once been a great empire of warriors, but it seems they never learned to cook. Typical Acehnese food is spicy, cooked with chilies and reminiscent of a lesser form of Padang cooking. For the best in town, head 17 km east to **Rumah Makan Ujong Batee** at Jl Krueng Raya. It's a Chinese-run seafood restaurant with Acehnese food served Padang style on the table. A feast for four with cold beer will cost $20 to $50. In town, the night market on Jl A Yani serves typical Indonesian dishes like *nasi goreng, fried noodles, gado gado and sate* for $1–$2. Several moderately priced Padang style restaurants can also be found along Jl A Yani. For Chinese and Western style food, try the **Aroma** on Jl Cut Nyak Dhien. For Acehnese food, try the **Aceh Specific** on Jl T Cut Ali.

SERVICES

The **Tourist Information Office** (Dinas Pariwisata office) is at Jl Tgk Chik Kuta Karang No 5. It has a good range of brochures and tries hard to give information and assistance ☎ 23692.

For **tours and travel**, the most established travel company is **Krueng Wayla** on Jl Sri Ratu Safiatuddin 26 ☎ 22066, 22150. It offers a variety of tours, and can organize a stay at Dieter's Tree House hideaway (see *The West Coast*).

SHOPPING

There is not a lot of Acehnese antique silver jewelry left to buy, but you could try Jl Perdagangan

115 near the mosque. Also try **Toko Daud** on the same street ☎ 22794. They have a selection of traditional Acehnese swords and weapons. Other shops in the street make gold jewelry and can copy or design items. Around the market are shops selling fruits, food and fabrics. A shop in the back of the Losmen **Aceh** sells modern stitched Aceh handicrafts.

GETTING AROUND ACEH

Probably the best way to see Aceh and traverse the area is to head north by the road through Gunung Leuser National Park to Banda Aceh, then return to Medan via the west coast. Others have ventured north as far as **Ketembe** (to stay in the jungle), then returned by rafting or road to **Kutacane**, then headed west to **Tapaktuan** and north to Banda Aceh.

Weh Island

At the very north of Sumatra lies the island of Weh, better known by the name of its main town, **Sabang**. The idyllic island has begun to attract a steady trickle of visitors who have learned by word of mouth of the available pleasures. Most travelers head straight to the lovely beach at Iboih, opposite the **Pulau Rubioh** marine reserve. People stay for days or weeks at a time.

Most of the attractions are concentrated around the north of the island at the **Iboih Beach** area. Several small holiday resorts have opened up on the hilly slopes above the beach where A-frame cottages cost around $1 per night. The set evening meals of fish, vegetables and rice cost another dollar while other traveler-type favorite dishes are available throughout the day. Try **Patimah's** in Iboih village for a good deal.

The bordering 1,300 ha **Iboih Nature Reserve** (where few people bother to go) is a refuge for wild pigs, monkeys, Nicobar pigeons and flying foxes, with a dirt road which ends abruptly in a cliff overlooking the Indian Ocean. Although the reserve's land stocks are diminishing slightly with the advent of more tourist accommodation, it is still worth a visit.

GETTING THERE AND AWAY

A daily 3 pm ferry leaves from the port of **Krueng Raya**, about 35 km from Banda Aceh, leaving the island for the return trip at 9 am. The amazingly cramped minibus ride (33 people, counting the driver, on our trip) takes about an hour and costs $1. Minibuses leave the market until around 1 pm. The pleasant ferry trip takes 2.5 hours. On the return journey in the calm, still morning, a school of dolphins followed the boat for around 20 minutes, delighting the passengers with their cheeky antics. Economy fare is around $2.50, although the much less crowded first class, around $3.50, is better value. The ferry docks at **Balohan**, about 12 km south of Sabang from where there is plenty of transport into town.

ACCOMMODATIONS

Budget and Moderate

There are three places to stay in Sabang town. The central **Pulau Jaya** on Jl Teuku Umar has 47 rooms, prices from $8–$20 ☎ 21344. Most popular with travelers is the **Losman Irma**, which has 15 clean rooms with outside bathrooms. It's on Jl Seulawah 1 ☎ 21235. Prices from $2–$3. Popular with Dutch tourists is the 30-room **Holiday** Hotel, clean and Chinese-run in Jl Perdagangan Belakang 1 ☎ 21131. The other cheap hotels which once inhabited the area are no longer operating.

FOOD

There is a limited selection of Chinese and Acehnese eateries. Travelers tend to congregate at friendly **Yulie's** Coffeeshop beneath the Wisma Irma, where local English speaking "guides" wait for each new batch of visitors. These places serve the ubiquitous fried rice and noodles, plus some local dishes. Without doubt, the best place in town is the **Dynasty** Restaurant. Open each evening, this charming old Dutch house has tables both inside and out and a range of excellent Chinese seafood dishes, cold beer (not always easy to get in Sabang), and well trained, friendly waiters—an oasis of civilization. The setting is far more attractive than other spots in town, yet prices are comparable.

Iboih Beach

The most popular spot on the island, Iboih is the center of a fast growing travelers' center. Several small operators are running chalets and restaurants with basic but palatable food. All chalets are located on a shady hill overlooking the beach and nearby marine reserve of **Rubiah Island**. It is quite easy to swim to the island for snorkeling, but beware of strong currents at tide changes.

Lovely coral gardens close to Rubiah contain giant clams, lionfish, octopus, barracuda, stingrays, reef-fish and a variety of colored corals. Stingray Diving operates a center at Iboih, with all equipment and boat transport to surrounding dive spots. Both snorkeling and diving gear can be hired from the center at fairly reasonable prices.

DIVING AND TOURIST INFORMATION

Source of all tourist and dive information is **Pak Dodent** of the Stingray Dive Center, right next to Losmen Irma in Sabang. He can tell you (in English) about dive sites, what to see and where to go both around Pulau Weh and on the Sumatra mainland. Stingray Dive has two centers, the main one based at Iboih Beach from where excursions can be arranged to nearby dive sites. Reports on dives are mixed as unfortunately, the Sumatrans have discovered the magical properties of dynamite as an effective way to catch large numbers of fish quickly and effortlessly. This "buang boom" fishing has a disastrous effect on the reefs.

However, the coral gardens around Pulau Rubiah in the marine reserve are in good condition, with 30–40 meter walls. The more distant **Pulau Rondo** has walls of around 30 meters with some big fish and sharks. The best months for calm and clear seas are from March to May, while September and October are clear with some rain. Apart from dive excursions, Stingray can also offer day trips (or longer) to Sabang's outlying islands such as **Pulau Breueh**, and longer trips to the **Pulau Bunyak** group and **Pulau Simileau** off Aceh's west coast. Stingray Dive Center: Jl T Umar No 3, P.O. Box 42, Sabang, Aceh, Sumatra ☎ (0652) 21265, fax (0652) 21333. Jakarta line ☎ (021) 5700272.

The West Coast

The road south from Banda Aceh passes through dozens of idyllic rural villages along the rugged west coast. The thatched roofs of traditional houses (*rumah adat*) can be seen along the roadside, half hidden behind verdant gardens of fruit trees and flowers. Close to the capital are several nice beaches, popular on weekends, but there are more beautiful spots further south.

Camp Europa is a private hideaway with houses in the treetops on a secluded beach! Run by German Dieter with his Indonesian wife Nurma, it makes a pleasant escape for a few days or more. Pity about the caged *orang utan* and sun bear in the compound. Prices from $7–$12 per day with mostly European meals and snacks. Dieter organizes trekking excursions into the jungle, snorkeling and river rafting, and there is plenty of wildlife nearby. Camp Europa can be found at Kuala Doe (Lageun), 500 m from the main road, (10 km north of Calang), or book at PT Krueng Wayla Tours, Jl Sri Ratu Safiatuddin ☎ 22066, fax 32139.

Meulaboh

Just 250 km south of Aceh, along a good, panoramic road, Meulaboh is a town with little to recommend it except for being the departure point for boats to Simeulue Island. Around 16 km to the north at **Lhok Bubon** is a growing surfers' mecca. Try the Losmen **Mustika** at Jl Nasional for $3. Hotel **Melagau** on Jl Iskander Muda, close to the bus station, has rooms with AC and TV from $10–$120.

Tapaktuan

One of the most beautiful little harbor towns on Aceh's west coast, Tapaktuan is fast becoming a popular stopover. Surrounded by jungle-covered mountains, and with magnificent panoramas, the town is centered on a natural harbor filled with many colored fishing boats.

Two km to the north of the town is a superb long white sandy beach complete with coconut palms. About 5 km to the south is the beautiful Seven Steps Waterfall—a popular local attraction. Accommodation is of the simple hotel/*losmen* type, but facilities are adequate. Try the **Panorama Standard** Hotel with rooms from $5–$10, some rooms have AC and satellite TV. **Jambu** Losmen, Losmen **Bukit Barisan** on Jl Merdeka (near the harbor) or the **Putra Bongsu** on Jl Adam Kamil all cost around $5 per night. There are restaurants close to the harbor.

Tapaktuan to Sidikalang

This route (and routes on to **Berastagi** or **Medan**) follow a good road. It takes around five hours by minibus, fare $4, or $2 by regular bus.

Takengon

The road south from **Takengon** passes through the massive Gunung Leuser National Park, through vast tracts of primary jungle. The road passes from **Bireuen** to **Takengon** before heading south-east through the middle of the rugged island. Buses leave early morning and evening from Banda Aceh for the approximately 8-hour journey to Takengon, which costs $4. If there is no direct bus, get down at Bireuen on the main highway and take a local bus for around $1.50, the trip takes three hours.

Around Takengon

Several *losmen* around Takengon are available for $3 per night, although the **Renggali** Hotel (28 rooms) overlooking the lake has rooms for $15–$30, and boasts the facilities of a star-rated hotel. It offers tennis, fishing, water-skiing and power boats, and credit cards are accepted. Book locally by calling ☎ (0643) 21144, 21630, 213-52 or through the Griyawisata Group in Jakarta ☎ (021) 7397417. Other new hotels are being developed in the area.

Boats are available for hire on **Lake Tawar** and a two-day hike around the lake is possible. Other trips include forays to the hot springs (20 km), **Loyang Koro Cave** (6 km) and **Mengaya Waterfall** (20 km). From Takengon the bus to **Lumut** takes around 4 hours and costs $2, to **Blangkejeren**, $6 and 6 hours although the 30km stretch between **Ise Ise** and **Godang** is best tackled by jeep. This is virgin jungle and tigers roam about after dark! Basic accommodation is available at most of the settlements along this road.

At **Lumut**, Losmen Toko costs $1.50 per night. It is possible to get a lift south to **Rikit Garb** with local roadworkers. At **Ise-Ise**, the resthouse costs $3 per night. At **Godang**, it's possible to stay with the village chief (*kepala desa*) for around $1.50 per night. From Rikit Garb, the bus to **Blangkejeren** costs $1 (20 km). Tuesday is market day when there is plenty of local transport and the town is busy and bustling. At Blangkejeren try the Losmen **Wahyu** at $3 per night. The bus to **Ketembe** costs around $1, and to **Kutacane**, $1.50.

Gunung Leuser National Park

It's possible to stay in the giant 800,000 ha National Park at the **Ketembe Base Camp**, a perfect base for jungle trekking. Travelers who have stayed here have reported sightings of wild *orang utan* and a good variety of other wildlife including gibbons, *luk luk* (reputedly a kind of flying dog), monitor lizards and hornbills. There are numerous badly-marked trails from the base camp to hot springs and waterfalls, and if you are lucky, to a freshly blooming Rafflesia. All visitors are advised to hire a guide for around $5 per day. They sometimes have basic camping equipment and sleeping bags available.

To enter the National Park, all visitors need a permit, obtainable at the PHPA office in Tanah Merah, 15 minutes by minibus from Kutacane at the *Department Kehutanan* (forest department) Office. Each permit costs 50 cents and you'll need three photocopies of your passport. Stay at the Base Camp, Wisma Ikut or Wisma Wisa Wisata. Losmen Leuser also offers very basic facilities for $1.50 per night. If you are traveling north, ask for a Mr Zalil in Blangkerjeren who can organize jeep transport and guides.

Kutacane

A small town, Kutacane has the main attraction of being close to the National Park. Several basic accommodations include Wisma **Renggali** on Jl Besar for $1 per night, or the more expensive Hotel **Bru Dihe** on Jl Cut Nyak Dien, which has rooms from $6 with fan and AC for $10. W*arungs* and small restaurants near the bus station.

— *Jill Gocher*

The Western Highlands area is one of the most beautiful in Sumatra. With its terraced rice paddies, striking architecture, lakes and volcanoes; its craft villages and the well-maintained culture of its Minangkabau inhabitants, it is rightly one of Sumatra's most developed tourist areas, with well-organized tourist facilities. *See pages 141–173.*

Padang

Telephone code is 0751.
Friendly, attractive and clean, Padang often serves as a base for tourists heading to the Minang Highlands. It's a compact, low-rise city with a pleasant, sea breezy esplanade and good tourist facilities. It's staunchly Islamic so behave politely and dress accordingly.

GETTING THERE AND AWAY

By air. Merpati/Garuda fly daily to and from **Jakarta** ($115), **Batam** ($60), **Medan** ($70) and **Palembang** ($75), and thrice weekly to and from **Singapore** ($110). There are thrice weekly flights to and from **Pekanbaru** ($29). **Sempati** fly to and from Jakarta daily ($115), so do **Mandala** ($100). **Pelangi Air** fly to and from Jakarta ($150), four times a week to and from **Kuala Lumpur** ($107), and on to **Langkawi**, **Ipoh** and **Tioman**. From Pekanbaru, Pelangi fly to and from **Kuala Lumpur** and **Malacca** in Malaysia—$70 and $60 respectively. Offices: Garuda/Merpati is on Jl Sudirman 22 ☎ 23431. Mandala is at Jl Pemuda 29A ☎ 22350. Sempati is at Pangeran's Beach Hotel ☎ 25366.
By sea. Pelni Lines' passenger boat *Lawit* leaves Padang fortnightly on Monday for Jakarta. Pelni is at Jl Tanjung Priok ☎ 33624, fares are $20 economy class (dormitory, below decks but clean), $62 1st class (cabin for two, bath), $48 2nd class (cabin for four, bath).
By bus. Buses to most destinations leave from the terminal on Jl Pemuda. Fares are the same as from Bukittinggi. Buy tickets from the bus station or the **ALS** office opposite.

GETTING AROUND

Although a city, Padang has a small, compact center and it's easy to walk around. **Taxis** are metered and abundant, most journeys in town cost less than $2.50. There are local *bemos* for 10 cents, and pony *bendis* for $1.

ACCOMMODATIONS

Budget

Try the hotels along Jl Pemuda opposite the bus terminal. The **Hang Tuah**, **Tiga Tiga**, **Cendrawasih** and **Aldilla** are all convenient (Jl Pemuda also accommodates many travel agents) and offer rooms from around $5–$20. These are all large hotels with spacious sitting areas, restaurants and endless corridors of rooms and bathrooms. **Machudum's** Hotel on Jl Hiligoo is an old Dutch house, somewhat dilapidated, but with faded charm. Simple rooms from $5.

Moderate and Luxury

Hotel **Putri Bungus** on Jl Permindo is not very pretty, but the rooms are clean and good value at $7 economy (with bath) and $25 deluxe. Chinese, Padang and Western food. The new **Dipo International** on Jl Diponegoro (☎ 34261) is central, near the beach, has a travel agency, restaurant and shop. Sunset views from the top floor—and evening BBQ option. Rooms from $14–$25. **Wisma Mayang Sari** (Jl Jend Sudirman ☎ 22647) has rooms from $14–$30 with a choice of Western breakfasts. Clean, on the airport road. **Femina** Hotel on Jl Bagindo Aziz Chan (☎ 28861) is good value at $8–$27, clean and conveniently located. Hotel **Padang** along the road (☎ 31383) is housed in an old Colonial bungalow with gardens, and has rooms from $17. **Dymens International** at the airport has standard rooms from $24. **Pangeran's Beach** Hotel (☎ 51333) on Jl Ir H Juanda is the top hotel, with a great beachfront location, sea or mountain views, good (Western) food and pool. Rooms from $64 to $375 for a suite. **Pangeran's City** Hotel on Jl Dobi 3–5 (☎ 26233) is close to Chinatown and the city, has rooms from $20–$40, and also a good lively bar. The **Mariani International** Hotel on Jl Bundo Kandung (☎ 34133) has rooms from $16–$30, and luxury suites for $100. There's a bar, restaurant and satellite TV. The **Natour Muara** on Jl Gereja No 34 (☎ 25600) has plain and boxy terraces of rooms for $36,

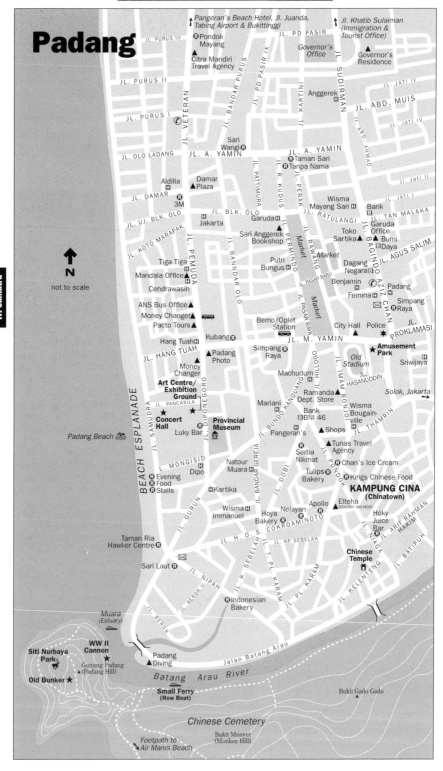

Padang

Pangeran's Beach Hotel, Jl. Juanda,
Tabing Airport & Bukittinggi

Jl. Khatib Sulaiman
(Immigration &
Tourist Office)

JL. PURUS III

JL. PD PASIR

Pondok
Mayang

Citra Mandiri
Travel Agency

Governor's
Office

Governor's
Residence

JL. PURUS II

JL. PD PASIR IX

JL. JATI IV

Anggerek

JL. SUDIRMAN

JL. ABD. MUIS

JL. PURUS I

JL. VETERAN

JL. KARTINI

JL. JATI IV

JL. OLO LADANG

Sari
Wangi

JL. A. YAMIN

JL. A. YAMIN

JL. ABD. AHMAD

JL. Jati IV

Taman Sari
Tanpa Nama

JL. PATTIMURA

JL. R. KUDUS

JL. PERAK

Aldilla

Damar
Plaza

Wisma
Mayang Sari

Bank

JL. JATI I

JL. TAN MALAKA

JL. DAMAR

3M

JL. BLK. OLO

Garuda

JL. RATULANGI

Garuda
Office

JL. UJ. BLK. OLO

Jakarta

Toko
Sartika

Bumi
Daya

JL. KOTO MARAPAK

Sari Anggerek
Bookshop

JL. PERMINDO

JL. BAGINDO AZIZ CHAN

JL. AGUS SALIM

Putri
Bungus

Dagang
Negara

Tiga Tiga

JL. PEMUDA

JL. BANDAR OLO

Market

Padang
Simpang
Raya

Mandala Office

Benjamin
Femina

Cendrawasih

JL. PASAR BARU

ANS Bus Office

Money Changer

Pacto Tours

Bemo/Oplet
Station

Market

City Hall

Police

JL. PROKLAMASI

Hang Tuah

Kubang

JL. PASAR RAYA

JL. M. YAMIN

Amusement
Park

JL. HANG TUAH

Simpang
Raya

Old
Stadium

Sriwijaya

Money
Changer

Padang
Photo

Machudum

JL. HASANUDDIN

Solok, Jakarta

Art Centre/
Exhibition
Ground

JL. PANCASILA

JL. DIPONEGORO

Mariani

JL. BUND KANDUANG

Ramanda
Dept. Store

Bank
BNI 46

JL. IMAM BONJOL

Wisma
Bougain-
ville

JL. THAMRIN

BEACH ESPLANADE

JL. SAMUDRA

Concert
Hall

Luky Bar

Provincial
Museum

Pangeran's

Shops

Padang Beach

L. MONGISID

Dipo

Natour
Muara

Serba
Nikmat

JL. DOBI

Tunas Travel
Agency

Chan's Ice Cream

JL. GURUN

Evening
Food
Stalls

Kartika

Tulips
Bakery

JL. PONDOK

Kings Chinese Food

KAMPUNG CINA
(Chinatown)

JL. BANDAR GEREJA

Wisma
Immanuel

Hoya
Bakery

Nelayan

JL. COKROAMINOTO

Apollo

Elteha
(courier service)

JL. NAGA

Hoky
Juice
Bar

JL. ARIF RAHMAN HAKIM

Taman Ria
Hawker Centre

JL. H.O.S.

JL. KP SEBELAH

Chinese
Temple

JL. BATIPUH

Sari Laut

JL. K. SEBELAH

JL. NIPAH

JL. T. PL. KARAM

JL. PL. KARAM

JL. KELENTENG

Indonesian
Bakery

JL. BEROK II

Muara
(Estuary)

JL. BEROK

Siti Nurbaya
Park

WW II
Cannon

Padang
Diving

Old Bunker

Gunung Padang
(Padang Hill)

Jalan Batang Arau

Batang Arau River

Bukit Gado Gado

Small Ferry
(Row Boat)

Chinese Cemetery

Footpath to
Air Manis Beach

Bukit Monyet
(Monkey Hill)

not to scale

N

4

W. Sumatra

suites for $50. There's a bar and restaurant, and also a travel agency.

FOOD

Naturally, there are plenty of **Padang** restaurants in Padang, home of the spicy, meat, fish and vegetable dishes now popular all over Indonesia. You pay for every dish you eat, and waiters always seem to charge very fairly. The **Simpang Raya** chain of Padang restaurants is a good starting place, there's one branch on Jl Bundo Kandung. **Tanpa Nama** on Jl Rohana Kudus also has tasty Padang food, and **Putri Balqis** on Jl Khatib Sulamain has the spiciest. **Pondok Mayang** on Jl Veteran is a good Javanese restaurant with a lovely garden setting—the roof is natural *atap* and umbrellas provide shade. **Taman Sari** on Jl A Yani is a bit pricier but has a great variety of noodle dishes. **Sari Laut** on Jl Nipah has good seafood. There are lots of Chinese *warungs* around Jl Niaga, and the **Apollo**, a good but expensive Chinese restaurant, is on Jl Hos Cokroaminto. **Kings** on Jl Pondok also serves good Chinese food. There are stalls galore around the **Pasar Raya** market area. There's a big hawker center at **Taman Ria** near the beach, at the beginning of the **Esplanade**, with all local dishes. Along the Esplanade after 4 pm, there are plenty of *warungs* which set up chairs and umbrellas on the seawall, and it's a pleasant place to enjoy the refreshing sea breeze as you try the BBQ prawns. For Western food, the **Pangeran's** Hotels are reputed to be the best—and the priciest. There are several bakeries around town, the best of which is **Hoya** on Jl Hos Cokroaminto. **Tulips** (Jl Pondok) is also good for snacks. The **shopping centers** all have large hawker centers and the supermarkets sell food and snacks, bread and even cheese.

NIGHTLIFE

Luky Bar, near Hotel Muara, is rather a dive but serves drinks and plays music. There aren't many bars as such outside of the hotels as Padang is strictly Muslim. However, there is one new nightspot called **HCC** with occasional bands, on Jl Khatib Sulaiman. There's a juice and cake bar called **Hoky** on Jl Niaga, and **cinemas** showing Hong Kong, Indonesia and US movies.

ARTS

The **Museum Adityawarman** on Jl Diponegoro has a few rather stale displays of Minang culture, crafts and arts. The **Arts Centre** across the road sometimes has dance and culture shows. There are classes on Sundays and you can see students practising martial arts and dance.

SHOPPING

Duta Plaza is one of the largest shopping centers in Padang, located on Jl Hiligoo. Others are **Matahari**, **Ramanda** and **Ambacan** in the same area—you can get nearly everything here, including clothes, batiks and even cheap handicrafts. The **Pasar Raya** central market has stacks of cloth and *batik* if you care to rummage and bargain. **Toko Arjuna** in the market stocks a wide range of textiles. **Danar Hadi Batik House** on Jl Pemuda No 39 is also very good. For souvenirs, antiques and handicrafts, try **Sartika** on Jl Sudirman, or **Abunawas** on Jl Iman Bonjol. Padang's antique shops offer the same range as Bukittinggi's—old sarongs, masks, chests and lamps, but wily shoppers can often get a sharper bargain in Padang. **Silda Arts and Gallery** on Jl Juanda also has a good range of local and Javanese arts. Silungkang in **Atom Shopping Centre** has baskets and embroidery.

SERVICES

There are **Tourist Offices** at Jl Khatib Sulaiman 22 (☎ 28711) and Jl Jend Sudirman 43 (☎ 34-231). The **Post Office** is on Jl Bagindo Aziz Chan, as is the **Telkom Office**. The **Immigration Office** is on Jl Khatib Sulaiman (☎ 21294). The **Nature Conservation Office** (trekking permits for Kerinci), is at Jl Raden Saleh (☎ 25136). The big **banks** are mainly situated along Jl Sudirman and Jl Bagindo Aziz Chan. There are **money changers** along Jl Pemuda. The main **Yos Sudarso Hospital** is on Jl Situjuh. There's the private (and more expensive) **Salasih Clinic** down from the Immigration Office on Jl Khatib Sulaiman. There are **travel agents**, (Pacto Tours, Natrabu, Tunas and Nitours), along Jl Pemuda. All run tours to the Padang beaches and Minang Highlands, charter cars and can put together packages for trips to Kerinci National Park, or Siberut. For **divers**, Padang Diving is at Padang Muara on Jl Batang Arau. At this small harbor, you'll find boats leaving for the **Mentawai Islands** and down the coast to **Bengkulu** and **Lampung**.

Padang Beaches

Traveling south of Padang, the coastline is surprisingly scenic considering its proximity to a city. The first decent beach is **Air Manis**, you can hike here from Padang Muara harbor in less than an hour. There's usually a simple homestay in the village. There are small islands off the coast—on **Banana Island** (*Pulau Pisang*) there are cottages for rent. A further 25 km south is pretty **Bungus Bay**, *bemos* run there for 50 cents, or charter a taxi. The beach is lovely, although a timber factory on one side of the bay hasn't improved its natural attractions. **Carolina** Guest

W. Sumatra 4

House (☎ 27900) is relaxing and peaceful, and has rooms from $8–$20. Further away from the factory, The **Bungus Beach** Hotel is slightly cheaper than Carolina. Both hotels are at km 20–21, Bungus. **Carlos** Hotel, close to Bungus Beach Hotel, also has rooms from $7. To the north of Padang, the best beach is **Pasir Jambak**. "Uncle Jack's" homestay caters for simple needs, but you need to walk in 1 km from the road to the homestay on Pasir Jambak.

Minang Highlands

Either Bukittinggi or Padang can be used as a base for exploring the Minang Highlands, a cool area with much to offer visitors. If you prefer a less touristy base, head away from Bukittinggi to one of the other highland towns. Nature lovers and walkers should head for Kerinci-Seblat National Park, which straddles west Sumatra and Jambi provinces (see *Jambi*).

Bukittinggi

Telephone code is 0752.
Bukittinggi, although small, has traditionally been a travelers' base and so offers an unusual range of facilities including hotels, restaurants, tour agents and shops. Bukittinggi is cooler, more convenient and more charming than Padang.

GETTING THERE AND AWAY

Bus services. There are frequent buses to and from Bukittinggi from most Sumatran towns. The roads are narrow and twisty and the going is slow, but the spectacular volcanic highland scenery guarantees a memorable trip. Sample prices are for air conditioned services, but there are also cheaper local services if you can bear no springs, no windows and probably, not much seat— Medan $12; Aceh $23; Prapat $9; Pekanbaru $4; Jakarta $20–$28, Bengkulu $12; Jambi $7, Palembang $16. Tickets from Aur Kuning bus terminal. Early morning, before 6 am, Padang buses wait in Jl A Yani.
Minibus. For shorter trips, for example to and from Padang, charter a minibus. Prices: $30 per bus to Padang, up to $140 for Prapat. Local jaunts are around $22 per bus per trip.

GETTING AROUND

Bukittinggi has a small, compact town center and it's easy to walk around, as the main street Jl A Yani joins Pasar Atas and the clock tower area which leads down to Pasar DiBawah. Maps are available at the tourist information office and from travel agents. Taxis can be picked up near the

clock tower—most have meters but make sure it's switched on! Pony carts or **bendis** throng the streets, $2 per hour or 50 cents a trip.The tiny ponies are well-kept and wear red pompom head-dresses. **Oplets** (local buses) are 10 cents per trip around town. For trips to local villages and sights outside Bukittinggi, it's worth considering a **minibus** charter. Local **bemos** go everywhere and fares are less than 50 cents to most outlying villages, but waiting for the bus to fill up and leave can be boring and time consuming. The bemo terminal is down the steps from Pasar Atas. For $30 a day a charter minibus can get you round many of the sights in the area. Most travel agents also run see-the-sights-in-a-day tours. **Motorbikes** can also be rented from most travel agents for around $8–$10 per day, and the local guides will even drive it for you if necessary.

TOURS

Jl A Yani is lined with travel agents selling day tours which take in the sights and local villages, bullfights and dances. The "Minangkabau" tours take in all the interesting craft centers, villages, architecture and panoramas. The average price per person per day tour is $10. The Maninjau tour is not such good value as it's very easy to get there by yourself. **PT Indowisata Cipta Permai** on Jl A Yani No 136 also offers interesting tours to visit the **Kubu** people in Jambi (see *Jambi Practicalities*) and also the beautiful Kerinci-Seblat National Park. **PT Batours** (Jl A Yani No 105) also has a selection of tours— Andi is a good, knowledgeable guide (many guides are little more than young groovers who run "tours" to their homes—interesting, none the less). All travel agents run tours to Siberut island (see *Siberut Practicalities*).

ACCOMMODATIONS

Budget

Jl A Yani is lined with cheap, clean, basic hotels haunted by travelers. Most of the rooms are basic boxes with bed (no air con is needed as the highland night air is cool) and little else. A few offer rooms with basic *mandi*, for example the **Grand** and the **Rajawali**, which also has a rooftop suntrap. All are convenient and offer rooms from $2–$5. The **Gangga**, **Tigo Balai** and **Murni** are fairly large and offer a range of stark rooms, some much better than others. All three are warren-like places with plenty of seating areas, and all three have a tourism service. The **Bamboo** Homestay is cozy and popular, **Tropik** is clean, and **Nirwana**, **Singgalang Inn** and **Srikandi** are all old, clean, cheap and basic, although the Singgalang has more cozy rooms

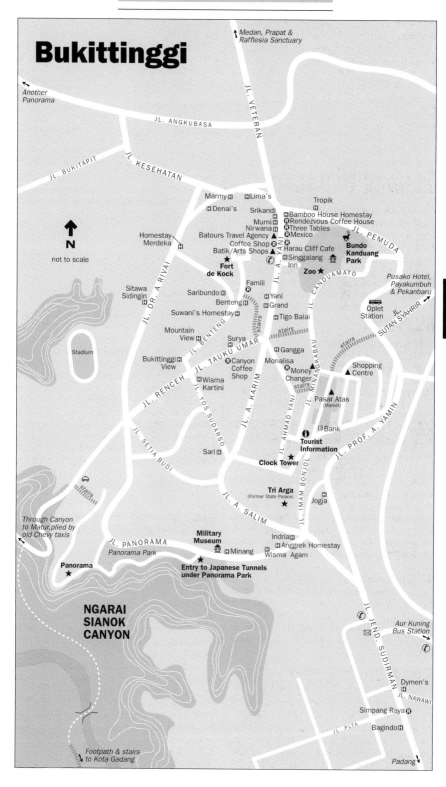

Bukittinggi

↑ Medan, Prapat &
Rafflesia Sanctuary

↖ Another
Panorama

JL. ANGKUBASA

JL. VETERAN

JL. BUKITAPIT

JL. KESEHATAN

↑
N

not to scale

Marmy 🄷   🄷 Lima's   Tropik 🄷
🄷 Denai's   Srikandi 🄷   🄷 Bamboo House Homestay
              Murni 🄷   🅡 Rendezvous Coffee House
Homestay   Nirwana 🄷   🅡 Three Tables
Merdeka   Batours Travel Agency ▲ 🅡 Mexico
        🄷   Coffee Shop 🅡 ▲ N   🄷 Harau Cliff Cafe   **Bundo**
             Batik/Arts Shops ▲   🄷 Singgalang   **Kanduang**
              ★   Inn   **Park**
            Fort   **Zoo** ★
            de Kock
Sitawa   Famili   JL. PEMUDA
Sidingin   Saribundo 🄷 🅡   Pusako Hotel,
            Benteng 🄷   🄷 Yani   Payakumbuh
        Suwani's Homestay 🄷   🄷 Grand   & Pekanbaru
                            🄷 Tigo Balai   Oplet
Mountain   Station
View 🄷   Surya   stairs
            🅡   🄷 Gangga
Bukittinggi 🄷 🅡 Canyon   Monalisa
View   Coffee 🅡 Money   Shopping
            Shop   Changer   ▲ Centre
        🄷 Wisma   stairs
        Kartini   ▲ Pasar Atas
                               (Market)
        Sari 🄷   🄷 Bank

        Stadium   ℹ
                              Tourist
                              Information
                         ★ **Clock Tower**

        🅿 stairs   **Tri Arga**
                     (Former State Palace) 🄷 Jogja
                              ★
Through Canyon
to Matur,plied by   **Military**   Indria 🄷
old Chevy taxis   **Museum**   🄷 Anggrek Homestay
                  🏛 🄷 Minang   Wisma Agam
            JL. PANORAMA
Panorama Panorama Park   ★
    ★   **Entry to Japanese Tunnels**
              under Panorama Park

NGARAI
SIANOK
CANYON
                              ↻ JL. JEND. SUDIRMAN
                                       Aur Kuning
                              ✉   Bus Station
                                          ↻

                                    Dymen's 🄷
                                  JL. NAWAWI

                        Simpang Raya 🅡
                              Bagindo 🄷

Footpath & stairs
to Kota Gadang   JL. PLTA   Padang ↘

(side tab) **W. Sumatra** **4**

with bath and shower for $11. Check out two or three hotels if you plan to stay a few days.

Moderate

There's a range of hotels offering rooms around $20–$25, all with bar and restaurant, TV and satellite, bathroom, hot water and telephone facilities. The **Gallery** Hotel on H Agus Salim Street ☎ 23515, has a good cafe and restaurant and is close to the market area.the small Minang-style **Nikita** Hotel serves European food, and is close to town on Jl Jenderal Sudirman, ☎ 23313. **Suwarni's** Guesthouse ☎ 23301, ($10), has a personal, friendly, homely environment, and Pak Suwarni can help with local information. **Benteng** Hotel ☎ 21115 is a boxy affair with a fairly charmless interior, but it's in a quiet spot up near Fort de Kock, and the meals are good. The **Mountain View** Guesthouse ☎ 21621, is friendly and clean, offers a great view and rooms for $10. **Merdeka** Homestay ☎ 21253, on Jl Dr A Rivai has very clean rooms from $6–$15, with hot water bathrooms —hot water can be a great plus as Bukittinggi's mountain water is often icy cold!

Luxury

The most upmarket hotel in Bukittinggi is Aerowisata's Hotel **Pusako** ☎ 22111 (standard $85, presidential suite $990). It's a new, local-style building set high on a hill outside Bukittinggi on the Payakumbuh road, with excellent facilities and dining rooms. **Denai** Hotel ☎ 21511, is a Minang-style building in town on Jl Dr Rivai. Although hardly local in style inside, it's tasteful, with a lovely garden. Prices range from $30 to $100, cottages $60. **Dymens** Hotel ☎ 21015 on Jl Nawawi (there's also a sister hotel at Padang airport) is a standard 3-star hotel with good facilities and has rooms from $35, suites from $60. Dymens has good but expensive restaurants. The **Bukittinggi View** ☎ 22277, offers a great highland panorama, and is small and personal. Room rates from $35 to $82.

EATING OUT

It's theoretically possible to stay in Bukittinggi without eating Indonesian food, as all the travelers' bars and coffee shops along Jl A Yani have Western-style snacks on the menu—tacos, chips, chicken, steaks, soups and sandwiches, plus Continental breakfasts. They also serve fruit salads, juices and basic Indonesian dishes such as fried rice and noodles, *cap cay* and *soto*, and prices range from $1.50 upwards. Most of these restaurants are popular gathering places, with music and drinks at night. Local guides hang out here, and can help to sort out trips and travel plans. Currently popular are the **Jazz and Blues Cafe**, the **Coffee Shop**, the **Three Tables**, the

Harau Cliff and the **Rendezvous**. For great cheap Padang and Indonesian food, head for the hawker stalls behind the market on market days—down the steps from the clock tower and follow the stalls until you smell it. Cheap and tasty. There are also small *warungs* which set up in Jl A Yani at night selling Padang style food, and the market area by the clock tower is the base for stalls selling grilled corn, *satay*, fruits and other snacks. The **Simpang Raya** Padang restaurants (there's a large one near the clocktower) are famous for their excellent Padang food, and this one also has good Western-style breakfasts. For Chinese food, the **Monalisa** on Jl A Yani is cheap and popular. For a splash-out meal, try one of the top hotels' restaurants.

SHOPPING

If you know your prices and know a little about old goods, then Bukittinggi can be a very tempting stopover. There are "antique" shops galore along Jl Minangkabau. Old sarongs, ceramics, lamps, *kain songket* and carved mirror frames jostle for position next to jewelry old and new, puppets, Javanese masks, basketware and rattan—even old ceremonial garments and belts. If you're lucky you get to see a new load brought in and have first pick. New souvenir-style goods mix with the genuine oldies. As well as **Beringin Arts** and **Tiga Putra** on Jl Minangkabau, try the **Minang Art Shop** on Jl A Yani, and also **Krisna Art**. For new clothes, designer batik and souvenirs, try the **Sumbar Indah** Art and Gift Shop at 103 Jl A Yani, or **Batik Chicoc** next door, which has modern-style hand-drawn batik sarongs and clothes. For general shopping and cheap souvenirs, the market is the place. Big markets are held on Wednesday and Saturday, and if you can carry it, you'll be able to buy it here, from cheap watches and shoes to rattan mats and ornamental fans. There's also a large market at Lawang on Monday and Friday. For clothes, slippers and bags, there's a row of souvenir shops in the square behind the clocktower.

SERVICES

The **Tourist Office** is in a small Minang-roofed building behind the clocktower. They know when weddings and bullfights and cultural dance performances are being held, but in general, the travel agents are more knowledgeable and efficient. The telephone office (**Telkom**) is at Jl M Syafei, open 24 hours, also fax service. There are private "*Wartel*" telephone offices all over Bukittinggi, there's one on Jl A Yani which also sells stamps and runs a postal agency. There are several **hospitals** such as the Rumah Sakit Umum on Jl Dr A Rivai or the Rumah Sakit Umum Pusat on Jl Jend Sudirman. **Banks** and **money changers** change cash currency. Travel agents handle credit card advances, cash and travelers cheques too. The major banks are all sited around the clocktower, and all change travelers cheques, but the rates aren't that good and the service isn't that speedy. **Flights** can be booked at any travel agent, but there's also a **Garuda** office at Dymens Hotel on Jl Nawawi.

ARTS, CULTURE AND NIGHTLIFE

The main nightlife is eating, watching the world go by or having a few beers in the travelers' bars to the sound of Bob Marley tapes. On certain nights every week, there are cultural **dance** performances, ask at The Coffee Shop or Yani Tours on Jl A Yani. **Bullfights** are held on Tuesday and Saturday afternoons at Kotobaru village —there are organized trips or you can simply take a local *bemo*. Weddings, cultural performances and ceremonies open to the public will be advertised in the Tourist Office.

SEEING THE RAFFLESIA

Don't let anyone tell you that it isn't flowering as blooms are unpredictable, so check out the Rafflesia sanctuary less than an hour away. Either charter a taxi to Batang Palupuah ($12) or take a *bemo* (30 cents), then walk. For $1, there are many willing local boys who know the bloom's whereabouts. Wear good shoes.

Lake Maninjau

A two-hour journey from Bukittinggi, the large, still Lake Maninjau is a favorite resting and hanging out place. It is smaller and slightly less spectacular than the grand, imposing Lake Toba in North Sumatra, but it is certainly quieter and more restful. It's popularity these days is such that there are now no fewer than 17 homestays and small cafe-restaurants around the lakeside, but the atmosphere of the old lakeside villages is still sublimely peaceful.

GETTING THERE AND AWAY

From Bukittinggi, take a local *bemo* to Aur Kuning Terminal (10 cents). The Maninjau buses leave from the far side of the terminal, fare 40 cents. Look for the "Harmoni" bus company. Most Bukittinggi travel agents also run Maninjau tours for $10 per person, which stop off at the various panoramas and places of interest on the way. But even on the public *bemo*, if you ask the driver nicely he'll stop at **Embun Pagi** panorama so you can take photos. A minibus charter is $22 one way, $35 round trip. It's also an easy day trip by motorbike ($8 per day).

ACCOMMODATIONS

Budget

The *bemo* drops you off at a T-junction on the lakeshore, which is Maninjau village. To the left, you'll find a few cheap guesthouses, plus several cafe/bars catering for tourists and serving local and Western food and drinks. There's **Davinsi** Coffeeshop and Homestay, which overlooks the lake and has a pretty seating area. **Dillie** homestay is new and clean, and has pleasant balcony terraces overlooking the lake. The attic rooms are huge. Prices at most of the Maninjau hostels range from $1.5–$2. The **Amai** Guesthouse is an old Dutch home set back from the lake on the other side of the road, no lake view, but it's very charming and clean and the owners are friendly and helpful. To the right of the T-junction are the bulk of the guesthouses, some right on the lake shore, some set back across the road which runs round the lake —bemos and the few cars there are simply zoom along this, unfortunately. Of the fourteen or so there are to choose from, the **Palantha** Homestay and Coffeeshop has lakeside views, and the **Riak Danau**, one of the first you come to, also has a great location on the lake front in the *padi* fields. Some homestays, like the **Panurunam**, are set up in modern family homes which contrast with the majority of Maninjau's pretty old wooden houses. Just walk along the lakeside road and check them out. There are also plenty of restaurants along this stretch. It takes about 20 min to walk to the furthest homestay.

Moderate

Maninjau village boasts a couple of more upmarket hotels. The **Maninjau Indah** (☎ 26471) has rooms from $10 to $30. It's well located on the lakefront and has a good restaurant and coffeeshop. **Speedboat** rentals are $20 per hour, and the hotel also has rental **canoes** and **pedaloes** for $2.50 per hour. The **Pasir Panjang Permai** has upmarket cottage style accommodations on the lakefront for $25–$30, and also a lovely lakeside restaurant and tennis courts. **Embun Pagi** Cottages on the crater rim high above the lake also offers cottage style accommodations from $25.

FOOD

On the T-junction corner, by the terminal, is Rumah Makan **Gumalah**, which offers good, cheap local dishes and some Western food. Many of the traveler-style bar-coffeeshops have cozy, convivial atmospheres—try the **Rezza** Coffee Shop or **Bobo's** to the left of the T-junction, or, to the right, the **Maninjau View** Coffee shop has a nice location in the *padi*, and the **Palantha** Coffeeshop also has great lake views. The **Riak Danau** Coffeeshop serves Indian and Padang food, most of the others serve the standard travelers menu of simple local dishes and sandwiches, tacos, burgers, fruit juices and pancakes. Prices are reasonable at about $1.50 per simple meal. Along the road there are *warungs* selling *satay* and grilled corn.

GETTING AROUND

Walking is the best way. Local *bemos* run along the lakeside road, fare 10 cents. **Mountain bikes and motorbikes** can be rented from Bobo Coffeeshop on the left of the T-junction, cycles $2 per day, bikes $7–$10. **Canoes** can also be rented from Beach Homestay or from locals, bargain hard. There's a **ferry service** from beside the Maninjau Indah Hotel to other lakeside *kampungs*, but it's irregular. Rent **speedboats** from the Maninjau Indah. **Hike** from Maninjau round the north of the lake to **Muko Muko** on the far shore, about 16 km. The trip round the south point of the lake and back (around 60 km) takes at least two days.The road is rough but tarmac is promised soon. There's also a very infrequent *bemo* to Muko Muko, the site of the holy hot springs. There's a good *rumah makan* just before the village, but no accommodation apart from a *losmen* in Batu Angin 2 km further on, unless you ask in the *warungs*, which sometimes have rooms. The **trek** to the **waterfall** above the lake takes 45 min, turn off the road after Palantha Guesthouse and walk up.

SERVICES

There's a **Post Office** 40 m down from the T-junction on the way to the Maninjau Indah Hotel. The **Telkom** office is on the corner by the T-junction. **Bank Rakyat Indonesia** changes cash and travelers cheques—slowly! **Simple** Coffee Shop to the right of the T-junction has a basic travel service and can book flights, buses and tours (or at least they have all the information). The Maninjau Indah Hotel offers charter **taxis** ($40 per day) and day tours. There's a batik course at **Khethek Batik** Shop opposite the Simple coffee shop. Local tailors' shops sell good batik cloth. There's a bookshop and laundry at **Mesra** Restaurant, and you can also buy the English language *Jakarta Post* here!

Batusangkar

Traveling along roads lined with coffee, clove, cinnamon, cabbage, corn, banana and rice plantations, it's about 50 km to Batusangkar, a lively market town. It's well located for visiting the cultural sites of the Minang area, but the town is not that charming in itself and so attracts few tourists other than those who pass through on their sight-seeing trips.But it's ideal for those seeking a respite from touristy Bukittinggi.

ACCOMMODATIONS

Batusangkar's hotels are all in the budget to moderate range, all fairly new, small, clean and plain, with basic facilities. **Hotel Parma** (☎ 713-30) has rooms from $3.5–$10. It's on Jl Hamka and offers a restaurant and room service. Hotel **Pagaruyung** across the road (☎ 71533) has rooms from $10 to $30—these rooms are comfortable. It's very clean and the restaurant isn't bad. Hotel **Yoherma** down the street (☎ 71130) has rooms from $4–$11, the top rooms with bathroom and TV.

FOOD

For cheap Padang food, try the **Purnama** Restoran on Jl Sukarno Hatta. It's cooler and fresher upstairs. There's also a **Simpang Raya** Padang restaurant on Jl A Yani. Otherwise, just wander down the main street and through the large market area which is filled with coffee houses and *warungs*. Several Padang-food *warungs* are also clustered around the central park near the Tourist Information Office.

SERVICES

The **Tourist Information Office** is at Jl Pemuda No 1, and has plenty of leaflets. The **Post Office** is on Jl Sutoyo near the Tourist Office. There's a **Telkom** office on Jl Terminal Baru. Local **buses** leave from the terminal 2 km out of town. For long distance buses, go via Bukittinggi or Solok. For getting around town, there are pony carts (**bendis**) or **bemos**.

Lake Singkarak

Lacking the tranquillity of Lake Maninjau, but with its own peaceful charm, Lake Singkarak is a calm, cool place surrounded by rice terraces. It's a beautiful drive down from Batusangkar, past many large old Minangkabau houses which are still occupied by families. The lake can be reached by *bemo* from Padang Panjang or Batusangkar, ask to be dropped off near Ombilin. There are plenty of *bemos* traveling along the lakeside road, hop on to travel the length of the lake. A chartered vehicle is ideal for touring this area.

ACCOMMODATIONS

The **Singkarak Sumpur** Hotel ☎ 82529 is the most upmarket hotel, with a very pleasant lakeside swimming pool, chalet-style terraced rooms and a lakeside restaurant. Watersports and fishing are on offer. Room rates are from $20–$40. The much simpler **Jayakarta** Hotel ☎ Padang 27279, has rooms from $9–$14, and a terrace right on the lakeside, but the landscaping leaves much to be desired. There's a 24 hour bar/restaurant, or nip next door to the Padang *rumah makan*. W*arungs* line the lakeside road. Boats charter for $5 per hour.

Payakumbuh

Few visitors stay in Payakumbuh, but it's a good base for exploring the **Harau Valley**. There's also a swimming pool and, outside the town, caves, traditional villages and craft centers, **Batang Tabik** poolside resort, **Mt Sago** (for keen climbers) and a tea plantation. To get to Payakumbuh, take a *bemo* from Bukittinggi. It's a 45-minute trip and costs 30 cents.

ACCOMMODATIONS

If you want to explore the Harau Valley with its wildlife and waterfalls, stay at **Rizal's**, a comfortable family homestay. Rizal acts a guide. Look for Paritrantang No 71, Lingkungan III, the house is behind the Anrico Bank on the main street. Rizal can organize bicycle tours and treks. Ms Zurni Boer from the Tourist Information Office also runs a homestay and tours—Jl Pacuan No 6, Labuh Buru ☎ 92131. Other hotels include the unaptly named **Flamboyan** ($7 per double room). **Bunda Kandung** Hotel (☎ 92711) has rooms for $7, so do *losmen* **Harau** and **Asia Baru**. There more classy **Mangkutu** hotel with a view, with rooms from $15, is opening up just outside town—ask at the **Tourist Office** on Jl Olah Raga No 1 ☎ 92907. There are plenty of *warungs* on Jl Sudirman. There's a good market on Sunday. Payakumbuh is also known as a craft center, see the baskets, bird cages and rattan goods on sale everywhere. There's embroidery at **Widjaya** on Jl A Yani, and *kain songket* and bamboo artifacts in the market. There's a handicraft village at **Andeleh**, half an hour's journey by *bemo*.

Climbing Gunung Merapi

To climb the volcano (which last erupted only ten years ago and buried three villages) start from Kotobaru between Bukittinggi and Padang Panjang. Report to the police, who'll tell you if the volcano is dangerous and off-limits. Take water, warm clothes and good shoes. Guides are usually needed and can be found in Bukittinggi—look for someone with experience. Walk or drive to the Relay Station at 1,200 m. Climb at night with a torch, or during the day. After a bamboo bridge across a gully, the ascent begins through primary forest. This thins out near the 3,000 m

summit due to recent volcanic activity. Tents can be pitched here. It takes around 5 hours to the summit with its craters and superb views. Don't wander off unless the volcano is quiet. Conditions change rapidly, so heed the guide.

Climbing Mount Singgalang

Another active and less temperamental volcano is Mt Singgalang. Most people climb at night but there's no reason to do this as the best views of the crater lake at Telaga Dewi and the forest are seen at sunrise or sunset when the mist lifts. Start the ascent from Kotabaru, and then go on to Pandai Sikat and hitch a ride to the relay station 5 km further on. There's a coffeeshop here at the start of the popular climb. It's possible to camp below the crater. Sights include the lake and views of the surrounding volcanoes. Take warm clothes and water.

Climbing Mt Tandikat

It's possible to camp inside the crater of Mt Tandikat. The tracks are hard to find so take a guide, for example Pak Lelo or his son—ask at Gantiang Singgalang, 7 km from Padang Panjang. Hike from the stream at Sungai Ulua Aia, up through the forest, for about 4–6 hours. Climb during the day and camp overnight. Pak Lelo can accommodate climbers, but don't forget to contribute. Trek past monkeys, moss forests and swampy land. There's a lake with a camping place, although it's an active site with steam eruptions and dead trees.

Solok

Solok is a pleasant, busy town. If you're exploring the **Twin Lakes** of Lake DiAtas and Lake DiBawah, stay over at the quiet, detached Hotel **Caradek** on Jl Perpatih Nan Sebatang ☎ 2093. Rooms with TV, hot water, breakfast and AC go for $24, down to $5 for simple rooms. The energetic manager Gusriwanto runs an impromptu **travel service**, dispenses maps and is generally very helpful. Other hotels are the **Sinar Timbulun** on Jl Dahlan, a large old rambling Dutch bungalow with courtyards and gardens ($3–$5), and the modern, clean **Ully** on Jl Syeikh Kukutt ☎ 20026, which has clean, simple rooms from $7–$13. There are plenty of **banks** in town, and the **Telkom** office is behind Bank Raykat Indonesia on Jl Sudirman. The **Post Office** is on Jl Sukarno, as is the **Tourism Office**, at Jl Sukarno No. 30. For eating, there are plenty of *kedai kopi* and foodstalls in the **Pasar Raya** area, and the restaurant **Pondok Tovina** on Jl Raya Bypass, a short distance out of town, has good Javanese food. The taxi stand is next to the *bemo* station off Jl Sukarno (for **Siberut**, see over).

— *Julie Heath, Andreas Peters and Laurie Scott*

Siberut

Most visitors to Siberut go with a group tour, as it can be difficult to get around on your own—especially for non-Indonesian speakers. Independent Siberut travelers were once very few and far between, and although it's now more common to visit the island without a tour group, it can be difficult to bargain for reasonable prices for river trips, and a tour can often be cheaper. Language can also be a barrier, and non-Mentawai speakers may not learn much about the culture without a guide.

Although it's becoming much more common to visit Siberut these days, it's still considered to be a trip for the more adventurous traveler. The boats are far from luxurious, the accommodation is very basic, and is customarily with Mentawai families in a traditional native *uma* or village, sleeping on the open verandah on a mat. There's quite a bit of trekking and a lot of mud, a fair few leeches and plenty of far from *cordon bleu* meals.

Living closely together with a small group of people for 10 days can also bother some individuals, especially if there are group tensions and conflicts—as there often are. If you don't like the idea of an organized tour company group, put together your own small group of compatible people and find a reliable guide to lead the group yourselves.

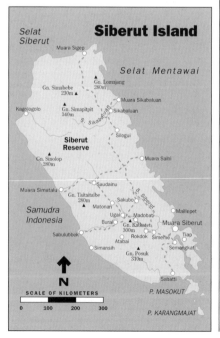

Siberut Island

Selat Siberut

Selat Mentawai

Samudra Indonesia

Siberut Reserve

Gn. Simabebe 230m

Gn. Simapitpit 340m

Gn. Lomajang 280m

Gn. Sinolop 280m

Gn. Taitaitaibe 280m

Gn. Katkatet 300m

Gn. Posuk 310m

Muara Sigep

Muara Sikabaluan

Sikabaluan

Silogui

Muara Saibi

Saudainu

Sakubo

Matonan

Ugai

Madobat

Bural

Rokdok

Atabai

Simansih

Simenie

Tiap

Semangkat

Maillepet

Muara Siberut

Muara Simatalu

Sabulubbek

Kagologolo

S. Sikabaluan

S. Siberut

Sabatti

P. MASOKUT

P. KARANGMAJAT

N

SCALE OF KILOMETERS

0   100   200   300

By sea. Ferries leave from Padang's Muara harbor two or three times a week for **Muara Siberut**. The *Sumbar Rezeki* leaves on Mon and Thurs at 8 pm, the fare is $7 for a cabin, $5 deck class. It's a 10–12 hour trip, so a cabin is recommended, otherwise it's difficult to sleep. The return ferry leaves Siberut on Tuesday and Friday at 8 am. If you're traveling independently, be sure to buy a ticket early from the Muara harbor as the boat is nearly always crowded, or book ahead with one of the Padang travel agents.

Visitors arrive in Muara Siberut, the island's largest town. There are seven basic *losmen*—try **Syahrudin's** place, **Muara** Guesthouse, **ANTO** Guesthouse or **Ucung** Guesthouse. All charge around $5 per night, although Muara also has rooms for $10. There's another *losmen* up the coast at Malepet Beach, a family house which charges $7 per group.

From Muara Siberut, the first stop for tour groups is usually **Rokdok**, a village that's very quickly come under the influence of the Government's development program. From here, there's a 4-hour speedboat trip to **Madobat**, although at low tide, the river trip is accompanied by a 2-hour hike.

From here, groups usually trek to various different local villages, spending at least 10 days on the island. The going can be tough, often there are no actual paths. Tracks are cut through the jungle, and there's an excess of mud, leeches, fallen logs, slippery log bridges and poles across swampy, wet areas. There are also rivers to wade through. But the consolations are the wildlife, the beautiful waterfalls and rockpools, ideal for refreshing dips, the friendly people, the culture and the isolation of the jungle.

Many of the people who live on Siberut's coast are settlers, transmigrants and fishermen who brought trades with them, and so the larger coastal towns have shops and *warungs*—**Sikabaluan**, in the island's north, has a large hawker stall market with tasty Sumatran food. The beach here is long and unspoilt—it's possible to stop off for a few hours on the way back to Padang as the ferry calls in here.

The interior villages, however, rarely have shops. The Mentawai have traditionally lived by hunting and gathering, raising sago and barter, although today they do also sell wood, sago, rattan and other goods to the larger coastal towns and to the Sumatran mainland. Most families still live in traditional houses or *uma* in traditional villages, and tourists visiting the village sleep on the covered verandah out front—villagers still keep their pigs and chickens under the house, so the sleeping arrangements can be very cozy! Meals are also taken with the family, although the guide will also bring along basic foods to cook as the family supplies will be limited, and also maybe unappealing to Westerners.

BEHAVIOR

Mentawai people are very friendly, but it's as well to remember a few basics. First, don't go to the toilet in the river or close to the house—and cover up the traces afterward. Don't bathe naked or scantily clothed, and do wear clothes in the villages. Don't leave your rubbish behind, and don't give out elaborate presents—cigarettes suffice, but *not* for children. Don't wear jewelry unless you are happy about losing it in a swap—Mentawai's love bracelets, bangles, necklaces, earrings and beads and will surely ask to keep yours in return for a local trinket which may not compare in value in your eyes. If you're in doubt about giving presents or money, ask the guide.

As usually happens when an area opens up to tourists, the locals will come to expect some form of payment, which your guide should arrange for. If you'd like to give something away, or get asked for something of yours, ask the guide to handle it. Extravagance will only make bargaining harder for those tourists who come after you. Don't take photos without asking permission first.

TRAVEL AGENTS AND TOURS

Siberut tours are big business as the number of tourists visiting the island has grown amazingly over the past five years. Every travel agent in Padang and Bukittinggi now offers a Siberut tour. Most follow a very similar 10-day itinerary, and organize tickets, permits, accommodation, food and porters.

The average going rate per person is around $125 for 10 days, $100 for 7 days. Perhaps one of the better travel agents in Bukittinggi for Siberut trips is **Batours**, as Andi, the manager, is a knowledgeable guide. Budi from **Yani** Tours and Travel has also been taking groups to Siberut for many years.

Nusa Mentawai Tours in Padang offers slightly more upmarket trips on a charter boat—$540 per group of up to 12 for 10 days. Although the boat is more comfortable than the public ferry, visitors still need to sleep in traditional Siberut houses—there's no way in to the remoter villages without trekking. Nusa Mentawai's rates for a trip using public transport are $435 per group of up to 12. Nusa Mentawai also run tours to other Mentawai islands—**Sipora**, **Pagai Utara**

and **Pagai Selatan**. Boat charter rates available—Nusa Mentawai is at Jl Batang Arau No. 53, Padang ☎ 28764.

TRAVELING ALONE

It can be a tough trip for those traveling alone, but rewarding. One of the main problems is the language. Whilst the coastal villagers and some of the younger children may speak Indonesian, the inner villagers mostly do not, and it can be difficult for independent travelers or groups to arrange for their food and accommodation. It's much easier with a guided group. Plus, lone visitors miss out on explanations and demonstrations of cultural importance, and the villagers themselves may be more wary of unaccompanied guests.

EQUIPMENT AND SUPPLIES

But there's a great sense of adventure in lone jungle trekking. If you do decide to visit alone, make sure you're well equipped—as indeed all visitors should be. You'll need mosquito net, torch, sheet, insect repellent, malaria tablets, cooking utensils, first aid kit, trekking shoes and a rain mac. It rains a lot and you'll certainly get wet and muddy during the day, so keep dry, clean clothes for night-time and sleeping. You'll also need photocopies of your passport for reporting to the police in Muara Siberut. You should check about permits with the Padang tourist office and the police in Padang before you leave, and they may want passport photos of yourself. You'll need to be able to speak at least some basic Indonesian if you intend to get anywhere off the beaten track. The tourist information office in Muara Siberut should be able to give you some useful information. You'll also need money—the hire of a longboat for the up and down river trip is around $75—try asking at the *losmen* in Muara Siberut. The full trip will probably cost at least $160. Plenty of cigarettes are handy for presents and bargaining. Mentawai guides will bring you into the jungle for about $10 per day—most younger ones can speak Indonesian. Without the services of a guide and porters, you'll also need to carry your own supplies and food. It's possible to eat with the Mentawai families in return for tobacco, but don't bank on this. Many meals with be cooked on the campfire—but you get the freedom to really get off the beaten track and explore the jungle.

GETTING AROUND

You'll need to find river transport. It may be possible to share the boat with an organized tour group. Arrange a time for the boat to come and collect you from upriver.

— *Julie Heath*

5 Riau PRACTICALITIES

INCLUDES PEKANBARU, BATAM, BINTAN AND RIAU ISLANDS

Riau is a province made up of an archipelago lying on Singapore's doorstep, providing an exciting stepping stone to either Java or Sumatra, and a mainland area rich in oil. The mainland's capital city of Pekanbaru is developing rapidly. Batam and Bintan islands feature in the Government's development plan—Batam for industry and tourism, Bintan for tourism. The best way to get around Riau is by boat. Where once trips to outlying islands could take days in slow wooden fishing *sampans*, the increasing prosperity in Riau has brought fleets of high speed ferries. But the old, slow boats are still there for the budget-conscious or the romantic. The main entry ports are Pekanbaru (by air), Sekupang, Nongsa and Batu Ampar on Batam, and Tanjung Pinang and Bandar Benten on Bintan, all which give visas on arrival. *See pages 177–193.*

Batam

Telephone code is 0776.
With the exception of the pretty resort strip at Nongsa, Batam is currently a rather unattractive island which resembles a large building site. Attractions are duty-free shops, seafood centers and many good hotels.

GETTING THERE AND AWAY

By air. A mere 30-min ferry ride from Singapore, Batam plans to be one of Indonesia's premier development zones. Although Batam's small Hang Nadim airport currently caters only for domestic flights, a big international terminal is part of Batam's short-term planning. Domestic flights by Garuda, Sempati and Merpati can occasionally be cheaper than flights to Indonesian destinations from Singapore. Tickets can be bought at the airport (the airport accepts Visa and Mastercard). There are several daily flights to and from **Jakarta** ($108), and daily flights to and from **Pekanbaru** ($45) and **Bandung** ($120). Also three or four times a week to and from **Palembang** ($60), **Pontianak** ($80), **Balikpapan** ($160), **Medan** ($90), **Banda Aceh** ($130), **Padang** ($62), **Jambi** ($60) and **Bangka** ($60. Sempati duplicates most routes for roughly the same fares. SMAC fly to **Ranai** on Pulau Natuna, check for fares, and have an on-off service to Riau Islands **Singkep** and **Karimun**. Offices: **Garuda/Merpati** Jalan Sultan Abdul Rachman Blok H-14, Batam. ☎ 456585. **Sempati** Jl Imam Bonjol Blok I No 6 Kodya Batam (☎ 459725).

By sea. Ferries to Batam's Sekupang port leave Singapore's World Trade Centre terminal around every 40 mins between 8 am and 7 pm. The last ferry from Sekupang to Singapore is 6 pm Singapore time. The trip takes about 40 mins, and the fare is $18 return, $12 one way (from Batam, it's $13). There are several ticket agents upstairs in the World Trade Centre terminal— try Channel Holidays ☎ 2702228, or Kalpin Tours ☎ 2714866. Ferries are less frequent to Batu Ampar, but the fare is the same. There are also services to Nongsa where the beach resorts are. The fare is $18 one way,$30 return.
Speedboats to and from **Tanjung Pinang** on Bintan Island leave from **Telaga Punggor** (whilst the old **Kabil** terminal is renovated) on the other side of the island, hourly at $5 for the half hour trip.

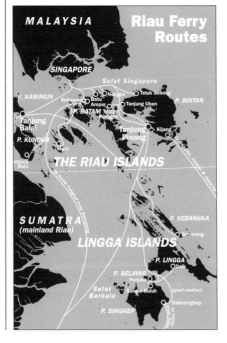

Riau Ferry Routes

MALAYSIA · SINGAPORE · Selat Singapura · P. KARIMUN · Teluk Sebong · BATAM · Tanjung Uban · P. BINTAN · Tanjung Balai · Tanjung Pinang · Kijang · P. KUNDUR · THE RIAU ISLANDS · SUMATRA (mainland Riau) · P. SEBANGKA · LINGGA ISLANDS · P. LINGGA · P. SELAYAR · Selat Berhala · Dabosingkep · P. SINGKEP

Taxi fare to and from Kabil is $5 per car. Speed boats to and from **Tanjung Balai**, Karimun (and from there on to **Selat Panjang** and **Pekanbaru**) leave from the wooden **Sekupang Pier** to the left of the Singapore ferry terminal. The fare to Tanjung Balai is $8. There are also daily fast ferries to **Kuala Tungkal** on Jambi's coast, just below the Riau border. These leave from the same pier, and the fare is $25 for the five-hour trip. Direct buses link Kuala Tungkal to Jambi town—an interesting route into Sumatra.

GETTING AROUND

There are **Metro** buses but they're rare, as are the people who are likely to tell you where to find them, so expect to rely on taxis. These are everywhere, both shared taxis and charter taxis. The fare from Sekupang to the main town of **Nagoya**, where the hotels and shops are, is $3 or $4 per car. To **Kabil** the fare is $5 per car, and to the **airport**, $4. Be prepared to bargain very hard if you don't want 'tourist' prices. The bigger resorts and marinas have courtesy buses which take you either free or for a token (usually $1) fare. They wait at the ferry terminal.

ACCOMMODATIONS

Budget and Moderate

Batam has a few budget hotels and guest houses around Pasar Pelita, Nagoya, none of them very nice. **Sederhana** Penginapan, Komplex Pribumi 1 ☎ 457149 has rooms without bath from $8. **Star Internasional** Hotel at Komplex Sri Jaya C9, has rooms for $15 without bath, with fan ☎ 457372.

Expensive

As far as fairly decent hotels go, Batam is not really very good value. The cheapest are **Horisona** Hotel at Jalan Sultan Abdul Rachamn, Komplex Lumbuj Rezeki Blok E No 1–7 ☎ 457111, which has air-con rooms with bath for $30 but there's a service tax on top, and the **Ramayana** Hotel, Komplex Batama B1 F1 ☎ 4568880, which has rooms for $50 with breakfast. There are clean and very comfortable hotels (some, like the **New Holiday Inn** and the **Nagoya Plaza** are 4-star, with 4-star prices) all over Nagoya—as the biggest, brightest buildings on the long main street, they are not easy to miss—but as Nagoya isn't the most charming town in Indonesia, it's maybe better to splash out a little and stay in one of Batam's beach resorts at **Nongsa**, the prettiest corner of the island by far. The resorts are busy at the weekend, and often far cheaper if you book a package tour in Singapore. **Turi Beach Resort**, Nongsa, has pretty Bali-style chalets in a lovely setting complete with

pools, seasports and all facilities. 156 rooms, price from $120 weekdays ☎ 310078. **Batam View** at Jalan Hang Lekir, Nongsa, has rooms at $80–$120 per night. Facilities include pool, tennis and squash. **Sei Nongsa Beach Resort** starts at $70 for a cottage room, $90 deluxe. Facilities include pool and restaurant. There are also cheaper beach bungalows on **Kasu Island**, 10 minutes from Sekupang by speedboat. Contact Mr Supardi on ☎ 321762 for prices and to book. The **Hilltop** Hotel at Jalan Ir Sutami, just outside Sekupang and with great Singapore views, has rooms at $80 ☎ 322482. Facilities include a pool, karaoke and a lounge and restaurant. **Sekilak** Resort, 15 min from Sekupang by boat, is a pleasant, *kelong* style hotel built on stilts in the sea. It offers rooms, food and watersports. Call Singapore ☎ 22-21097 or Batam ☎ 458762. **Waterfront City** at Tanjung Uncang near Sekupang offers a marina, AC tent and chalet accommodation, a clubhouse, bungee jumping, waterskiing, go-karting, windsurfing and sailing. New golf resorts open regularly, check Singapore travel agents.

FOOD AND NIGHTLIFE

There are a couple of fast food-type local restaurants in the Sekupang ferry terminal, but if you're waiting for a ferry and fancy a meal, try **Pondok Batam** just outside and across the road from the terminal. It has good local food at reasonably uninflated prices. **Nagoya** town boasts the best variety of eating places, from Dino's Italian **pizza and pasta** restaurant, in a lovely, bamboo-finished open air setting above Regina Palace Disco behind Studio 21 cinema, to **Kentucky Fried Chicken** on the busy, long main street of Jl Raden Patah. There are Padang cafes galore—the **Roda Lestari** in Jl Ali Haji Blk A No 4 is really good—plus the usual motley collection of food stalls and *warungs* which pop up from nowhere at night on street corners. **Jl Sungai Harapan** just outside Sekupang has a good selection of Padang cafes, too. For seafood, go to **Batu Besar** on the coast down from Nongsa—the **Silera Wisata** and **Simpani** are two of the best restaurants. There are also seafood places at **Batu Ampar** and **Pantai Telaga Punggur**, which looks out over a small island near Kabil. There's a large food center at **Pujusera Nagoya**, and a steak house at the side of New Holiday Hotel. There are plenty of **bars** and karaoke joints, the haunts of the growing resident ex-pat and Singaporean community, which open till late every night, as do the hotel bars and discos. **Skyline Disco** behind Studio 21 cinema is the chic place, full of young groovers. **Anne's** eating House in Komplex New Holiday Blok C, No 7, is a nice, clean and friendly Western-style cafe serving good local and Western snacks quite cheaply. Most of the hotels offer Chinese,

Indonesian and Western food. There's even a Japanese restaurant near the Gelael supermarket on Jl Raden Patah. The rapidly developing new **Batam Centre**, a new town and business centre, already has one good restaurant, **Tithes**, serving Sundanese and Chinese food.

Bintan

Telephone code is 0771.
Bintan's main town of Tanjung Pinang is a pleasant, bustling trading town with a rather old-fashioned atmosphere. The beaches are the island's main attraction, and pleasant new resorts and hotels are springing up along the coasts.

Tanjung Pinang

GETTING THERE AND AWAY

By air. Merpati and Sempati fly thrice weekly from and to Jakarta ($106) and Pekanbaru ($55). The **Merpati/Garuda** office is at Jl Bintan No 44, Tanjung Pinang ☎ 21267, fax 21269; **Sempati** is at Wisma Riau Hotel, Jl Yusof Khahar No 8 ☎ 23715, fax 24082. **SMAC** (Jl Jend A Yani ☎ 22798) has an on-off service to **Dabo**, Singkep Island, and more definite flights to **Ranai**, Natuna Island ($97), **Bangka** ($60) and **Jambi** ($68). A taxi to the airport near **Kijang**, 20 km from Tanjung Pinang, costs about $4–$5.

By sea. Ferries leave for Tanjung Pinang from Singapore's **World Trade Centre** daily at 9.35am, 10.00am and 2.55pm. Return fare: $65, one way $52; the trip takes about two and a half hours. Tickets can often be bought for less from Singapore travel agents, try Concorde Travel ☎ 5602866 or Auto Mas ☎ 2922870. There is a $3 fee to pay for reconfirming your return ticket in Tanjung Pinang, essential on busy weekends.

There is also a ferry service from the new Tanah Merah ferry terminal to Bandar Benten Telani terminal in Bintan's north, the site of the new beach resorts. It departs on weekends at 9am, 3.30pm and 7pm, less frequently on weekdays. Return: $54, one way: $35 ☎ 345 1210. There's a well-worn but less advisable route to Tanjung Pinang **via Batam**. From Sekupang, take a 40-minute **taxi** ride to Kabil ($5). At **Telaga Punggor** (Kabil is being renovated), fast speedboats usually crammed full to bursting cross to Tanjung Pinang in half an hour for $5, last boat: 5 or 6 pm. There's also a slower ferry called **Bestari** ($4), and a *very* slow wooden boat ($1.50). There are also wooden boats ($1.50) and speedboats ($3) to **Tanjung Uban**, north Bintan Island, from where you can catch a bus to Tanjung Pinang ($1), a two-hour journey. Some buses take a scenic route via the beach.

ONWARD PASSAGE

By sea. The **Pelni** ferry service to Jakarta and Sumatra now operates once a week. The boat leaves each Sunday morning, 8 am from Kijang

Tanjung Pinang

harbor. It reaches Jakarta in 30 hours, and the economy fare is $18, 1st class $70. To **Dumai**, on Sumatra's Riau coast, the ferry leaves Friday at 10 pm, and reaches Sumatra in 10 hours. The fare is $11 economy class. Tickets can be bought from the Pelni office at Jalan Jend A Yani, just go round to the back and you can get a ticket without having to queue. You can check the schedule in Singapore at the Pelni office (☎ 2726811), but no tickets are sold there. There are many private ferries to Jakarta, services stop and start, but lately only the **Samudera Jaya** is running. It leaves from the town harbor, the fare is $40. The agent's office is at Jl Pelantar I No. 10 ☎ 23862, or ask at **Netra Service** agent in the harbor area. There's a fast boat, the *Maharani,* to **Dumai** via **Selat Panjang** every Wednesday from the town harbor, 7 am. There are also speed ferries to **Pekanbaru** via **Selat Panjang** every day, fare $16 to Selat Panjang, where there are onward connections by slow boat ($6) and speedboat to Pekanbaru. Ferries to **Tanjung Balai**, **Karimun** leave the town harbor at 10 am every day; the trip takes three hours. The fare: $11. From there there are also connections to Selat Panjang, Dumai and Pekanbaru.

GETTING AROUND

Tanjung Pinang has a small centre and is easy to walk about. **Minibuses** go anywhere round the town in a 6–7 km radius for Rp300 a trip but there are no routes, just find one that's going roughly your way—a good way to get a free scenic city tour thrown in. **Motorbike taxis** or *ojeks* hang about at corners on the main street, the fare is Rp500 a trip in town. The **bus terminal** is 7 km from the town at Batu Tujuh (ask for terminal Uban). Buses leave frequently for **Tanjung Uban,** some via **Trikora beach**, fare $1.50. There are also shared taxis to **Kijang** from the main street in Tanjung Pinang ($1 per person) until about 12 am. Public taxis to **Trikora** at 11 am cost $1.50 from the taxi termianl on Jl. Teuku Umar. *Bemos* or **taxis** can be chartered hourly or daily by bargaining.The fare is $4 per hour in town, more outside. To **Trikora**, a taxi or *bemo* costs between $10–$15.

ACCOMMODATIONS

Moderate and Luxury

New hotels and resorts are popping up like mushrooms all over Bintan, although as yet, none are super-luxury. A huge resort, being built on the northern **Pasir Panjang** beach, will offer the first 5-star accommodation in 1996, although some smaller new resorts in this project are already open (*see Bintan Beach International Resort*). But for now there's no shortage of comfortable hotels in and around town. From the harbor as you arrive, you can't miss the big new **Sanno** Hotel, rising like a white box above the old stilted *kampung* houses. It's right in the heart of town near the markets. Rooms are $35 plus, due to glitzy marble and gilt finishes. The older **Wisma Riau** on Jl Yusuf Khahar ☎ 21023, also in town only 5 mins from the harbor, has rooms from $15–$40 The **Sampurna Jaya** Hotel ☎ 21555, opposite, has comfortable rooms with bathtubs and hot water from $20–$40. **Tanjung Pinang** Hotel, simple but recently renovated and close to the markets, has rooms from $15–$40 ☎ 21238. **Riau Holidays Indah** ☎ 2-2644 has rooms from $25; you can take your harbor photos from a lovely back terrace overlooking the old, wooden part of town. On a hill overlooking the sea and Penyengat Island, the **Sadaap** Hotel ☎ 22357 has rooms with a view from $20, and also a pleasant terrace restaurant. Much more upmarket, with a pool and very pleasant rooms, is the new **Hilltop** Hotel on Jl Ciptadi ☎ 24221.

At the 10 km marker, 10 km outside town, is the stylish **Royal Place** Hotel ☎ 27555, arguably the best in town but in a slightly odd location on the Trikora beach road. Closer to town, but still within a 3–4 km radius of the town's centre, there's a whole crop of new places—the very pleasant **Bintan Beach Resort**, at Km 4, with a sea view (although not a swimming beach) and a huge pool and poolside restaurant, has nice, tasteful rooms from $80 ☎ 23661. The rest offer a similar grade of accommodation—hot and cold water bathroom, TV—often satellite—bar, karaoke and coffee shop at least. The **Paradise** Hotel ☎ 24213 ($35–$60) has a noisy, lively karaoke bar. **Rainbow** Hotel has little cottages, rooms from $20–$40 ☎ 21982. Others such as the **Garden** Hotel, **Asean** Hotel, **Wisma Kartika** and the **New City** Hotel offer rooms at roughly the same rates, and with similar facilities. The small **Tourist Information Office** in the harbor as you arrive has all the details, and arranges bookings. It's usually cheaper to book these hotels from Singapore as part of a package. Many Singapore travel agents run good value Batam and Bintan tours which include transport, hotels and meals.

Budget

There are plenty of budget accommodations, as Tanjung Pinang is a place for travelers to wait for the boats which leave frequently for Java and Sumatra. Most of these basic *losmen* are close to the main street and walking distance from the harbor. **Johnny's** and **Bong's** off Jl Bintan down a small alleyway are friendly family homes with a few rooms and small dorms, $5 and $2 per person respectively, including breakfast. **Rommel's** (further up the alley, same price) is larger. **Lobo's**, further up the road is an old, rambling, run-down house, same prices. A few cheap hotels: **Sempurna Inn**, Jl Yusuf Khahar, has rooms with *mandi* for $8, so does the garden-style Hotel **Surya** on Jl Bintan.

Up the coast in **Tanjung Uban** are: **Wisma Bahari**, Jl Martadinata, ($12) and **Penginapa Roma Jaya**, Jl Yos. Sudarso 31, ($12).

FOOD

Although it's a bit more expensive than other parts of Indonesia due to the influence of Singapore, there's still plenty of good, cheap food in Tanjung Pinang. During the day, coffee shops and *warungs* around the town sell all kinds of local food. **Kedai Kopi Pinang** on the main street of Jalan Merdeka has wonderful *prata* with a delicious sauce.There's also wonderful *tempe* and *tahu* in coconut curry. The large, airy coffee shop at the corner of Jl Bintan and Jl Merdeka serves local dishes and fruit juices, and is a popular hanging out place. **Pagi Sore** on Jl Merdeka also has *roti prata* with more traditional side dishes. **Bali** on the main street and the cafe next to Sempurna Inn on Jl Yusuf Khahar have good Padang food. Near the market, on the road to Pelantar III, the **Segara** serves fresh fruit juice and ice-cream. On Jl Tambak there's the **Steak House** restaurant with AC. **Hana Ria**, on the road out to Trikora, has good inexpensive food and a garden and boating pool for kids to play in. Early evening, the small **Sunset** night market by the harbor is a relaxing place to have coffee and *sate* and watch the sun set over Penyengat Island. This night market doesn't have much choice of food, but it's lit by kerosene lamps and is pleasantly unbustling. Further round the bay on Jl Hang Tuah is another open-air **Sunset** restaurant, with the usual drinks, local dishes and a great view. Very quiet and peaceful. Later on, there's a large, bustling **night market** on Jalan Teuku Umar, with all kinds of Indonesian and Chinese food, and seafood—$5 per portion for sweet and sour crab or pepper crab. There's also barbecued squid, prawns and fish, plus the usual *nasi* and *mee goreng, soto, mee rebus* and *cap cai*. Outside town there are scattered smaller night markets, two of the best being **Meja Tujuh and Potong Lembu**, which have Chinese and Indonesian food. For seafood, the restaurant at **Teluk Kriting**, the Sungai Enam, on Jl Usman Harun 16 is the most popular. Pricier than the night market, with prices around $10 per head, it has more elaborate dishes, and you dine on stilts over the water. Just along the road is the similar **Seafood Centre**, and there are other seafood places near Kijang, for example the **Sungai Enam** Seafood restaurant. Take a taxi.

SERVICES

The **Tourist Information Office** is in the ferry terminal building.There are several **banks**, and perhaps the most efficient is the **Lippobank** on Jl Merdeka. For changing money, the many **money changers** on Jl Pos and Jl Merdeka give better rates. The banks often make a fuss about wanting to see the receipts. Bank **BCA**, down by the market at Pelantar III, gives Visa and Mastercard cash advances before 12.30 am. The main **Post Office** is on the corner of Jl Pos. The telephone office (**Telkom**) is just round the corner past the harbor on Jl Hang Tuah, and open 24 hours. It sells cards for the town's cardphones, which connect directly to Singapore. There are also *wartel* telephone offices (private telephone services) on Jalan Tambak and at Meja Delapan, also 24 hours. There are many **travel agents** (try **Bunga Tanjung Tours** if you need transport or hotel packages arranged) and **shipping agents** around the town and in the harbor area which can arrange tickets for onward journeys. **Netra Service** on Jl Samudera, the street leading down to the harbor, can arrange for most ferry tickets, and **Toko Osaka** and **Toko New Oriental** on Jl Merdeka represent the agents for the Singapore ferries. The **Pelni** office is at Jl Jend A Yani, 5 km out of town. The **Immigration Office** is at Km 4, outside town. There's a public **swimming pool** at Km 5, just ask the *bemo* driver for 'kolam berenang'. For a day member's rate of $2 plus the fees, the pool, tennis courts and other facilities of Bintan Beach Resort, 4 km out of town on Jl Pantai Impian, can also be used.

NIGHTLIFE

Apart from the lively night markets, the main one being open until the early hours and acting as the local pub and general meeting place, there are several discos. **Pantai Impian** (Dream Beach) on the street of the same name is small and friendly. **Stella Disco** is also small and friendly, and **Kartika Hotel**, **Bintan Beach Resort** and a few other hotels boast karaoke bars and discos. There's a plush new cinema, **Studio 21**, on Jl Sutami, and opposite are a couple of very pleasant cafes serving cheap local food. The 'Villages of Joy' at Km 24 also offer a lively social scene, although the participating clientele is mainly Singaporean. **Siantan** Coffeeshop on Jl Kembodja, 2 km from the town and behind Stella disco, is the late night joint, often open until 5 am.

Trikora Beach

Bintan's east coast beaches are beautiful and unspoiled, stretching for miles with nothing but fishing villages to disturb the peace.The road to **Trikora Beach** has been upgraded and there are now shared daily taxis from the town terminal every day, fare $1; five buses a day from the Uban terminal 7 km out of town, fare $1 (look for the *Tepindo Jaya* buses), and charter taxis, fare $10. A motorbike *ojek* one way costs $5. Motorbikes can usually be hired in town, ask at Rommel's Guesthouse.

At present the **Trikora Beach Resort** is in the process of being upgraded and extended. It has a lovely beachfront setting, pool, tennis and restaurant, and chalets with AC, TV, and bathroom ☎ 22446. Rooms are from $45. Motorbikes can also be hired here, $20 per day. The **Tricora Country Club**, km 38, **Tricora Beach**, ☎ 771-22446, has rooms at $45-98.

There are several basic, cheap guest houses on the beach. First, at Teluk Bakau, 35 km from the town, there's **Bukit Berbunga Chalets**, simple wooden chalets with *mandi* inside, price from $7 per person including food. Drinks on sale. Next door **Yasin's** has chalets from $7 per person and up, depending on the accommodation. The price also includes three meals a day—fish, rice and vegetables. There's a small shop/bar at Yasin's. For eating out, the Trikora Beach Resort has a rather expensive and poor value restaurant, simple dishes like *mee goreng* costs $5. Further on there is the Rumah Makan **Trikora**, a seafood restaurant built on stilts stretching out into the sea, where the food is good and fresh. They have crab, fish, squid and seafood straight from their own traps on the jetty, as well as fried rice and the usual vegetable dishes, plus ice and cold drinks. Around $5 per person minimum. The villages of Kawa, Teluk Bakau and Malangrapat offer one or two coffeeshops serving basic food, otherwise it's down to what the guesthouses can provide.

Bintan International Resort

The beautiful beaches along the Northern coast of Bintan, are currently being developed into an upmarket resort. For now, already opened, are a large kelong restaurant, and the **Mayang Sari** resort, with 100 AC chalets from $120, S'pore ☎ 7328515, fax: 7323959 and the **Mana Mana Beach Club** and watersports center, which offers diving (from $24/person), windsurfing (from $10/hr.), and sailing (from $20/hr.), boat tour ($80/hr.), snorkel sets ($8/day), and a banana boat from $3.50/hr. Direct ferries run to the new, nearby Bandar Benten Telani terminal from Singapore's Tanah Merah Terminal. Call Singapore ☎ 2212328 for information.

In 1996, several new resorts will open. **Banyan Tree Bintan** ☎ 2266123, is being developed at **Tanjung Said** on a 240-ha elevated seafront site. It will have 27 luxuriously appointed Balinese-style villas, perched on hill slopes amidst lush tropical surroundings and constructed partially on stilts to provide breath-taking views overlooking the sea; villas with jacuzzi from $400, and three 2-bedroom pool villas from $660. Its facilities are to include a swimming pool, tennis courts and wind surfing. Also scheduled to open in 1996 is Bintan Lagoon Golf & Country Club ☎ 2212328.

Mapor Island

Popular now with tourists is **Pulau Mapor**, one and a half hours east by small boat, from Kijang, off the coast of Bintan. Mapor is a small, quiet island with lovely clear water and very good snorkeling. **Ronny's Beach Bungalows** offer basic accommodation, around $7 per person including three simple meals (ask at Rommel's Guesthouse for information). There's also a diving club on Mapor, near the main village of Niayang, which will open fully in 1996. But mainly, visitors share this tranquil island with only its 300 residents. Take a morning fishing boat from Kijang (in front of **Pantai Indah** restaurant on Jl Barek Motor). The fare is $1.50.

Karimun (Tanjung Balai)

A small, pretty town, you can reach Tanjung Balai from Singapore, Batam or Bintan. The harbor is it's nub, and is often visited by splendid old Makassar schooners. There are big plans for Karimun, but they concern oil and industry, not tourism, as Karimun is well placed to service Singapore's oil and petroleum industry.

Wisma **Gloria** rambles up a hill overlooking the harbor, layers of terraces and gardens housing simple rooms, the cheapest $5 ☎ 21033. **Wisma Karimun** ☎ 21088 and **Holiday Karimun** Hotel☎ 21165 are the biggest and most expensive hotels, both with good restaurants, bars and discos, and the rates are from $20–$30 respectively. Wisma **Purnama** at Jl Pelabuhan No 38 has rooms with fan for $10. Wisma **Harmoni** at Jl Pelabuhan No 5 also has rooms with fan from $5. Wisma **Nusantara** looks awful at the front but has a nice cafe terrace at the back, overlooking the sea. Rooms are $7 (Jl Nusantara No 194). You can get around the sights—the inscription, the beach and the swimming pool—by bus, although the rickety old wooden buses take their time. Look at the front of the buses for destinations, and go via **Meral** for trips outside town. Taxis are also available, but you'll have to bargain rather hard. It's about $25 for the trip to the beach and back.

There's a **night market** at **Puja Sera**, overlooking the harbor. There's also a **night market** on

Jl Pelabuhan with the usual mix of Chinese and Indonesian food. Along the road from the harbor to Wisma Gloria, there are also *warungs*. There are coffee shops and **Chinese seafood** restaurants along Jl Trikora.

SERVICES

For day trips, there is the **beach** and the **swimming pool** at Bukit Balai Permai. There are some lovely old buildings, shophouses from the 20's, Singapore style, and old Dutch colonial buildings, now the school and the government offices. There's a large **bank** at Jalan Trikora, and also ferry **ticket agents** along Jl Trikora and in the harbor. **Island Adventures** Travel organizes adventure trips which include mountain biking and sea sampanning (a *sampan* is a small wooden Indonesian kayak) in these Western Riau islands. Accommodation is at a basic base camp on Pulau Parit ☎ 3362163 in Singapore, ☎ (0778) 457994 in Batam.

Lingga Archipelago

Once considered off the beaten track, the islands of **Lingga** and **Singkep** are now only a few hours away from Tanjung Pinang by fast ferry. Yet they're still very quiet, Lingga especially. But Lingga's unique history as the one-time home of the Malay sultan's graand court and its reputation for magic, not to mention its ruins, waterfalls, beaches and virgin jungles, give the island a forgotten appeal that can't fail to inspire romantics.

GETTING THERE AND AWAY

Once reached via Dabo on Singkep Island, you can now travel to Lingga direct. Ferry services tend to vary tremendously due to breakages and sudden stoppages, but there is usually at least one boat running. (Ask at Netra Service in the harbor for accurate information on current sailings to Singkep, every day by SuperJet at 1 pm from the town harbor, fare $10, and Lingga.) The trip to Singkep takes three or four hours, and passes many smaller Riau islands. They get prettier and more mountainous, mistier and more mysterious as you go south.

Visitors to Lingga should take the ferry to Pancur, a busy little trading town built on stilts, and from there take a *sampan* ($1.50) across the bay and down a mysterious, mangrove-lined river to Resun, a tiny jetty that suddenly pops out of nowhere. *Ojeks* ($1.50) wait here to take you the half hour to the main town of Daik. There are also direct, but rather slow, boats between Lingga and Tanjung Pinang. The small wooden

Bintan Permai sails to Daik via Penuba ☎ 21314, fare $7. A handful of cargo boats sail overnight to Daik, check with the harbormaster.

Dabo Singkep

There are small boats every day between Daik and Lingga, leaving when the tide's high, fare $1.50. The open sea trip takes 2 hours, depending on the waves. Fast ferries leave Tanjung Pinang daily at 1 pm. The fare is $9, and during the windy season when Dabo harbor is out of use, the boats will stop at **Sungai Buluh**, 30 km from Dabo. There's a connecting bus. To Tanjung Pinang, ferries leave at 9 am, or an alternative is to take the bus to **Jago** on Singkep's northern tip, past some pretty beaches, bays and *kampungs*, and cross by *sampan* to **Pulau Penuba** (75 cents). Penuba is a small, pretty island with one guesthouse, the **Wisma Penuba**, set up on the hill overlooking the harbor. From Penuba take the old wooden *Bintan Permai* to Tanjung Pinang, a 10-hour trip which costs $6, leaving from Penuba at 12.30 am (the same boat leaves Daik at 10 am). From Dabo, there are also boats several times a week to **Jambi**.

ACCOMMODATIONS

There are three places to stay in **Daik** town. **Wisma Daik** is near the Camat's offices, and has rooms up to $10. It's near to Daik village, known as **Kampung Cina**, where the shops and cafes are. Eureka Travel in Singapore, specializing in adventure tours, also have a guesthouse, packages include food and guide (book in Singapore ☎ 4625077). Lastly, there's **Pak Amadi's** hotel, which is none too salubrious, but has rooms at $3 per night. It's in Daik's tiny main street. There are coffee shops and warungs along the street—at the far end, near the Chinese temples, is one of the best, a Chinese place with good seafood and vegetables, built on a back terrace which sticks out over the Daik River.

Dabo is something of a ghost town these days. There are several hotels, none very nice, and most noisy. **Wisma Gapura** at Jl Perusahaan No 14 ☎ 21136, has rooms from $3. **Sri Indah** round the corner has rooms from $3, but is especially noisy. **Sempurna**, above a restaurant on the road from the harbor, is also noisy, and the same price. **Wisma Timah**, up the hill behind the main town off Jl Pemuda, is nicer, calmer and quieter, but more expensive, as is closeby **Wisma Singkep**. **Wisma Kaya Dharma** has double rooms for $3.50. One of the best places to stay is **Pak Rustam's** large, rambling, friendly and calm house favored by travelers. The family will find you an empty room to sleep in, make you feel at home and cook for you for $5.

There are indifferent coffee shops all over Dabo, and two **night markets**. One is no more than a few stalls gathered round the communal TV in the town's square off Jl Merdeka, the other, known as **Kaparinyo**, is round the corner off Jl Pramuka, and offers much more choice. For entertainment, look for posters advertising traditional arts or dances at the open-air **Taman Seni** theater. There's an open air cinema called Mandala on Jl Pramuka for whiling away quiet evenings. By day, the beaches close by the town at **Batu Berdaun** and **Tanjung Jodoh** (the quieter of the two) are clean and pleasant, and an ojek costs about $1 to either one. In the evenings, eat fresh grilled fish on the beach with the locals. There's no longer a bank operating in the town, so remember to take enough money for the stay, (since the closure of the tin mines some years ago, Dabo has been getting quieter and quieter), but there's still a post office off Jl Pahlawan, and a **Telkom** office.

Pekanbaru

Telephone code is 0761.
Pekanbaru, capital of Riau, is a booming oil town and one of the main gateways into Sumatra. There's a well-worn route from Singapore to Pekanbaru, and so on to other spots in mainland Sumatra, via the nearby Riau islands. Tourist and transport facilities are improving, but the province's great rivers are still vital for transportation. Pekanbaru is a pleasant base for exploring Riau's sights.

GETTING THERE

By air (international). Garuda Airlines fly to and from **Singapore**, $100. Pelangi fly from **Kuala Lumpur** (KL) four times a week, $70. Sempati fly to **KL** four times a week, also $70.
By air (domestic). Pekanbaru's Simpang Tiga airport is busy with Merpati and Sempati flights to and from most Indonesian cities. Sample fares are **Jakarta** $125, **Medan** $70, **Palembang** $80, **Batam** $55, **Padang** $40, **Tanjung Pinang** $65. SMAC flies to **Jambi** for $58 and **Rengat** for $30. Book Merpati, Pelangi and Sempati flights at Kota Piring Kencana Travel on Jl Sisingamangaraja 3–7. SMAC is at the bottom end of Jl Sudirman near the harbor.
By bus. Buses arrive and leave from **Bukittinggi** (and the Trans-Sumatra Highway) and **Padang** round the clock, $3 for the scenic 5–6 hour journey. Buses to **Jambi** (10 hours) and on to **Palembang** are just as frequent. The bus terminal is on Jl Nangka, and there are numerous ticket agents there. There are also buses to **Butun** on the Riau coast (3 hours) which connect with direct speedboats to **Batam** Island, which is just a half hour ferry from Singapore.
By sea. Slow ferries, river boats and newer speedboats operate services down the Siak river and on to the **Riau Islands**, transit point for **Java** or **Singapore**. Call at the ferry terminal at the end of Jl Sudirman by the river to check sailing times and prices—$12 for a slow boat up to $30 for a speedboat. These services nearly all sail down the Siak River to **Selat Panjang** on Tebingtinggi Island (see *Riau Islands Practicalities*). From there, fast and slow boats continue on to **Sekupang** on Batam Island, **Tanjung Pinang** on Bintan Island, and **Tanjung Balai** on Karimun Island. Buy a ticket straight through to Riau, or change boats at Selat Panjang if you wish to travel by fast and slow boats.

GETTING AROUND

Pekanbaru city itself has a compact center and it's easy to walk around. **Taxis** are metered for around town journeys; a short trip should be around $2. The bug-like orange *bajaj* taxis are good for short trips ($1–$2). The **buses** are Rp400 a trip, *oplet* Rp250. Taxis can be chartered in town ($4–$5/hour), more for outside town trips. A full day costs $25–$30 per vehicle. A **minibus** from a travel agency listed below for day outings will cost around $50 /day.
By ferry/speedboat. Riau's many rivers are used for transport, and boats leave all morning and early afternoon for destinations along the River Siak, and for connections to other rivers. Check at the harbor and ferry port for accurate details of the many sailings.

ACCOMMODATIONS

Budget and moderate

The **Pekanbaru City** Hotel is on a quiet side street away from Jl Sudirman's traffic. It's spartan and barracks-like, but has clean, serviceable rooms from $12–$50. The more expensive room are comfortable. Discounts available—ask. Late check-out facility, taxi service, travel agent. All rooms with AC. Jl Sam Ratulangi ☎ 33093. Hotel **Anom** is a typical plain but spacious Indonesian style hotel with clean rooms from $12 to $25 with AC, *mandi* and for $1 extra, an old TV! Good Chinese restaurant. Jl Gatot Subroto ☎ 36083. Hotel **Bandarusami** on Jl Sisingamangaraja ☎ 22475 has light rooms with windows, AC, satellite TV and "guest room" for $20–$25. Cheaper rooms with fan from $12. Free breakfast. Central and friendly. Also central, dark and basic but clean and comfy is Hotel **Afri** on Jl Setia Budi ☎ 33190. TV, stereo, breakfast, AC and phone for $15. Located in a pleasant old part of town near some good restaurants.

For budget travelers, **Poppies Homestay** on Jl Cempadak near the bus terminal is popular. It's a big, clean, friendly house with cosy rooms from $2.50 per person. Home cooked food and information available. Recommended. If it's full, there are other homestays and cheap hotels in the area, ask at Poppies. Opposite the terminal on noisy Jl Nangka are basic and boxy but clean hotels like **Linda** which have rooms for $5 upwards.

Luxury

The **Mutiara Merdeka** is one of the best hotels in town, overlooking the Siak River yet located close to the city area. Large pool, quality restaurants serving Western and local food, bar, karaoke and all facilities. The decor tries to reflect Riau cultural influences rather than bland international style. Rooms from $65–$200. Jl Yos Sudarso 12A ☎ 32526, fax 31272. The **Indrapura International** is a rather boxy looking hotel, but very comfortable with pool, good Western, local and Chinese food, bar and disco. Full facilities. Convenient city location. Rooms from $45–$155, Jl Dr Sutomo No 86 ☎ 36233, fax 38906. The **Sri Indrayani** is a smaller, 50-room, welcoming hotel with a Riau flavor, set back from off the road in a quiet garden. Pub, restaurant and tennis. City location. Rooms from $25–$100. Jl Sam Ratulangi ☎ 35600, fax 31870. The **Tasia Ratu** is centrally located, a fairly new building with good facilities—coffee shop serving Western and local food, full room facilities. Jl KH Hasyim Ashari No 10 ☎ 33431, fax 38912. Rooms $25–$70.

FOOD

As is usually the case, the best restaurants are in the top hotels, especially those catering for Western food. The **Mutiara Merdeka** and **Indrapura** have good local, Western and Chinese food. For a good selection of Chinese and seafood try **Pelita Pantai** Floating Restaurant by the ferry harbor at the end of Jl Sudirman. Reasonable prices—prawns, fish and crab from $2.50 per portion. Also in that area of town, on Jl Sudirman and Jl Juanda respectively, are the **Medan** and **Jumbo** seafood restaurants, good food and reasonable prices. The **Ky-Ky** is a small pleasant 'Family steak house' on Jl Sudirman, Western influence and cosy interior. Up near the cheap *losmen* on Jl Nangka is the **Selero Bagindo**, a pleasant, cheap coffee shop with tables outside selling all the usual local dishes, and fruit juices. There's a large hawker center called the **Pekanbaru Food Centre** next to the cinema on Jl Sudirman, open late afternoon and well into the evening for all kinds of cheap local food. There are many *warungs* and coffee shops in the market area.

There's no shortage of tasty, spicy Padang food in Pekanbaru. There's the **Kurnia Baru** on Jl Sudirman, and **Sari Bunda 88** on Jl Gatot Subroto, right near the Anom Hotel. There's a steak house next door to the **Sari Bunda 88**. On Jl Sudirman at Bumi Sakti Plaza there's the **Holland Bakery** selling breads, cakes and sweets, and also a burger and juice bar.

SERVICES

The **Provincial Museum** just outside town on Jl Sudirman has displays of *Melayu* culture. **Banks** are mainly located along Jl Sudirman. Changing US and Singapore $ is no problem, other currency travellers cheques you may need to shop round. **Bank BCA** and **Lippobank** are usually efficient. There are **money changers** in the area of the gold stalls in the central market. The **Telkom** office is on Jl Sudirman, so is the **Post Office**. There are plenty of *wartels* (private telephone offices) around the town's central streets. The **Tourist Information Office** is on Jl Diponegoro, in the administrative complex by the Governor's office. The **Immigration Office** is on Jl Kh Amad Dahlan. There's a **swimming pool** at Jl Hang Tuah, for **golf**, contact Caltex.

Travel agents can organize tours to the Riau mainland sights, and also run tours over into West Sumatra, (Padang, Bukittinggi and the Minang Highlands) and to Jambi (to visit the Kubu people and the beautiful Kerinci Seblat National Park). Try **Kota Piring Kencana** on Jl Sisingamangaraja 3–7 (☎ 21382), or **CPS Tour** on Jl Sudirman 211 ☎ 31866.

Hospitals are at Jl Diponegoro, or try the

Caltex hospital on Jl Yos Sudarso. There's also a private hospital on Jl Mustika. There are **department stores** and **supermarkets** on Jl Sudirman and Jl Nangka, selling bargain clothes, snacks and cakes, drinks, souvenirs, cheap handicrafts and sarongs, and books.

NIGHTLIFE

The only real bars are those in the top hotels, although there's also the **Plaza Pub** in Plaza Shopping Centre and the **Shangri-la Karaoke** on Jl A Yani. The **Pekanbaru Food Centre** is also a lively nighttime meeting place. There are several **cinemas** in town, most show a few Western movies as well as the local fare.

SIDETRIPS

The **Siak Sri Inderapura** can be reached from Pekanbaru by bus (2.5 hours), speedboat 1.5 (hours) or ferry (4 hours). Ferries leave from the harbor. **Siak** town offers accommodation in basic hotels, there's one by the Siak harbor, and also a restaurant. From here it's a short walk to the Siak Palace. It's possible to shop here for textiles, souvenirs and handicrafts. The town has a colorful market. Most travel agents offer this tour.

Public transport is also available to the sights of Riau. To **Bukit Suligi Reserve**, take the bus to Rantau Beringin (3–4 hours) and then a *bemo* to **Tandun**. There look for an *ojek* or a local truck, or trek for one and a half hours into the reserve. There are basic guest houses and simple student accommodation in the forest for keen wildlife spotters.

To **Muara Takus** temple, the bus takes 3–4 hours, head for **Kototengah**, off the main road which leads north-west from Bankinang. Take the bus from the bus terminal, or charter a taxi for the day $30–$50. Muara Takus is not that far from Bukit Suligi, and both can be visited in a day if you have transport.

The Elephant Training Center at Sebanga, Duri, is also four hours' journey away from Pekanbaru. Take the Dumai bus which leaves every hour from the main terminal. On the way stop off at Wana Bahkti, 18 km outside Pekanbaru, to see natural forest and wildlife. Most Pekanbaru travel agents offer very reasonable one or two days all-in tours to these Riau attractions.

To see the tidal waves, set out for **Pankalanbaru** on the Kampar River. Take the bus from the terminal, fare $1 and the journey takes an hour or so. Then take a boat (5 hours) to **Teluk Meranti**. There's a public wooden ferryboat. Basic accommodation is available in the village, ask around. Allow enough time around the full moon to see the wave.

Rengat

Rengat is a small administrative town in the center of Riau province, on the River Indragiri. It's quiet, pleasant and friendly, and offers a refreshing glimpse of small town Malay life in an area unaltered by tourism. There's a small lake 4 km outside the town, with a new hotel and a small lakeside cafe. This is a recreation spot for locals on a Sunday.

In town there is a pretty riverfront with afternoon and evening foodstalls, and many old, traditionally built wooden houses. There are restaurants, banks and a Telkom office, and a big, busy, colorful and cheap market. Passenger boats go up the river to Tembilahan, where there are sea connections to Batam in the Riau islands. From the Riau Islands there are connections to Java, Kalimantan and to Singapore.

GETTING THERE AND AWAY

Take the bus from Pekanbaru 's main terminal at 2 pm ($3, 4 hours). The bus travels via **Air Molek**. From Rengat, night buses carry on to Jambi, (6 hours) and from Jambi on to Palembang. Buses also travel frequently to and from Rengat over to Padang in West Sumatra.

ACCOMMODATIONS AND FOOD

Rengat's Hotel **Bintang Tujuh** on Jl M Boya is good value with rooms from $2.50 up to $18. It's old and rather dark, but it has character and it's clean, and the cheap rooms have balconies. The pricier rooms all have AC, hot water and satellite TV. **Sari Bunda** on Jl Yos Sudarso has comfortable rooms with bathtubs and hot water, AC and TV for $25 upwards. Good restaurant. **Wisma Bunda**, not so fancy as Sari Bunda, has decent rooms from $6, $12 for AC. **Hotel Embun Bunga** is a quiet old colonial bungalow in gardens by the river. The new, gleaming white **Danau Raja** Hotel is built overlooking the pretty lake 4 km outside town, and has well decorated rooms for $30, restaurant coming up soon.

Ask at Digitec Computers on Jl Arif Rachman Hakim 9 for tour advice—they're a group of locals who are setting up a travel co-operative. Free or very cheap accommodations.

The **Talang Mamak** are Riau's 'primitive' tribe. To visit them, either charter a car ($35) or take the bus to Pangkalan Kasai on the Jambi road, then ask the villagers where the tribes are and walk in. The only accommodations are with local families in their huts, or back at the main villages. The bus goes straight on to Jambi from there, leaving Rengat 5 pm and arriving at Jambi late evening. Or travel in the other direction back to Rengat, and so on to Pekanbaru or over to West Sumatra.

— *Julie Heath*

6 Jambi PRACTICALITIES

INCLUDES KERINCI-SEBLAT NATIONAL PARK

Jambi is a pleasant, small but booming city on the banks of the great Batang Hari river. With improved communications—a daily speedboat from Batam, Riau (on Singapore's doorstep) and new, well surfaced roads, entering Sumatra via Jambi is a viable alternative which offers an interesting glimpse of unspoilt, rural Indonesia. The beautiful Kerinci-Seblat National Park, now easily accessible, is a major attraction for walkers and nature lovers alike. *See pages 197—205.*

Jambi

Telephone code is 0741.
There's none of the oppression, traffic and general hassle of other Indonesian cities in Jambi, although as a developing city, it boasts enough facilities to make tourists comfortable.

GETTING THERE AND AWAY

By air. Merpati has flights every day to and from **Jakarta** ($82), and also three times a week to and from **Batam** ($60). The Merpati agent is on Jl Dr Wahidin 95 ☎ 22303. SMAC on Jl Rangkayo Hitam 26 ☎ 22804 has flights to **Rengat** and **Pekanbaru**, and depending

whether the service is on or off, to **Batam**, **Palembang** and **Medan**. Sultan Thaha Airport is about 8 km to the city's south, taxi $2.50. Public transport is available outside the airport.
By bus. Thanks to a fast, surfaced road running from Pekanbaru to Jambi via Rengat, and on to Palembang, Jambi is now reasonably approachable. It's about 9 hours to or from **Pekanbaru** ($8), 4 hours to or from **Palembang** ($3 upwards) and about 28 hours to or from **Jakarta** (prices from $11). Long distance buses leave from terminal **Simpang Kawat** on Jl M Yamin, shorter hops from **TAC** terminal on Jl Bojonegoro.
By sea. From the small port of Kuala Tungkal on Jambi's coast there are daily speed boats to **Batam**, leaving at 10 am ($22), with a connecting minibus service to and from Jambi

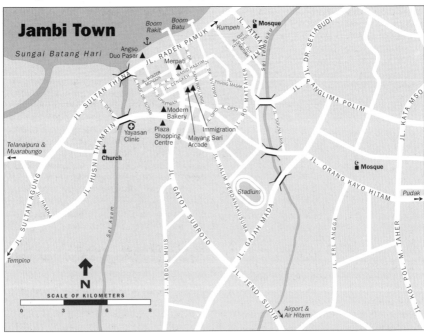

Jambi Town

SCALE OF KILOMETERS
0   3   6   8

($2.50), two hours. For information and pick-ups, call Marina Express on Kuala Tungkal ☎ 217-74. There's also a branch office at the Simpang Kawat bus terminal in Jambi. The trip to Batam takes 6 hours. Three times a week, there are also speedboats to and from **Tanjung Pinang** on Bintan island. There are cargo passenger ferries to Riau or South Sumatra, check with Pelni on Jl Sultan Thaha, near the harbor.

GETTING AROUND

Jambi is a small city and it's pleasant simply strolling around the central streets, squares and market places. For trips further afield, there are *dokars*—small carts driven by red tasselled ponies. Each trip is around $1. *Oplets* or local minibuses start from the market area and in front of the river harbor, and are routed by color—red, yellow, blue and green. Ask at the terminal for your route, fare is 10 cents. A small fleet of battered-looking local **taxis** hangs out on the corner of Jl Mr Assaat, the fare is about $1.50 per trip or $4 per hour. For day charters, Kijang cars are available for around $30–$35 per day—either charter one direct from Terminal TAC, or ask at your hotel or a travel agent.

ACCOMMODATIONS

Budget and Moderate

Jambi's accommodation is adequate but nothing to get excited about. Hotel **Adipura**, recently opened on Jl Brojonegoro, is a welcome addition, set on a quiet street, with a reasonably quality finish and a bit of regional character and flavor about the buildings. Rooms with all facilities, including bath tubs and stereo, range from $20–$35. In the center of town, Hotel **Abadi** (Jl Gatot Subrato ☎ 25600) looks remarkably unprepossessing from the street frontage, but there's a whole new wing at the back with restaurant and karaoke, and in fact it's one of the best hotels in town with all facilities and rooms from $25 upwards. The **Surya** is located over an indoor multi-level carpark, and the restaurant is supposed to be good if you can make it up all the stairs. Rooms from $12. Outside the town to the west and in the new suburb of Telanaipura, where wide, tree-lined roads are home to the province's administration offices, there are a number of rather characterless hotels in the $20–$30 price range, their main recommendation being that the location is quiet, but still close to the town center. These are the Hotel **Telanaipura**, **Merdeka** Hotel and the more traditionally styled **Marisa**, which has overrun its old bungalow and moved into the new block behind. All these out of town hotels stand in their own grounds. The best of these is **Mata Hari** on Jl Sultan Agung ☎ 20457 which has hot and cold water, TV and decent beds in all but the economy rooms. Prices from $14 to $55 for a two-room suite. For those on a tight budget, there's the **Pinang** Hotel on Jl Sutomo in the heart of town, old and rather gloomy, but clean, well kept and with a bit of character about it, rooms go from $8 with fan. There's communal TV, breakfast, and "bar" room service. The **Kartika Jaya** across the road is newer and more modern, with a loud bar, a disco, and a restaurant. AC rooms start from $12.50 up to $30.

SERVICES AND INFORMATION

The **Tourist Information Office** is on Jl Basuki Rahmat, (Kotabaru). If you are persistent, they have information on what to see and do outside of Jambi town, and can even help with travel arrangements. The **Provincial Museum** is about 4 km out of town on Jl Sri Sudewi. The **Immigration Office** is down by the market area on Jl Sam Ratulangi. The General **Post Office** is on Jl Sultan Thaha, and for telecommunications, the privately-run *wartel* telephone offices are most conveniently located—they're found on all the main streets in town. The **Telkom** office is at the base of the easily spotted tall radio antenna which dominates the town center. There are plenty of **banks** in town, all change US and Singapore dollars readily. There's a **swimming pool** at Jl Selamat Riyadi and a **sports center** in Kotabaru. The **hospitals** are at Jl Gen Supratno ☎ 22364 and Jl Dr Setiabuda, and the Army hospital is at Jl Rd Mattheer. There's a large surgery at **Yayasan Bina Sehat Clinic** on Jl Thamrin, with several doctors in attendance.

TOURS

There's not exactly a roaring business doing tourist trips out of Jambi at the present time, although the province has plenty of sights, for example the once nomadic, primitive **Kubu** people to the west of the province. But there are a handful of travel agents who can put together a decent tour, a chartered vehicle and a guide for excursions. Try **Aquavita Jaya** Travel on Jl Gatot Subrato ☎ 26524 or **Mitra Kencana** Travel on Jl Sutomo. **Jayapura Jayakarta** Tour and Travel ☎ 23369 on Jl Wahid Hasyim is also helpful. Local sights: opposite the Governor's office at Telanaipura there's a traditional wooden house in Taman Mayang Mangurai.

FOOD

There are a number of restaurants in Jambi outside of the usual hotel eateries. **Es Jumbo** on Jl Dr Wahidi offers all the usual *mie* and rice dishes, plus *martabak*, *sate* and fruit juices. The town is full of *mie* and *nasi* places, *kedai kopi*

Jambi 6

and *warungs*, and with such a mixed population, the food's mixed too—Chinese, Jambi, Indian and Malay. **Pinang Merah** on Jl Prof Sri Sudewi is known for its local Jambi dishes. The best Padang food is at **Simpang Raya** on Jl Raden Mattahir, but try also **Safari** restaurant on Jl Dr Wahidin for good Padang food. A second Safari on Jl Veteran also has Padang food, and a more exclusive menu in the aircon room upstairs. For Chinese food, the **Terkenal** on Jl Mr Assaat has a good selection of Chinese dishes, as does **Viktoria** on Jl Sultan Iskander, which is air-con, cool and comfortable with a rather bland but clean environment. A seafood meal for two should be no more than $10. **Sari Wangi** on Jl Sudirman and **Sangkuriang** at Sipin (a suburb of the city) have sizzling grilled seafood—all the taxi drivers know them. There's also a selection of bakeries—**Peraneis** on the corner of the **Mayang Sari** arcade offers cakes, breads and fried chicken. The arcade is worth a visit, it's full of stalls and shops and still retains its old style cast iron lampstands and shophouses. The **American Bakery** on Jl Gatot Subrato has pizza, donuts and cake, and the **Modern** French bakery on Jl Thamrin has a good line in cakes and breads, and also a place to sit down. Right opposite the **Modern** is an old wooden house built on a wooden floor with a glass conservatory in front—sandwiched in between the new plazas. Sit down in front behind the shutters and have a refreshing iced lime juice as you marvel at the chaotic jumble that makes up a typical big Indonesian town. For hawker stall food, the **Mayang Sari** arcade, and the town's city squares, are full of stalls, day and night, and the night market stays open until 3 am. Down by the market, near the river, stalls also sell fried snacks day and night. **Kentucky Fried Chicken** is at Dinza Plaza Shopping Centre.

ENTERTAINMENT

Apart from the night markets and sitting about in the squares, the many **cinemas** are the main attraction. Many show good Western movies along with Chinese and Malay fare. As for bars, the **Selamat** on Jl Sisingumajah and the karaoke bar **Lido Palace** are popular, as is **Ceasar Palace** karaoke on Jl Gatot Subrato. The **Kartika** and **Surya** Hotels have discos at weekends.

SHOPPING

The market area around Jl Supratman has great stalls bursting with bargains—terracotta, basketwares, woven mats, ceramics. For fruit and the atmosphere, go to **Angso Duo** market in front of the harbor. The **Mandala** Supermarket is at Jl Mr Assaat, and the **Plaza** Shopping Centre, which offers cheap souvenirs amongst its wares, is on Jl Thamrin. There's a traditional village

across the river, **Mudunglaut**, which has traditional woven crafts to sell. The easiest place to see and buy batik is at the **Handicraft Centre** on Jl Dr Sri Sudewi, which also has traditional Jambi wicker and bamboowork, and sometimes precious stones.

Outside Jambi Town

If you've time to explore Jambi province, other attractions include the eight temples in the temple complex at **Muara Jambi**, a 20-min river trip from Jambi. There's also a small archaeological museum. For river boats, ask at the river port in Jambi, or take the regular service to **Muara Sabak**. Further down the river, a three-hour trip, is the **Berbak Nature Reserve**, the place for keen bird-watchers and wildlife spotters. Less than an hour's speedboat ride from **Nipah Panjang** on Jambi's coast is the lovely **Pulau Berhala** with clean sandy beaches and traditional fishing villages. Near **Bangko**, the Batang Asai River is used for whitewater sports.

The Kubu

To visit the traditionally nomadic Kubu people, although far fewer of them still live the old life today, head for **Bangko** on the way to Sungai Penuh and Kerinci National Park. You'll need to ask around to find out where in their reserve the Kubu are. Or arrange a trip through a travel agent in Jambi, Padang or Bukittinggi. Near Bangko is also the traditional village of **Rantaupanjang**. It's said to be more than 500 years old, and the residents keep many old heirlooms. Further north at **Rantaupandan**, the Rafflesia flowers.

Kerinci-Seblat

The Kerinci-Seblat National Park is an area of outstanding beauty. Many visitors climb Kerinci, although it's by no means an easy stroll, the ascent and descent taking two days. But there's plenty besides Kerinci itself to see in the park area, and some new accommodations have made it easier to explore the park more fully.

GETTING THERE

Sungai Penuh is the main town in the Kerinci area. From Jambi, take the bus to Sungai Penuh via Bangko. From there take a local bus 50 km to the village of **Kersik Tuo**, an hour away, near the Karo Ayu Tea Plantation. The fare is $2.50 and the buses leave in the afternoon. If you'd rather stay in the pleasant, larger town of Sungai Penuh, with its interesting market and tasty night food stalls, stay at **Mata Hari** Hotel, a large, rambling old bungalow with clean, stark rooms for $3. **Yani**, closer to the main square, has old but clean rooms from $5, or the more comfortable **Lempur**, used by tour groups, has rooms with AC and *mandi* from $9.

Kersik Tuo is a small, friendly highland village, home to a group of Indonesians running a co-operative travel and information service called **Eco-Rural Travel**, sponsored by the World Wildlife Fund. Ask for the guide Bajairi Robertus, and he'll send you to one of the five or six homestays run by co-op members in the village, average price $3 per person, meals extra. The group are well informed about the Kerinci Park and its wildlife, and can arrange treks to see all the Park's natural attractions (swamplands, tea plantations, areas of rare flora and fauna, primary forest) with guides, food and camping equipment included in the package price. Also equipment rentals.

They can also advise on exploring, on climbing Kerinci, on trekking alone, and have excellent maps and local guides. The various trips include visits to crater lakes, springs and handicraft villages, swamps and river treks. Most take two or three days, and the average price including guide is less than $10 per person per day.

Mt Kerinci and Lake Gunung Tujuh

Kerinci National Park boasts incredible scenery and many species of wildlife. To climb Mt Kerinci, allow two days and take the southeastern route to the 3,805 m summit, Indonesia's fourth highest. Start from Kersik Tuo. It's possible to climb all year round, bring warm clothes and water for the lower slopes. Climb 6 hours to the camp. It's two hours to the summit next day, and the final ascent is tricky—one local climber died some years ago. Watch out for sulphur fumes. The view is well worth the effort, get there before sunrise.

Lake **Gunung Tujuh** is a crater lake which can be reached by a short bus ride and a brisk 3–4 hours' walk from Kersik Tuo. Start the trek from the village of **Pelompek** 12 km from Kersik Tuo (15 cents by *bemo*). It's only a few km up the track to a quiet get-away-from-it-all rest house in a simple wooden stilt building with a large verandah, guestrooms with beds, and facilities for woodfire cooking downstairs. The *mandi* is out by the nearby river. To check into the "Gunung Tujuh" Resthouse, ask for Mr Matatar Ides when you report at the Park Post (on the track) to Mr Solok, who issues a pass for 50 cents. Mr Ides collects the $1.50 per person accommodation fee. From the resthouse, it's possible to trek to the lake and other parts of the Park. The forest teems with wildlife, and local village boys are only too keen to guide you for less than $1. To climb to Lake Gunung Tujuh, a 3 km by 4 km dramatic crater lake, lonely and surrounded by forest, take the track from the guesthouse. The return climb can be done in a day, but it's also possible to camp. Monkeys and gibbons are common sights. The crater rim is at 2,100 m, there's a short descent to the lakeside. To climb **Mt Hulujujuhan**, the steep peak visible in the distance, cross the lake by the boat of one of the locals fishing at the lake—bargain first!
— *Julie Heath*

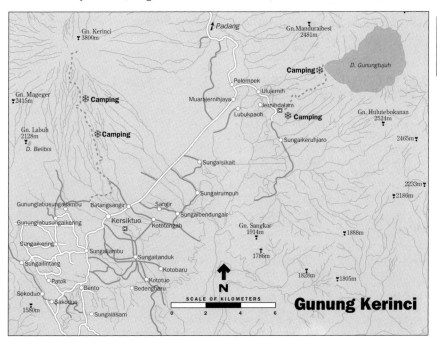

Gunung Kerinci

7 South Sumatra PRACTICALITIES

INCLUDES PALEMBANG, LAKE RANAU, BANGKA AND BELITUNG

Palembang, the capital of South Sumatra province, is a large, busy and not very attractive city. Its main interest for tourists lies in its history and local handicrafts—it attracts many more business visitors than it does sightseers. It's hot and hassly, and also, unlike cosmopolitan Jakarta, tourists can attract a lot of attention as they're still relatively rare. Outside Palembang, improving roads mean that it's relatively easy to travel around the province, and beautiful spots like Lake Ranau, and the islands of Bangka and Belitung, are much more easily accessible. Accommodation outside of these islands, or Palembang itself, tends to be rather simple. *See pages 209—221.*

Palembang

Telephone code is 0711.
Many travelers can find bustling, noisy and crowded central Palembang a little stressful. There are two sections to the city, on the north and south sides of the Musi river, named Ilir and Ulu respectively.

GETTING THERE AND AWAY

By air. Merpati fly six times daily from and to **Jakarta** ($65), four times weekly from and to **Padang** ($72) and **Medan** ($119). Three times a week from and to **Bengkulu** ($41), and once a week (Thurs) to/from **Bandar Lampung** ($36). There are also daily flights from and to **Pangkal Pinang** on Bangka Island ($27), Batam ($60), and regular connections with **Dumai** ($70), **Belitung** (Tanjung Pandan) ($52), **Jambi** ($29), **Rengat** ($58) and **Pekanbaru** ($71). The airport is 12 km out of town, a taxi costs $4.50. Buy a taxi voucher so you don't get overcharged.
By bus. Buses leave round the clock for **Jakarta**. The average fare for an air-con bus is $16, same price to **Bandung**. Check at the Terminal Bis Tujuluh for very regular buses leaving to **Padang**, **Medan**, **Jambi** and **Lubuklinggau** on the Trans-Sumatra Highway. Most bus journeys are long and gruelling—Jakarta 24 hours, and Padang at least 20 hours depending on the roads. Buses off the Trans-Sumatra Highway are not so regular. Local buses such as those to **Lahat**, close to the Pasemah Megaliths, (4 hours) leave regularly from the Pasar Burung bus terminal. The **DAMRI** bus service office is on Jl Kapt A Rivai ☎ 35418. **ALS** on Jl Diponegoro Baru 100 ☎ 350029. ALS has a range of AC buses island-wide, and to Jakarta. For distance taxis, call **Eka Taxi** on ☎ 357263, Jl Letkol Iskandar), chartered or shared taxis available.

By train. Kertapi station is 4 km to the Ulu side of the city—it's a place you should keep a close eye on your belongings. The Sriwijaya Express (fare $8) to Lampung is relatively comfortable and hassle-free. The day trains (the Rajabasa Express) are much cheaper ($2.50), but more crowded. There's also a morning and afternoon train to **Lubuklinggau** ($2—$5) on the Trans-Sumatra Highway, where you can transfer onto a bus for Padang or Jakarta, so cutting out some of the grueling road trip. Trains continue on to Lahat, fare $3.50.
By boat. Jetfoils ($12–$15, 4 hours) leave every morning at 8 am and slower ferries leave in the afternoon (overnight slow boat, $4–$5) from Boom Batu harbor and sail down the Musi River to **Mentok** on Bangka Island. Call PT Carmeta Ampuh ☎ 313790.

GETTING AROUND

Palembang's local city transport is a fleet of open sided *bemos* known as **kijangs**. They run on a complicated one-way system. Different routes use different colored *kijangs,* and fares are 10 cents. There are also local **city buses** and **taxis** —taxi fares start at around $1 for a short town trip. Taxis can be chartered for around $3.50 an hour, bargain hard. For short hops and getting around in the backstreets, take a **becak**, fare around 50 cents, or less if you're a good bargainer. Agree on the price first—make sure it's per *becak*, not per person!

ACCOMMODATIONS

Palembang's hotel accommodations are not really very good value, but it is worth splashing out a few extra dollars on a decent, quiet hotel with a few facilities so you can recover from the city's hassles and find a little peace. Try bargaining, often the hotels aren't full.

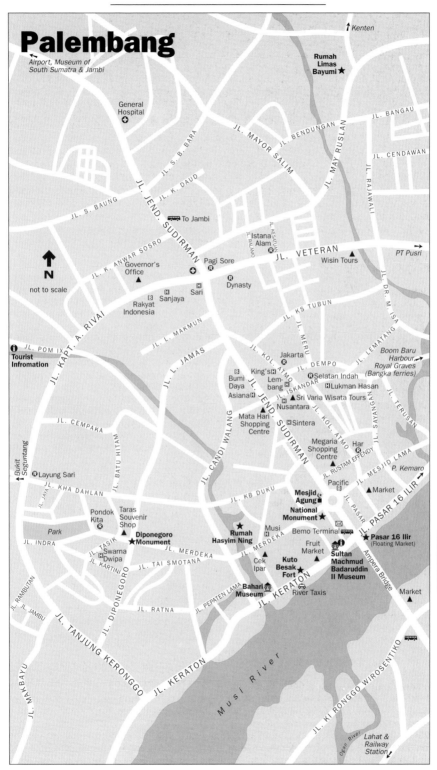

Palembang

Airport, Museum of
South Sumatra & Jambi

↑ Kenten

**Rumah
Limas
Bayumi** ★

General
Hospital ✚

JL. BANGAU

JL. MAYOR SALIM

JL. BENDUNGAN

JL. MAY RUSLAN

JL. CENDAWAN

JL. S. B. BARA

JL. K. DAUD

JL. JEND. SUDIRMAN

JL. S. BAUNG

To Jambi

JL. RAJAWALI

Istana
Alam

JL. RIALMO

JL. KESTURI

JL. VETERAN

PT Pusri →

Wisin Tours ▲

N
not to scale

JL. K. ANWAR SOSRO

Governor's
Office ▲

Pagi Sore
Ⓡ

Dynasty

JL. DR. M. ISA

Sari Ⓗ

Sanjaya Ⓗ

Rakyat
Indonesia Ⓑ

JL. KS TUBUN

JL. L. MAKMUN

JL. MERU

JL. LEMATANG

Boom Baru
Harbour,
Royal Graves
(Bangka ferries)

Tourist
Infromation
ℹ JL. POM IX

JL. KAPT. A. RIVAI

JL. L. JAMAS

JL. KOL. ATMO

Jakarta
Ⓡ

JL. DEMPO

Selatan Indah Ⓡ

Lukman Hasan Ⓗ

JL. SAYANGAN

JL. TERUSAN

King's Ⓗ Ⓑ

Bumi
Daya Ⓡ

Lem-
bang

ISKANDAR

Sri Varia Wisata Tours ▲

Asiana Ⓗ

Nusantara

JL. CEMPAKA

JL. BATU HITAM

Mata Hari
Shopping
Centre

JL. KOL. ATMO

Sintera Ⓗ

Bukit
Seguntang

Layung Sari Ⓡ

JL. JAYA

JL. KHA DAHLAN

JL. CANDI WALANG

JL. JEND. SUDIRMAN

Megaria
Shopping
Centre

JL. RUSTAM EFFENDY

Har

JL. MESJID LAMA

P. Kemaro

Pacific
Ⓑ

Market ▲

Pondok
Kita Ⓡ

Taras
Souvenir
Shop

Park

JL. INDRA

Diponegoro
★ Monument ▲

JL. KB DUKU

JL. MERDEKA

Rumah
Hasyim Ning ★

Musi
Ⓗ

Mesjid
Agung ■

National
Monument ▲

Bemo Terminal 🚌

JL. PASAR

JL. PASAR 16 Ilir

Pasar 16 Ilir
(Floating Market)

S. Sumatra
7

JL. TASIK

Swarna
Ⓗ Dwipa

JL. KARTINI

JL. TAI SMOTANA

JL. MERDEKA

Cek
Ipar ▲

Kuto
Besak
Fort ★

Fruit
Market ▲

Sultan
Machmud
Badaruddin
II Museum ★

Ampera Bridge

JL. RAMBUTAN

JL. JAMBU

JL. DIPONEGORO

JL. RATNA

JL. PEPATEN LAMA

Bahari
Museum ★

JL. KERATON

River Taxis 🚗

Market ▲

JL. MAKBAYU

JL. TANJUNG KERONGGO

JL. KERATON

Musi River

JL. KI RONGGO WIROSENTIKO

Ogan River

Lahat &
Railway
Station →

Budget

The basic **Riau** Penginapan at Jl Dempo 409C (☎ 352011) is clean but dowdy—with small singles (no bath, no fan) from $5. You get what you pay for with Palembang cheapies. **Asiana** on Jl Sudirman, above a row of dingy shops, has bleak rooms for $5. There are plenty of others, ask for recommendations at the Tourist Office.

Moderate

Hotel **Sintera** on busy but very central Jl Jend Sudirman (☎ 354618) is a basic but fairly clean characterless hotel in the typical terraced-style shophouse with rooms from $7 to $20 with AC and bathroom. In the same style, class and price range is the **Sari,** also on Jl Sudirman (☎ 353-319). The **Sriwijaya** on Jl Letkol Iskandar (☎ 354-193) is a warren of boxy rooms, the cheapies overlooking (and overhearing) a school. But clean and helpful, with rooms from $10 to $25, all with bathroom and including breakfast if you like getting up at 5.30 am.

Luxury

Swarna Dwipa on Jl Tasik (☎ 313322) is one of the most pleasant hotels. It's just outside the city, quiet and with a bit of colonial style, good facilities (pool, bamboo bar, restaurant). Rooms from $28–$50, suites $100 plus. The **Sanjaya** on Jl Kapt A Rivai (☎ 350634) offers full facilities like pool, bar and restaurant and gym. Also shops and travel agents with airline agents. Modern and boxy, but decent rooms from $45 to 85, suites $100 plus. **Kings** Hotel on Jl Kol Atmo (☎ 310033) is also relatively new, clean and efficient, with a good coffeeshop and central location. Full facilities. **Lembang**, also on Jl Kol Atmo (☎ 363333) is another modern box with a glitzy lobby, but comfortable rooms from $42–$120 for a suite. Chinese restaurant, coffee shop, bar and disco. All hotels have 21 percent tax to add on to quoted prices.

SERVICES

The **Provincial Tourist Service** is at Jl Pom 1X (Komplek Taman Budaya Sriwijaya) ☎ 357348. The **Regional Tourist Office** is at Jl Rajawali 22 ☎ 358948. There's also another small tourist office behind the Sultan Mahmud Baharuddin Museum near the riverfront (☎ 358450). It's worth a visit to the first office, the friendly staff will turn out *en masse* to help you, and some of the printed information for the South Sumatra province is refreshingly up to date and well presented. The main **banks** are along Jl Jend Sudirman and Jl Kapt A Rivai, all change cash and travelers cheques—at least popular currencies like USD and Sterling. Outside Palembang, in South Sumatra, it's not so easy, be warned. There's a large **Telkom** office on Jl Sudirman and numerous *wartels* (telephone offices) around the city. **Hospitals** are plentiful—the public city hospital is at Jl Sudirman, as is the Charistas hospital. There are several **pharmacies** along Jl Sudirman and in the shopping centers. **Fitness** centers are mostly found in the hotels—Swarna Dwipa, Sanjaya and Kings. For **golf**, contact Pertamina ☎ 313233, it has several courses. There's also a **sports complex** and **swimming pools** at the cultural park which houses the Tourist Office at Jl POM 1X. **Travel agents** can organize tours, and can help with visiting cultural performances. Try Wisata Indah on Jl Veteran 172C (☎ 353811), PT DBS on Jl Sudirman No 10C or Sri Varia Wisata on Jl Letkol Iskandar 16A (☎ 313708).

FOOD

The best Western restaurants are in the top-rated hotels. **Kings Palace** in Kings and Sriwijaya in the Sandjaya Hotel both do good, pricey Chinese food. There's good, reasonable set Asian and Western menus every night at the Swarna Dwipa Hotel's **Seguntang** Restaurant, also a good lively bar. Around the central junction of Jl Sudirman and Jl Letkol Iskandar, right in the hotel and shopping zone, there are coffee shops galore, serving Palembang and Indonesian regulars. Try **Lily** on Jl Letkol Iskander. On the ground floor of **Matahari** shopping center is a cheap, cool restaurant serving all local dishes, Chinese food, fruit juices and desserts. There are also several bakeries, one "French," and a **KFC** upstairs. All the shopping centers have clean, cheap restaurants or food centers with a wide variety of dishes. The supermarkets sell a surprising variety of Western style edible bits and pieces. There are *sate* places along Jl Iskander near the Jl Sudirman junction. **Jakarta** Restaurant on Jl Kol Atmo has Chinese and local food at reasonable prices, it's cool but karaoke-noisy. **Istana Alam**, down Jl Veteran, has good food that you can eat in your own little *pondok* (hut). Live music most nights. For Indian-style *paratha*, *dal* and curries, try one of the many **Har** restaurants in the town. For vegetarian food, try **Chandra** on Jl Veteran.

SHOPPING

Palembang is particularly famous for its textiles and unique red-black-and-gold lacquerwares. Don't leave town without some.

Textiles

Songket is a cotton or silk fabric, usually in a single colour, overlaid with a floating design in gold or silver threads. Most of the weaving is done at home by women on backstrap looms.

Before the war every Palembang girl was expected to wear a self-woven *kain* (wraparound skirt) and *selendang* (shoulder scarf) on her wedding day. Unmarried girls wore *songket* as a head-covering. There are 16 traditional designs, mostly named after flowers—like *bunga cina* (Chinese flower), *bunga jatuh* (fallen flower), *bunga tabur* (drum flower) and *bunga intan* (diamond flower). Pricewise, *songket lepus* is the most expensive, *bunga cina* the next and *bunga intan* a little cheaper.

Jumputan pelangi (meaning "rainbow") is tie-dyed cloth for which Palembang is famous. It is prepared using Chinese silk or fine local cotton. Small beans are tied into the cloth, and the knots are dipped in different dye baths. The result is an intricate geometric pattern of stars, circles, diamonds and paisley on a red, green or purple background. Some of the best pieces have a dark maroon or purple background. As with *kain songket*, *pelangi* comes in sets—a *kain* (approx 180 x 90 cm) and *selendang* or shawl (200 x 40 cm) range from $25 to over $100, depending on the quality of material and workmanship. Be warned that the colors may run on the cheaper ones.

Prada (meaning "gilded") is a type of batik, usually on fine silk, distinguished by intricate designs in gold paint—often triangular. These are rarely produced today, though expensive antique pieces can sometimes be found.

To see *songket* weavers at work, go in the morning to **Cek Ipar** at Jl Ilir Syuro 141, 4 km from the roundabout. Catch a brown minibus from Jl Rumah Bari and ask to be let off at Cek Ipar. The selection is good, but if you have time go to **Songket Husin Rahman**, a small shop a little way back from Cek Ipar where the prices are lower. Wealthy Jakartans shop at both these places so the prices are high. Not much change out of $75 for a *kain* and *selendang* set. Prada is also sold at both places.

A good place to shop for these textiles and other local artifacts is **Taras** on Jl. Merdeka. See the owner, Pak Hamid, who speaks good English and can provide useful information on getting around Palembang. Open till 8.30 pm. Try also **Songket Palace** in the Megaria Shopping Center on Jl T P Rustam Effendi, and **Sumatra Shopping Centre** in Pasar Ilir. Both have a variety of local fabrics. For the cheapest *songkets*, take a bus to Tanjung Batu where they are made, about 70 km south of Palembang. Ask at the tourist office for directions.

Lacquerwares

The introduction of lacquerware to Palembang can probably be traced to gifts brought to the king of Srivijaya by Chinese imperial envoys. Palembang lacquerware is distinguished by distinctive gold-and-black designs on a deep red background. All designs relate to Chinese and Indonesian folklore. The large *jilin* or golden phoenix is associated with a life free of problems; the lion signifies strength; flowers signify beauty; letters and scrolls stand for Buddhist learning; butterflies are for the joys of the night —love, sleep and sweet dreams.The lacquer process is complex, requiring 10 steps from start to finish, involving three or more people. Work on a single piece can take four days. The most complex items are reproductions of Srivijayan period furniture and tall jars.The first stage involves sealing the wooden core with red ochre, rubbing it down and coating it again. After the second rub-down the craftsman draws the design. Then the background is painted with China ink. The unique local lacquer is made from ant's nests mixed with methylated spirits in a proportion of 2:1, left to stand for three days. The murky brown liquid is filtered and three successive coats are applied; each one dried in the sun and gently rubbed smooth with sandpaper. Finally, two more coats are applied with a thinner mixture of ant's nest to spirits at 1:2. After drying in the sun, the product is ready.

Most pots are of mahogany but ceramic, which is cheaper, is also used. Prices range from $5 for a small sugar bowl up to $1,000 for a 1.8 m pot. The best mahogany is from **Sebalik** village up the Musi River, near Gasing Laut. There is significant demand in Palembang for reproduction lacquered furniture, bordered by scroll-like flowers in gold.

For a wide selection of quality lacquerwares, go to Palembang's **Serelo** area where many shops sell a range of antique and craft items. **Mir Senen International** at Jl H M Amin 39 is a good starting point. See the owner, who speaks good English and can take you to local craftsmen and designers. Try also **Mekar Jaya** on Jl Slamet Riyadi, which probably has the largest selection of lacquerwares in Palembang, and if you go before 4 pm you can see the craftsmen at work behind the shop.

Rattan products

The *tikar* mats produced here originate in a small village outside Palembang called Gasing Laut. The mats are distinguished by simple red-and-green checked designs and are produced by women at home. A good place to start is Mir Senen International (see above). For a wide range of rattan handicrafts and furniture, go to Kampong 2 Ilir and 3 Ilir. **Siti Zahara** on Jl Cut Nyak Dhien 16 Ilir Barat II, 3 km from the city, has excellent but expensive rattan furniture and can arrange export.

Shellcrafts

The latest craft to arrive in Palembang is shellcrafts. Lampshades, wall hangings, plaques, ashtrays and many other items are produced using delicate, opaque shells. The factory moved here from the Philippines in 1990, and already employs over 700 people. The shells are from Surabaya, East Java, and must go through various processes: washing in acid, cutting, heating over charcoal until they are translucent, then dipping in hydrogen peroxide so they can be shaped into boxes. Painting is done with natural varnish. Finished goods are exported to Italy and sold in local department stores.

To see the craftsmen and women at work and buy at wholesale prices, go to **Kerang Indah** Rattan and Shells Handicrafts, Jl Tanjung Banten 127, 16 Ulu. Cross the Ampera Bridge to the south and turn left to Plaju. Continue for 2 km and turn right for about 500 m. Ask for Pak Sudjono or Jaime Taguba, the Philippine consultant.

Antiques

For a good selection of antiques—from porcelain cups to old grandfather clocks—and a wide selection of local hunting and farming implements, visit the antique shops in the Serelo area. Try **Sriwijaya Antique and Art Shop** at Jl H M Amin 43. A short walk brings you to Jl Faqih Jalahuddin—a narrow street with old buildings lined with antique shops. Hard bargaining is required as well as a tight grip on your wallet!

NIGHTLIFE

The **Lembang** and **Kings Hotel** both have nightclubs, but hostesses abound. **Kings Palace** restaurant and **Sandjaya bar and restaurant** have karaoke, as do a few of the more upmarket, air-con restaurants. There are plenty of cinemas, **Plaza 21** often has quite recent Western movies. The **Swarna Dwipa bar** is the happening place at weekends—an expat haunt. Ask at the hotel for discos, which come and go, or change names, rather quickly. Or ask at the Tourist Office for those recommended to tourists.

CULTURE

It's difficult to get to see **traditional dances** or **rituals**, they're rare as only rich families can afford them—for example at weddings. But you'll usually be welcome if there is a traditional wedding going on—ask at the Tourist Office. The **Bidar races**, in which long rowing boats race along the river, are held on anniversaries such as National Day, 17th August.

Lahat

Lahat can be used as a base for visiting the Pasemah Plateau, site of the megalithic remains. Frequent buses pass here going north and south on the Trans-Sumatra Highway. The bus takes 4 hours, price $3. The night train,

which is the same price, leaves Kertapi station at 8 pm, and there's also a pricier day train. Buses leave from the Pasar Burung Terminal every hour or so. Lahat Buses leave in the morning from Lahat's terminal to Pagaralam, the main town of the Pasemah region, or charter a taxi for the day for $20–$25.

ACCOMMODATIONS

Mediocre at best. There's really only one main street—Jl Mayor Ruslan—and most of the hotels either front or back this street, where the bus terminal also is. **Hotel Permata** is probably best value, with dark but clean rooms for $6 upwards. There's a restaurant next door. **Nusantara** is a little more upmarket, with rooms from $9, larger, more comfortable and also clean. **Simpang** is poky, smelly and old, **Simpang Baru** is more comfortable and cleaner. Rooms with *mandi* and ancient TV for $8 upwards.

FOOD AND SERVICES

There are *warungs* all along the main street, and a small, pleasant night market lit by kerosene lamps in the *pasar* area after sunset. Cheap rattan and basket products are on sale in the market. For information on the surrounding area, including the **elephant training camp** 28 km away, the many caves and waterfalls, also cultural dance and the Pasemah Plateau, look for knowledgeable Mr Kursni at the **Lahat Tourist Office** on Jl Letnan Amir Hamzah No 150 (☎ 22469), a short *becak* ride from the town.

Pagaralam

A busy little town very close to the Pasemah Plateau megaliths, with a maze-like *pasar*, surrounded by fertile rice and vegetable fields. Expect attention from locals. There are many simple restaurants—for Padang food try **Dua Putra** on Jl M Ruslan. There's a **Telkom** office and **banks**, but it's not wise to guarantee money changing facilities in small towns. Great spot for *bonsai* fans—there are several enthusiastic practitioners and clubs in town. The bus terminal is less than 2 km from town. The trip from Palembang takes 8–10 hours, fare $2.50. Local buses leave in the morning from Lahat to Pagaralam, fare less than a dollar. A taxi can be chartered for the day trip, including visiting the megaliths, for $20–$25. From Pagaralam, buses continue on to Bengkulu. To travel south, backtrack to the Trans-Sumatra Highway.

ACCOMMODATIONS

Losmen **Mirasa** is the most pleasant place to stay. The lady owner speaks good English, is friendly and can organize cars, bus tickets and taxi pick-ups and guides at sensible prices. The place is a family house with great home cooking. A pleasant place to pass the evening without hassle and with a cold beer. Simple rooms in the maze-like house from $3–$12. Hotel **Dharmakarya**, despite its rather garish external decor, offers pleasant terraced rooms in a nice garden setting for $6 upwards. Both hotels have decent restaurants, and there are plenty more in town. There's also the rundown **Telaga Biru** hotel right in town near the market, downstairs is one of the Palembang bus agents.

VISITING THE MEGALITHS

It's easiest to charter a car for the visits—a few of the sites are within walking distance of the town, but most aren't. Public transport is slow and unreliable. $10–$12 is the average price for a taxi, and add a few dollars for guiding—the staff at Losmen Mirasa know good guides. Many young locals know less than tourists do about the stones, so choose carefully! There's some rice *padi* walking to do, with plenty of attendant mud, so wear sensible shoes. A "donation" of Rp1,000 is expected,to contribute to the stones' upkeep. The keepers will find you.

Climbing Mt Dempo

Gunung Dempo (3,159 m) dominates the Pasemah Plateau. Get your permit in Pagaralam from the police office, or ask the staff at Losmen Mirasa, who can also arrange guides. Either climb overnight, or during the day and spend the night at a campsite below the crater rim and lake. Take a *bemo* to **Kampung Dua** on the tea estate, and then walk to Pembibitan tea nursery. The track is signposted. The steep climb to the campsite takes 5–6 hours. Take water and warm clothes if camping. There's a super view from the crater rim.

Baturaja

A fairly large, busy town, there's no reason to stay here. But if you do, there are plenty of hotels. Try **Kencana II**, **Kurnia** or **Horison**, all clean, typical local hotels with stark boxy rooms and simple facilities, located in the compact center of town. Rooms from $4 to $15 for AC and mandi. **Banjarsari**, 15 km outside town on the country road to Muara Enim, is a better, quieter place to stay, clean rooms from $9.

Lake Ranau

Lake Ranau is a beautiful, cool lake resort set among terraced rice paddies in the shadow of the Bukit Barisan range. Like a small Toba without the tourist influx—yet. There are plenty of interesting caves, waterfalls and villages in the area, or you can simply relax and swim in the lake with its hot springs. Good value.

GETTING THERE

From Baturaja's main street, take a minibus—last trip 4 pm daily but it's best to start much earlier or you might find yourself stuck half way—to **Simpang Sender** or **Banding Agung**, both lakeside villages. Simpang Sender is closest to the better, but pricier accommodation. Banding Agung offers pleasant, cheaper *losmen* but none with a real lakeside position. It's a slow, windy trip from Baturaja through pretty villages. For a local adventure, or if your bus has to wait over for passengers, stop off at **Muara Dua**, a small *kampung* with a few *warungs* around the single square, and a very friendly local population, most of whom will sit and talk with you, or play local songs. A touch of real rural Indonesia. Stay at Losmen **Indonesia**, above the square's restaurant, an old, dark wooden house with creaky 4-posters, for $3. The minibus continues on to the lake in the early morning. From Simpang Sender, take a local *bemo* or taxi to the hotel, **Wisma Pusri**, and turn in the long drive. To rejoin the Trans Sumatra Highway, or if approaching from the south, the route is via Liwa and Bukit Kemuning.

ACCOMMODATIONS

Wisma Pusri on the SE shore of Lake Ranau is the pleasantest place to stay. Large well-furnished chalets with bathroom, fan and a large balcony set in lovely gardens overlook the tranquil lake, $18 per chalet. It's cool enough at night for blankets, and the main reception has a good restaurant with home cooking at reasonable prices, and a small bar. Poor travelers are allowed to camp or stash a mattress in the meeting room on occasion. Friendly Manager Pak Suwarso has good English and local knowledge. The odd group from Jakarta or Lampung stays at the weekend. Boats for hire. Next door is the run-down **Wisma Putri**, an old building with great potential but sadly neglected. If it's open, $5 per room. **Banding Agung**, a poor village with a small market, a few *warungs* and a lakeside location, offers cheaper accommodation. There's Wisma **Seminung Permai**, near the lake and *warungs*, homely and clean Penginapan **Danau Indah**, a lovely old house with small rooms and a spacious, pleasant lounge area, from $1.50. The **PU Mess** near the lakefront offers a few rooms in a spartan but clean house, with a friendly Javanese family in attendance. Including good home cooking, $5 per person. (**Bangka** and **Belitung**, see over.)

— Julie Heath, David Booth, Nancy Caldwell

S. Sumatra

7

Bangka

Bangka's beaches are among the finest in Indonesia. The island also has good hotels, and the place is just waiting to be "discovered."

Pangkalpinang

Telephone code is 0717.
A small but busy town, Pangkalpinang is Bangka's administrative and commercial center. It's pleasant, but the beaches around nearby Sungailiat remain the island's biggest attraction.

GETTING THERE

By air. Merpati flies to and from **Jakarta** twice a day (1 hr/$70). Sempati flies to and from Jakarta on Tues and Fri (same fare). Merpati has daily flights to and from **Palembang** ($30), and **Batam** flights twice weekly ($65). Sempati flies to Batam on Tues, Wed and Thurs ($60). Deraya flies to and from neighboring **Belitung** island every day ($25). If it's running, SMAC fly to and from Batam, **Tanjung Pinang** and **Dabo Singkep**, check with a travel agent for details.

The airport is 6 km south of town on the road to Koba. Taxi drivers crowd around as you step outside. Bargain hard; a ride into town should cost $4. To the beach hotels it costs $8 (Parai Tenggiri) and $15 (Remodong) but if you have advance bookings they pick you up.

By sea. Every week, a Pelni passenger ship sails from **Jakarta** to Mentok on Bangka's west coast ($18), to **Tanjung Pinang** (on Bintan Island, opposite Singapore) and **Belawan** (Medan). The same trip is done in reverse, also weekly. There are also ferries between Pangkalpinang and Tanjung Pinang, fare is $45, and the trip takes 12 hours.

Ferries (9 hrs/$4) and jet foils (3 hrs/$11) travel up and down the Musi River and across the Bangka Strait between **Palembang** and Mentok twice daily. Jet foils depart Palembang at 8.30 am and 10 am. From Mentok, a 3–4 hour bus ride brings you to Pangkalpinang, Sungailiat or Belinyu. Take the DBS bus ($2.50) from the ferry terminal, it leaves directly to the town. There may not be a local bus for a while from the terminal 1 km away. There is also a ferry from Palembang to Kayu Arang, on Bangka's north coast (near Belinyu), close to the beach resorts and only an hour from Pangkalpinang.

A ferry also travels to Pangkalpinang from Tanjung Pandan (**Belitung**) every Wed and Sun (10 hrs/$7), and returns to Belitung on Fri and Mon, leaving in the afternoon.

GETTING AROUND

Pangkalpinang is small enough to explore on foot. The main street, Jl Sudirman, runs north-south, and everything is here—restaurants, bakeries, shops, banks, airline offices and travel agents. Stop in at **DBS Tour & Travel**, or one of its neighbors, to inquire about tours and car rentals.

Old buses and minibuses run all over the island and are cheap (under $1 to anywhere on the island) but service is infrequent, once or twice in the mornings only between main towns (the exception is between Mentok and Pangkalpinang). If you have time this is fine; otherwise hire a car. Rates are negotiable. Expect to pay $25 for local trips, and up to $65 a day.

ACCOMMODATIONS

There is no shortage of hotels in Pangkalpinang but none is very nice and you are better off in the beach resorts. The best in town is the **Menumbing** (65 rooms) Jl Gereja ☎ 22990, 22992. $10 to $28; the cheaper rooms at the back are pleasanter. If this is full, try the **Wisma Jaya II** (10 rooms), Jl Mangkol 10 ☎ 21656, offering private bath and TV for $15–$24. **Wisma Jaya I** (10 rooms) Jl Depati Amir 8 ☎ 21696, is housed in a large, old, rambling house with some character, and there is a garden restaurant which features live music on Saturday nights. $9–$38. The but new and clean **Bukit Shofa** (23 rooms) Jl Masjid Jamik 43 ☎ 21062, has small, noisy rooms with *mandi* for $3.50 to $5, but the place is characterless.

Bangka

Kayu Arang
Ferry
to Palembang
Romodong
Beach
Laut Cina Selatan
Teluk Klabat
Matras Beach
Bakit
Belinyu
Hakok(Parai Tenggiri) Beach
Teluk Kampa
Pusuk
Pugul
Hot Spring
Sungailiat
Mt. Menumbing 415m ▲
Terentang
Plangas
Kapuk
Baturusa
Mentok
Ferry
to Palembang
Tempilang
Petaling
Kotakapur
PANGKAL PINANG
Ferry to Belitung
Pangkol
Cape Selokan
Koba
Cape Berikat
Payung
Airbara
Lubukbesar
Batu Betumpang
Kepoh
P. LEPAR
Toboali
Sadai
Cape Baginda
Cape Kait

N

SCALE OF KILOMETERS
0   20   40   60

FOOD

Bangka offers a wide variety of delicious, fresh seafood. Wild boar or monkey meat—a local cure for rheumatism—are occasionally served.

Restaurant **Asori** on Jl Kampung Bintang is the best place for seafood. Try their crabs in oyster sauce and steamed prawns. Another good seafood restaurant is **Tirta Garden** on Jl Lembawai; the place is pleasanter but the food not as tasty. There's also karaoke here. **Bukit Raya**, on the road to the airport, also specializes in seafood, as does **Hew Ko Sui** on Jl Kep Bintang Dalam RT XII. **Anggrek** on Jl Mayor Syafrie Rachman offers fried chicken, *gado gado* and more local dishes. Down by the market area there are several cheap, clean Chinese coffee shops. Sweet and savory bread rolls and croissants are sold in the **French Bakery** on Jl. Sudirman. The **Dutch Bakery** across the road offers more substantial fare. The **Wisma Jaya** garden restaurant is cheap and pleasant.

SHOPPING

The studio of **Tjoeng Khoen Foe**, Jl Sudirman (☎ 22581), sells miniature boats, Malay houses and other objects of beaten tin. **Peltin**, the smelting firm, has a shop at the airport selling pewter crafts. Although it is less pure than Tjoeng's tinwares, the pewter is lead-free, cheaper and more durable, and there is greater variety. *Akar bahar* is the root of a mangrove plant—fashioned by coastal villagers into walking sticks, bracelets and other accessories.

SERVICES

Most **banks** and **travel offices** are on Jl Sudirman. The **Tourist Information Office** is on Jl Sudirman in Sungailiat (☎ 92496). There are **Telkom** offices and **Post Offices** in Pangkalpinang and Sungailiat.

Bangka Beaches

Most visitors come to Bangka for the gleaming white beaches. **Parai Tenggiri Beach**, 33 km north of Pangkalpinang, boasts a spectacular rock-studded bay and the island's biggest hotel. Within walking distance is long and sandy Matras Beach. **Romodong Beach** is past Belinyu on the north shore—clear, calm waters and endless sands. Book in advance to ensure a room and an airport pick-up. Add 15.5 percent tax and service to the prices below. **Parai Beach** (100 rooms) is Bangka's newest resort—modern bungalows in an idyllic setting. Swimming pool, disco, watersports. $45–$75; $15 surcharge on weekends. You can book in Jakarta ☎ (021) 356025, fax: 356383, or

through the Bangka office ☎ (0717) 92133, 92134, fax: 92155. **Romodong Beach** (10 cottages) has pleasant AC cottages in a landscaped garden facing the sea. The restaurant serves good seafood. Cottages are $23 to $43. Busy on weekends; book on ☎ (0717) 21573; or in Jakarta ☎ (021) 5604150, fax: 594469. **Tanjung Pesona Resort** (☎ 92313), **Bangka City Hotel** (☎ 92090) and the **Uber Beach Hotel** (Pantai Teluk Uber) in Sungailiat all offer good restaurants and accommodation from $20.

Tanjung Pandan (Belitung)

Telephone code is 0719.
Belitung's beaches, if anything, are even nicer than those on Bangka. Hotel and travel facilities are developing quickly.

GETTING THERE AND AROUND

Tanjung Pandan is small enough to explore on foot. *Bemos* go around town for Rp200. Rent an old car for $20 to $30 per day. There are daily flights and twice weekly ferries from Bangka.

ACCOMMODATIONS

The best hotel in town is **Martani** (45 rooms) Jl Yos Sudarso, ☎ 432, with clean and spacious, AC rooms for $14–$28; smaller rooms with fan for $7 to $10. **Wisma Dewi** on Jl Srivijaya is a rambling old family mansion with 12 simple, clean rooms. It has a warm, cozy atmosphere and a good restaurant. $8.50 to $11 with AC and shower, breakfast included. **Wisma Timah** on Jl Melati is the tin company's guesthouse. If they are not full, the cottages can be rented for $15 including meals.

Belitung Beaches

The west coast beaches around Tanjung Pandan have brown sand and are polluted, so head for the great beaches on the north or southwest. **Tanjung Kelayang**, 27 km north of town, has the best beaches on the island. If you have a car, stay for the sunset. To get to Tanjung Kelayang by public transport, take a minibus to Tanjung Binga (24 km), where you can catch another one to the beach. You can stay at the **Kelayang Beach Hotel**, which has 14 large rooms with showers for $7.50 to $10. Several more large resorts are being developed in this area, and will shortly open.

Gembira Bay is a lovely beach 60 km south of town. Head for **Membalong** (45 km) where you can get another *bemo* to "Teluk Gembira." As yet, there is no hotel—you can stay later if you charter a taxi, as the last minibus returns late afternoon.

— *Amir Sidharta, Sandra Hamid, Julie Heath*

Bengkulu PRACTICALITIES

INCLUDES REJANG LEBONG DISTRICT

8

Bengkulu is a small, laid back, spacious and friendly town, with a forgotten colonial history and a sleepy air. It's growing rapidly, but as yet there's no high rise development or big shopping complexes. But it's just big enough to offer services such as the odd department store, travel agents and decent hotels. There are no traffic hassles and the pace is slow and leisurely. Within minutes you can be out of the town and on the beach or in the highlands. Telephone code is 0736. *See pages 225–229.*

GETTING THERE AND AWAY

By air. There are now twice daily flights to and from **Jakarta** ($85), and also flights several times a week to and from **Palembang** ($60). The main **Merpati** office is in Hotel Asia on Jl A Yani ☎ 21901.

By road. There are buses from the new Air Sibakul terminal 8 km out of town to and from **Palembang** ($7–$10) via **Pagaralam**, to and from **Lubuklinggau** on the Trans-Sumatra Highway ($2–$4), and from **Padang** via **Sungai Penuh** ($5). Except for the trip east to the Trans-Sumatra Highway, bus journeys to Bengkulu take many long, usually overnight, hours as the roads are badly surfaced, narrow and windy. In addition, the buses are anything but express. Tickets can be bought at the bus terminal at Air Sibakul, or from the many bus ticket offices along Jl Bali. The DAMRI bus office is on Jl Kalimantan. Most of the services pick up passengers in town before they get to the terminal. There's no railway to Bengkulu, but there is a train from Palembang to Lubuklinggau, which is only 6 hours bus journey from Bengkulu.

By sea. Arriving by sea, there are boats connecting Bengkulu to Padang. Check out Pelni, which may stop off, or a passenger-carrying cargo boat. Check at the Pulau Baai harbor 14 km outside the town. From here, there are boats to Enggano Island.

GETTING AROUND

Walking is the easiest way, as the town is small, and sights such as Fort Marlborough and the Jamik mosque can be seen on foot. *Bemos* or *oplets* rides in town costs 10 cents. There are *becaks* for short distances, bargain hard, fares start at 50 cents. Pony cart or *bendi* fares also start from 50 cents. **Taxis** can be chartered for out of town trips for the day ($20–$25) or the hour ($4) from hotels or travel agents, or simply by asking the driver. Most vehicles in

Bengkulu are willing to turn into taxis at a moment's notice. One way trips to the local attractions close to town should cost no more than $1–$2.

ACCOMMODATIONS

Moderate and Budget

The best accommodation is on the beach just outside the town. The sea is OK for swimming, but it's the fresh breeze and the stunning sunsets over the water that make the location so welcoming. **Nala Seaside Cottages** (Jl Pantai Nala 133 ☎ 21855) has comfortable chalets with sea view, air-con and bath for $14–$45 (the VIP chalets have TV and hot water). Ask for cheaper rooms at the back, $7. There's a pleasant cafe and bar, a tour and travel service, and room service! Ask for Rozi, he's a great guide and available for tours when he's not working. Hotel **Horison** is on the hill overlooking the beach, it's new and glaringly white and looks like a hospital. The rooms are clean and comfortable, and range from $23–$42. Hotel **Pantai Panjang** along the beach is an older place with recreation facilities and comfortable, all-facilities rooms. Prices from $20 to $40. It's pleasant and well located. In the town, the new, clean Hotel **Niaga** (☎ 24852) on Jl S Parman 408 has rooms for $16–$30, all with hot water, TV and AC. There's a restaurant serving European, Chinese and local food, and 24 hour room service. Hotel **Dena**, which claims to be the one-time second home of Raffles, has pricey rooms ($40 and up), and an upmarket dress policy—no pajamas allowed in the corridors! It's on Jl Fatmawati. Hotel **Asia**, Jl A Yani (☎ 21091) is convenient, has a restaurant and travel agent, and the rooms are clean. Rates are from $11–$43. For the cheapies, try the Kampung Cina area. Penginapan **Aman** on Jl Pendaikian is an old barracks of a place with dingy but clean rooms and bathrooms, and has rooms for $2.50.

8

Bengkulu

There's also a pleasant and clean homestay on Jl Kenaga 99 at the very good **Ragil Kuning** Indonesian restaurant (☎ 22682). It's friendly and the rooms go for $3.50.

FOOD

There are *warungs* all over town, especially around the Fort area and Jl Abidini. There are many *sate* and *mie goreng* places on Jl Supratman. The **Si Kebayan** restaurant on Jl Sudirman is a pleasant *pondok*-style (small huts) place selling Javanese food. Javanese fare is also on offer at **Sri Solo** on Jl Supratno. For Chinese food at reasonable prices, try **Sari Rasa** Rumah Makan on Jl A Yani—around $10 for two for a meal of fish, vegetables and chicken. There's a sister restaurant two doors away serving tasty *mie* dishes—also good value. For snacks, try the **Ghandi Bakery**—good breads and cakes. For treats like chocolate and cakes, try **Puncak** department store, behind the clothes store at Jl Supratno No 6A. Also alcoholic spirits. For seafood, there's an excellent *warung* which opens in front of the mosque on Jl A Yani in the evenings. The Hotel **Niaga** has a good Western restaurant, and there are Padang places, such as the well-known **Simpang Raya**, on Jl Supratno.

NIGHTLIFE

Bengkulu doesn't offer much, but it isn't lights out at dusk. Apart from the hotel bars, the best of which is probably the **Horison** which has live music, there's the **Sweet Pub** 6 km out of town, ask the taxi to bring you to km 6. There's the **Monaco Disco** on Jl S Parman. One of the best bets for an evening out is the **Nala Seaside Cottages** cafe and bar, which is pleasant and open 24 hours for any late night tipplers.

SHOPPING

The **Puncak** Department Store on Jl Supratno has a surprisingly wide range of cheap rattan and bamboo wares. Also decorative fans and sarongs. There's also a good selection in Pasar Minggu if one is prepared to scrummage around. **Gedung Kerajinan** is a Handicraft Centre next to the Pantai Panjang hotel on Jl Pantai Nala, with touristy handicrafts. There's a good shop for rummaging in on Jl Putri Gadang Cempaka—the **Gadang Cempaka** stocks old and new sarongs, musical instruments, chests, jewelry and lots of tack. Gold is a good buy in Bengkulu—check out the goldsmiths in Kampung Cina.

SERVICES

The **Tourist Information Office** is at Jl Pembangunan 14 ☎ 21272. There are travel agents who handle tours and flights—Swadaya on Jl S Parman, or **CSH 88** Travel on Jl Supratno 88 ☎ 22385. There are **banks** and **money changers** along Jl A Yani and Jl S Parman, also on Jl Supratno. Bank BCA on Jl Supratno and Bank Bumi Daya are probably the most accommodating. There's a big public **hospital** on Jl Padang Harapan, and a **polyclinic** on Jl A Yani. The **Immigration Office** is on Jl Pembangunan Padang Harapan. The **Forestry Office** (PHPA) is on Jl Mahoni, and issues permits to visit the National Parks. The **Post Office** is on Jl S Parman. The **Telkom** office is on the corner of Jl R A Hadi, and there are also private telephone offices (*wartel*)—there's a large one on Jl Supratno.

SIDETRIPS

To see sights such as **Danau Dendam Tak Sudah**, take local transport (10 cents) or a $1 taxi. **Pulau Tikus** can be visited by the day, charter a local boat from the town harbor near the fort. A one day charter is around $20, and the journey to the island takes an hour. There's a deserted beach, no one around but the lighthouse keepers. Bring your snorkel and some food and water. To **Curup**, main town of the **Rejang Lebong** district, take a local bus for $1.50 from the town *oplet* terminal, or charter a car early in the day if you don't want to overnight there ($25). The trip takes three hours, and the area is probably best visited for two days rather than one, as there's a lot to see. There are a handful of *losmen* in Curup, around the bus terminal. Try the **Kinantan** or **Sriwijaya** for basic rooms. Slightly more expensive is the Penginapan **Garuda** on Jl Kartini, but the best—and most expensive—is the Wisma **Sarinah** on Jl Basuki Rachmad 99. There are cafes and *warungs* in the main street—Setia Utama serves good, cheap local food.

To climb **Bukit Kaba**, which periodically, if infrequently, erupts and kills people (so be warned), head for Kampung Bukit Kaba and look for a reliable local guide to bring you to **Sumber Urip**, where you start climbing. It's not a difficult climb—go up early morning and come down at lunch time. The view from the top is worth the climb. From Curup, the trip on to **Muara Aman**, the old gold mining village, takes three hours and costs $1.50. Muara Aman is a good base for exploring the **Tambang Sawah** highlands—an excellent area for walkers. There's a limited choice of accommodation in Muara Aman—try **Trido** for the cheapest rooms, **Sukma Jaya** for the priciest (☎ 8), on Jl Pelabuhan. To see the **Rafflesia** flower, head for either **Pagar Gunung**, **Kepahyang** (in the Rejang Lebong district) or **Taba Penanjung** in North Bengkulu. Charter a taxi or take local *bemos* from the town terminal. The flowers can be in bloom any time.

— *Julie Heath*

9 **Lampung** PRACTICALITIES

INCLUDES BANDAR LAMPUNG, WAY KAMBAS & KRAKATAU

Lampung province is well worth a visit as it's surprisingly well endowed with good value hotels, tourist sites, national parks, beaches and facilities. Teluk Betung and Tanjung Karang are the two towns which now combine to form the pleasant, hilly, spacious capital city of Bandar Lampung. Many of the scenic coastal villages have a Javanese flavor, and the province's main attractions include the famous Krakatau volcano and a large elephant training center. *See pages 233—243.*

Bandar Lampung

Telephone code is 0721.
The two city halves are joined by the main road of Jl Raden Intan, you'll see the colorful tiled boundary wall beside the road. The city area is pleasant and easy-going, and as it's rather small, in no time you're out in green suburbs.

GETTING THERE AND AWAY

By air. There are at least six daily Merpati flights between Bandar Lampung and **Jakarta** ($32). Bandar Lampung's Branti Airport is 25 km to the city's north, take a taxi for $5 or a

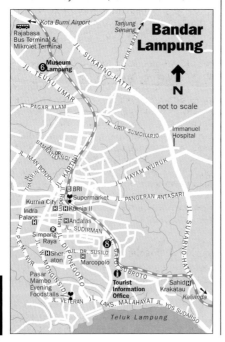

bus for $1. There are also daily flights from and to **Palembang**, and connections to several other Sumatran destinations from there ($45).
By sea. There are round the clock ferries to **Merak**, Java, from **Bakauheni** at Lampung's tip, 85 km from Bandar Lampung (BL). The ferry crossing takes less than two hours and the fare is $15 for cars, $1.50 for passengers. There's also a jetfoil service to and from Jakarta, leaving Jakarta in the mornings and BL in the afternoons, at 2 pm. Call ☎ 31437 for more information, fare $15. Several door to door taxi companies do the BL–Jakarta trip, including ferry, faster than the bus services. **Dynasty Taxi** offers charters to Palembang, Bakauheni and Jakarta ☎ BL 45674/69, Jakarta ☎ 5680986, so does **Taxi SB90** ☎ 31926, 31676, Jakarta ☎ 4721146. The fare is $10–$12 per person.
By train. There are night and day trains to Palembang. The night train is the most comfortable, fare $10, the trip takes 10 hours.
By bus. The main bus terminal is Rajabasa, 12 km from town, and can be reached by DAMRI service 2 from Jl Raden Intan, or by taxi. The *mikrolet (bemo)* station is next door. All long-haul buses leave from Rajabasa, round the clock for Jakarta (fare $8) and other main towns.

GETTING AROUND

Local **bemos** do the usual about town routes (double fare over the boundary). Larger DAMRI **buses** also serve the city and Rajabasa bus terminal. Taxis can be chartered for about $4–$5 per hour. **Taxis** wait in front of the Marcopolo Hotel. Day taxi or **minibus** charters are available from hotels and travel agents, prices from $40.

ACCOMMODATIONS

Budget

The **Malaya** Losmen on Jl Tongkol, in the maze of small streets near the bay, has rather dingy rooms from $3.50. The **Kenanga** on Jl Kenanga (☎ 481888) and the **Wijaya** on Jl Seraya (☎ 521-63) both have the usual boxy rooms for $9. The **Sriwijaya** on Jl Kalimantan (☎ 481046) has rooms for $10 and up. There are other stark and simple cheapies near the train station on Jl Kota Raja. Basic Losmen **GunungSari** has rooms from $4.

Moderate

Kurnia II is a fairly new hotel with basic facilities—free breakfast, small lobby shop and communal TV lounge. The plain rooms are clean, $9 for a room with *mandi* and inefficient fan. The **Kurnia City** across the road is a little more expensive and offers a pool. $10–$15. Both on Jl Raden Intan, convenient for a shopping center and transport. Just along the road is **Andalas** Hotel. Good AC rooms with *mandi* from $12.50.

Expensive

A good selection of hotels, and the best value for money. The **Sheraton Inn Lampung** is a low rise, resort style development set around a large pool. All facilities, including tennis and a gym. Rooms from $80. Jl Wolter Monginsidi 175, ☎ 486666, fax 486690. The **Marcopolo** is not so well finished, but has a superb location high on a hill and with a view and a large pool. Open-air terrace cafe and bar, friendly atmosphere. Good value at only $15 upwards, $44 for a suite. Restaurant, AC and room service. Jl Dr Susilo, ☎ 62511, fax 54419. The **Indra Palace** is another centrally located low-rise hotel, but without the quality appeal of the Sheraton. Full facilities, pool, restaurant and pub. Rooms from $50. Jl Wolter Monginsidi 70 ☎ 62766, fax 62399. The **Sahid Krakatau** on Jl Yos Sudarso by the bay also has a swimming pool, restaurant, bar and full room facilities, rates from $30.

SERVICES

The friendly and helpful **Tourist Information Office** is at Jl WR Supratman No. 39 Gunung Mas ☎ 482565. The **Merpati** office is at Jl Kartini 90 ☎ 63419. The **Immigration Office** is at Jl Diponegoro No 24. The **Forestry Office** is at Jl Teuku Umar ☎ 73177. There are six **hospitals,** two on Jl A Rivai, one on Jl Gatot Subroto, one on Jl Soekarno-Hatta, one on Jl W Monginsidi and one on Jl Teuku Umar. The **Museum** is at Jl Teuku Umar. **Banks** can be found all over the city, but it can be tricky changing travelers' cheques. Try banks **BCA** or **BRI** on Jl Raden Intan, which will oblige (US or Sterling, certainly) or suffer a worse rate in the hotels. The **Post Office** is at Jl Ahmad Dahlan 21, the **Telkom** at Jl Majapahit. There are private *wartels* (telecommunication service offices) all over town. For **tours and travel services**, contact **Femmy** Tours on Jl W Monginsidi ☎ 482593 or PT **Sahid Tours** on Jl Yos Sudarso ☎ 487114. For an adventure package, try **Kalpataru Adventure** in Jakarta, who will arrange special trips to Krakatau, etc. Jl Galur Sari, 11/5C Jakarta 13120 ☎ 021 8198989, fax 8583712.

NIGHTLIFE

There are **cinemas** which show Western movies, try Studio 21 on Jl Kartini. The **Swiss Pub and Disco** is popular, on Jl Yos Sudarso, as is the **Oya Disco and Karaoke**, same street. The bars in the star-rated hotels, particularly the Indra Palace, are lively.

FOOD

To eat in a busy and pleasant setting, try the **Pasar Mambo** night market, with its street stalls selling all local dishes including fresh Chinese seafood at *warung* **Tio Ciu**, rice and noodles, crab, prawn and fish at reasonable prices at many of the others. After dinner, have a cold beer and listen to the non-hassly buskers. The main hotels all have top restaurants—the Sheraton's **Kebun Raya** serves great Indonesian food, and the Marcopolo's terrace cafe is a pleasant hang-out. For Chinese food, try the **Golden Dragon** on Jl Yos Sudarso. **Cookies Corner** on Jl Kartini is a neat and tidy European-style cafe with checked tablecloths and a European patron. Very clean and serves chips, burgers and local favorites, toast and toasted sandwiches. There are Padang restaurants in abundance. There's a **Kentucky Fried Chicken** at Jl Sudirman. **Restaurant Garuda** on Jl Kartini has good, filling, cheap local food.

SHOPPING

Kings Supermarket chain sells everything from snacks to shampoo, suntan oil and souvenirs. There's one on Jl Raden Intan. The busy central **market** of Pasar Baru, which sells textiles, clothes and household goods, is always worth a visit. For arts, **Lampung Art Design** on Jl Kartini is good, as is **Mulia Art Shop** on Jl A Yani. Also try **Melati Art Gallery** on Jl Way Rilau, or the **Art Market** in the Saburai Sports Hall on Jl Sudirman if it's on. There's a **Tapis** weaving center at the airport.

Outside Bandar Lampung

The beaches just outside the city, for example scenic **Pasir Putih** 16 km away, are pleasant enough, but the best beaches begin south of the city at **Merak Belantung**. If you're traveling on the bus, which leaves from Rajabasa and goes via **Panjang** Terminal outside town, get dropped off at the junction of the road which leads down to the beach (ask for Merak Belantung), and take a motorbike taxi down to the beach ($1) or walk the two kilometers. It's a lovely clean beach but the once pleasant chalet accommodation now has an eerie air of neglect. If you want to stay with the spiders, the caretakers claim that they'll cook for you.

Kalianda

10 km further south, once back on the main road, is an attractive, friendly, fishing village which you can use as a base for exploring **Krakatau** and the quiet, pretty islands of **Sebuku** and **Sebesi**.

Stay at the **Beringin** Hotel, a pleasant old family home in a rambling Dutch bungalow with spacious covered garden courtyards and large rooms with *mandi* from $3.50. The helpful family will arrange a trip to Krakatau at reasonable rates, plus other trips such as climbing Mt Rajabasa. If you prefer more privacy, the new glaringly white concrete **Kalianda** Hotel at the top of the road which leads down to Kalianda, has functional, clean but hardly cosy rooms from $12, (*mandi*, AC available), but it's a 1 km walk to the simple *warungs* and food stalls along Kalianda's main street. There are a few other basic hotels in town—try **Fajar** and **Sudi Mampir**, along the street from Beringin, if Beringin is full. There's a **bank BNI** and a **Telkom office** in Kalianda. To visit and bathe in the pools at the **Way Belarang** sulphur springs, take an *ojek* (motorbike taxi) or walk the 3 km up the hill at the side of Beringin Hotel. There's a small entrance charge, but the waters are very relaxing. There are hot springs in town near the beach too, just behind the shopping street where the fishing boats pull up to the beach—dip feet in carefully, the water can be very hot.

Krakatau and Anak Krakatau

These famous volcanoes can be reached either as part of a tour from Bandar Lampung or by arranging your own transport to and from either Kalianda or **Canti**, a quaint little fishing village a few kilometers south of Kalianda, and chartering your own fishing boat. The large wooden boats from Canti are available for $100–$120, but can take 10 people. It's possible to take a smaller boat from Bakauheni, at the Java ferry terminal, for $50—the Beringin Hotel can arrange this. But be careful, this is a smaller boat and not for the faint-hearted, as it's a four hour trip out and much longer on the return journey (6–8 hours) because of the tides, and it can be very choppy. Take food and water. See phosphorescence and fireflies. If you depart from Bakauheni, stop off at the coral gardens of **Pulau Harimau** near Bakauheni terminal. There's a Krakatau Festival with fishing, dancing and sport in mid-July. The return trip from Krakatau

passes **Sebuku** and **Sebesi** islands, ideal for swimming and sunning. There's simple accommodation on Sebesi island (around $20 per chalet). There's a public ferry to and from both islands from Canti every day for less than $1.50.

Krui

A small, pleasant fishing village on the Lampung coast below Lake Ranau, in the **South Bukit Barisan** national park (*see South Sumatra Practicalities*), and with a distinctly Javanese flavor. The bus from **Bukit Kemuning** on the Trans Sumatra Highway travels to **Liwa**, from where the road descends to the coastal plain. It's an appalling bumpy road, hacked out of the cliff, so choose a bus with springs. It's 2–4 hours depending on the state of the road. The beach at **Krui** is wonderful—long, white and clean and the sea is blue with strong breakers and white surf. Stay at **Sempana Lima** Hotel on Jl Kesuma, a short walk from the beach through the *kampung*. The **Gembira** Hotel further down the street is cheaper but much scruffier. Walk around the town avoiding bullock carts, eat at the many *warungs* and shop at the market—batik is cheap. There's a budding tourist service at the Sempana Lima, ask about boats to **Banana Island**, where *kain tapis* weavers work. Buses leave every day to Liwa and on to the Trans-Sumatra Highway, and bus ticket offices are along the main street.

The Way Kambas Nature Reserve

This can be reached from Bandar Lampung or Kalianda in about two hours. The trained elephants are on show most mornings and afternoons, especially Sundays. Get a permit first from the forestry office in Bandar Lampung, or arrive at the park office in **Kadangsari** during office hours. Either charter a car—cheaper from Kalianda ($12.50) or take the bus to **Panjang** (50 cents) and then to **Tridatu**. A four-wheel drive vehicle is recommended. About 12 km inside the park is **Way Kanan** (*way* means river in Lampungese), where there's a very simple guesthouse. A motorbike *ojek* as far as there costs $1.50. Bring food. The river trip down Way Kanan, ideal for wildlife spotting, is best done over two days, spending one night at Way Kanan.

Pugung Raharjo

To reach the archaeological park, charter a taxi (40 km from Bandar Lampung) or take the bus, travelling via **Panjang** terminal. See and pick pepper, cloves and coffee in the area if you have your own transport. At **Pugung Raharjo**, there's a museum, traditional architecture and prehistoric remains. This site is on the way to Way Kambas and both places can be visited in a day if you have transport.

— *Julie Heath*

Further Reading

ARTS AND CRAFTS

Barbier, J.P. and D. Newton (eds) *Islands and Ancestors: Indigenous Styles of Southeast Asia* (New York 1988).

Barbier, J.P. *Sumatra: The Batak People and Their Art.* (Dallas 1982). Exhibition catalog.

Barbier, J.P. *Tobaland; The Shreds of Tradition* (Geneva, 1983). A rambling discussion of Batak art and culture based on the author's five visits to North Sumatra in the 1970s.

van Dijk, T. and N. de Jonge. *Ship Cloths of the Lampung, South Sumatera* (Amsterdam 1980). Exhibition catalog.

Feldman, J. *The Eloquent Dead. Ancestral Sculpture of Indonesia and Southeast Asia* (Los Angeles 1985). Excellent chapters on Nias and Batak ancestral figures and their symbolism.

Hasibuan, J.S. *Batak Art et Culture* (Jakarta 1985). Lovely photos. An English edition is planned.

Hasibuan, J.S. *Primitive Art of the Ancient Batak* (Medan 1982).

Hitchcock, M. *Indonesian Textiles* (Singapore 1991). A good overview of traditional fabrics. Widely available in Indonesia.

Leigh, Barbara. *Hands of Time: The Crafts of Aceh* (Jakarta). Many illustrations and excellent discussions of how the crafts are made. Available in Jakarta bookshops.

Nias: Tribal Treasures. Cosmic Reflections in Stone, Wood and Gold (Delft 1990). Catalog of an exhibition held at the Museum Nusantara, Delft, with informative articles on sculpture, architecture, festivals, jewelry and folktales.

Niessen, S.A. *Motifs of Life in Toba Batak Texts and Textiles* (Dordrecht 1985).

Taylor, P.M. and L.V. Aragon. *Beyond the Java Sea: Art of Indonesia's Outer Islands* (Washington 1991). Excellent introductory text.

Waterson, R. *The Living House: An Anthropology of Architecture in South-East Asia* (Singapore 1990).

LITERATURE

Ambler, Eric. *Passage of Arms* (London 1959). A thriller about gun-running in Sumatra, by a master of the genre.

Clerkx, E. and W.F. Wertheim. *Living in Deli, Its Society as Imaged in Colonial Fiction* (Amsterdam 1990). A survey of (mostly Dutch) fiction set in North Sumatra early this century.

Conrad, Joseph. *Youth* (London 189?). Conrad's first novelette, in which he describes his initial impressions of the Indies, landing at Mentok on Bangka Island as a young seaman.

Lubis, Mochtar. *Harimau.*

Székely, Ladislao. *Tropic Fever* (New York 1937, repr. Singapore 1989). Autobiographical novel by a young Hungarian who worked as a tobacco planter in the Medan area around the turn of the century, it sensitively portrays the hardships endured by coolies and European overseers alike.

Székely-Lulofs, Madelon. *Coolie* (London 1932, repr. Singapore).

Székely-Lulofs, Madelon. *Rubber: A Romance of the Dutch East Indies* (London 1931, repr. Singapore).

PEOPLES OF SUMATRA

Bartlett, H.H. *The Labors of the Datoe and Other Essays on the Bataks of Asahan (North Sumatra)* (Ann Arbor 1973).

Collet, O.J.A. *Terres et peuples de Sumatra* (Amsterdam 1925). Offers a detailed description of flora, fauna, peoples and cultures.

Errington, F. *Manners and Meaning in West Sumatra* (New Haven 1984).

Graves, E. *The Minangkabau Response to Dutch Colonial Rule* (Ithaca 1981).

Hagen, B. *Die orang Kubu auf Sumatra* (Frankfurt 1908). The earliest major account.

Heidhues, Mary F. Somers. *Bangka Tin and Mentok Pepper: Chinese Settlement on an Indonesian Island* (Singapore 1990).

Josselin de Jong, P.E. de. *Minangkabau and Negri Sembilan. Socio-political Structure in Indonesia* (The Hague 1980).

Kipp, R. S. and R. (eds) *Beyond Samosir: Recent Studies of the Batak Peoples of Sumatra* (Athens, Ohio 1983). A collection of essays.

Loeb, E.M. *Sumatra: Its History and People* (Vienna 1935, Singapore 1972, 1989). A systematic study compiled largely from Dutch ethnographic sources; still very readable. The author spent five months on the Mentawais.

Singarimbun, M. *Kinship, Descent and Alliance Among the Karo Batak* (Berkeley 1975).

Snouck Hurgronje, C. *The Achehnese* (Leiden/London 1906). The classic work by a Dutch scholar who greatly influenced colonial policy during the wars with Aceh.

Sopher, D. *The Sea Nomads* (Singapore ?). Excellent description of the *orang laut*, their habitat and lifestyle.

Suzuki, P. *Critical Survey of Studies on the Anthropology of Nias, Mentawei and Enggano* (The Hague 1958).

Tobing, P.O.L. *The Structure of the Toba-Batak Belief in the High God* (Amsterdam 1956, 1963).

HISTORY AND ECONOMY

Bastin, John. *The British in West Sumatra 1685-1825* (Kuala Lumpur 1965). Selection of edited letters and reports from the British at Bengkulu.

Bellwood, P. *Prehistory of the Indo-Malaysian Archipelago* (Sydney 1985). A standard work.

Bowen, John. *Sumatran Politics and Poetics: Gayo History 1900-1989* (New Haven 1991).

Collis, M. *Raffles* (London, 1966). Wonderfully readable account of a fascinating man; poignantly describes Raffles' years in Bengkulu.

Cunningham, C.E. *The Postwar Migration of Toba-Bataks to East Sumatra* (New Haven 1958).

Dobbin, Christine. *Islamic Revivalism in a Changing Peasant Economy (Central Sumatra, 1784-1847)* (London 1983).

Franke, Wolfgang and Salmon, Claudine. *Chinese Epigraphic Materials in Indonesia, Vol. I: Sumatra* (Singapore 1988).

Gould, J.W. *Americans in Sumatra* (The Hague 1961).

Hal Hill (ed) *Unity and Diversity: Regional Development in Indonesia Since 1970* (Singapore 1990). A mine of information on Sumatra's economy, presented province-by-province. (Bengkulu and Jambi are not covered however.)

Lombard, D. *Le Sultanat d'Atjeh au Temps d'Iskandar Muda 1607-1636* (Paris 1967).

Marsden, W. *The History of Sumatra* (London 1783, 1811). The first scientific study in English of any Indonesian island. Not a light read, but a book you will come back to time and again to learn about the geography, flora, fauna, people and history of the island. Based in large part on the author's observations during an 8-year stay at Bengkulu. The substantially revised third edition of 1811 has additional material gleaned from informants in Sumatra. (Repr. Singapore.)

Maxwell, J. (ed) *The Malay-Islamic World of Sumatra: Studies in Policies and Cultures.*

Milner, A.C. *Kerajaan: Malay Political Culture on the Eve of Colonial Rule* (Tucson 1982).

Reid, A. *Southeast Asia in the Age of Commerce 1450-1680. Vol. 1: The Lands Below the Winds* (New Haven 1988).

Reid, A. *The Blood of the People: Revolution and the End of Traditional Rule in Northern Sumatra* (Kuala Lumpur 1979). An account of the massacre of the Malay aristocracy in an outburst of pent-up anger during the revolution.

Reid, A. *The Conquest for North Sumatra* (Kuala Lumpur 1969). Highly readable historical account of the Aceh wars.

Schnitger, F.M. *Forgotten Kingdoms of Sumatra* (Leiden 1938, repr. Singapore 1989). A good introduction to the antiquities of Sumatra. Written in a lively, first person style by an amateur archaeologist who himself discovered and excavated many Sumatran monuments. Touches also on legends, folktales and ethnographic details of the island's peoples.

Schnitger, F.M. *The Archaeology of Hindoo Sumatra* (Leiden 1938). A more technical work.

Thee, Kian-wie. *Plantation Agriculture and Export Growth: An Economic History of East Sumatra 1863-1942* (Jakarta 1977).

Wolters, O.W. *Early Indonesian Commerce: A Study of the Origins of Srivijaya* (Ithaca 1967).

Wolters, O.W. *The Fall of Srivijaya in Malay History* (Ithaca 1970).

NATURE AND ECOLOGY

Griffiths, M. *Indonesian Eden: Aceh's Rainforest* (Jakarta 1989).

Holmes, D. and S. Nash, *The Birds of Sumatra and Kalimantan* (Singapore 1990). A brief but comprehensive introduction.

King, B., Dickson, E.C. & Woodcock, M. *Field Guide to the Birds of South East Asia* (Collins). There is as yet no field guide for Sumatran birds, but this book covers the mainland, with a good deal of overlap.

van Marle, J.G. and Voous, K. *The Birds of Sumatra, An Annotated Checklist* (Checklist No. 10 from the British Ornithologists' Union, 1988). For all serious ornithologists.

Savage, V. *Western Impressions of Nature and Landscape in South East Asia* (Singapore 1984).

Whitten, A., D. Sengli, A. Jazenul and H. Nazaruddin. *The Ecology of Sumatra* (Yogyakarta 1984). An authoritative and richly-documented overview of the island's ecosystems.

Whitten, A. *The Gibbons of Siberut* (London 1982).

GUIDES AND TRAVELOGUES

Burton and Ward. "Report of a Journey into the Batak Country, in the interior of Sumatra, in the year 1824" in *Transactions of the Royal Asiatic Society* 1:485-583 (London 1827).

Dalton, Bill. *Indonesia Handbook* (Chico 1992). The backpacker's Bible, 5th edition.

Harfield, A. *Bencoolen; The Christian Cemetery and the Fort Marlborough Monuments* (London 1985).

Junghuhn, F. *Die Battakländer auf Sumatra* (Berlin 1847). One of the earliest explorers to the Batak highlands.

Maass, A. *Durch Zentral-Sumatra* (Berlin 1910). A classic work, 2 vols.

Modigliani, E. *Un Viaggio a Nias* (Milan 1890).

Salmon, C., D. Lombard and P. Labrousse, "Guide Archipel III: Palembang et Bangka" in *Archipel 15* (Paris 1978), pp.145-161.

About the Authors

Peter Bellwood is a Reader in Prehistory at the Australian National University, specializing in Southeast Asian and Pacific Prehistory. His books include *Man's Conquest of the Pacific* (1978), *Prehistory of the Indo-Malaysian Archipelago* (1985) and *The Polynesians* (1987).

David Booth has been traveling for work and pleasure since 1970. His work as a civil engineer took him to West Africa, the Middle East, the Caribbean and Papua New Guinea, whilst most of his pleasure trips were to Southeast Asia. Now he is a writer and English teacher, and moved to Jakarta in 1989.

John Bowen is Associate Professor of Anthropology at Washington University in St. Louis.

Ian Caldwell was educated at the School of Oriental and African Studies in London and holds a doctorate in Indonesian history from Australian National University. In the last ten years he has traveled widely in Indonesia, photographing and studying its pre-Islamic cultures. He is currently lecturer in Malay Studies at National University of Singapore.

Nancy Caldwell was born in India and grew up in Singapore. She has traveled widely in Asia and Europe. She obtained her BA from the United States, where she studied modern and primitive Indonesian art.

Janet Cochrane has been involved in Indonesia since 1979, including 6 years' work there in conservation, tourism and development, and 3 years as a producer with the BBC Indonesian section. She is director of a tour company, Detours, specializing in wildlife and cultural travel.

Alain Compost was born in France and has lived in Bogor, West Java, for many years. He specializes in nature photography and his work has appeared in many books and magazines, including *Paris Match* and *National Geographic*.

Robert Cribb, an Australian, studied Indonesian history at the universities of Queensland and London. His research included topics such as Indonesia's history of environmental protection. He is author of the *Historical Dictionary of Indonesia*.

Richard Davidson studied languages at Cambridge University before traveling in Asia and Africa as a journalist and safari guide. He spent 6 months in 1991 traveling in Indonesia.

Toos Van Dijk, a cultural anthropologist (Free University of Amsterdam), is a researcher at the Centre of Non-Western Studies at the University of Leiden. She is the author of various publications on the material culture of Indonesian peoples. Her PhD thesis concerned the symbolic system of the population of the Babar Archipelago, SE Moluccas.

Jerome Feldman is a professor of art history at Hawaii Loa College, specializing in the tribal arts of Indonesia and Oceania. His dissertation was on the architecture of Nias and he has edited and contributed to *The Eloquent Dead*, *Art of Micronesia*, *Islands and Ancestors*, *To Speak with Cloth* and *Nias Tribal Treasures*.

Annabel Teh Gallop grew up in Brunei Darussalam. She has been Curator for Indonesian and Malay at the British Library, London, since 1986 and has organized a number of exhibitions. She is co-author of *Golden Letters: Writing Traditions of Indonesia* (1991) and is working on a doctoral dissertation at SOAS, London University, on Indonesian historical novels.

Jill Gocher is a freelance photojournalist who studied photography in Melbourne, and has traveled and worked in Asia for over 10 years, contributing regularly to a number of magazines. Her favorite destination is Indonesia, and she has produced guides to Cirebon, Bandung and the Riau Islands.

Beatriz van der Goes studied Cultural Anthropology at the University of Amsterdam. She did field research from 1989-1990 among the Karo Batak of North Sumatra. Presently she is writing her PhD thesis at the Centre of Non-Western Studies of Leiden University.

Jay Goodfriend is a freelance photographer who splits his time between Indonesia and San Francisco. Since 1986 he has worked on a photo documentary exploring the relationship between culture and land use. He is researching a historical novel set in the Japanese era.

Sandra Hamid was born in Jakarta in 1962. She moved to Bali soon after finishing her degree at the Faculty of Social & Political Science at the University of Indonesia, and worked for a time at the Bali Hyatt. She is now a journalist for *Tempo* magazine, based in Jakarta.

Julie Heath took her Cultural Studies degree in England and is now a journalist based in SE Asia, contributing to Asian and European publications. She has lived in Riau, Sumatra for 6 years, and travels frequently in Indonesia.

Derek Holmes graduated in geology at Bristol University in 1960. He has worked as a land resources consultant since 1963, and in Indonesia since 1974. He is co-editor of *Kukila*, the bulletin of the Ornithological Society of Indonesia, and has authored two books on the birds of Java, Bali, Sumatra and Kalimantan.

Nico de Jonge studied Cultural Anthropology at the Free University of Amsterdam and is now a researcher at the University of Leiden. He is the author of various publications on the material culture of Indonesians. His PhD thesis studies the people of the Babar Archipelago, Southeast Moluccas.

Rita Smith Kipp is Professor of Anthropology at Kenyon College, Ohio, and she lived in a Sumatran highland village in order to write a dissertation on Karo weddings and funerals. She has written articles on Karo kinship and her books include *The early years of a mission; The Karo field* (University of Michigan Press, 1990).

Glyn Luntungan has lived in Indonesia intermittently since 1979. She was married in 1984 in Jambi and taught English before returning to Australia to teach Indonesian for two years. In 1988 she returned to Indonesia to live with her recently widowed mother-in-law in Jambi.

Edmund Edwards McKinnon trained in agriculture at Edinburgh and first came to Sumatra in 1960 as a rubber planter. He has a longstanding interest in archaeology and has traveled extensively throughout the archipelago. He holds a degree in History of Art from Cornell University and is currently consultant to the Director General of Culture, sponsored by the Ford Foundation. He lives with his family in Jakarta.

John Miksic holds a doctorate in SE Asian history from Cornell University and is lecturer in history at the National University of Singapore. He has spent many years conducting research in Indonesia under the auspices of the Ford Foundation and the Asian Cultural Council.

Kal Muller is a veteran photojournalist whose travels have taken him to more than 80 countries. For over 16 years he has explored and photographed the Indonesian archipelago. He has written several guides to the more remote islands of Indonesia.

Eric Oey was born in the United States and has degrees in mathematics from Brown University and in Indonesian language and literature from the University of California, Berkeley. He founded Periplus Editions in 1988 and is now based in Singapore.

Gerard Persoon studied Cultural Anthropology at the University of Amsterdam. He has traveled and worked in Indonesia; for instance three years on a development project in Siberut. He now works at the Environmental Centre of Leiden University.

Andreas Peters is a German journalist and musician who travels and plays extensively in Indonesia for several months each year.

Kunang Helmi Picard is an Indonesian freelance journalist based in Paris. She studied history,

law and political science in Bonn, followed by post-graduate studies in London and Hamburg. She now contributes to German, French, American and Indonesian publications.

Anthony Reid is Professor of Southeast Asian History at the Australian National University in Canberra. He has published several books and articles on the history of Sumatra. His most recent book is *Southeast Asia in the Age of Commerce, 1450-1680*.

Michael Richardson is the Singapore-based Editor for Asia of the *International Herald Tribune*.

Nicola Robertson is a graduate from Edinburgh University. Founder of Stage International, a group specializing in Eastern European Drama. She is writing a play set in the Mentawai Islands.

Gottfried Roelcke graduated in 1975 in geography from Hanover University, where he first befriended a number of Indonesian students. He visited Indonesia in 1977 and has lived in the country since 1982, working as a technical advisor in Samarinda, Padang and now Bandung.

Reimar Schefold studied cultural anthropology in Basel and Munich and carried out years of field research on Siberut and among the Toraja of Sulawesi. He is Professor of Cultural Anthropology at Leiden University and his research in Mentawai has resulted in numerous books and articles, museum exhibitions and a film for the *Disappearing World* series of Granada TV, UK.

Laurie Scott is an Australian traveler, trekker and climber who frequently tests himself against Indonesia's toughest mountain challenges.

Ilsa Sharp is a British-born journalist who has lived and worked in Southeast Asia for more than 20 years. She runs a writing agency and is an active member of the Malayan Nature Society.

Amir Sidharta was born in Jakarta. He received a BA in architecture from the University of Michigan and is currently a Fulbright Scholar undertaking an MA degree in museum studies at George Washington University.

Edward Van Ness was born in Bloomfield, New Jersey and has taught in Madras, India, at the Akademi Musik Indonesia in Yogyakarta, at Universitas Sumatera Utara and at Oberlin College, and is currently chairman of the music department at Nommensen University in Medan. He is author of several books, including a work on Javanese *wayang kulit*.

Roxana Waterson studied anthropology at Cambridge; her thesis was on the Sa'dan Toraja people of Sulawesi. She is author of *The Living House: An Anthropology of Architecture in South-East Asia*, and presently lectures in anthropology at the National University of Singapore.

Tony Whitten is a British ecologist who has lived in Indonesia for about 10 years and works with the Ministry for Population and Environment. He is co-author and editor of *The Ecology of Sumatra* and *The Ecology of Sulawesi* and is currently working on another volume in the same series, *The Ecology of Java and Bali*.

Index

Map Index